THE HEROIC LEGEND OF
ARSLAN

STORY BY
YOSHIKI TANAKA

MANGA BY
HIROMU ARAKAWA

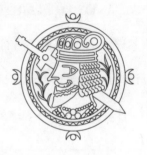

13

The Heroic Legend of
ARSLAN

Table of Contents

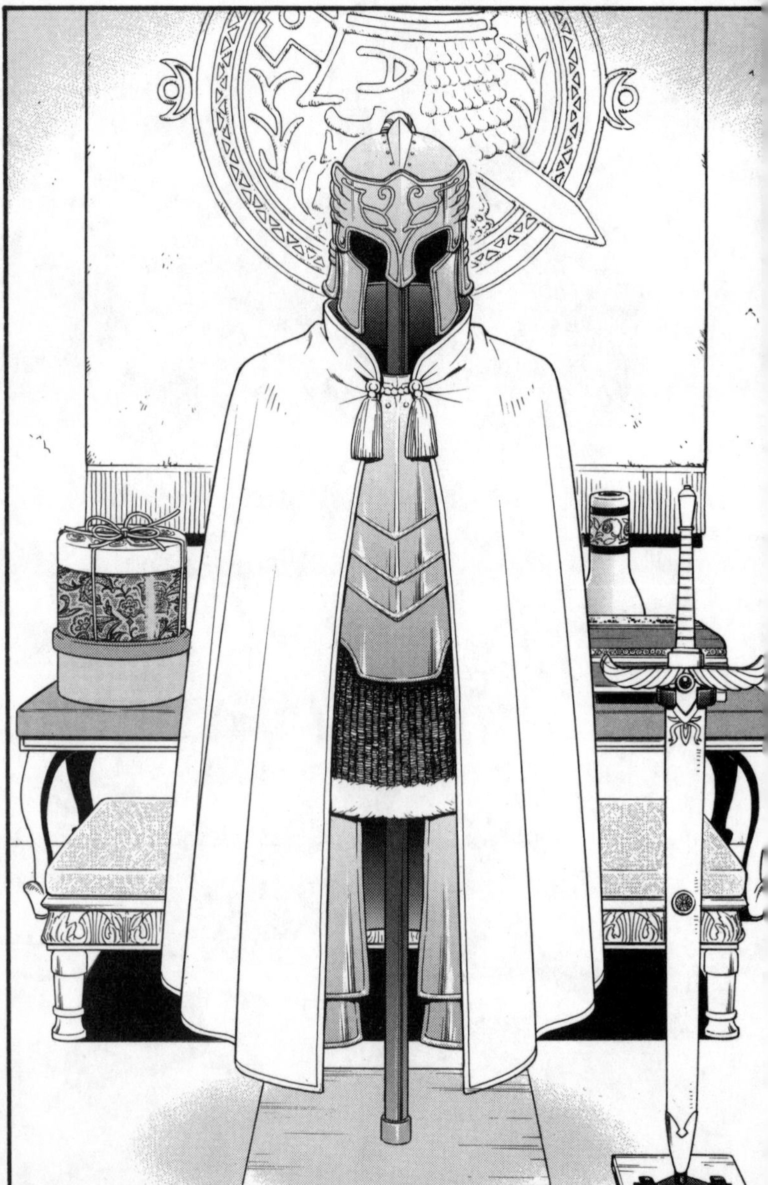

Chapter 77: Jubilation of Peshawar

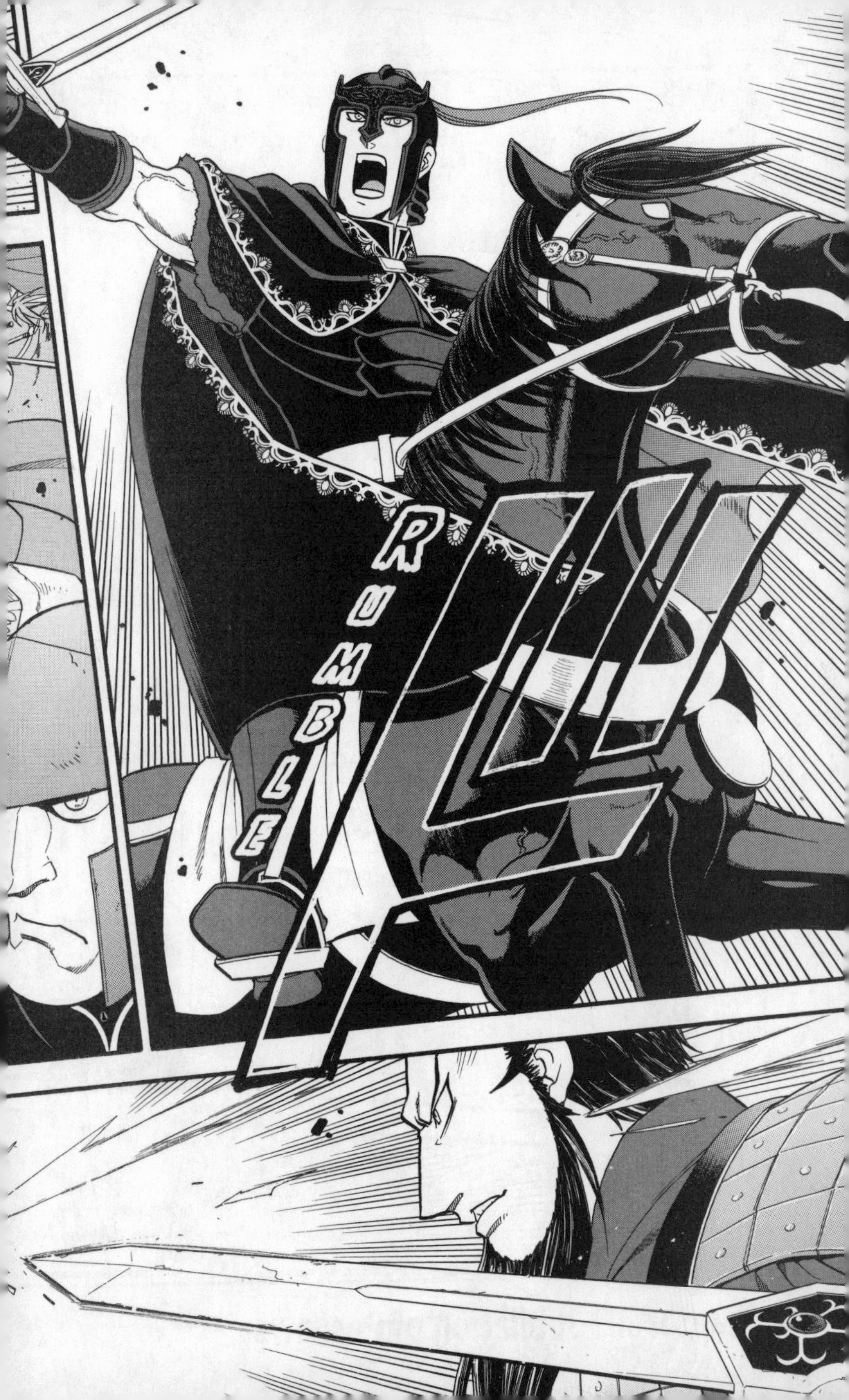
RUMBLE

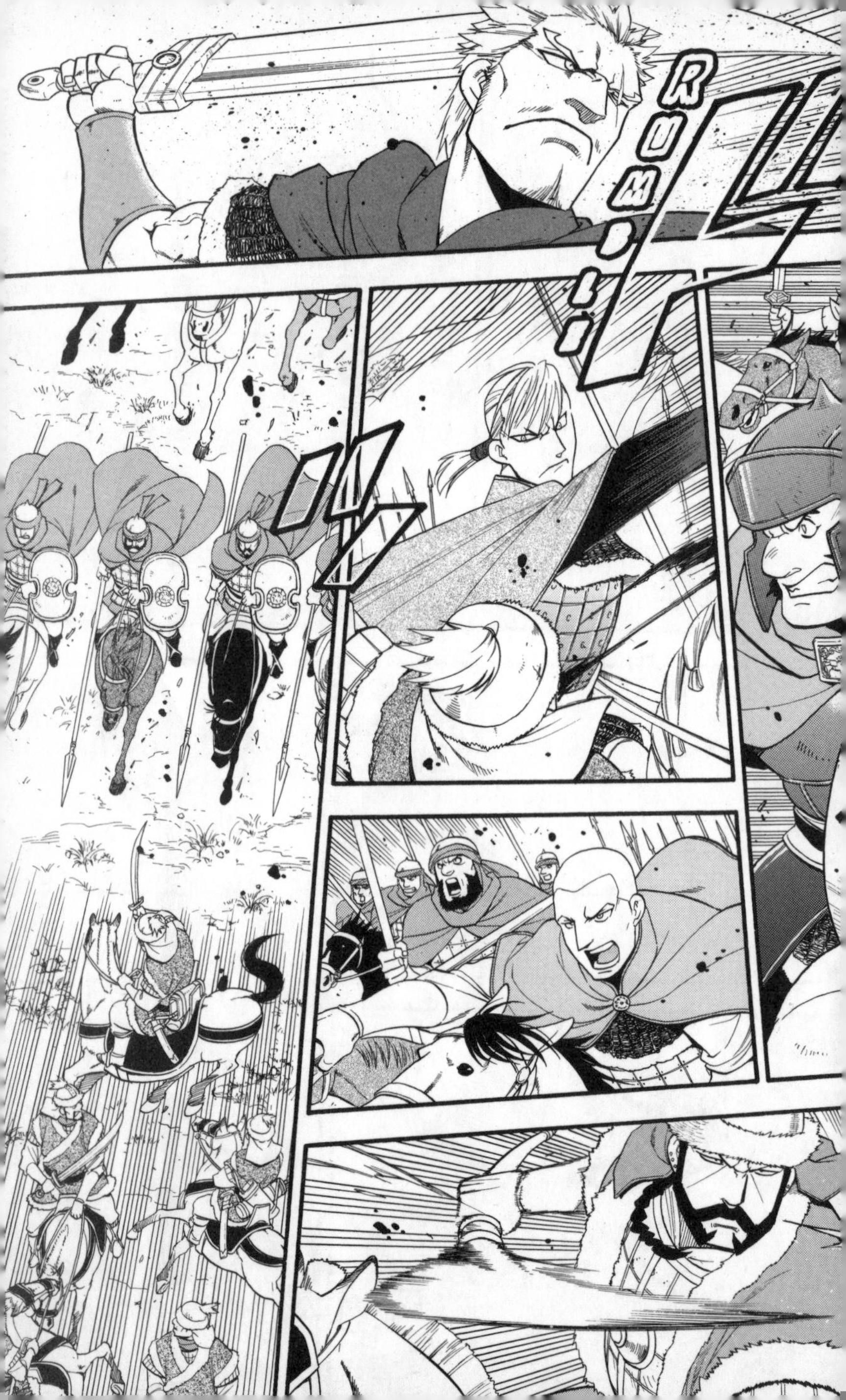
RUMBL

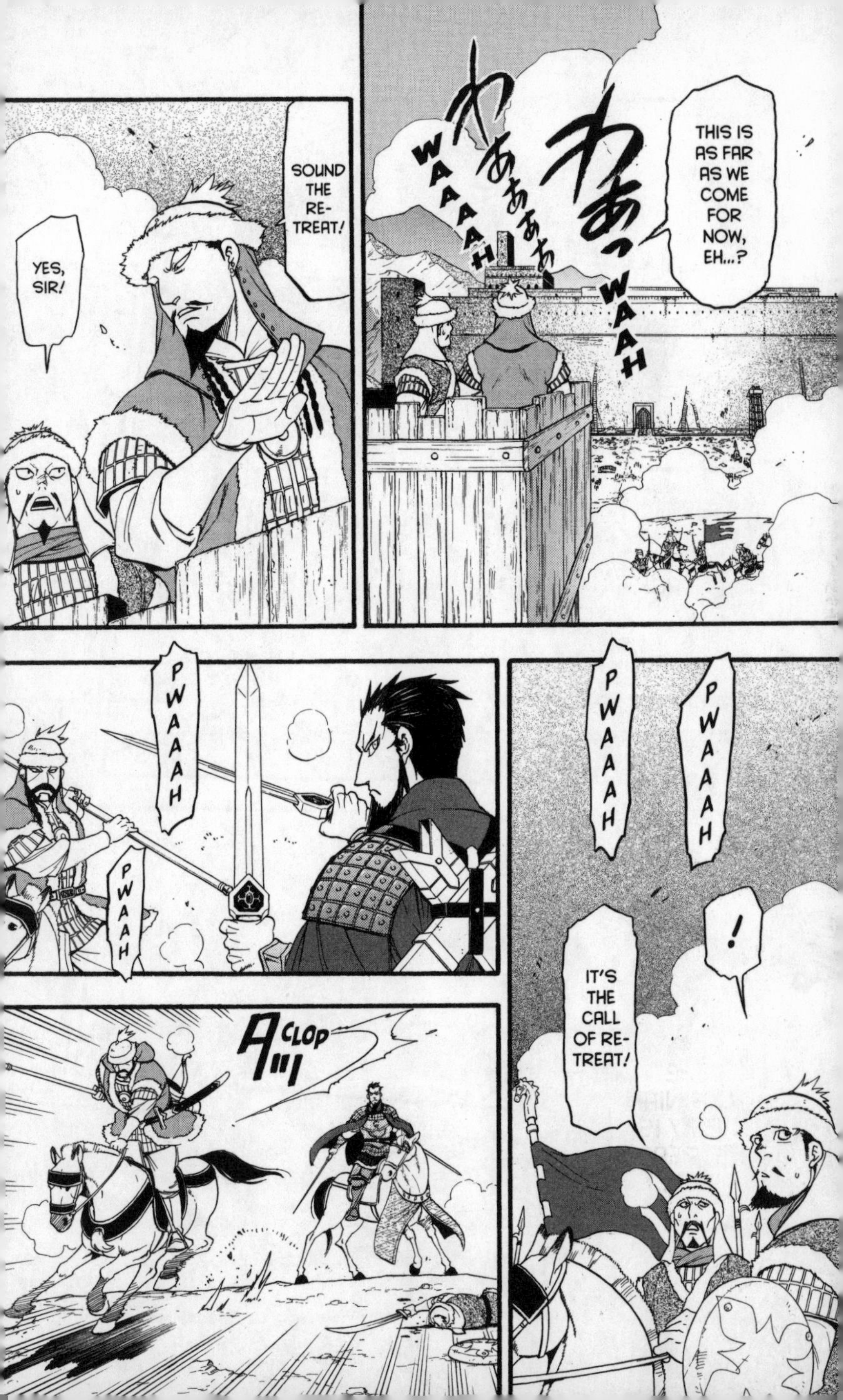
THIS IS AS FAR AS WE COME FOR NOW, EH...?
わぁっ
WAAH
わあああ
WAAAAH
SOUND THE RE-TREAT!
YES, SIR!
PWAAAAH
PWAAAAH
!
IT'S THE CALL OF RE-TREAT!
PWAAAH
PWAAH
CLOP

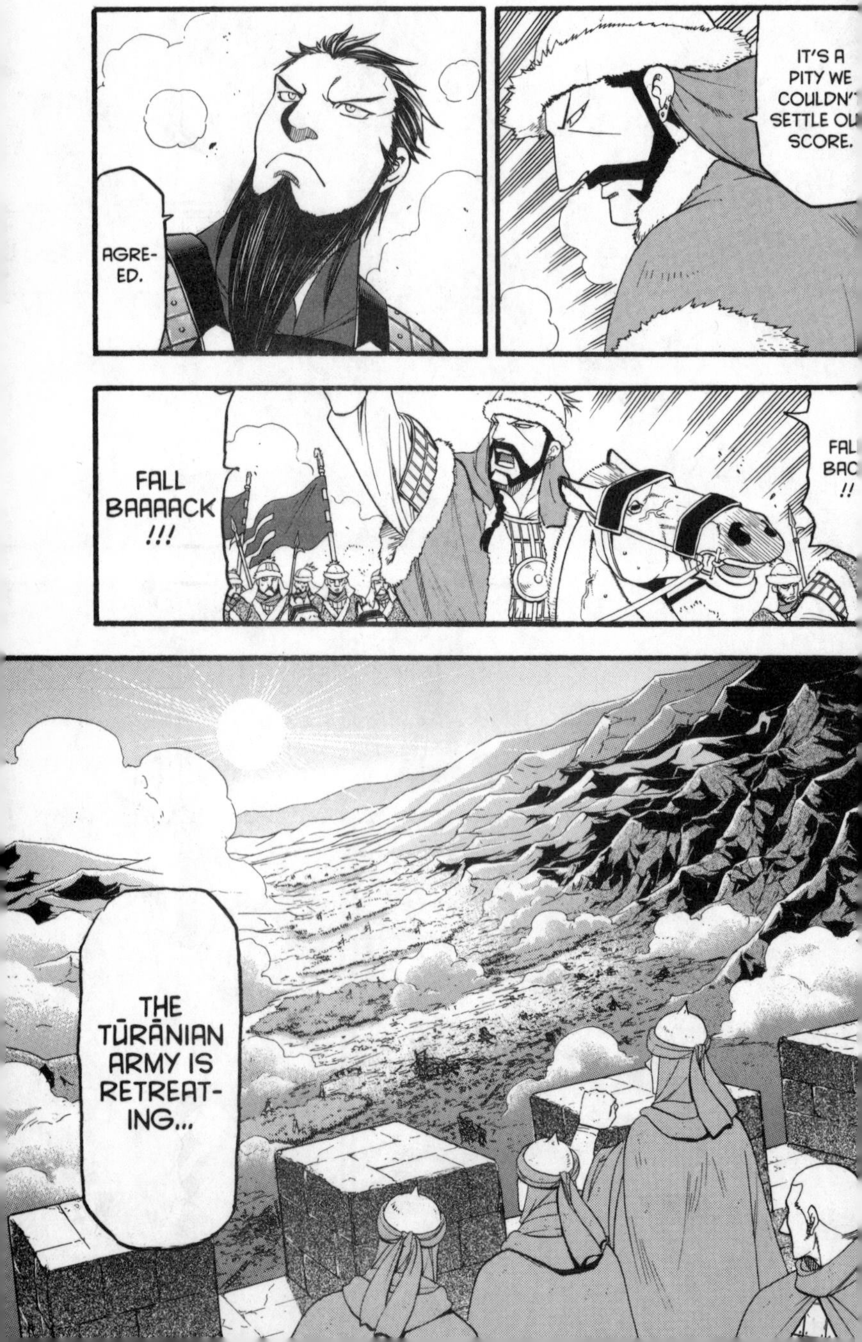
IT'S A PITY WE COULDN'T SETTLE OU SCORE.
AGRE-ED.
FAL BAC !!
FALL BAAAACK !!!
THE TŪRĀNIAN ARMY IS RETREAT-ING...

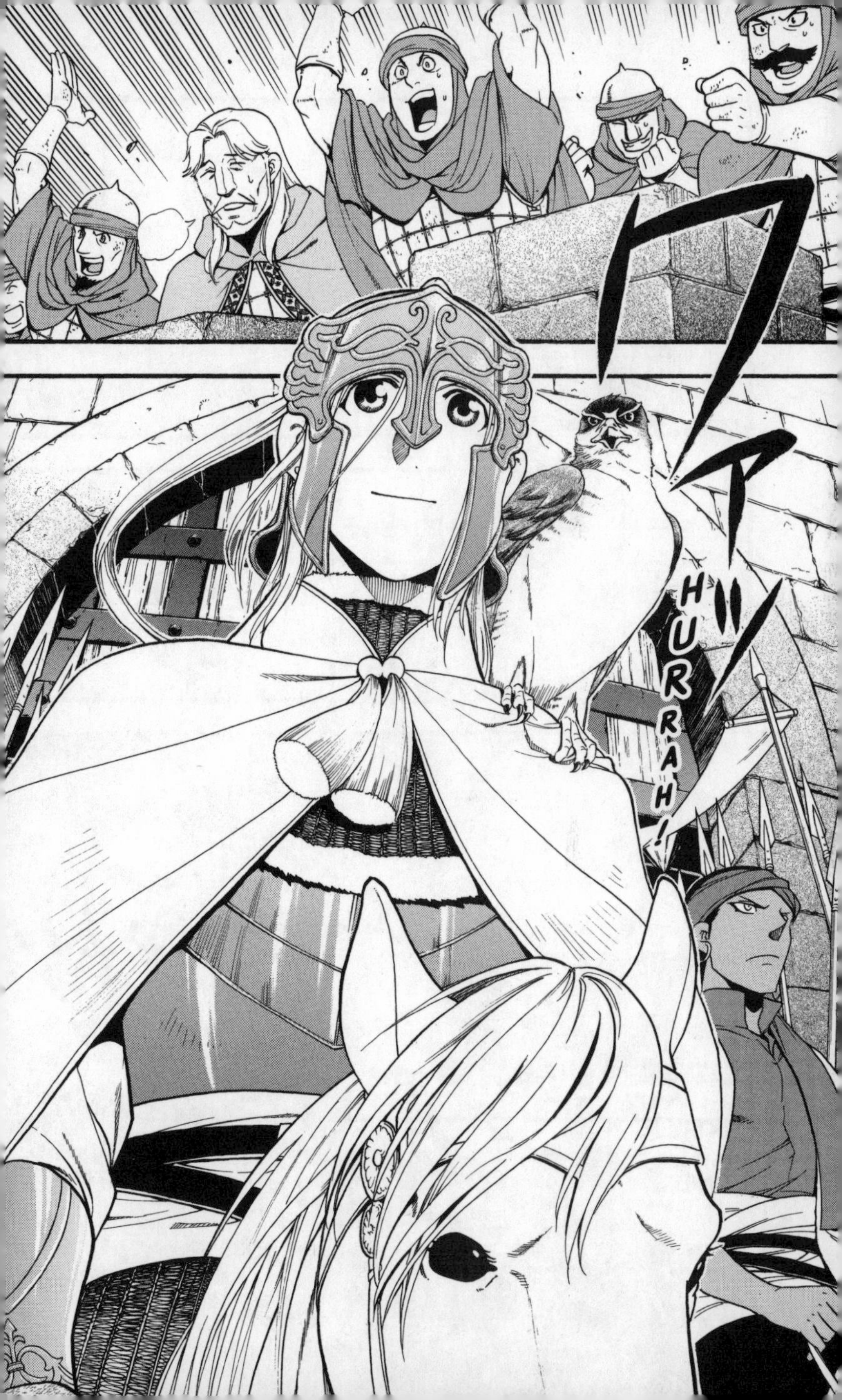
ワァッ
HURRAH!

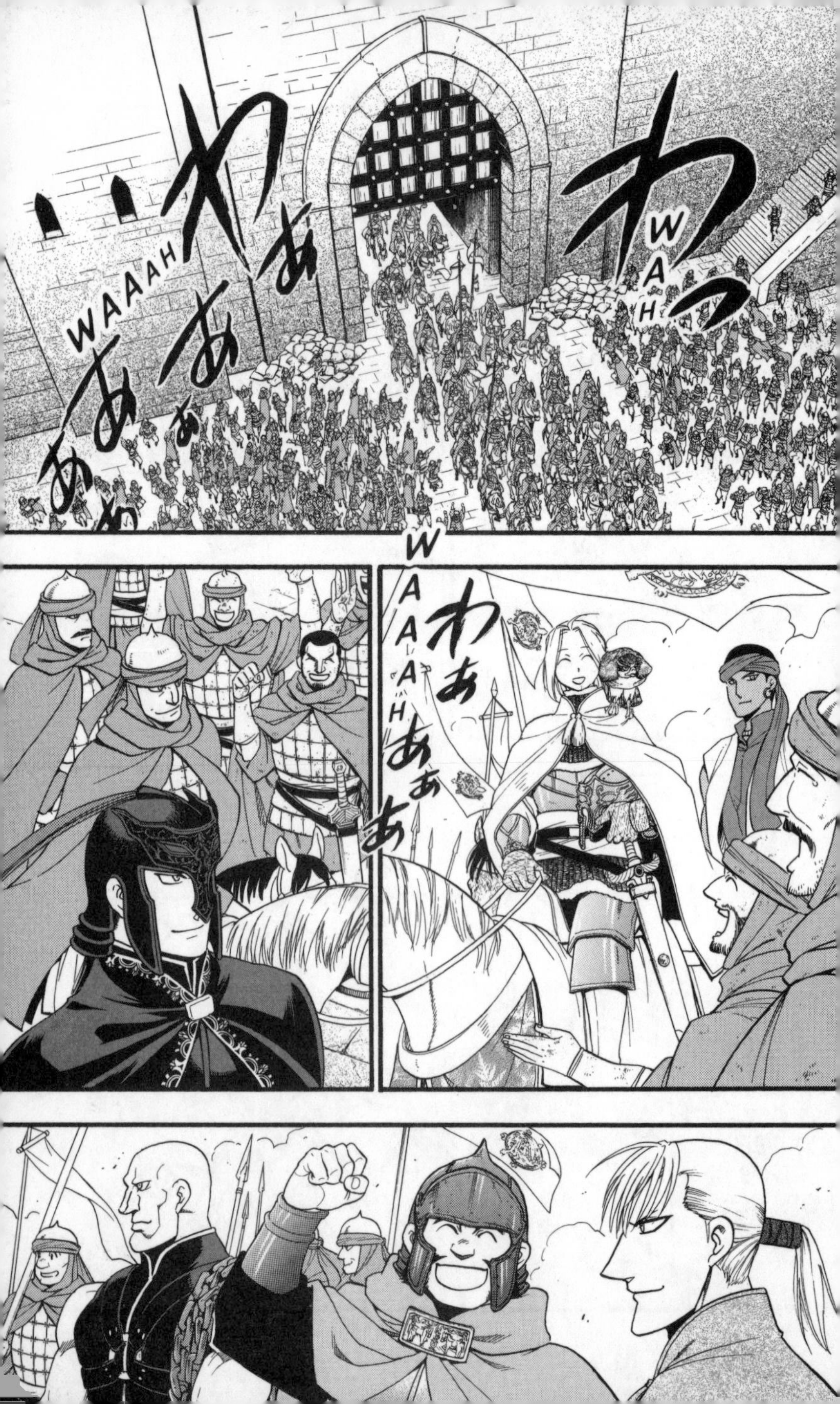
わっ
WAH
わぁぁぁぁ
WAAAH
わぁぁぁぁ
WAAAAH

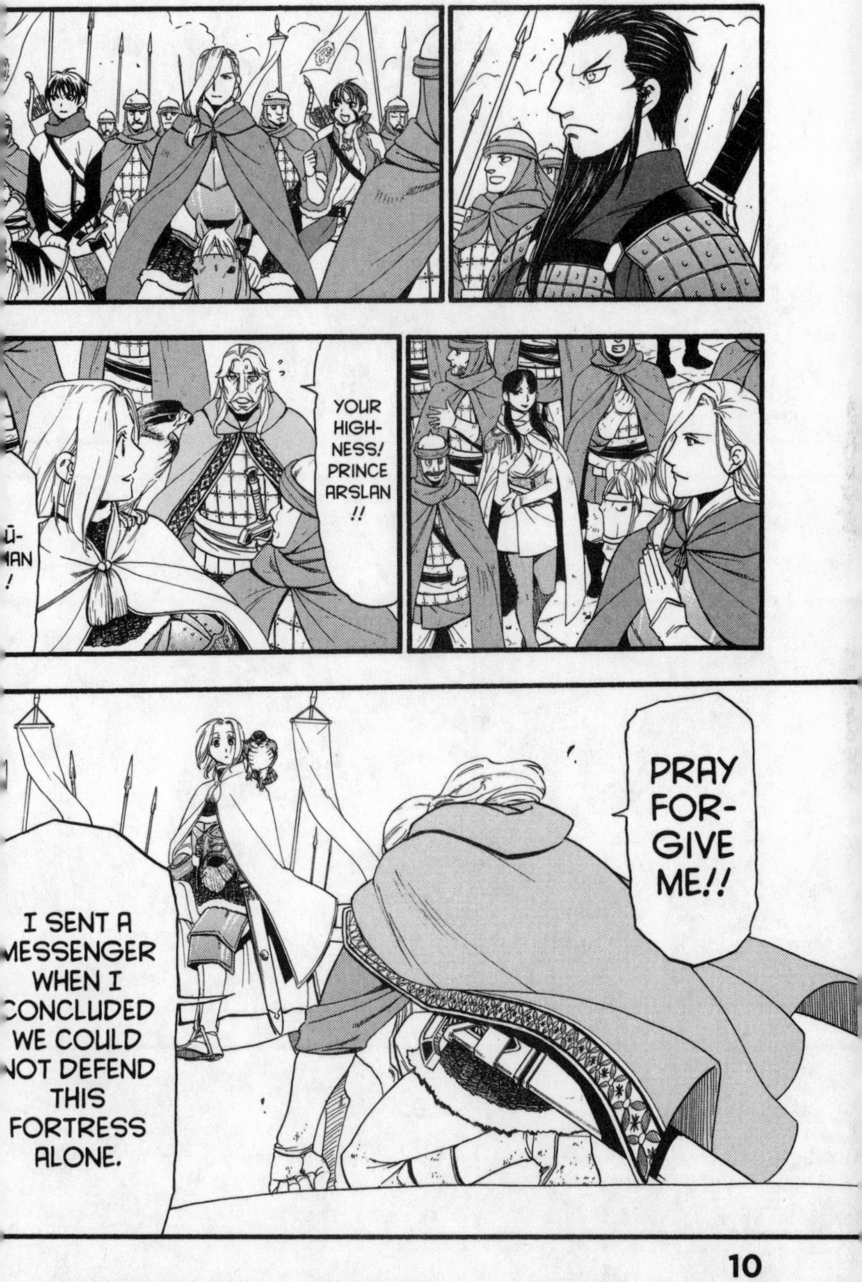
YOUR HIGHNESS! PRINCE ARSLAN!!
PRAY FORGIVE ME!!
I SENT A MESSENGER WHEN I CONCLUDED WE COULD NOT DEFEND THIS FORTRESS ALONE.

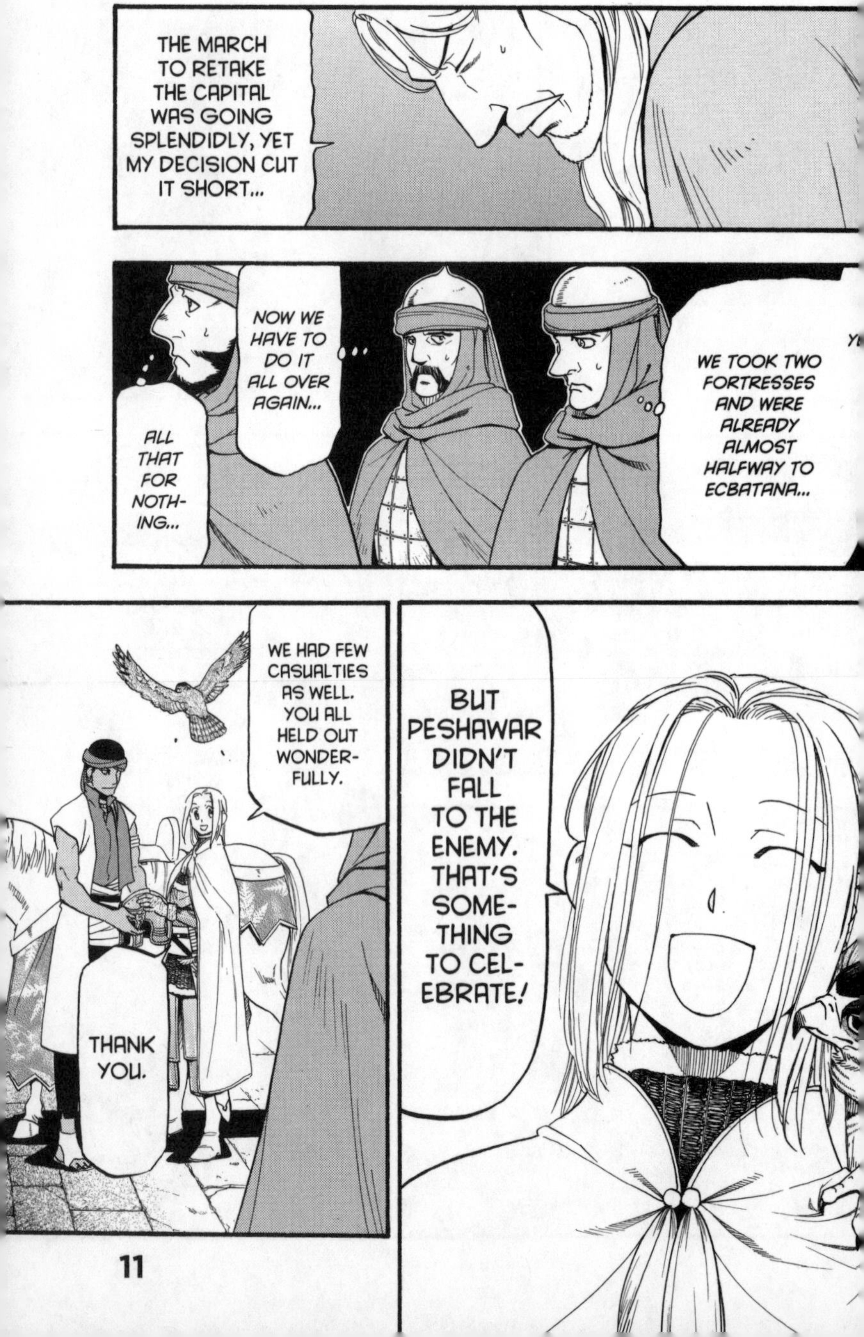

THE MARCH TO RETAKE THE CAPITAL WAS GOING SPLENDIDLY, YET MY DECISION CUT IT SHORT...
WE TOOK TWO FORTRESSES AND WERE ALREADY ALMOST HALFWAY TO ECBATANA...
NOW WE HAVE TO DO IT ALL OVER AGAIN...
ALL THAT FOR NOTHING...
BUT PESHAWAR DIDN'T FALL TO THE ENEMY. THAT'S SOMETHING TO CELEBRATE!
WE HAD FEW CASUALTIES AS WELL. YOU ALL HELD OUT WONDERFULLY.
THANK YOU.

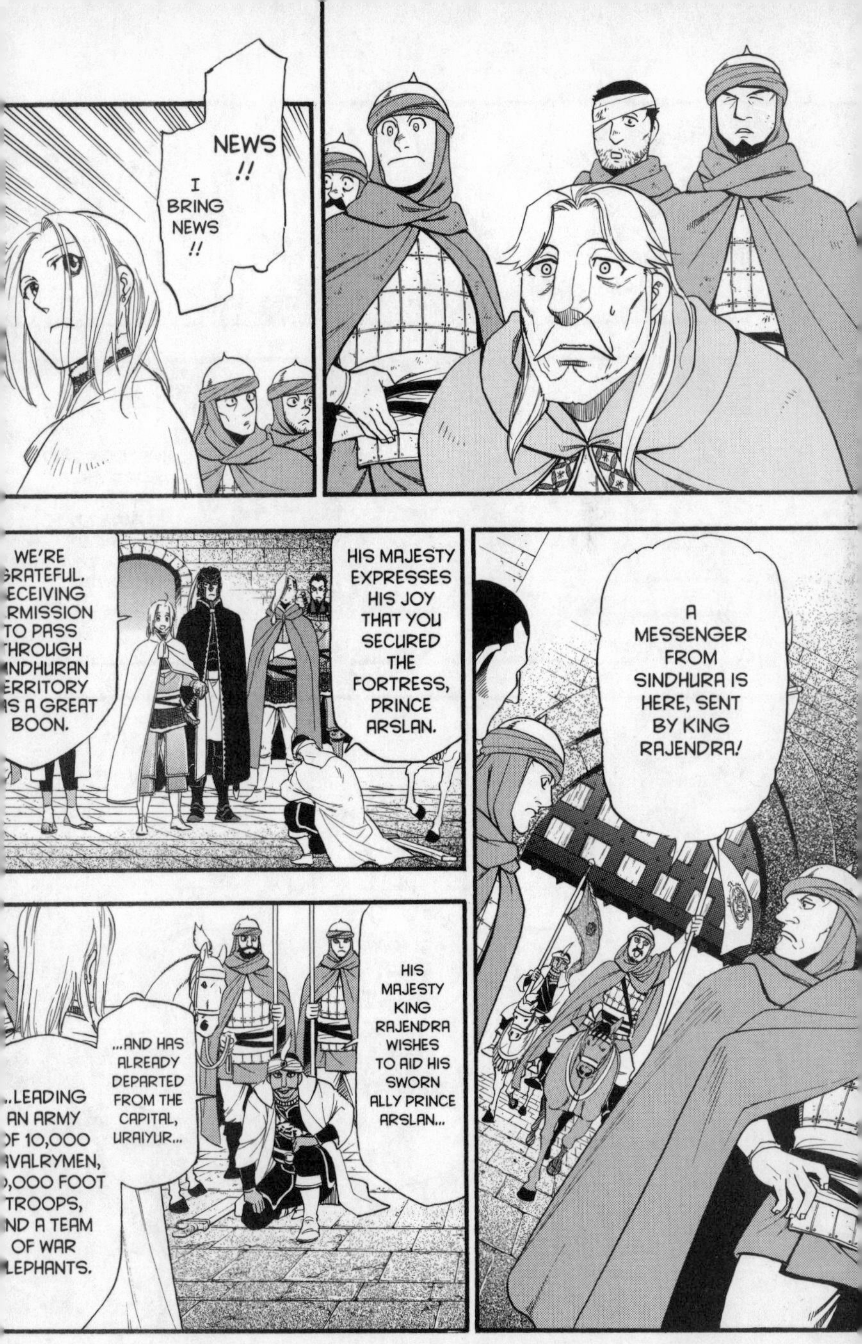
NEWS!! I BRING NEWS!!
A MESSENGER FROM SINDHURA IS HERE, SENT BY KING RAJENDRA!
HIS MAJESTY EXPRESSES HIS JOY THAT YOU SECURED THE FORTRESS, PRINCE ARSLAN.
WE'RE GRATEFUL. ECEIVING RMISSION TO PASS THROUGH INDHURAN ERRITORY S A GREAT BOON.
HIS MAJESTY KING RAJENDRA WISHES TO AID HIS SWORN ALLY PRINCE ARSLAN...
...AND HAS ALREADY DEPARTED FROM THE CAPITAL, URAIYUR...
..LEADING AN ARMY OF 10,000 VALRYMEN, ,000 FOOT TROOPS, ND A TEAM OF WAR LEPHANTS.

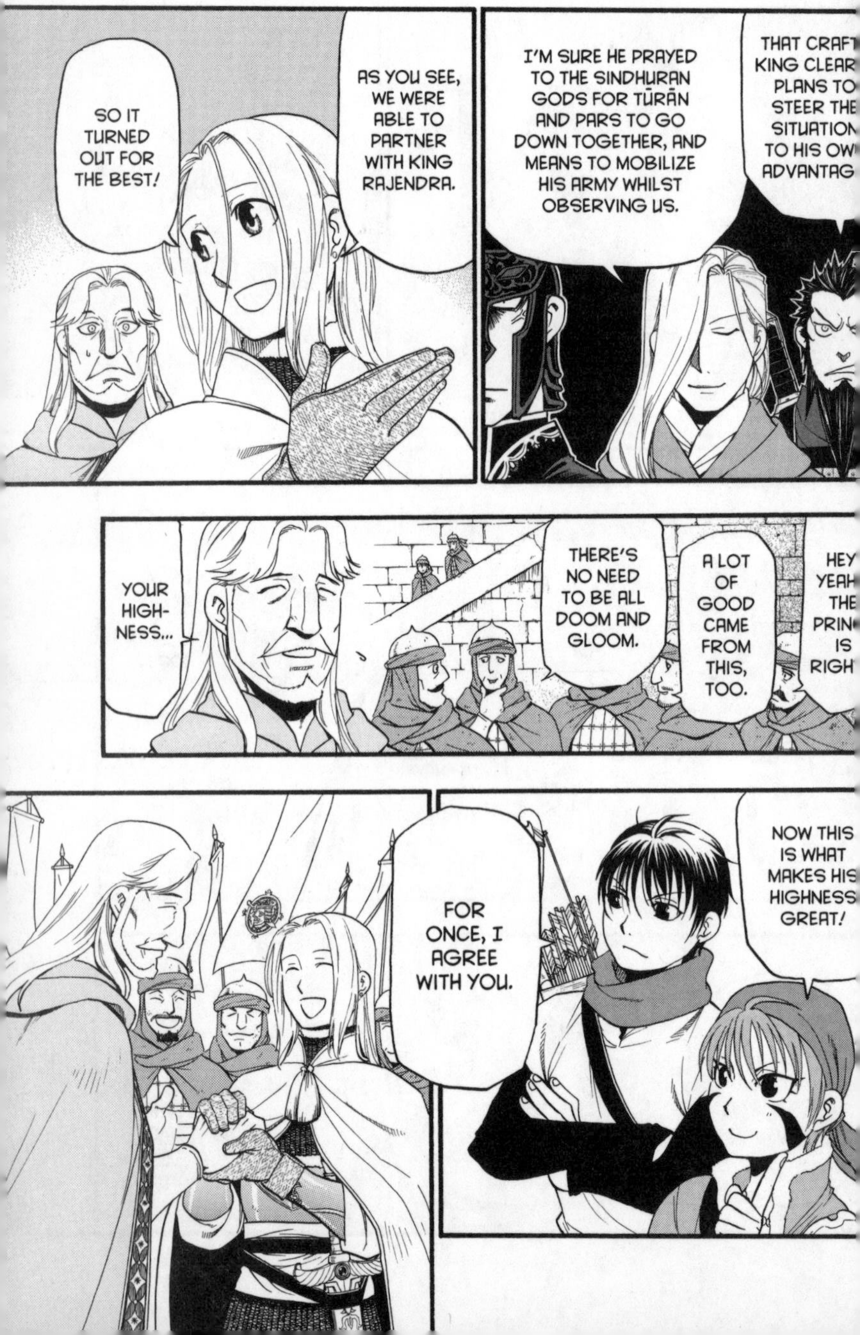
THAT CRAFT KING CLEAR PLANS TO STEER THE SITUATION TO HIS OW ADVANTAG
I'M SURE HE PRAYED TO THE SINDHURAN GODS FOR TŪRĀN AND PARS TO GO DOWN TOGETHER, AND MEANS TO MOBILIZE HIS ARMY WHILST OBSERVING US.
AS YOU SEE, WE WERE ABLE TO PARTNER WITH KING RAJENDRA.
SO IT TURNED OUT FOR THE BEST!
HEY YEAH THE PRIN IS RIGH
A LOT OF GOOD CAME FROM THIS, TOO.
THERE'S NO NEED TO BE ALL DOOM AND GLOOM.
YOUR HIGH-NESS...
NOW THIS IS WHAT MAKES HIS HIGHNESS GREAT!
FOR ONCE, I AGREE WITH YOU.

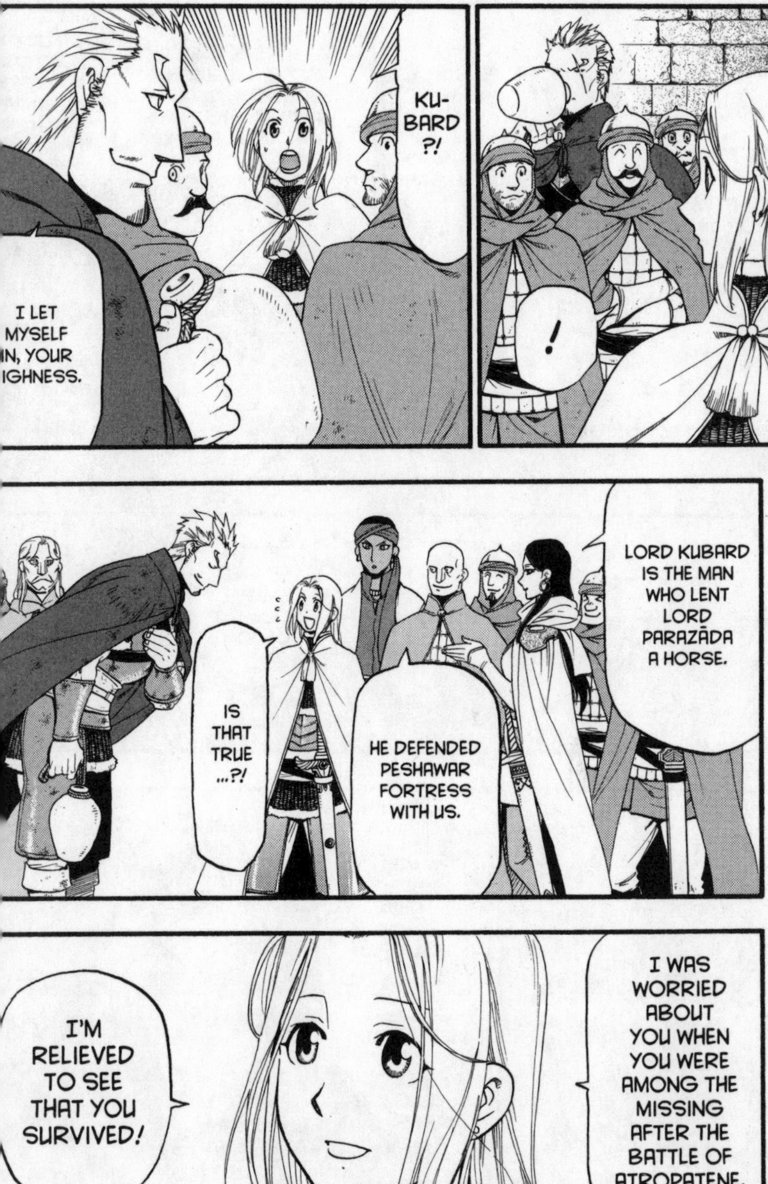
!
KU-BARD ?!
I LET MYSELF IN, YOUR IGHNESS.
LORD KUBARD IS THE MAN WHO LENT LORD PARAZĀDA A HORSE.
HE DEFENDED PESHAWAR FORTRESS WITH US.
IS THAT TRUE ...?!
I WAS WORRIED ABOUT YOU WHEN YOU WERE AMONG THE MISSING AFTER THE BATTLE OF ATROPATENE.
I'M RELIEVED TO SEE THAT YOU SURVIVED!

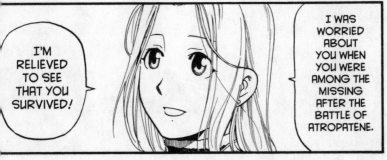

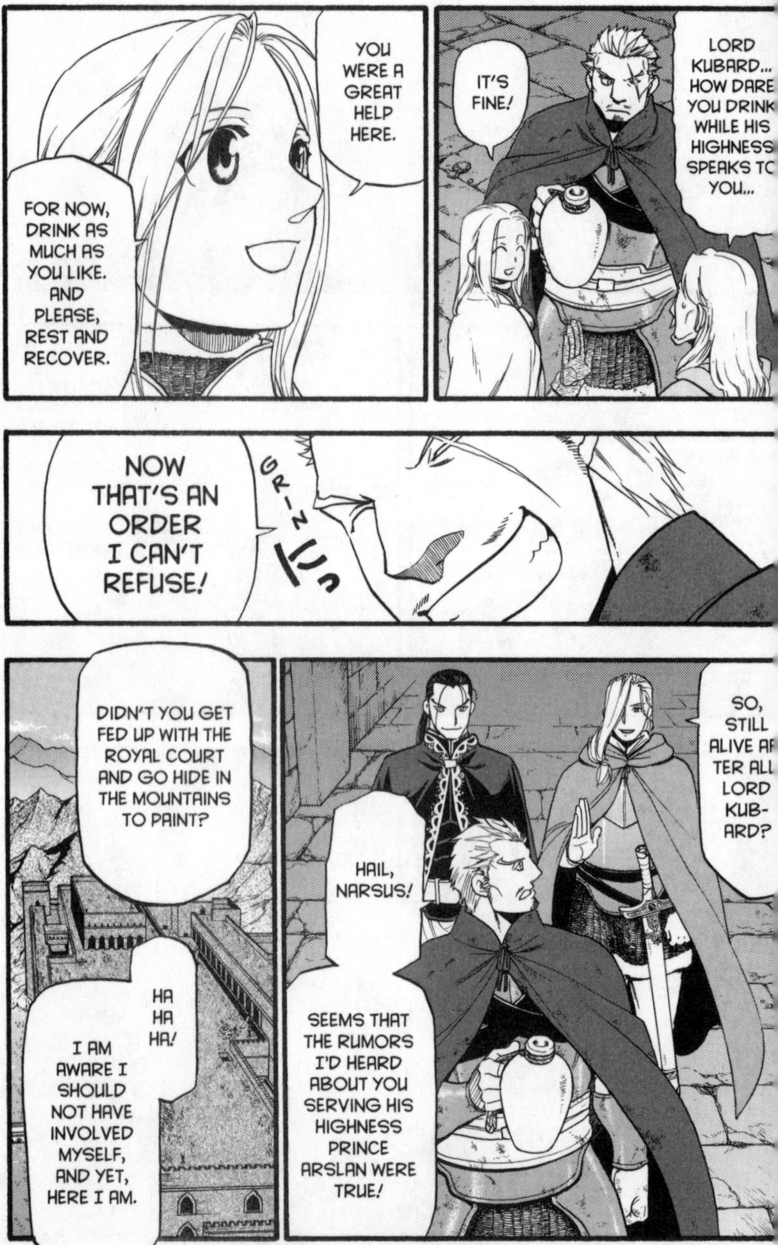
LORD KUBARD... HOW DARE YOU DRINK WHILE HIS HIGHNESS SPEAKS TO YOU...
IT'S FINE!
YOU WERE A GREAT HELP HERE.
FOR NOW, DRINK AS MUCH AS YOU LIKE. AND PLEASE, REST AND RECOVER.
GRIN
NOW THAT'S AN ORDER I CAN'T REFUSE!
SO, STILL ALIVE AFTER ALL, LORD KUB-ARD?
HAIL, NARSUS!
SEEMS THAT THE RUMORS I'D HEARD ABOUT YOU SERVING HIS HIGHNESS PRINCE ARSLAN WERE TRUE!
DIDN'T YOU GET FED UP WITH THE ROYAL COURT AND GO HIDE IN THE MOUNTAINS TO PAINT?
HA HA HA!
I AM AWARE I SHOULD NOT HAVE INVOLVED MYSELF, AND YET, HERE I AM.

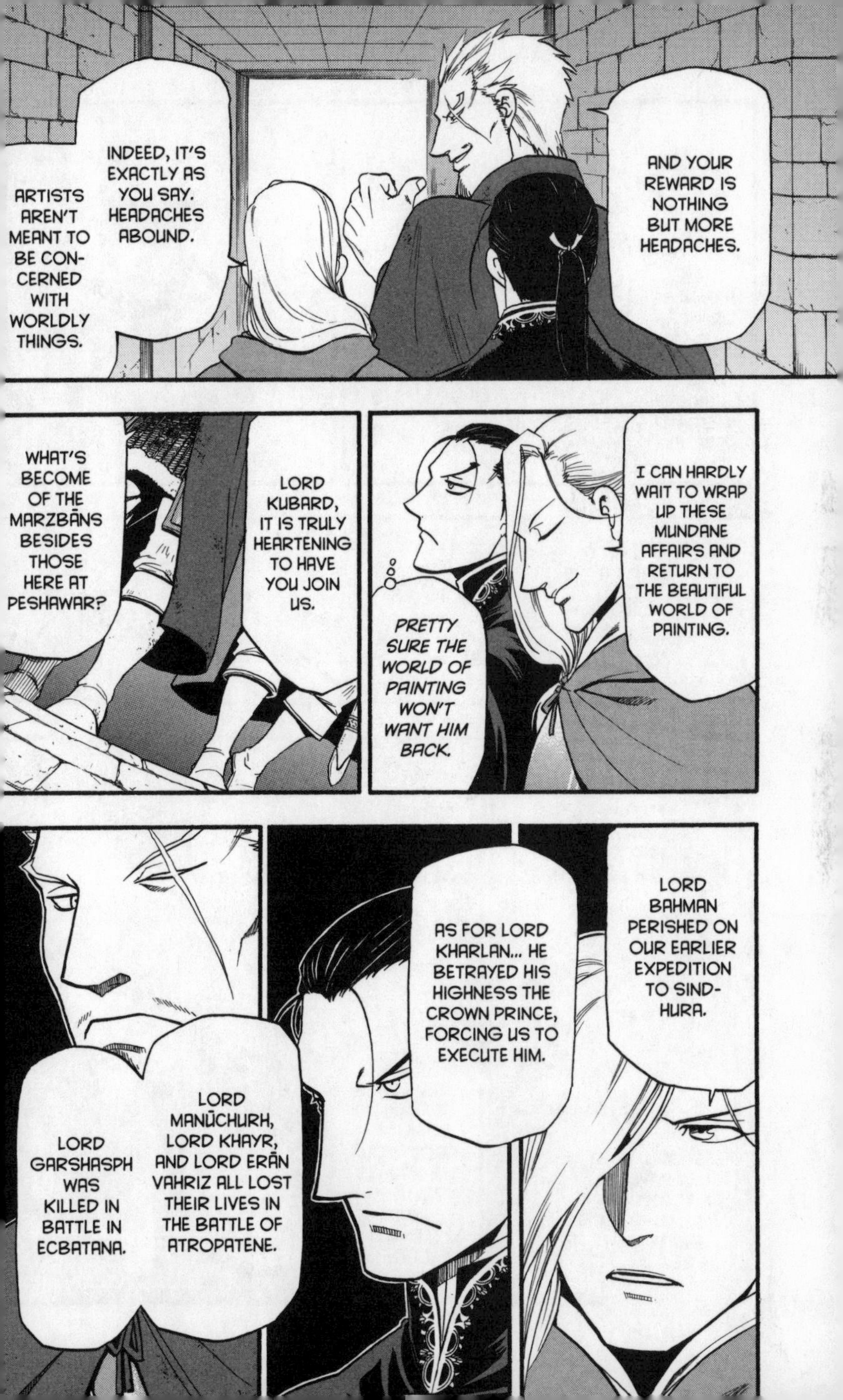
AND YOUR REWARD IS NOTHING BUT MORE HEADACHES.
INDEED, IT'S EXACTLY AS YOU SAY. HEADACHES ABOUND.
ARTISTS AREN'T MEANT TO BE CON-CERNED WITH WORLDLY THINGS.
I CAN HARDLY WAIT TO WRAP UP THESE MUNDANE AFFAIRS AND RETURN TO THE BEAUTIFUL WORLD OF PAINTING.
PRETTY SURE THE WORLD OF PAINTING WON'T WANT HIM BACK.
LORD KUBARD, IT IS TRULY HEARTENING TO HAVE YOU JOIN US.
WHAT'S BECOME OF THE MARZBĀNS BESIDES THOSE HERE AT PESHAWAR?
LORD BAHMAN PERISHED ON OUR EARLIER EXPEDITION TO SIND-HURA.
AS FOR LORD KHARLAN... HE BETRAYED HIS HIGHNESS THE CROWN PRINCE, FORCING US TO EXECUTE HIM.
LORD MANŪCHURH, LORD KHAYR, AND LORD ERĀN VAHRIZ ALL LOST THEIR LIVES IN THE BATTLE OF ATROPATENE.
LORD GARSHASPH WAS KILLED IN BATTLE IN ECBATANA.

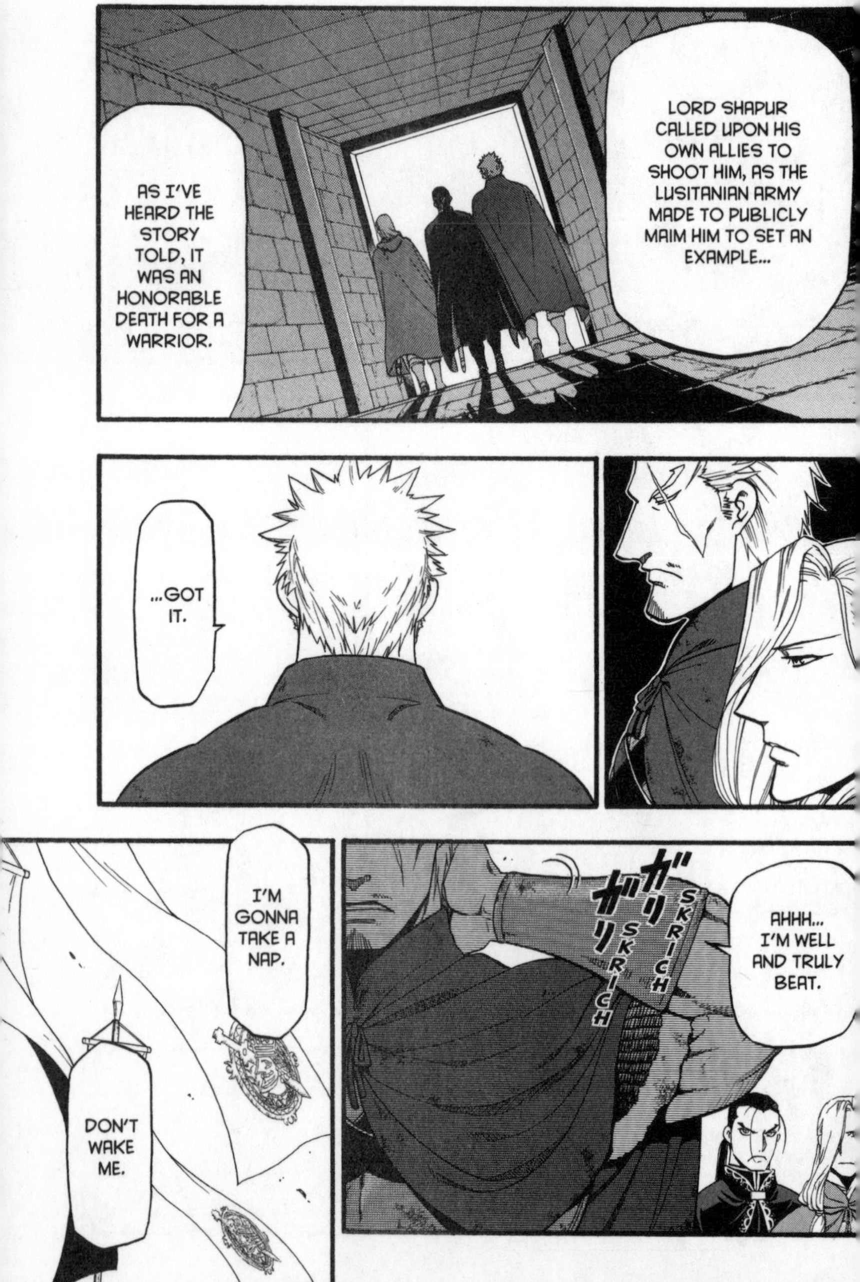
LORD SHAPUR CALLED UPON HIS OWN ALLIES TO SHOOT HIM, AS THE LUSITANIAN ARMY MADE TO PUBLICLY MAIM HIM TO SET AN EXAMPLE...
AS I'VE HEARD THE STORY TOLD, IT WAS AN HONORABLE DEATH FOR A WARRIOR.
...GOT IT.
AHHH... I'M WELL AND TRULY BEAT.
ガリ SKRICH
ガリ SKRICH
I'M GONNA TAKE A NAP.
DON'T WAKE ME.

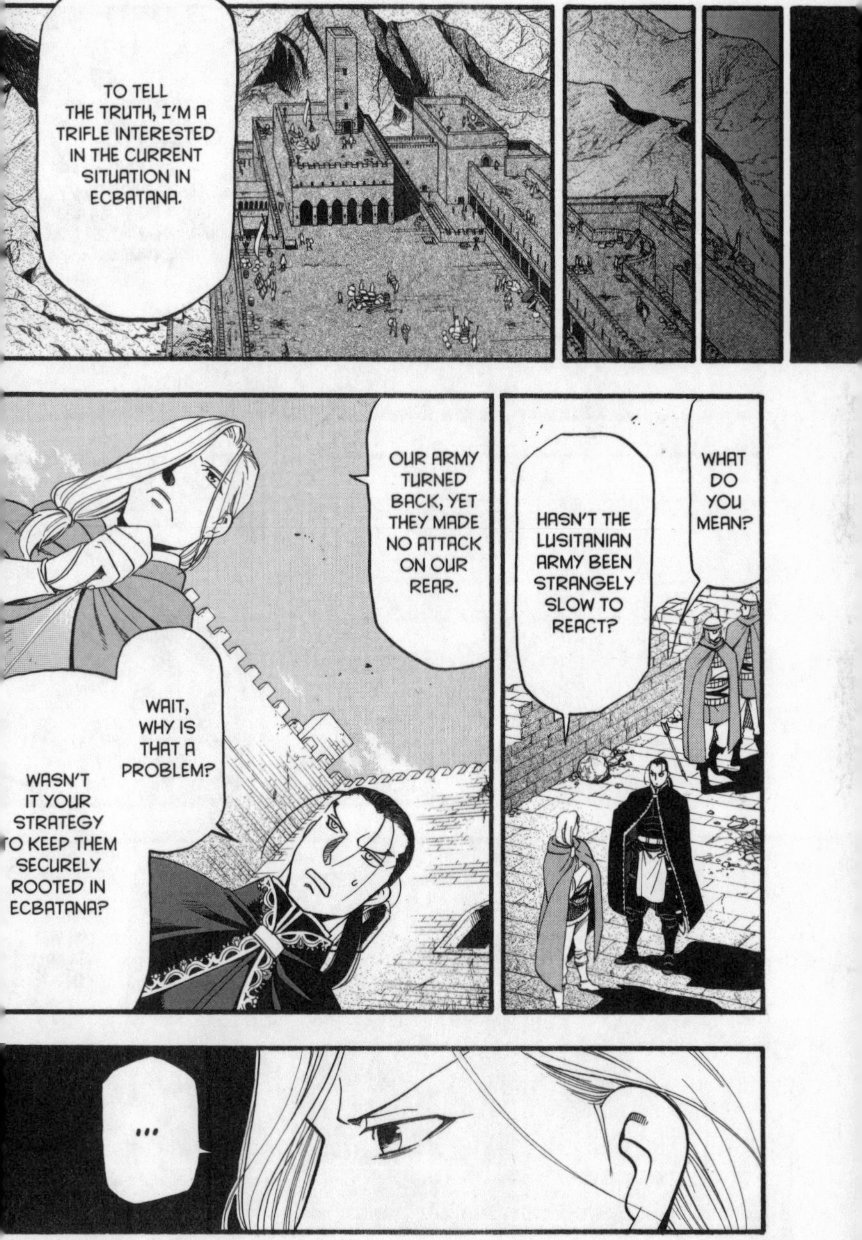
TO TELL THE TRUTH, I'M A TRIFLE INTERESTED IN THE CURRENT SITUATION IN ECBATANA.
WHAT DO YOU MEAN?
HASN'T THE LUSITANIAN ARMY BEEN STRANGELY SLOW TO REACT?
OUR ARMY TURNED BACK, YET THEY MADE NO ATTACK ON OUR REAR.
WAIT, WHY IS THAT A PROBLEM?
WASN'T IT YOUR STRATEGY TO KEEP THEM SECURELY ROOTED IN ECBATANA?
...

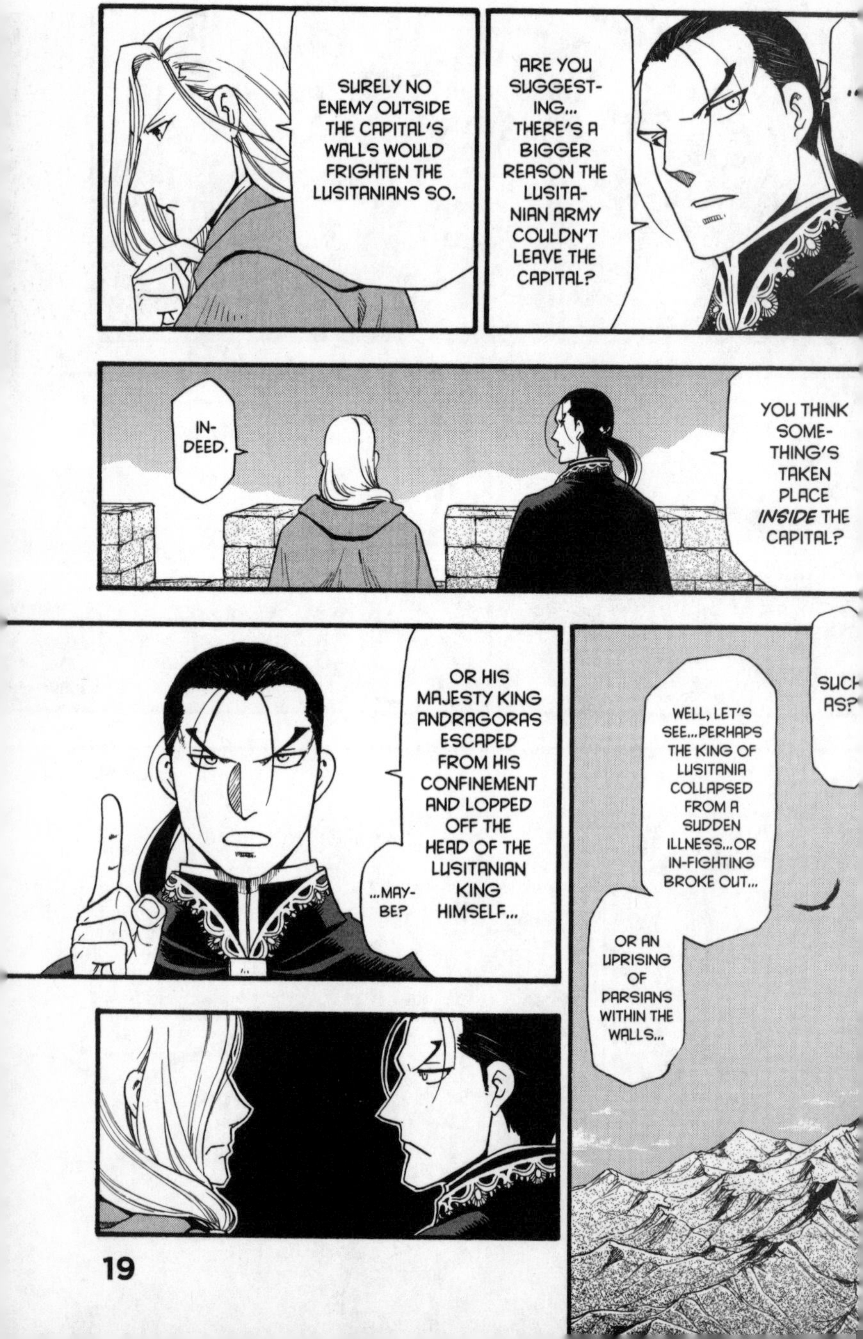

ARE YOU SUGGESTING... THERE'S A BIGGER REASON THE LUSITANIAN ARMY COULDN'T LEAVE THE CAPITAL?
SURELY NO ENEMY OUTSIDE THE CAPITAL'S WALLS WOULD FRIGHTEN THE LUSITANIANS SO.
YOU THINK SOMETHING'S TAKEN PLACE *INSIDE* THE CAPITAL?
INDEED.
SUCH AS?
WELL, LET'S SEE...PERHAPS THE KING OF LUSITANIA COLLAPSED FROM A SUDDEN ILLNESS...OR IN-FIGHTING BROKE OUT...
OR AN UPRISING OF PARSIANS WITHIN THE WALLS...
OR HIS MAJESTY KING ANDRAGORAS ESCAPED FROM HIS CONFINEMENT AND LOPPED OFF THE HEAD OF THE LUSITANIAN KING HIMSELF...
...MAYBE?

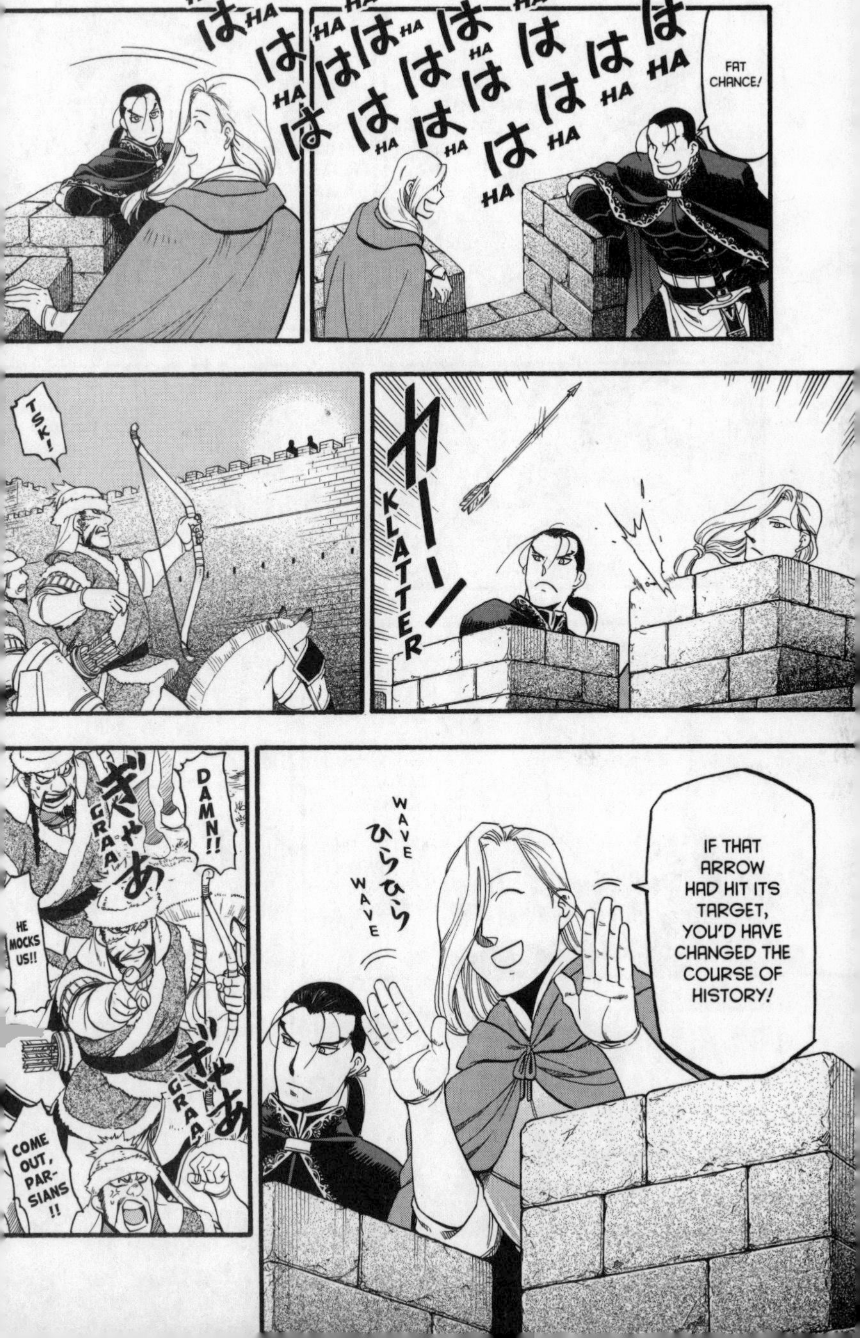

FAT CHANCE!
HA HA HA HA HA HA HA HA HA HA HA HA HA HA HA HA
ははははははははははははは
カーン
KLATTER
TSK!
IF THAT ARROW HAD HIT ITS TARGET, YOU'D HAVE CHANGED THE COURSE OF HISTORY!
ひらひら
WAVE WAVE
DAMN!!
ぎゃあ
GRAA
HE MOCKS US!!
ぎゃあ
GRAA
COME OUT, PAR-SIANS!!

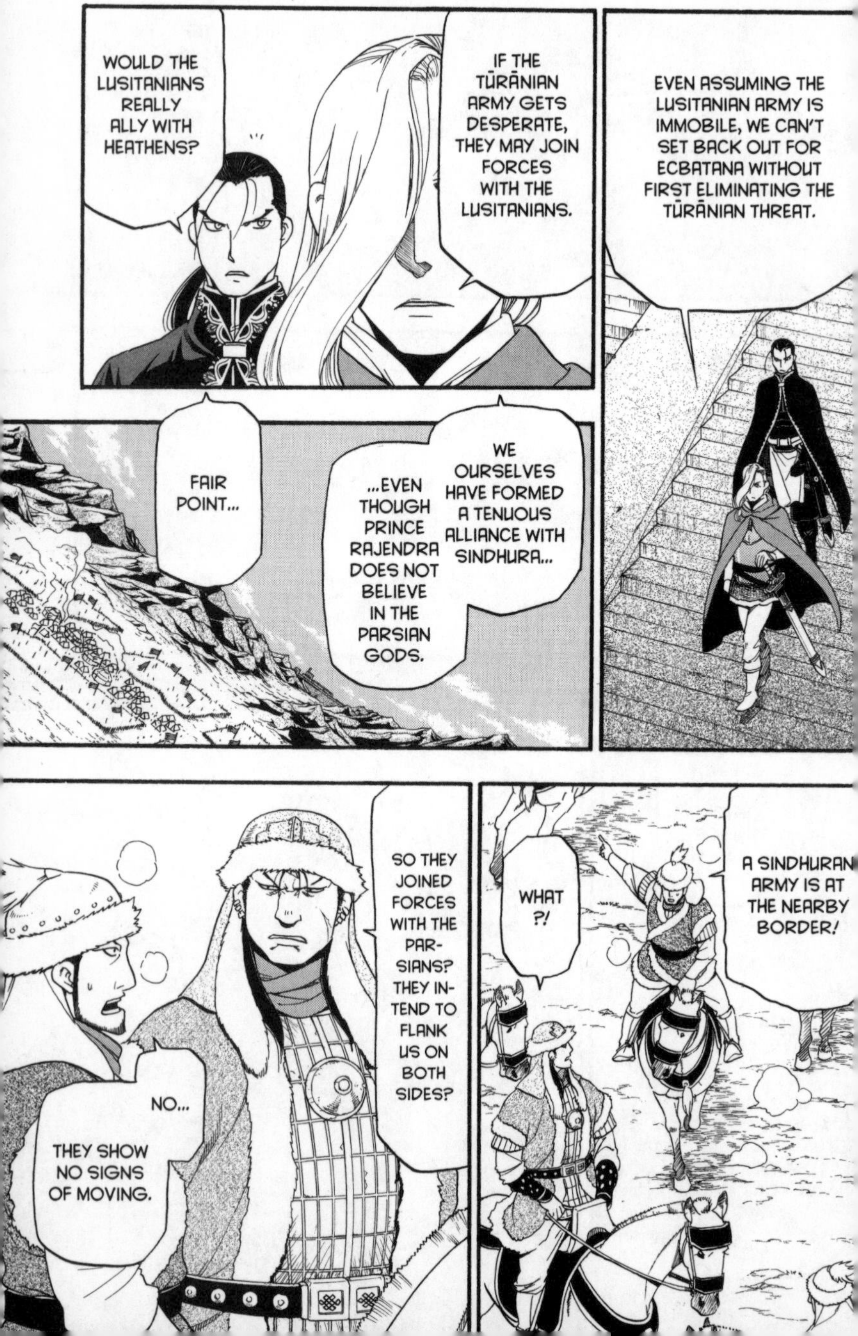
EVEN ASSUMING THE LUSITANIAN ARMY IS IMMOBILE, WE CAN'T SET BACK OUT FOR ECBATANA WITHOUT FIRST ELIMINATING THE TŪRĀNIAN THREAT.
IF THE TŪRĀNIAN ARMY GETS DESPERATE, THEY MAY JOIN FORCES WITH THE LUSITANIANS.
WOULD THE LUSITANIANS REALLY ALLY WITH HEATHENS?
WE OURSELVES HAVE FORMED A TENUOUS ALLIANCE WITH SINDHURA...
...EVEN THOUGH PRINCE RAJENDRA DOES NOT BELIEVE IN THE PARSIAN GODS.
FAIR POINT...
A SINDHURAN ARMY IS AT THE NEARBY BORDER!
WHAT ?!
SO THEY JOINED FORCES WITH THE PAR-SIANS? THEY IN-TEND TO FLANK US ON BOTH SIDES?
NO...
THEY SHOW NO SIGNS OF MOVING.

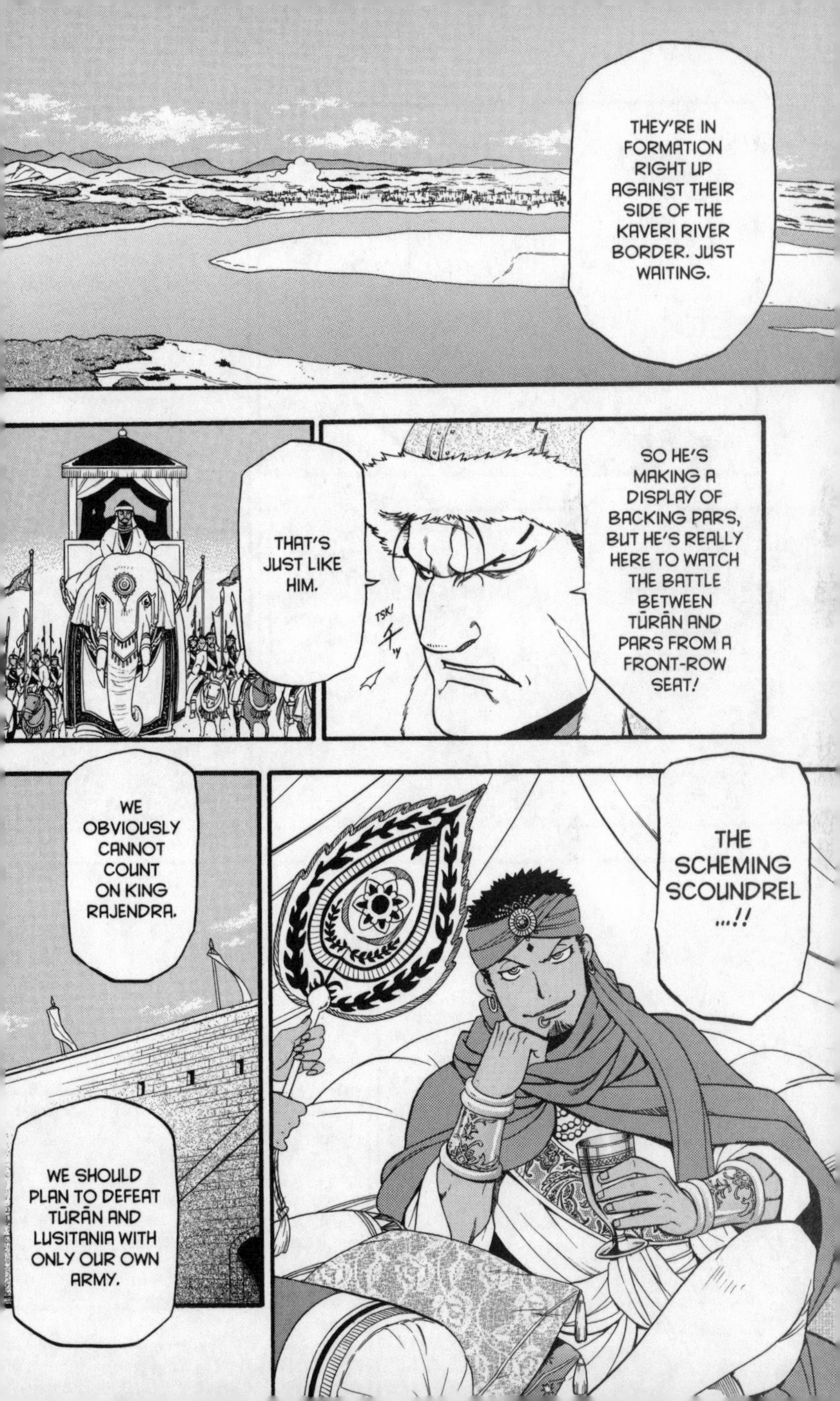
THEY'RE IN FORMATION RIGHT UP AGAINST THEIR SIDE OF THE KAVERI RIVER BORDER. JUST WAITING.
SO HE'S MAKING A DISPLAY OF BACKING PARS, BUT HE'S REALLY HERE TO WATCH THE BATTLE BETWEEN TŪRĀN AND PARS FROM A FRONT-ROW SEAT!
TSK!
THAT'S JUST LIKE HIM.
THE SCHEMING SCOUNDREL ...!!
WE OBVIOUSLY CANNOT COUNT ON KING RAJENDRA.
WE SHOULD PLAN TO DEFEAT TŪRĀN AND LUSITANIA WITH ONLY OUR OWN ARMY.

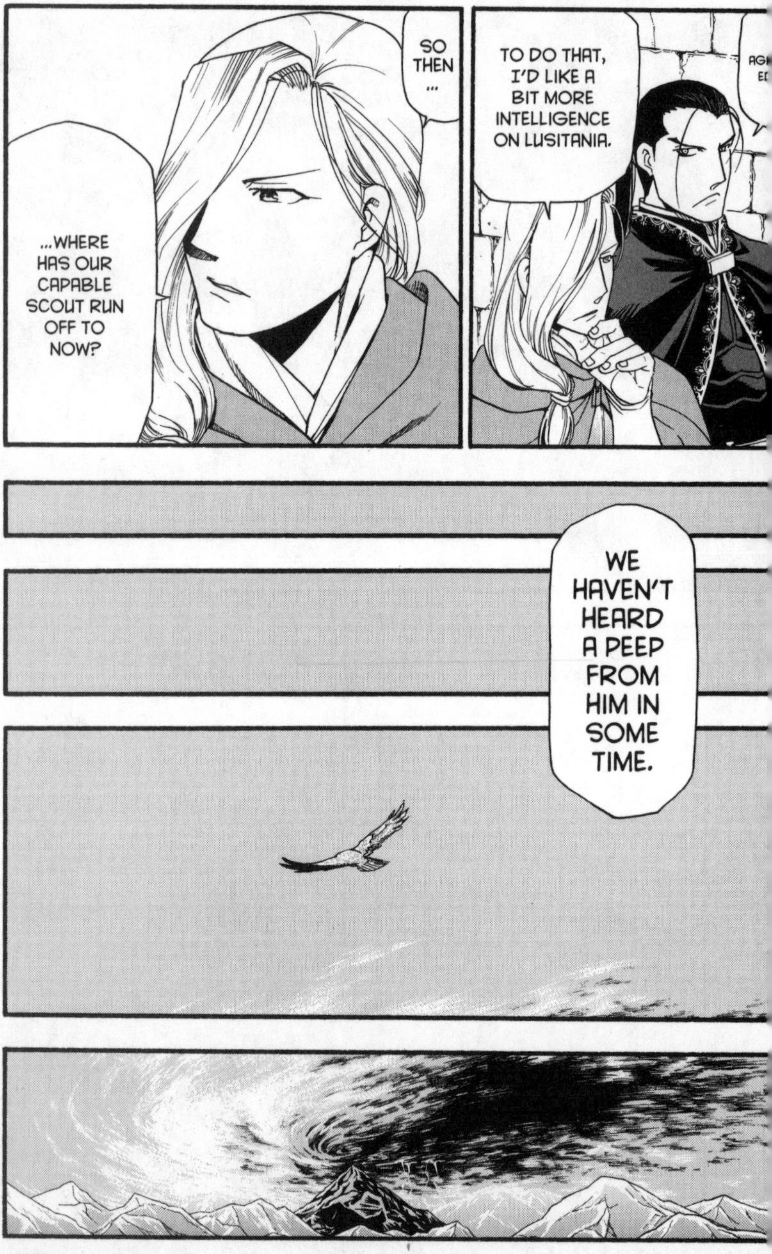
TO DO THAT, I'D LIKE A BIT MORE INTELLIGENCE ON LUSITANIA.
SO THEN ...
...WHERE HAS OUR CAPABLE SCOUT RUN OFF TO NOW?
WE HAVEN'T HEARD A PEEP FROM HIM IN SOME TIME.

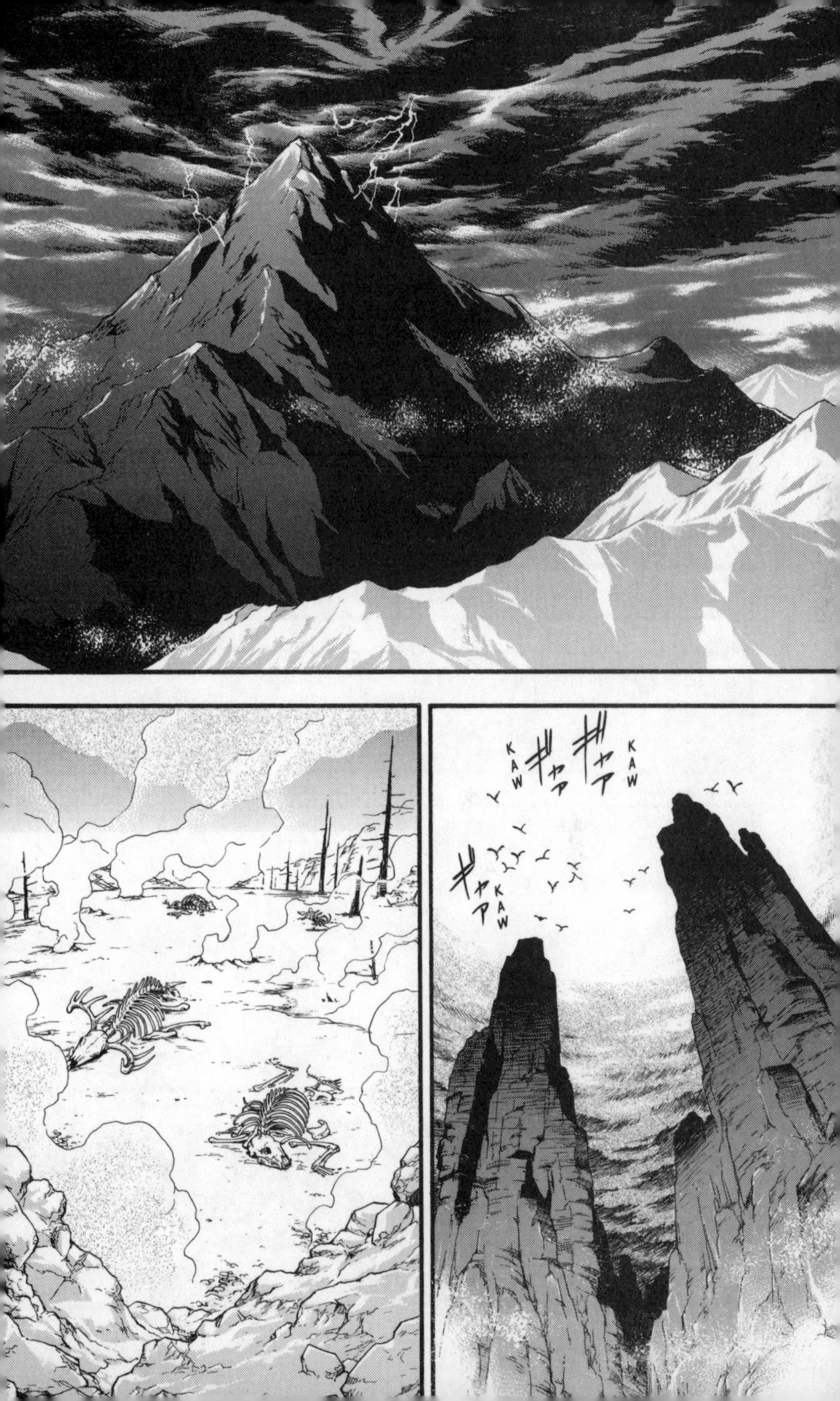

ギャア KAW
ギャア KAW
ギャア KAW

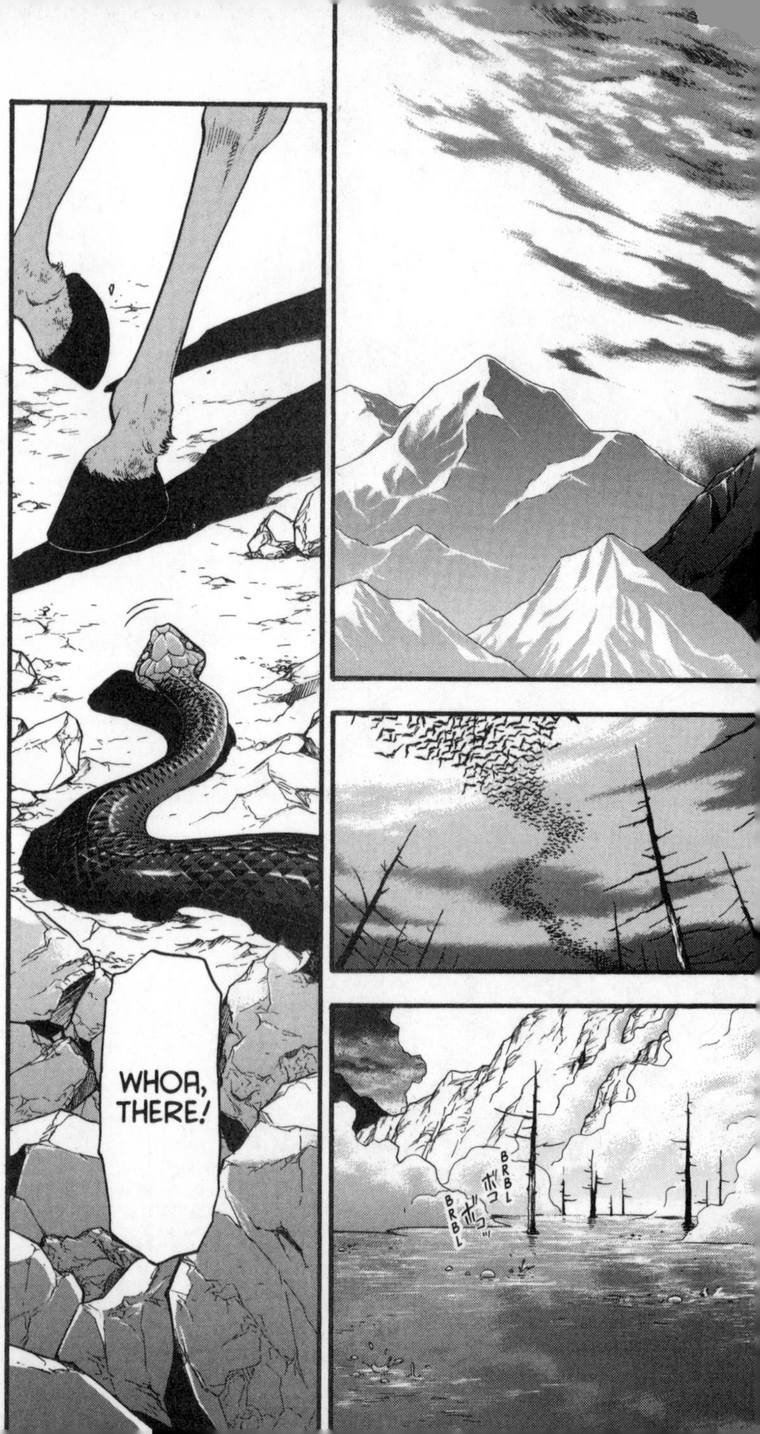
BRBL
ボコ
BRBL
ボコッ
WHOA, THERE!

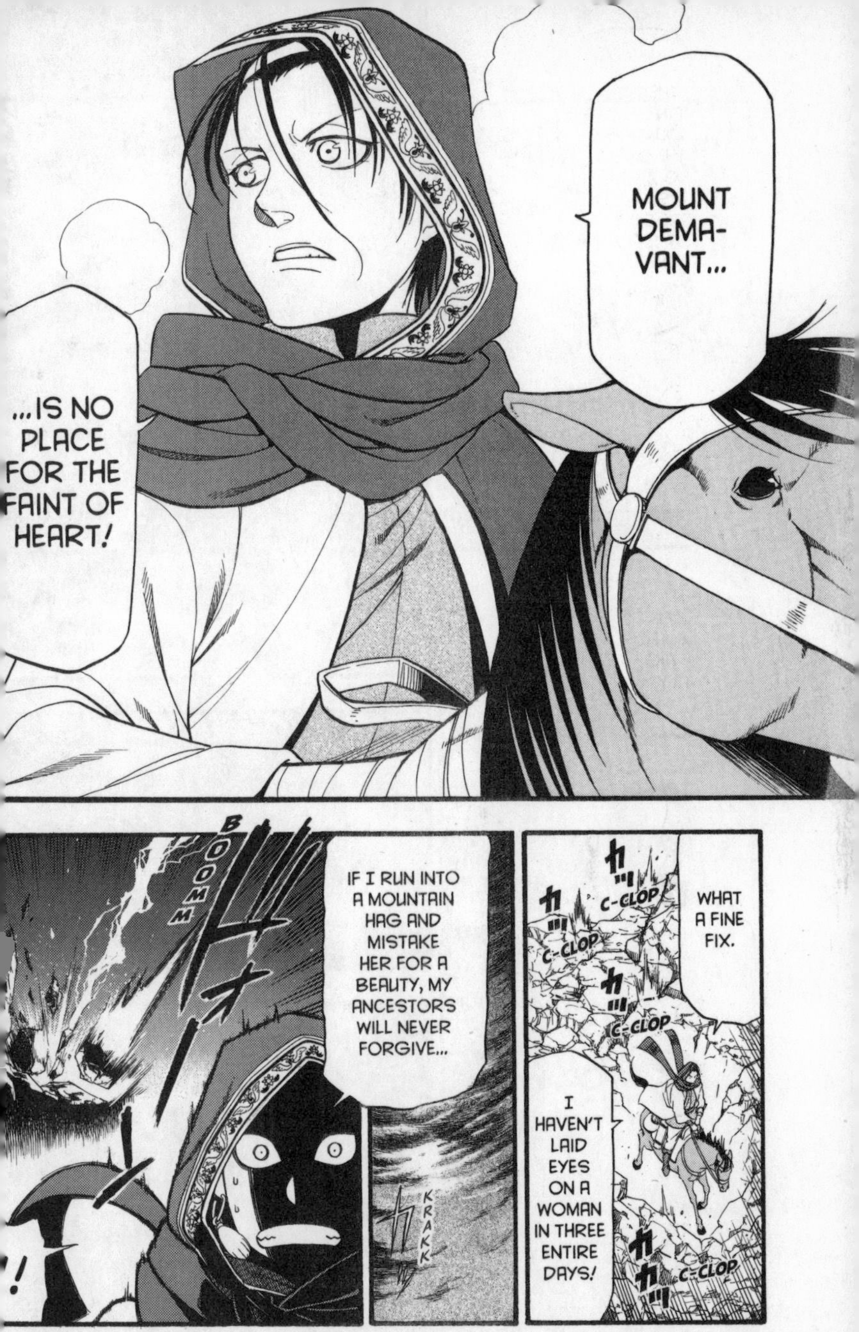

MOUNT DEMA-VANT...
...IS NO PLACE FOR THE FAINT OF HEART!
C-CLOP
C-CLOP
C-CLOP
WHAT A FINE FIX.
I HAVEN'T LAID EYES ON A WOMAN IN THREE ENTIRE DAYS!
C-CLOP
IF I RUN INTO A MOUNTAIN HAG AND MISTAKE HER FOR A BEAUTY, MY ANCESTORS WILL NEVER FORGIVE...
KRAKK
BOOMM
!

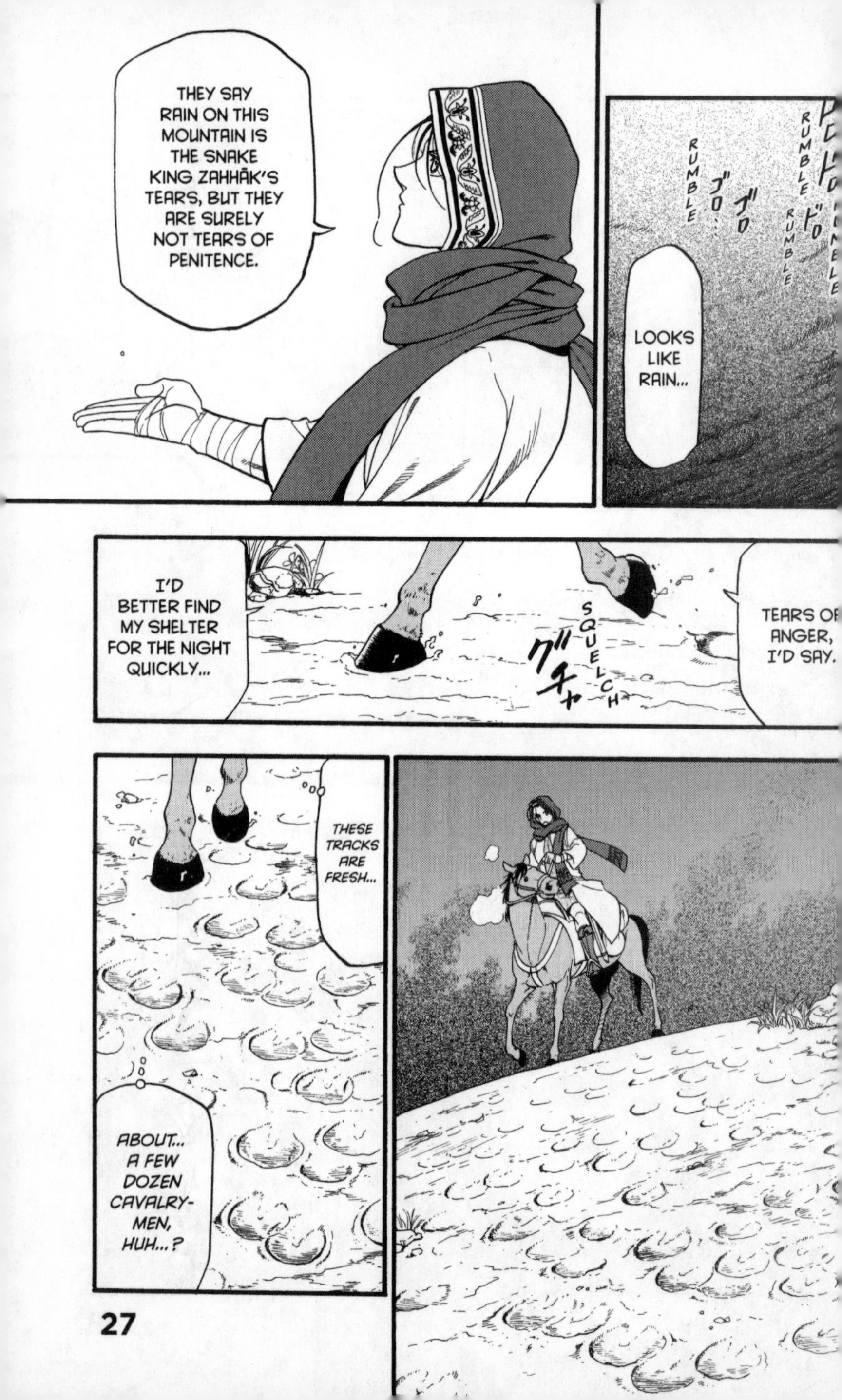
RUMBLE
RUMBLE
RUMBLE
RUMBLE
LOOKS LIKE RAIN...
THEY SAY RAIN ON THIS MOUNTAIN IS THE SNAKE KING ZAHHĀK'S TEARS, BUT THEY ARE SURELY NOT TEARS OF PENITENCE.
TEARS OF ANGER, I'D SAY.
グチャ
SQUELCH
I'D BETTER FIND MY SHELTER FOR THE NIGHT QUICKLY...
THESE TRACKS ARE FRESH...
ABOUT... A FEW DOZEN CAVALRYMEN, HUH...?

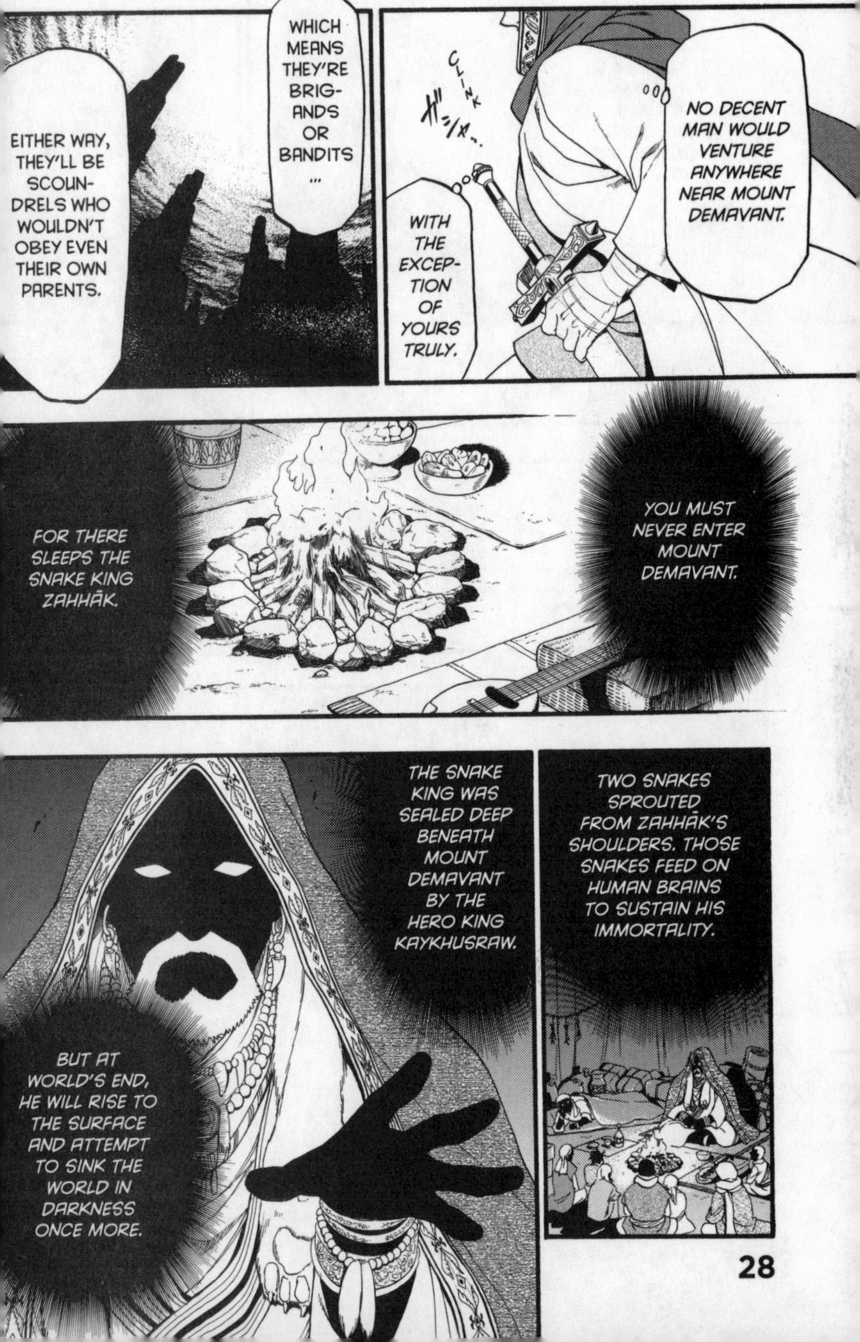

NO DECENT MAN WOULD VENTURE ANYWHERE NEAR MOUNT DEMAVANT.
CLINK
WITH THE EXCEPTION OF YOURS TRULY.
WHICH MEANS THEY'RE BRIG-ANDS OR BANDITS ...
EITHER WAY, THEY'LL BE SCOUN-DRELS WHO WOULDN'T OBEY EVEN THEIR OWN PARENTS.
YOU MUST NEVER ENTER MOUNT DEMAVANT.
FOR THERE SLEEPS THE SNAKE KING ZAHHĀK.
TWO SNAKES SPROUTED FROM ZAHHĀK'S SHOULDERS. THOSE SNAKES FEED ON HUMAN BRAINS TO SUSTAIN HIS IMMORTALITY.
THE SNAKE KING WAS SEALED DEEP BENEATH MOUNT DEMAVANT BY THE HERO KING KAYKHUSRAW.
BUT AT WORLD'S END, HE WILL RISE TO THE SURFACE AND ATTEMPT TO SINK THE WORLD IN DARKNESS ONCE MORE.

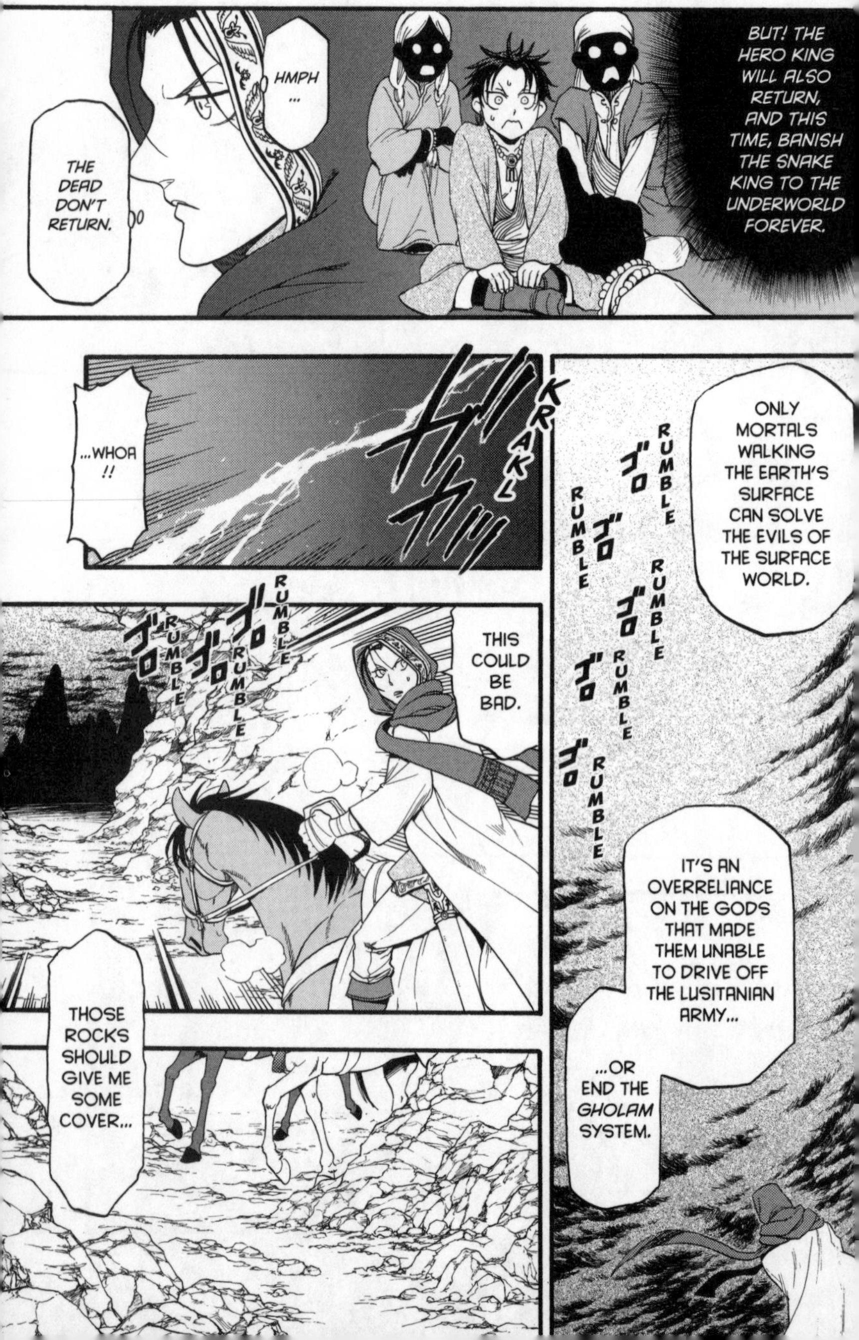

BUT! THE HERO KING WILL ALSO RETURN, AND THIS TIME, BANISH THE SNAKE KING TO THE UNDERWORLD FOREVER.
HMPH ...
THE DEAD DON'T RETURN.
ONLY MORTALS WALKING THE EARTH'S SURFACE CAN SOLVE THE EVILS OF THE SURFACE WORLD.
RUMBLE
RUMBLE
RUMBLE
RUMBLE
RUMBLE
IT'S AN OVERRELIANCE ON THE GODS THAT MADE THEM UNABLE TO DRIVE OFF THE LUSITANIAN ARMY...
...OR END THE GHOLAM SYSTEM.
KRAKL
...WHOA !!
RUMBLE
RUMBLE
RUMBLE
THIS COULD BE BAD.
THOSE ROCKS SHOULD GIVE ME SOME COVER...

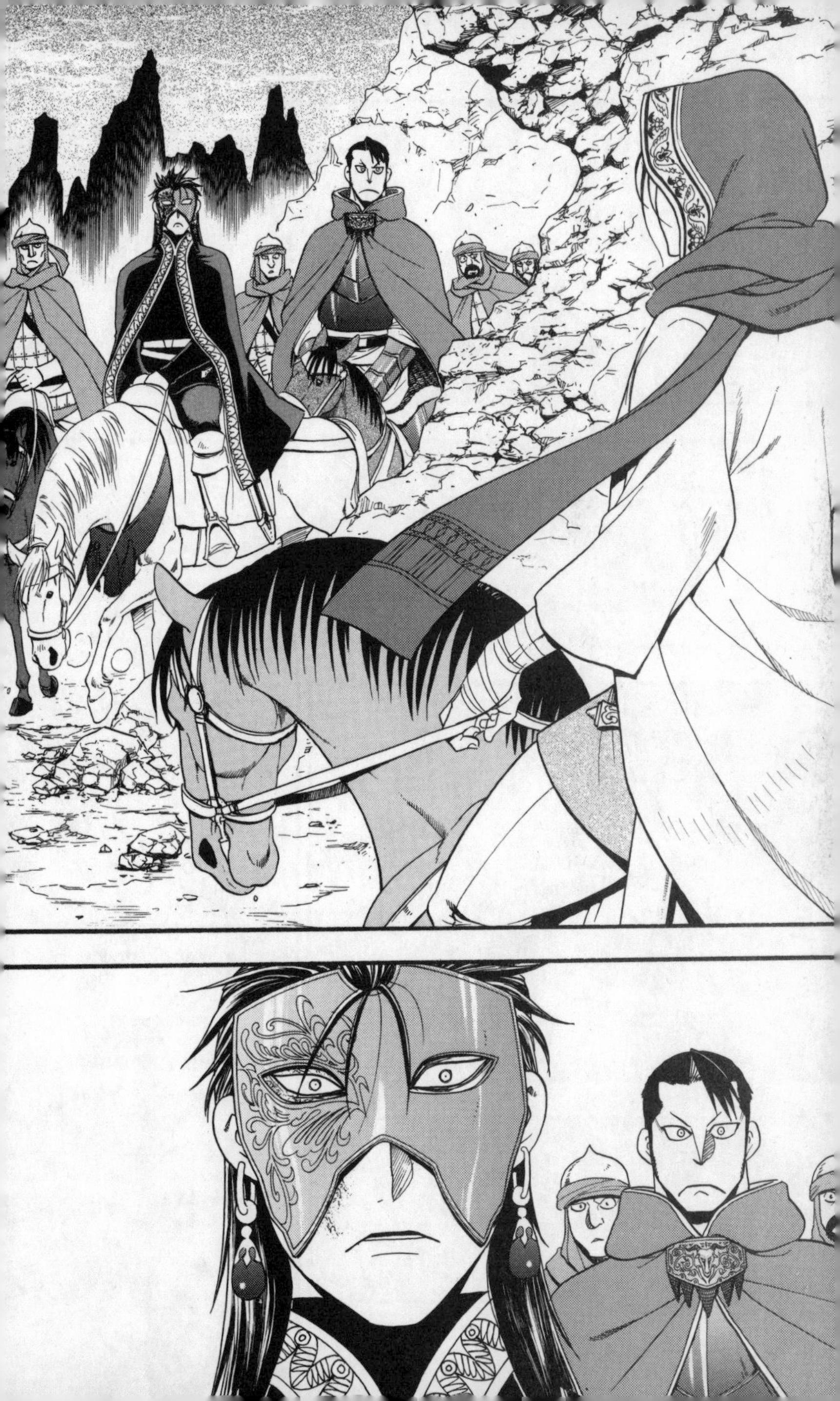

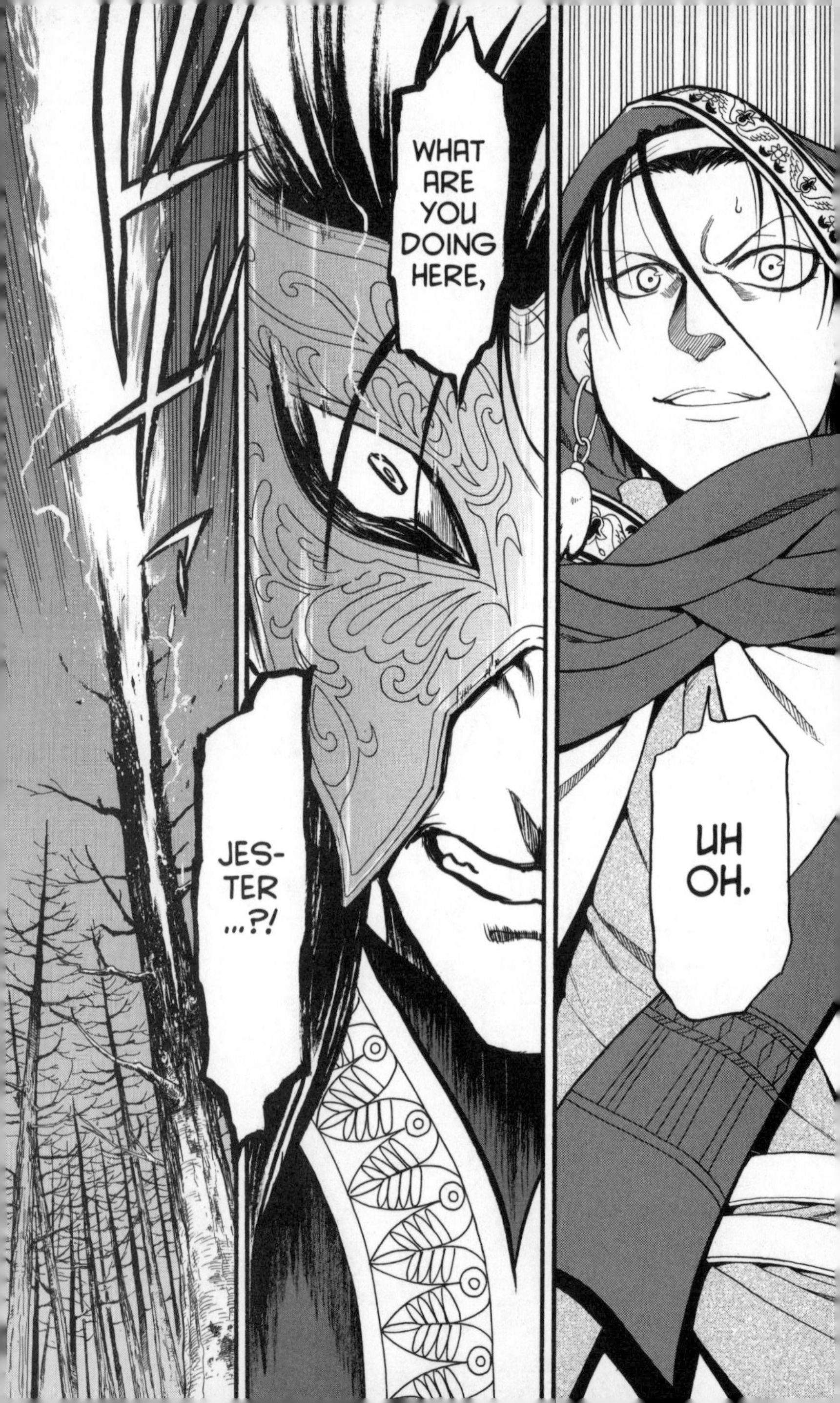
UH OH.
WHAT ARE YOU DOING HERE,
JES-TER ...?!

THE HEROIC LEGEND OF
ARSLAN

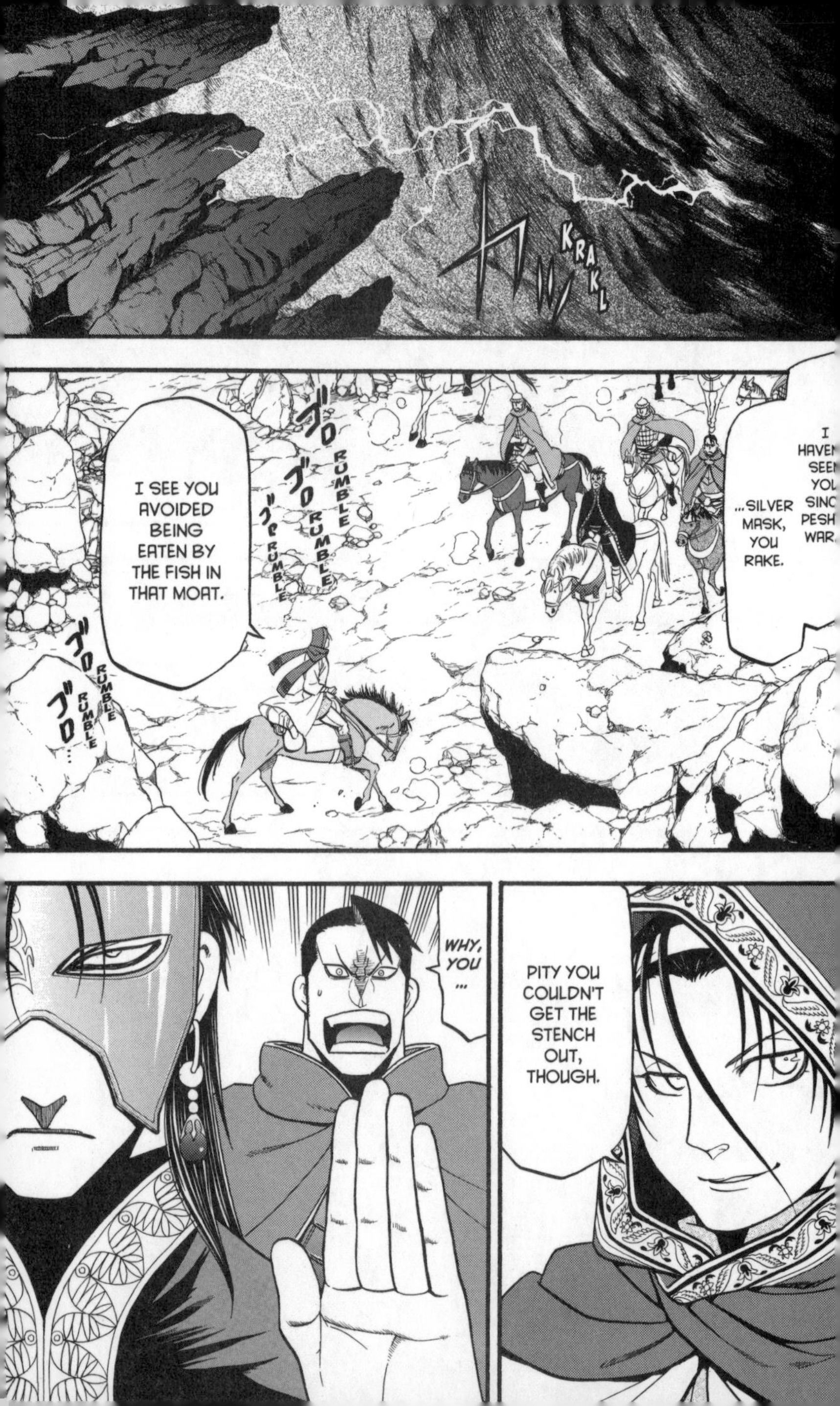
KRAKL
I HAVEN SEEN YOL SINC PESH WAR.
...SILVER MASK, YOU RAKE.
RUMBLE RUMBLE RUMBLE
I SEE YOU AVOIDED BEING EATEN BY THE FISH IN THAT MOAT.
RUMBLE RUMBLE
PITY YOU COULDN'T GET THE STENCH OUT, THOUGH.
WHY, YOU ...

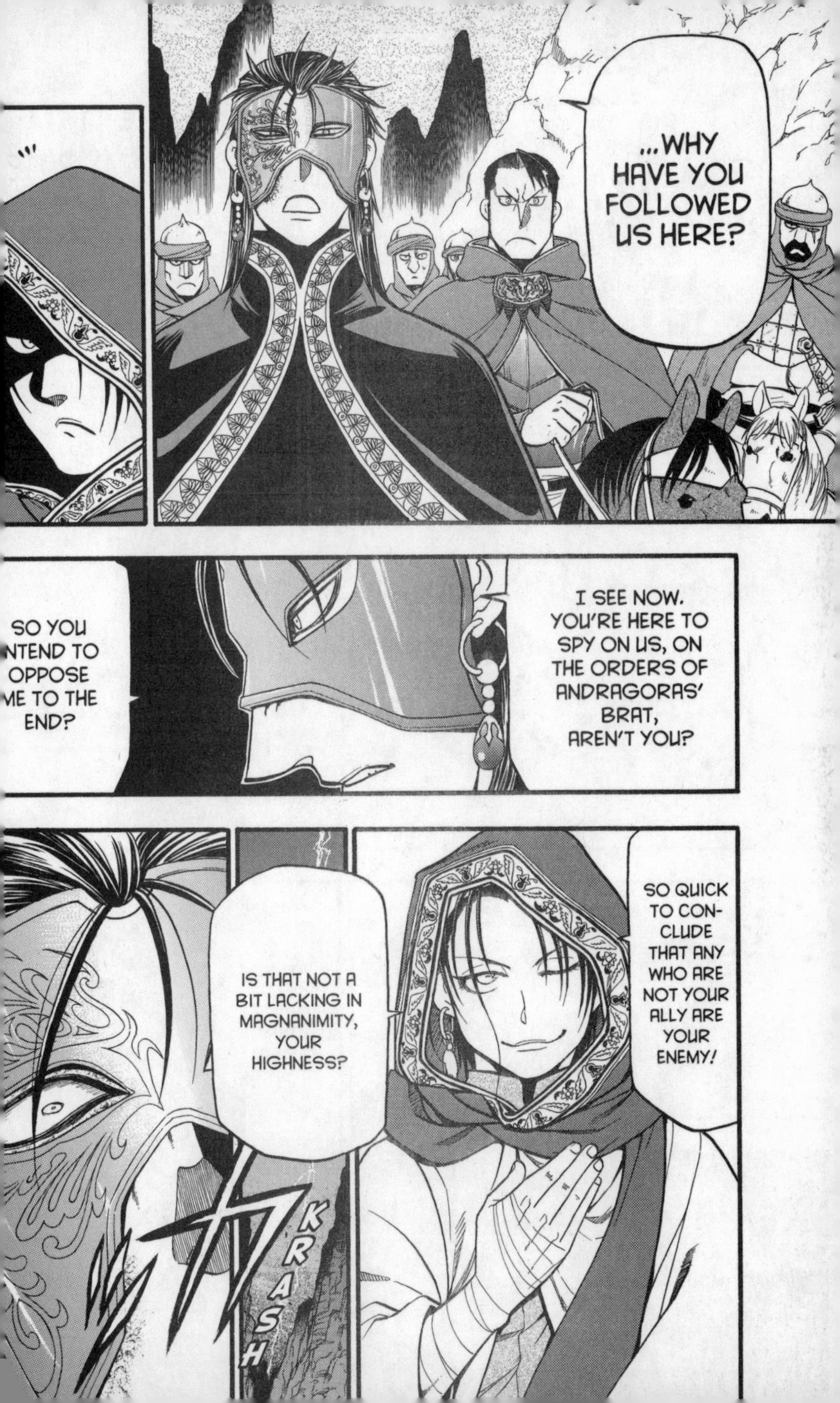
...WHY HAVE YOU FOLLOWED US HERE?
I SEE NOW. YOU'RE HERE TO SPY ON US, ON THE ORDERS OF ANDRAGORAS' BRAT, AREN'T YOU?
SO YOU NTEND TO OPPOSE ME TO THE END?
SO QUICK TO CON-CLUDE THAT ANY WHO ARE NOT YOUR ALLY ARE YOUR ENEMY!
IS THAT NOT A BIT LACKING IN MAGNANIMITY, YOUR HIGHNESS?
KRASH

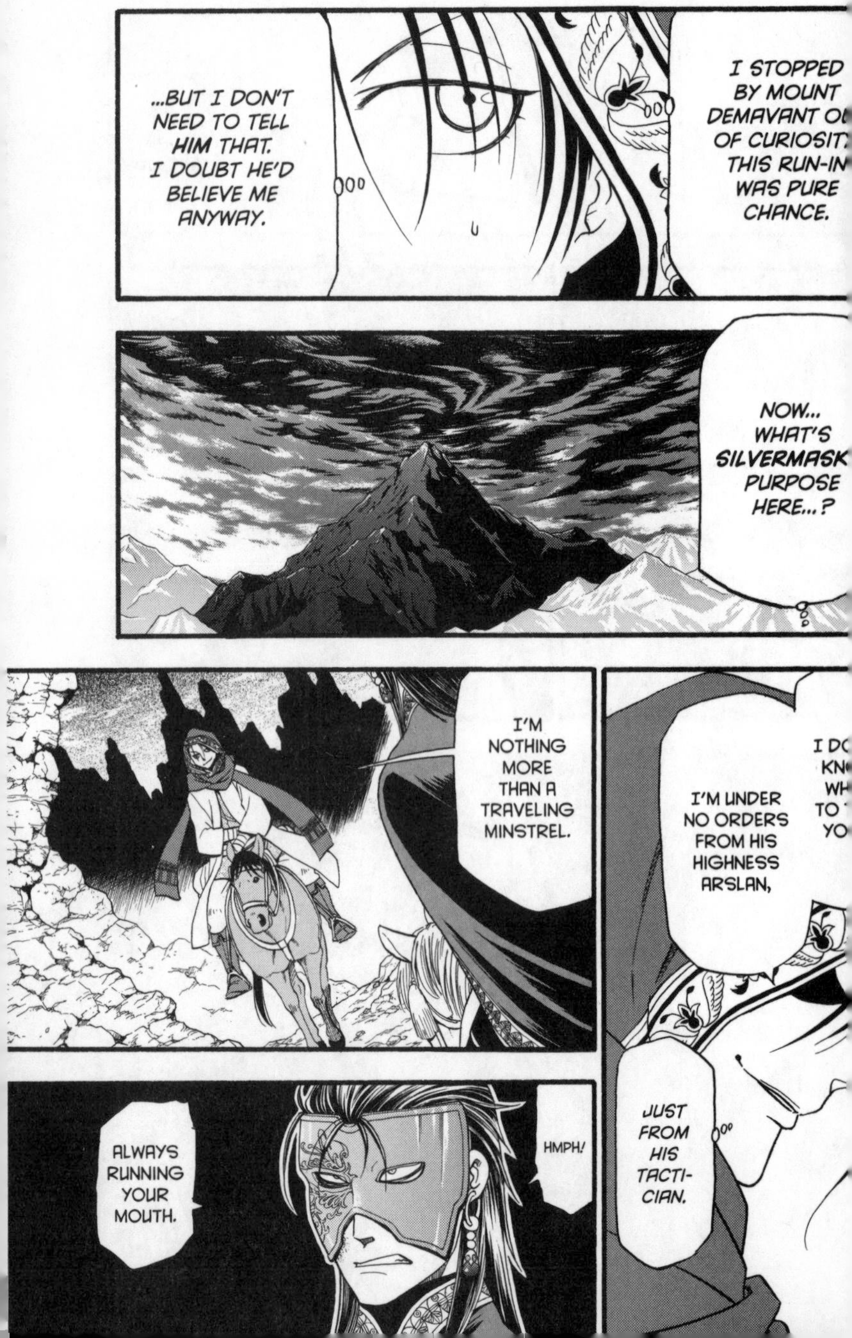
I STOPPED BY MOUNT DEMAVANT
THIS RUN-IN WAS PURE CHANCE.
...BUT I DON'T NEED TO TELL HIM THAT. I DOUBT HE'D BELIEVE ME ANYWAY.
NOW... WHAT'S SILVERMASK PURPOSE HERE...?
I'M UNDER NO ORDERS FROM HIS HIGHNESS ARSLAN,
JUST FROM HIS TACTI-CIAN.
I'M NOTHING MORE THAN A TRAVELING MINSTREL.
HMPH!
ALWAYS RUNNING YOUR MOUTH.

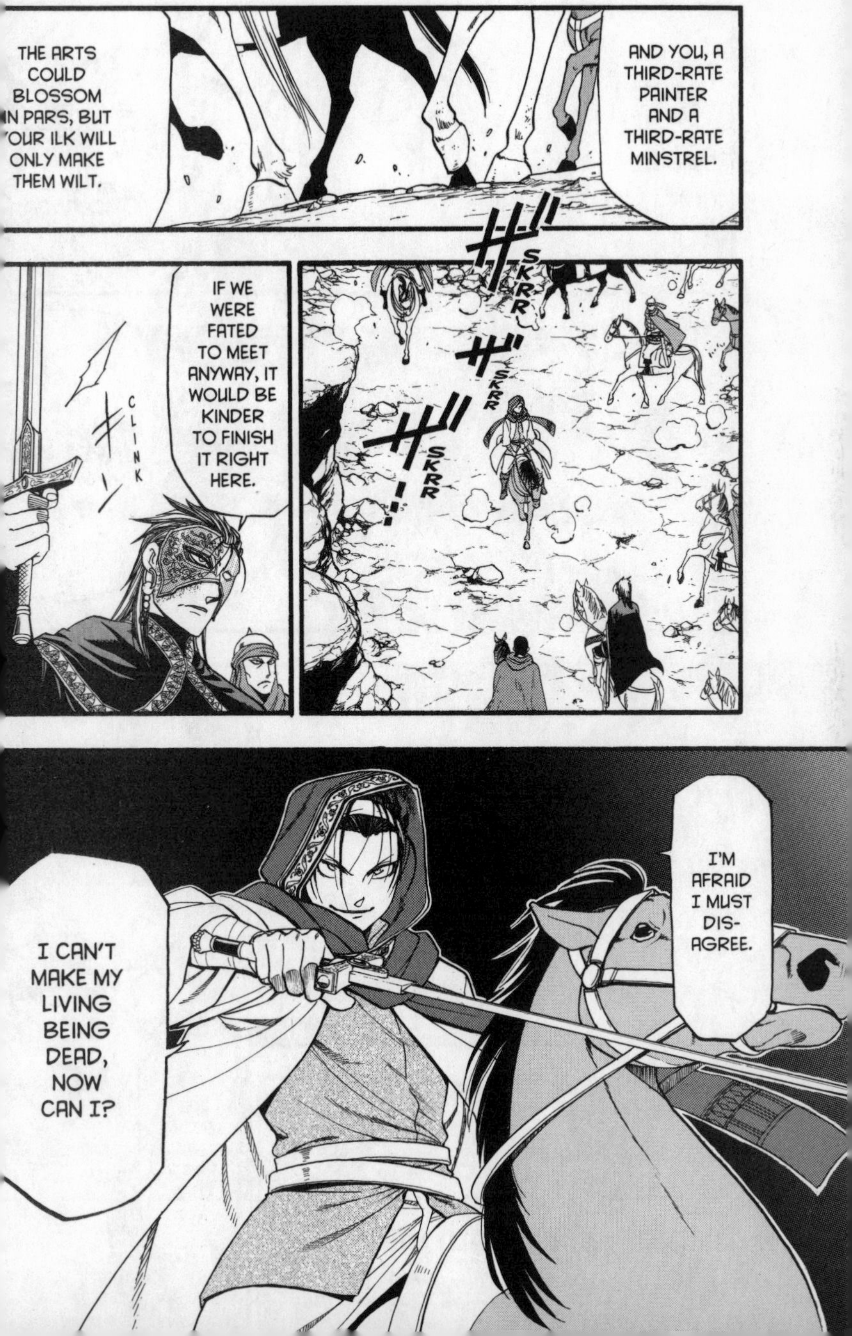
AND YOU, A THIRD-RATE PAINTER AND A THIRD-RATE MINSTREL.
THE ARTS COULD BLOSSOM IN PARS, BUT YOUR ILK WILL ONLY MAKE THEM WILT.
SKRR
SKRR
SKRR
IF WE WERE FATED TO MEET ANYWAY, IT WOULD BE KINDER TO FINISH IT RIGHT HERE.
CLINK
I'M AFRAID I MUST DIS-AGREE.
I CAN'T MAKE MY LIVING BEING DEAD, NOW CAN I?

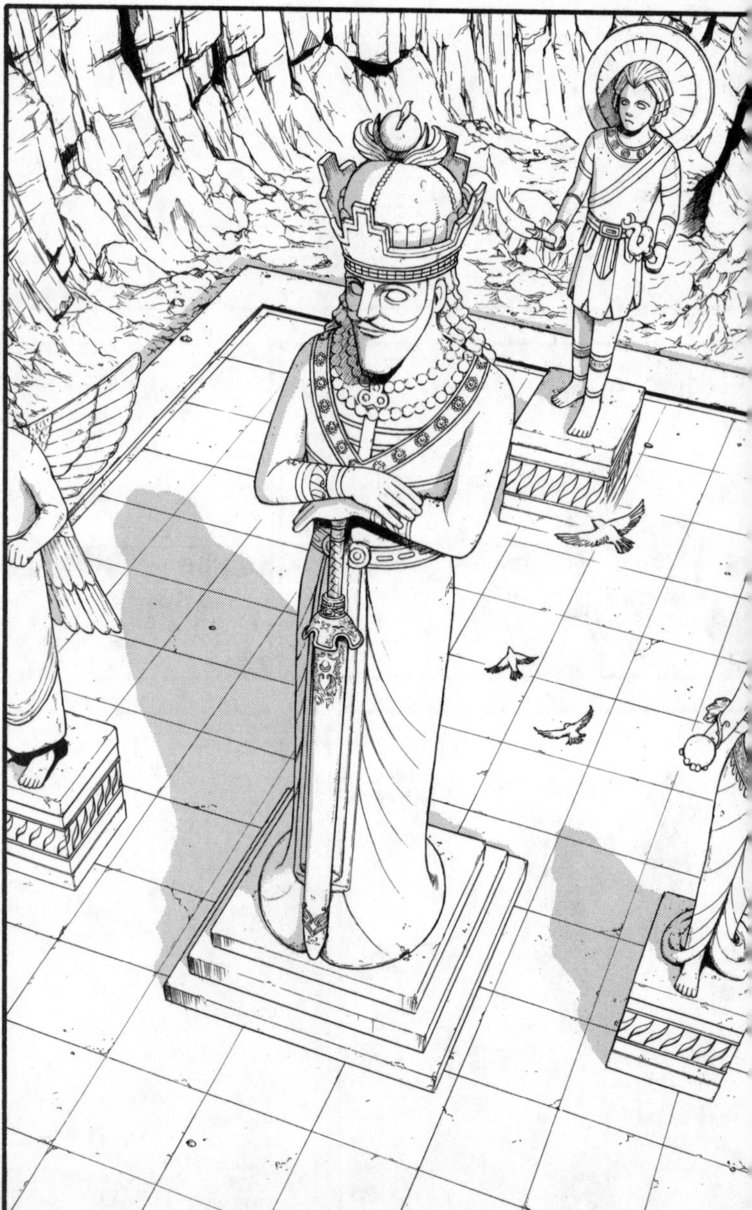

Chapter 78: Beneath the Tomb

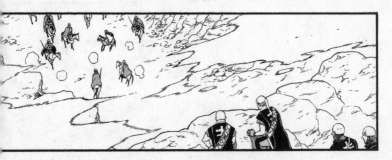

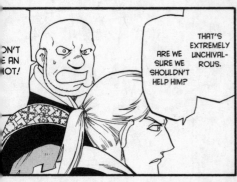

THAT'S ODD.
LOOKS LIKE THEY'RE IN A STANDOFF WITH ANOTHER PARSIAN.
WHAT ?!
THEY OUT-NUMBER HIM BY FAR!
THAT'S EXTREMELY UNCHIVAL-ROUS.
ARE WE SURE WE SHOULDN'T HELP HIM?
THEY'RE ALL WICKED HEATHENS. LET THEM KILL EACH OTHER!
WELL, YEAH...
BUT WE SHOULD HAVE SOME SORT OF ETIQUETTE FOR HEATHENS...
OUR JOB IS TO TRAIL HILMES IN SECRET TO FIND OUT WHAT HE'S SCHEMING.
DON'T FORGET HIS HIGHNESS DUKE GUISCARD'S ORDERS!

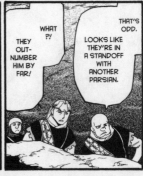

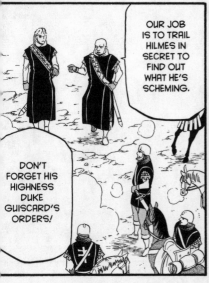

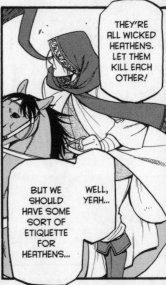

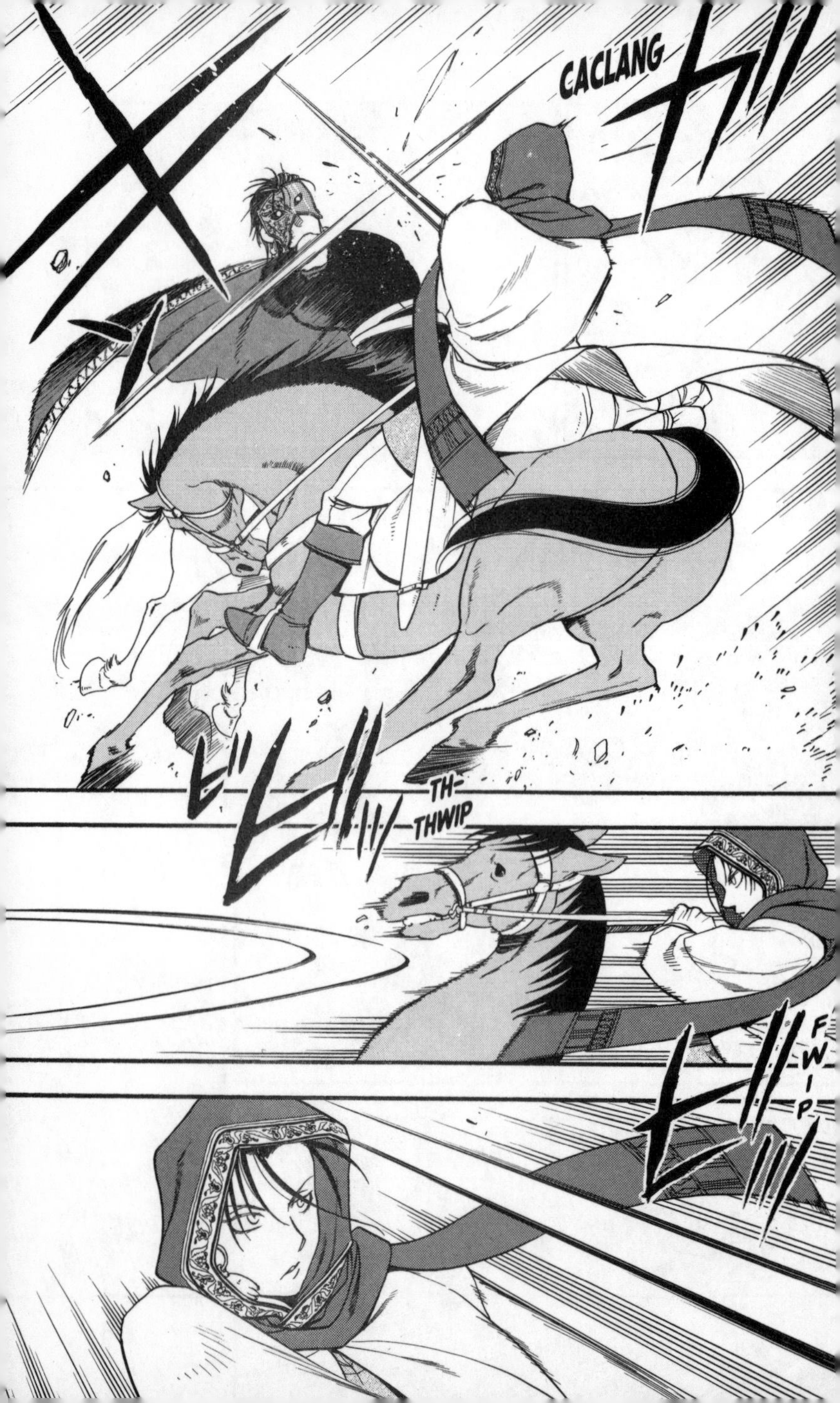
CACLANG
TH-THWIP
FWIP

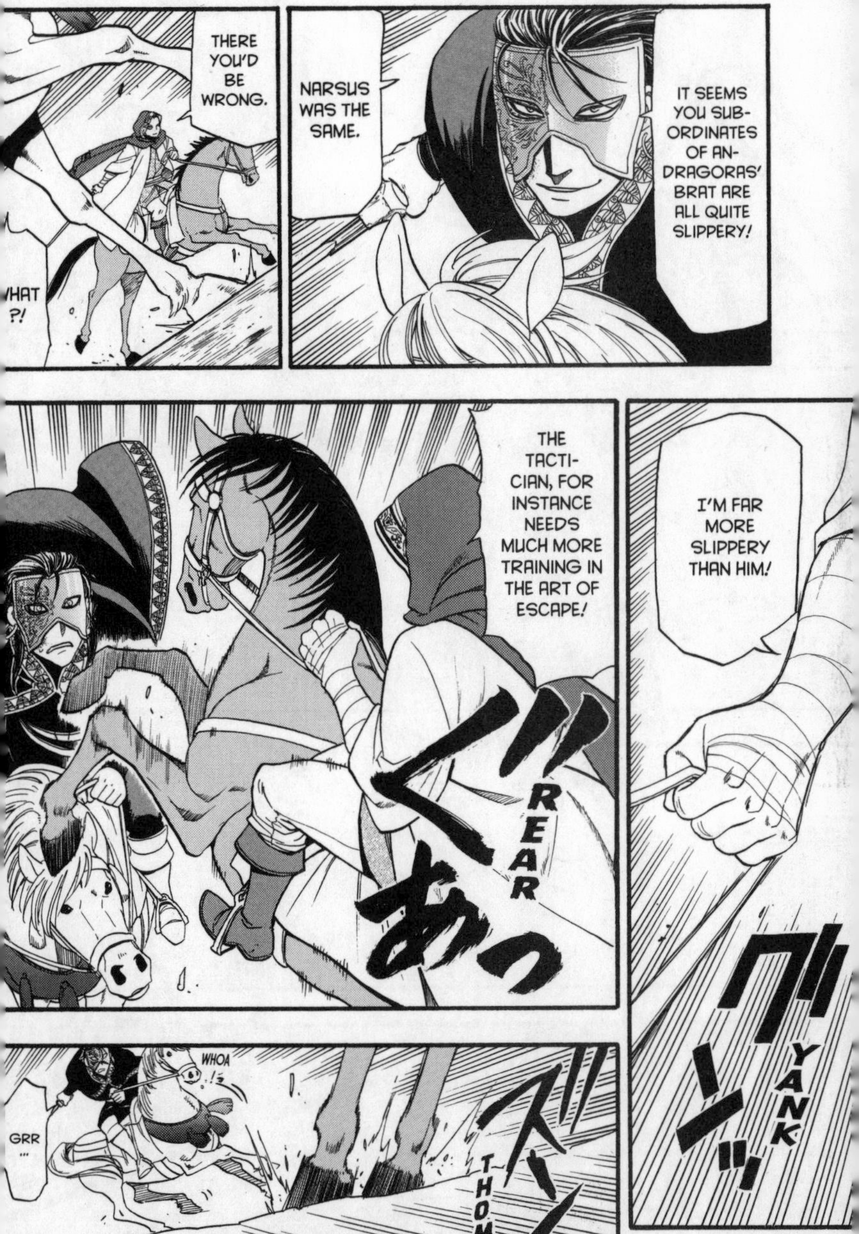

IT SEEMS YOU SUBORDINATES OF ANDRAGORAS' BRAT ARE ALL QUITE SLIPPERY!
NARSUS WAS THE SAME.
THERE YOU'D BE WRONG.
HAT ?!
I'M FAR MORE SLIPPERY THAN HIM!
YANK
THE TACTICIAN, FOR INSTANCE NEEDS MUCH MORE TRAINING IN THE ART OF ESCAPE!
REAR
THOMP
WHOA !?
GRR ...

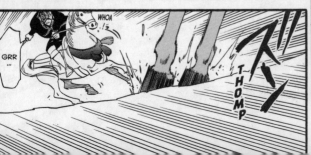

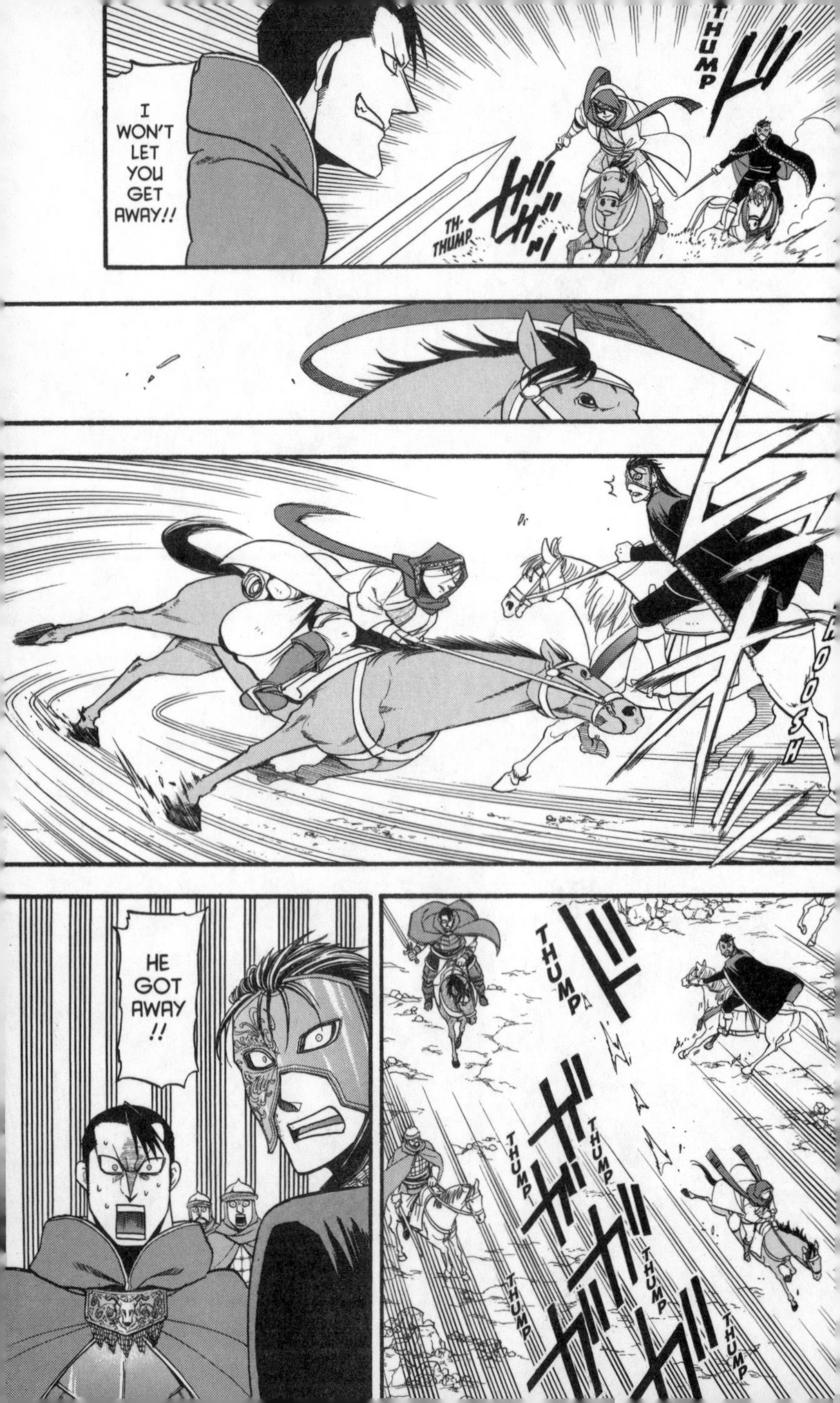
THUMP
I WON'T LET YOU GET AWAY!!
TH-THUMP
WOOSH
THUMP
THUMP
THUMP
THUMP
THUMP
THUMP
HE GOT AWAY!!

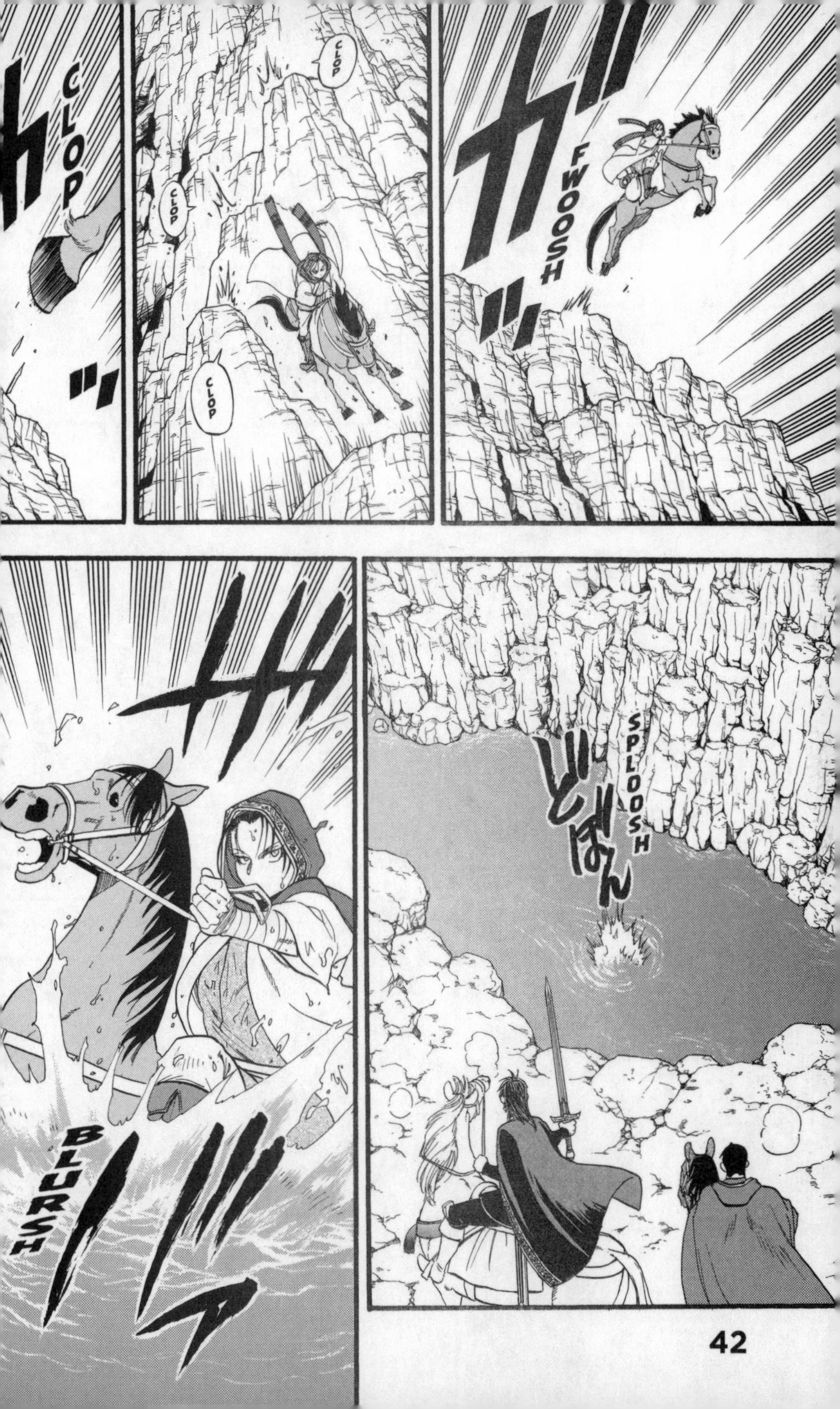
FWOOSH
CLOP
CLOP
CLOP
CLOP
SPLOOSH
どぼん
BLURSH

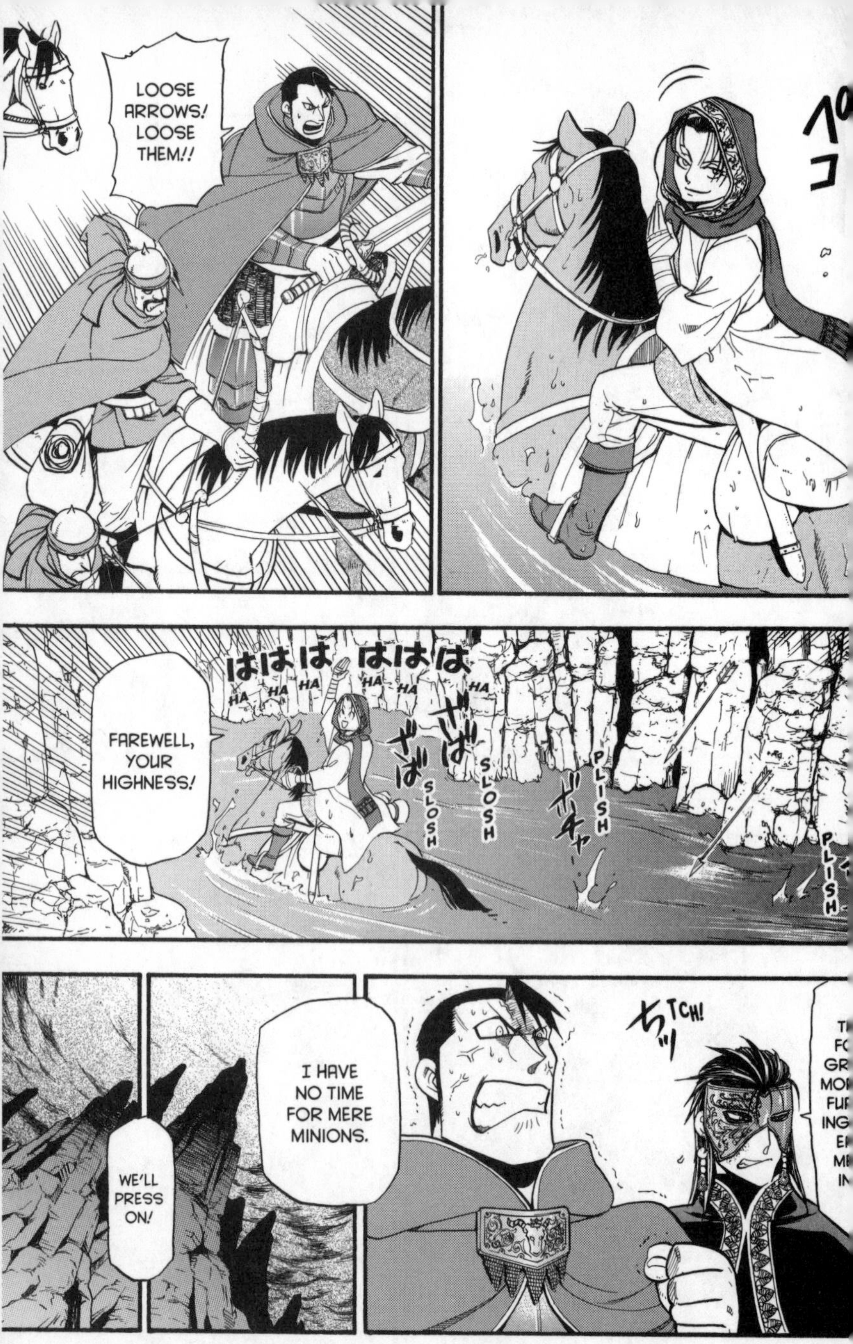
LOOSE ARROWS! LOOSE THEM!!
ははは ははは
HA HA HA HA HA HA
FAREWELL, YOUR HIGHNESS!
SLOSH SLOSH
PLISH
PLISH
TCH!
I HAVE NO TIME FOR MERE MINIONS.
WE'LL PRESS ON!

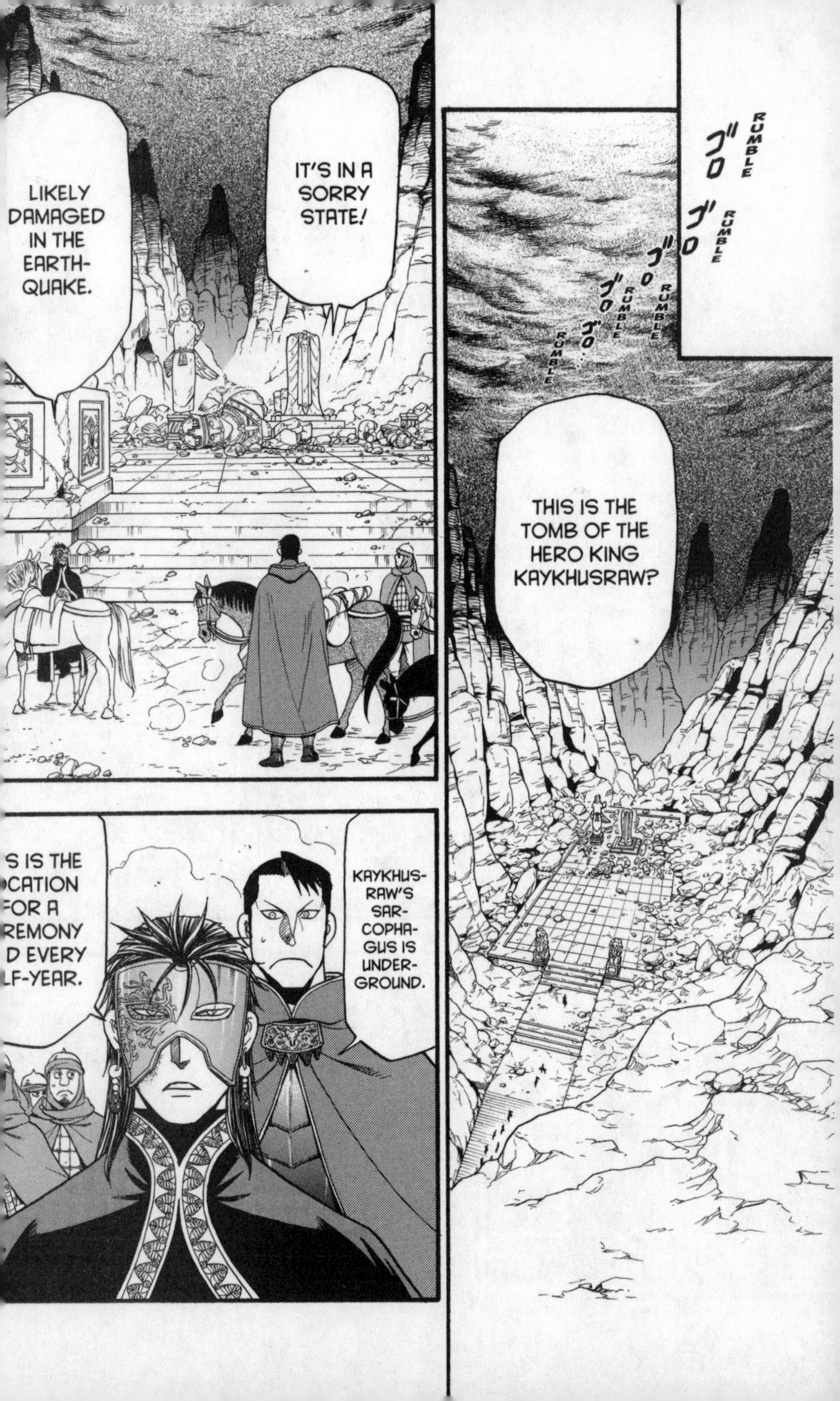

ゴロ
RUMBLE
ゴロ
RUMBLE
ゴロ
RUMBLE
ゴロ
RUMBLE
ゴロ…
RUMBLE
THIS IS THE TOMB OF THE HERO KING KAYKHUSRAW?
IT'S IN A SORRY STATE!
LIKELY DAMAGED IN THE EARTH-QUAKE.
KAYKHUS-RAW'S SAR-COPHA-GUS IS UNDER-GROUND.
S IS THE
CATION
FOR A
REMONY
D EVERY
LF-YEAR.

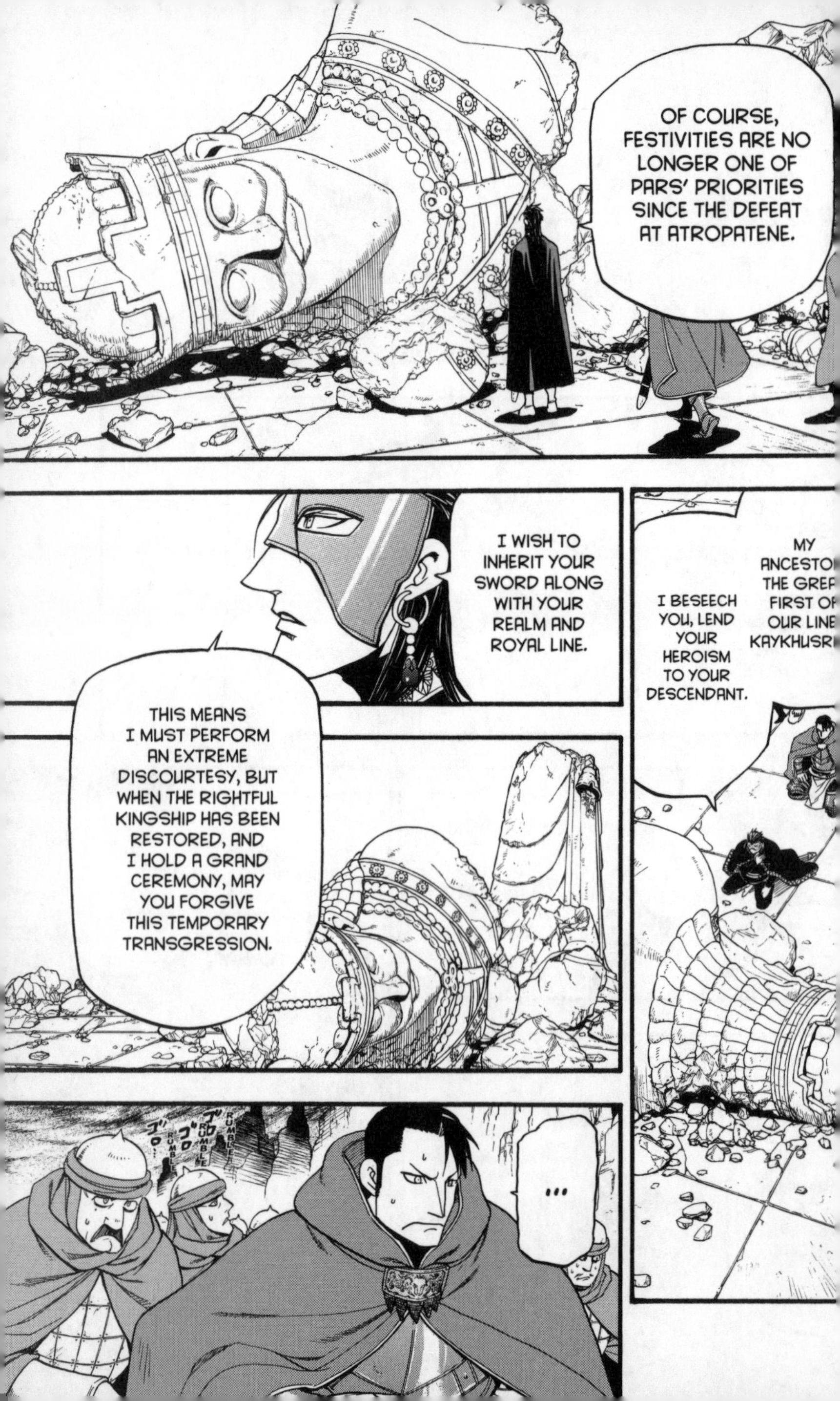
OF COURSE, FESTIVITIES ARE NO LONGER ONE OF PARS' PRIORITIES SINCE THE DEFEAT AT ATROPATENE.
MY ANCESTO THE GREA FIRST OF OUR LINE KAYKHUSR
I BESEECH YOU, LEND YOUR HEROISM TO YOUR DESCENDANT.
I WISH TO INHERIT YOUR SWORD ALONG WITH YOUR REALM AND ROYAL LINE.
THIS MEANS I MUST PERFORM AN EXTREME DISCOURTESY, BUT WHEN THE RIGHTFUL KINGSHIP HAS BEEN RESTORED, AND I HOLD A GRAND CEREMONY, MAY YOU FORGIVE THIS TEMPORARY TRANSGRESSION.
RUMBLE
RUMBLE
RUMBLE
...

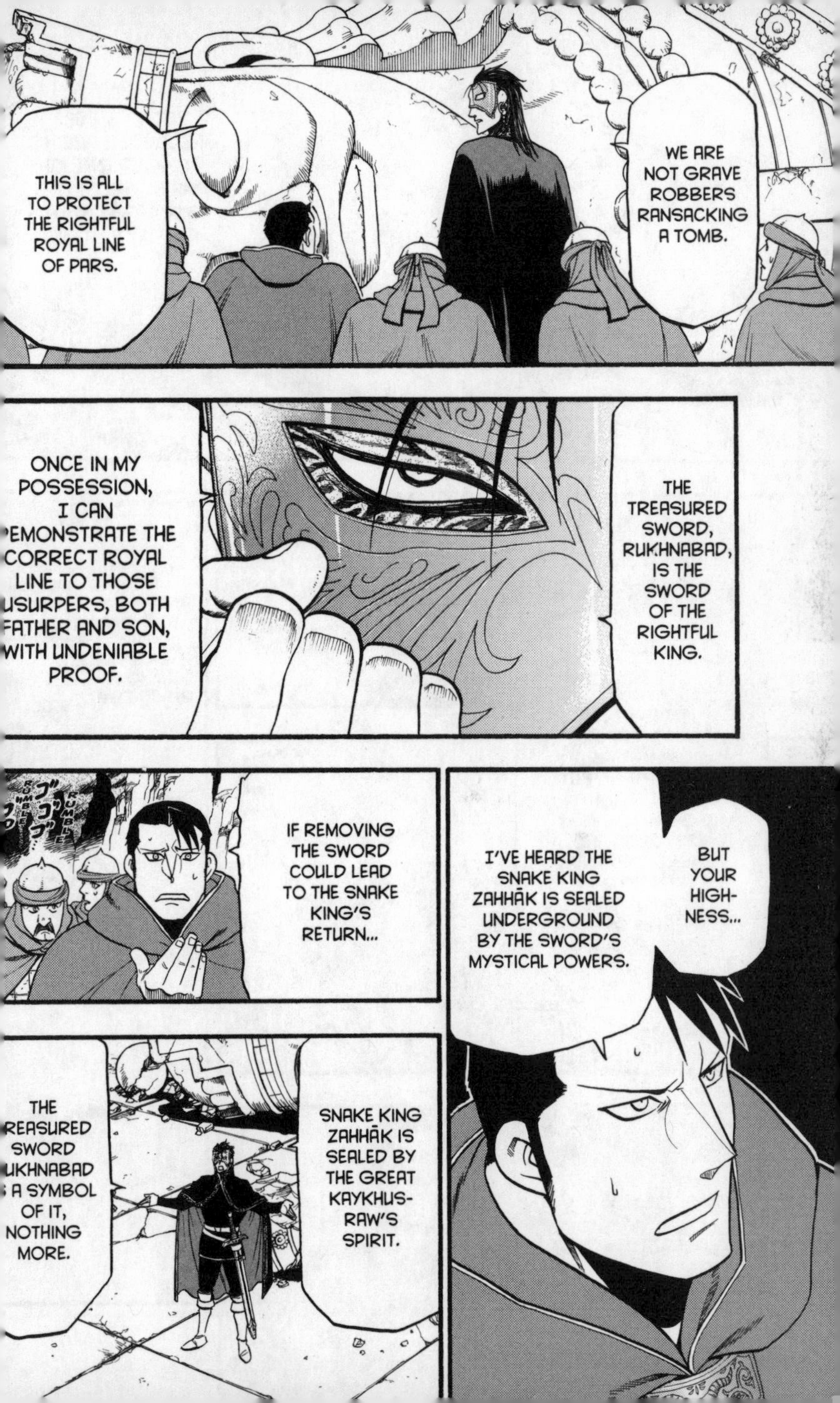
WE ARE NOT GRAVE ROBBERS RANSACKING A TOMB.
THIS IS ALL TO PROTECT THE RIGHTFUL ROYAL LINE OF PARS.
THE TREASURED SWORD, RUKHNABAD, IS THE SWORD OF THE RIGHTFUL KING.
ONCE IN MY POSSESSION, I CAN DEMONSTRATE THE CORRECT ROYAL LINE TO THOSE USURPERS, BOTH FATHER AND SON, WITH UNDENIABLE PROOF.
BUT YOUR HIGHNESS...
I'VE HEARD THE SNAKE KING ZAHHĀK IS SEALED UNDERGROUND BY THE SWORD'S MYSTICAL POWERS.
RUMBLE RUMBLE
IF REMOVING THE SWORD COULD LEAD TO THE SNAKE KING'S RETURN...
SNAKE KING ZAHHĀK IS SEALED BY THE GREAT KAYKHUS-RAW'S SPIRIT.
THE TREASURED SWORD RUKHNABAD IS A SYMBOL OF IT, NOTHING MORE.

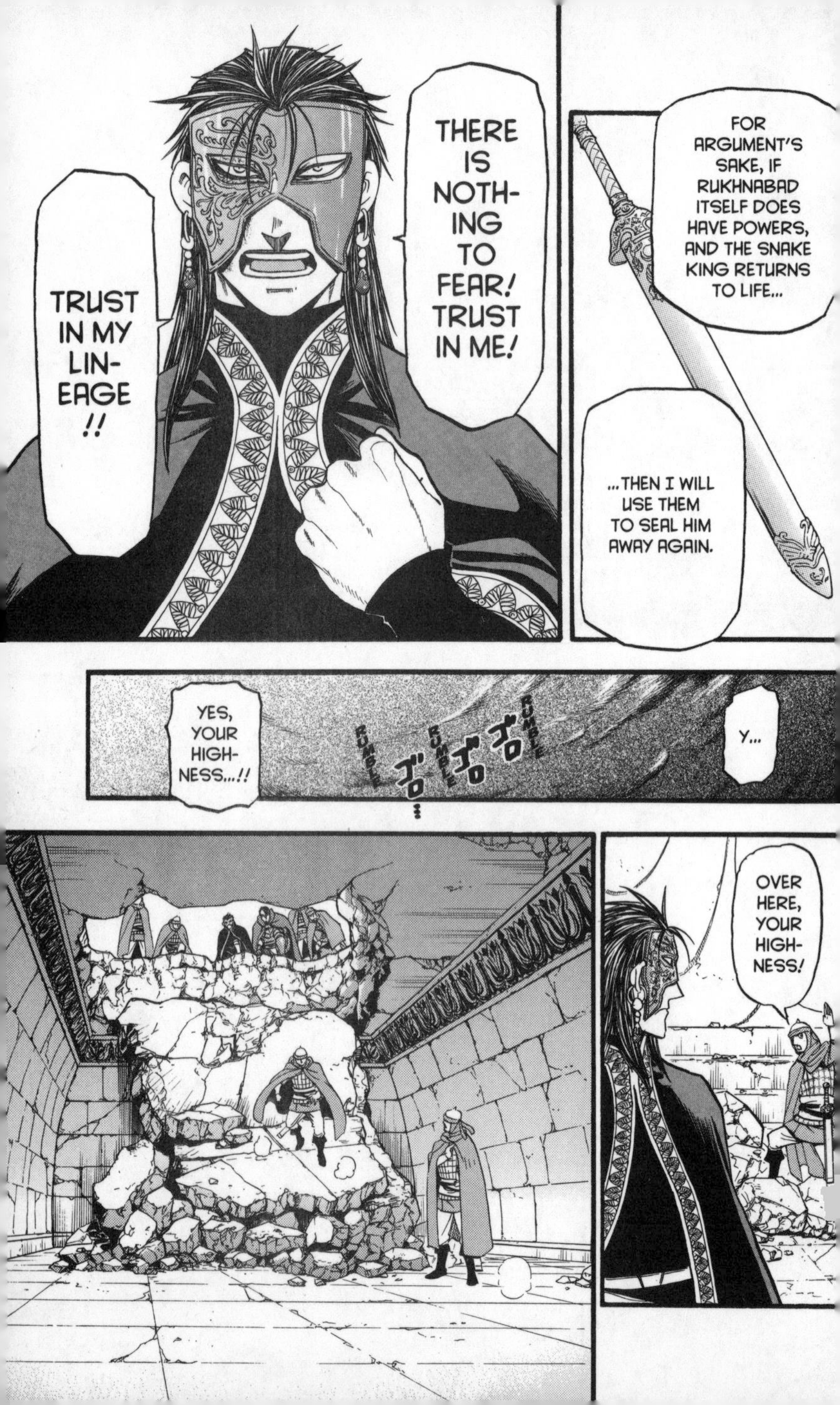
FOR ARGUMENT'S SAKE, IF RUKHNABAD ITSELF DOES HAVE POWERS, AND THE SNAKE KING RETURNS TO LIFE...
...THEN I WILL USE THEM TO SEAL HIM AWAY AGAIN.
THERE IS NOTHING TO FEAR! TRUST IN ME!
TRUST IN MY LINEAGE!!
Y...
ゴロ RUMBLE
ゴロ RUMBLE
ゴロ RUMBLE
YES, YOUR HIGHNESS...!!
OVER HERE, YOUR HIGHNESS!

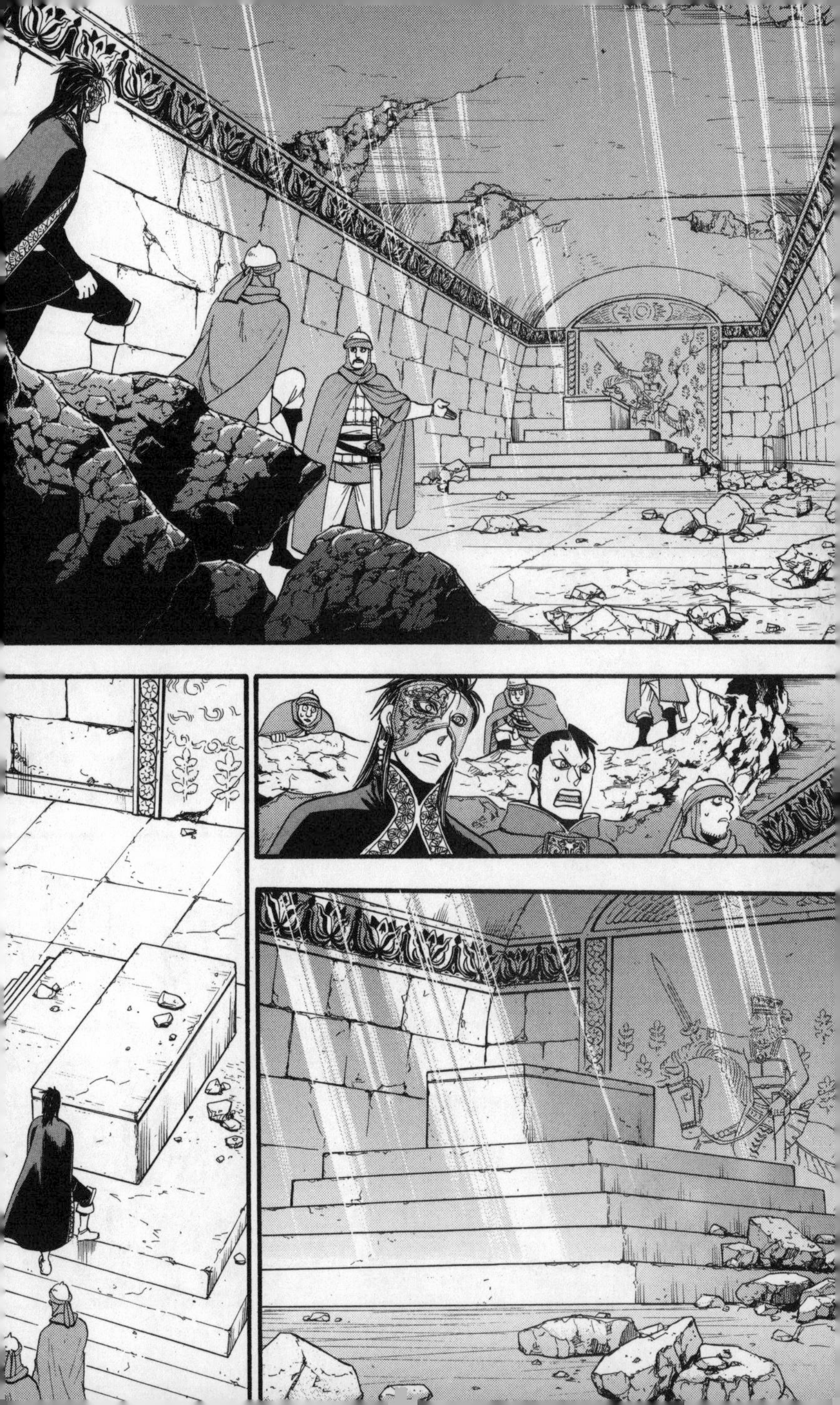

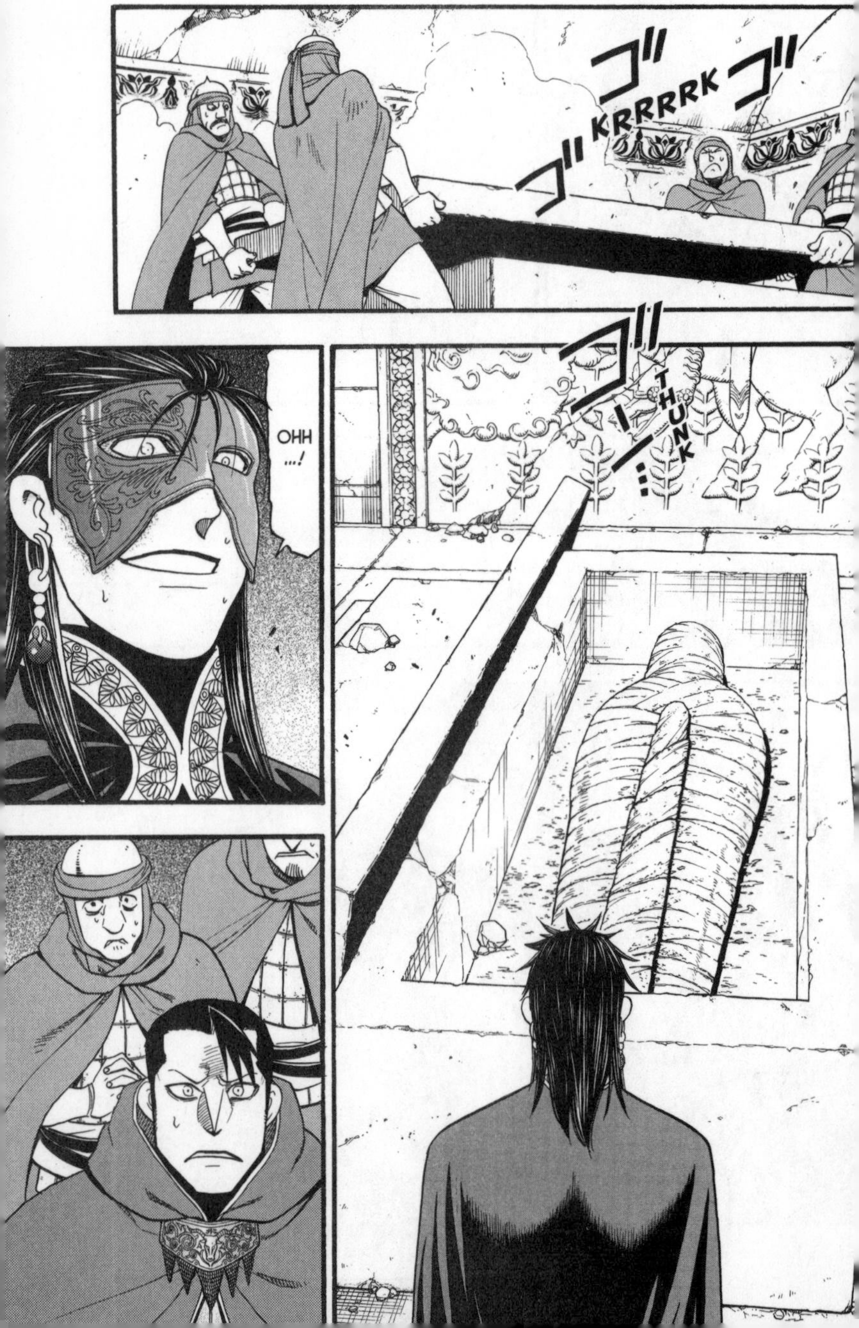

KRRRRK
THUNK
OHH ...!

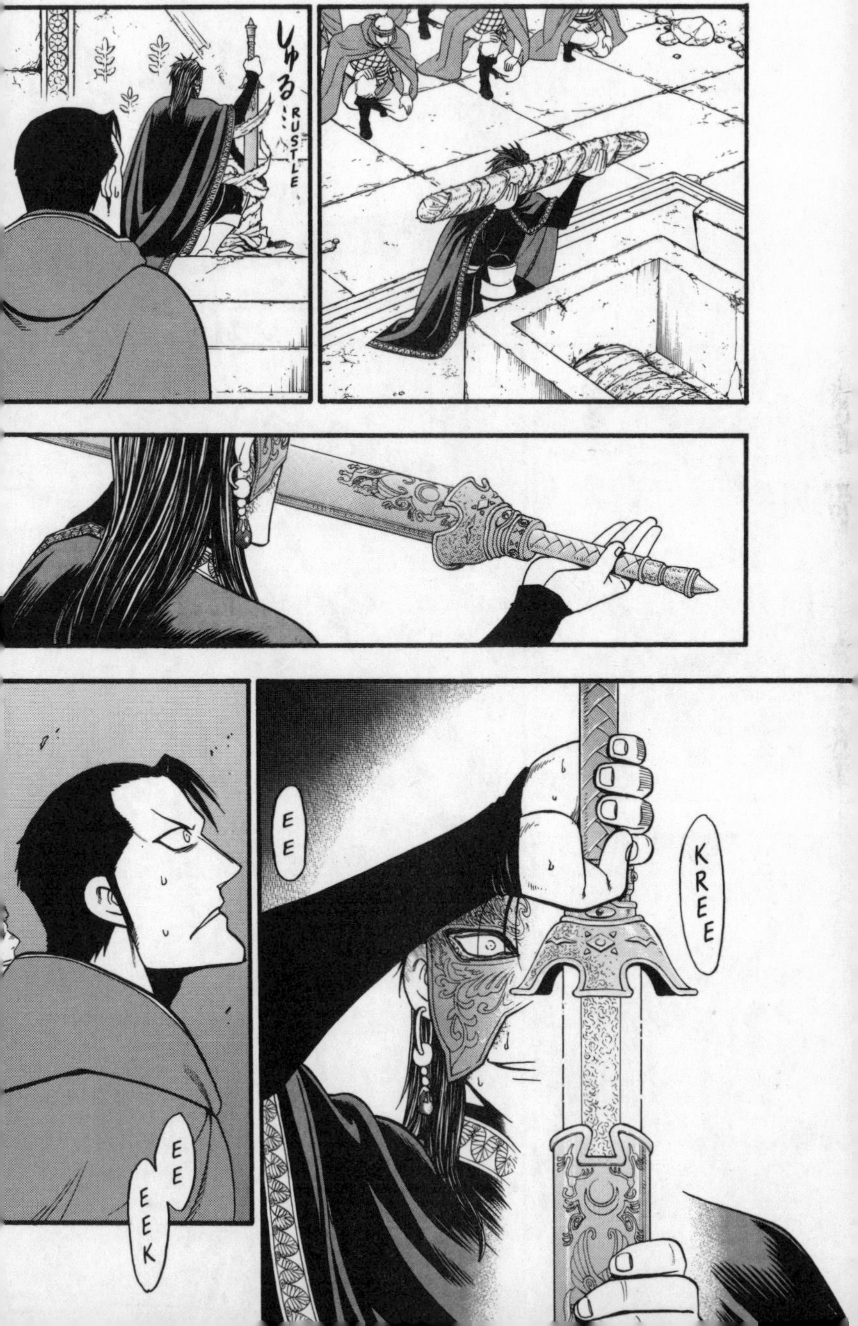

しゅる
RUSTLE
KREE
EE
EE
EEK

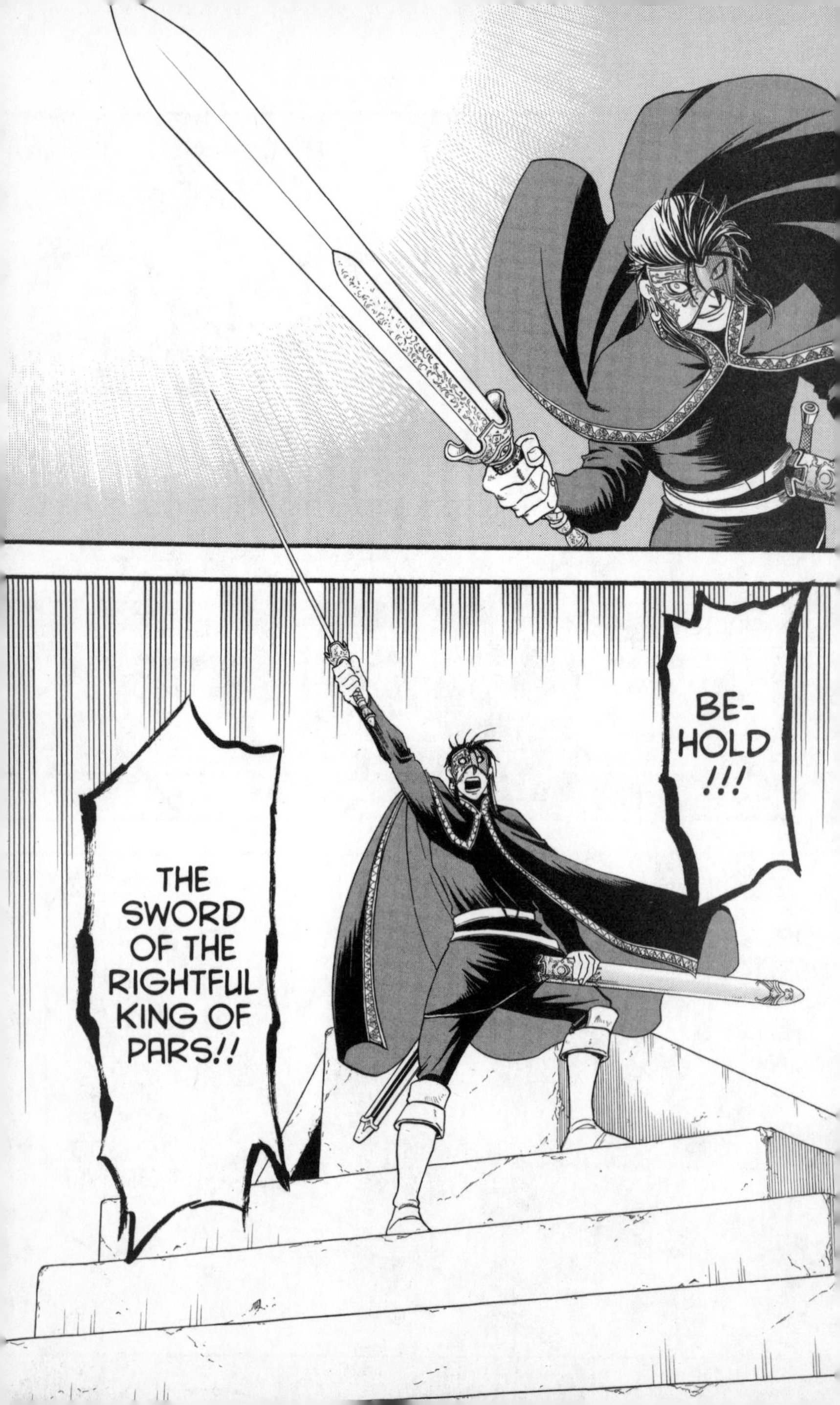
BE-
HOLD
!!!
THE SWORD OF THE RIGHTFUL KING OF PARS!!

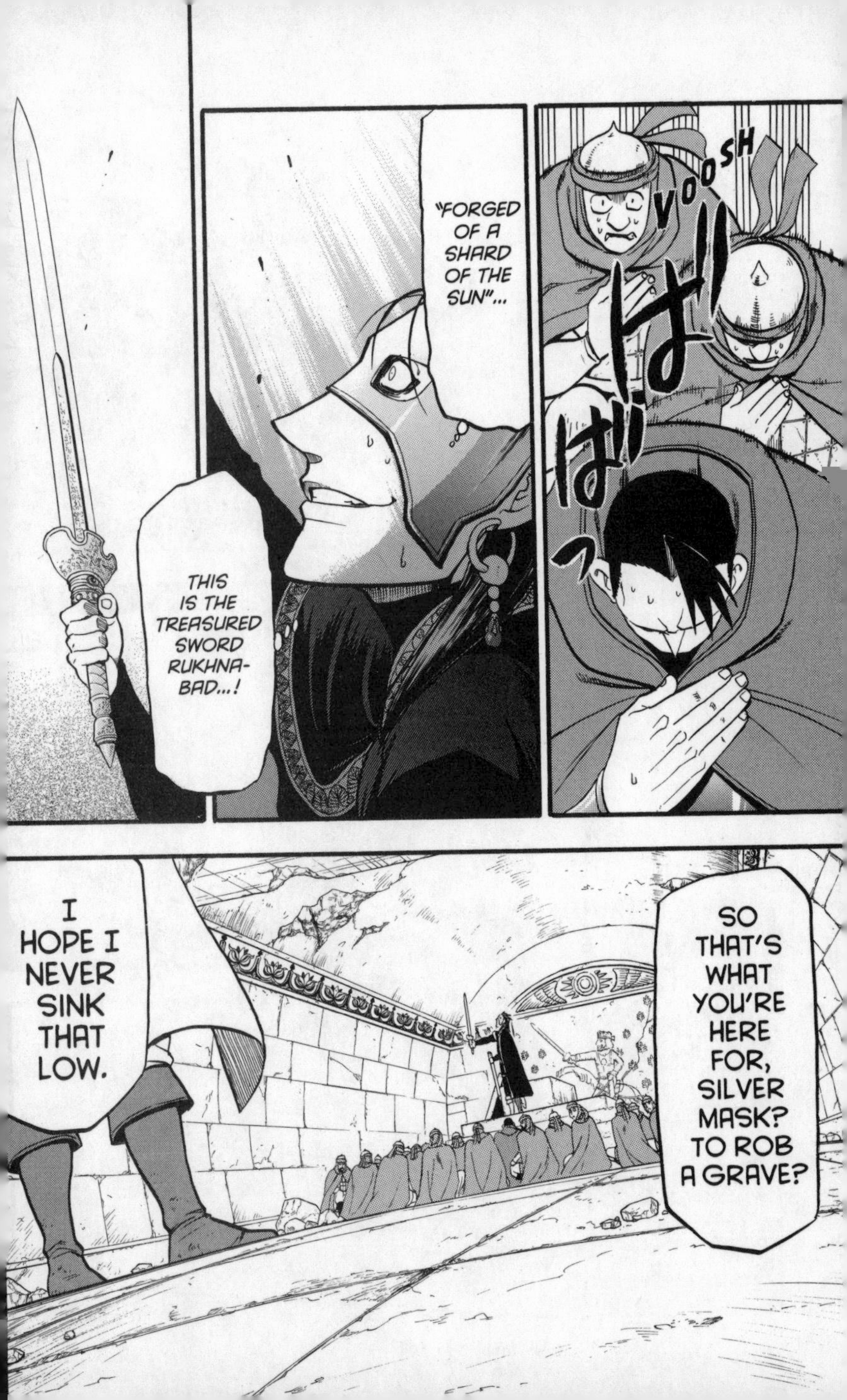
VOOSH
ぱぱっ
"FORGED OF A SHARD OF THE SUN"...
THIS IS THE TREASURED SWORD RUKHNA-BAD...!
SO THAT'S WHAT YOU'RE HERE FOR, SILVER MASK? TO ROB A GRAVE?
I HOPE I NEVER SINK THAT LOW.

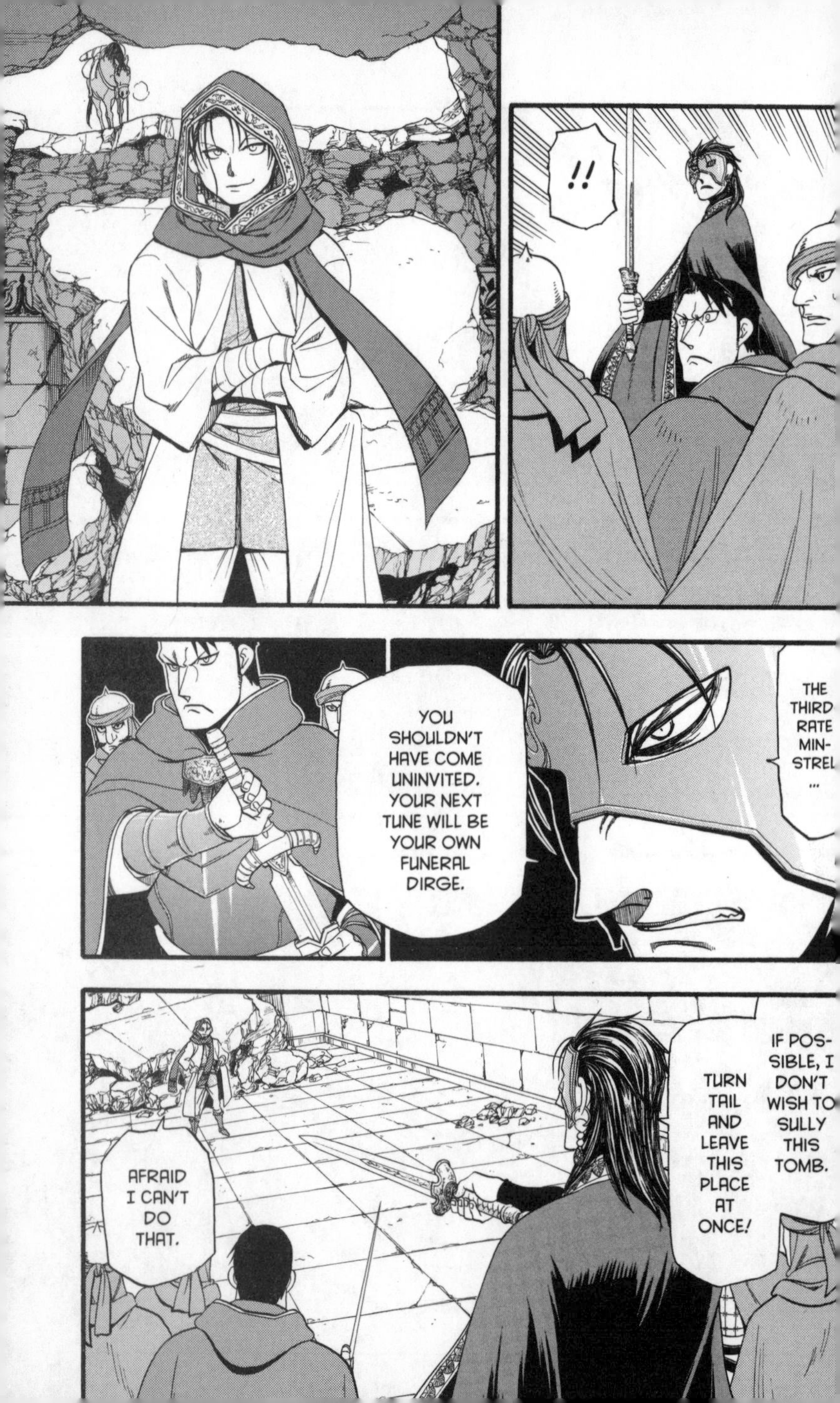
!!
THE THIRD RATE MIN-STREL ...
YOU SHOULDN'T HAVE COME UNINVITED. YOUR NEXT TUNE WILL BE YOUR OWN FUNERAL DIRGE.
IF POS-SIBLE, I DON'T WISH TO SULLY THIS TOMB.
TURN TAIL AND LEAVE THIS PLACE AT ONCE!
AFRAID I CAN'T DO THAT.

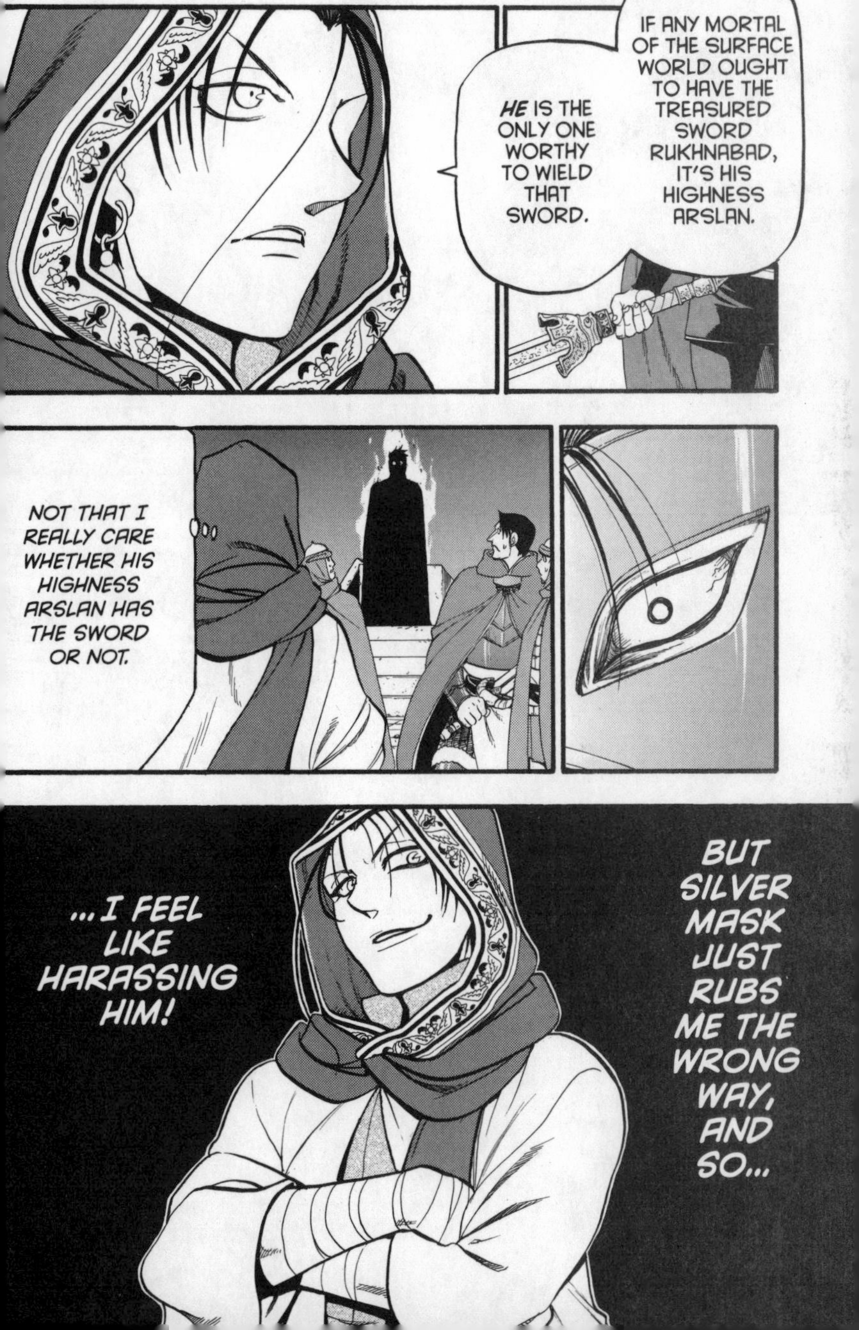
IF ANY MORTAL OF THE SURFACE WORLD OUGHT TO HAVE THE TREASURED SWORD RUKHNABAD, IT'S HIS HIGHNESS ARSLAN.
HE IS THE ONLY ONE WORTHY TO WIELD THAT SWORD.
NOT THAT I REALLY CARE WHETHER HIS HIGHNESS ARSLAN HAS THE SWORD OR NOT.
BUT SILVER MASK JUST RUBS ME THE WRONG WAY, AND SO...
...I FEEL LIKE HARASSING HIM!

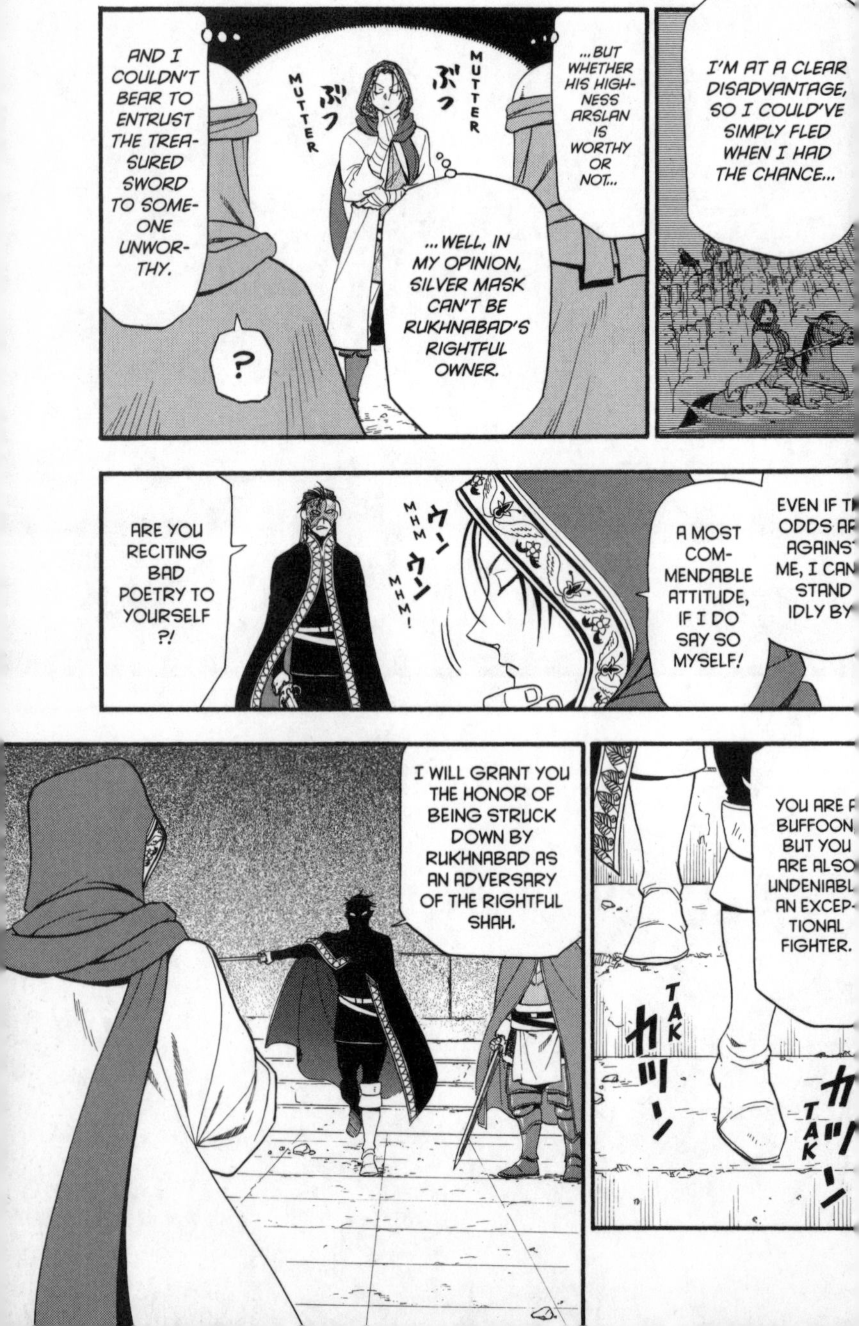

I'M AT A CLEAR DISADVANTAGE, SO I COULD'VE SIMPLY FLED WHEN I HAD THE CHANCE...
...BUT WHETHER HIS HIGHNESS ARSLAN IS WORTHY OR NOT...
ぶつ MUTTER
ぶつ MUTTER
AND I COULDN'T BEAR TO ENTRUST THE TREASURED SWORD TO SOMEONE UNWORTHY.
...WELL, IN MY OPINION, SILVER MASK CAN'T BE RUKHNABAD'S RIGHTFUL OWNER.
?
EVEN IF T ODDS AR AGAINS ME, I CAN STAND IDLY BY
A MOST COMMENDABLE ATTITUDE, IF I DO SAY SO MYSELF!
ウーン MHM
ウーン MHM!
ARE YOU RECITING BAD POETRY TO YOURSELF?!
YOU ARE BUFFOON, BUT YOU ARE ALSO UNDENIABL AN EXCEPTIONAL FIGHTER.
カツーン TAK
カツーン TAK
I WILL GRANT YOU THE HONOR OF BEING STRUCK DOWN BY RUKHNABAD AS AN ADVERSARY OF THE RIGHTFUL SHAH.

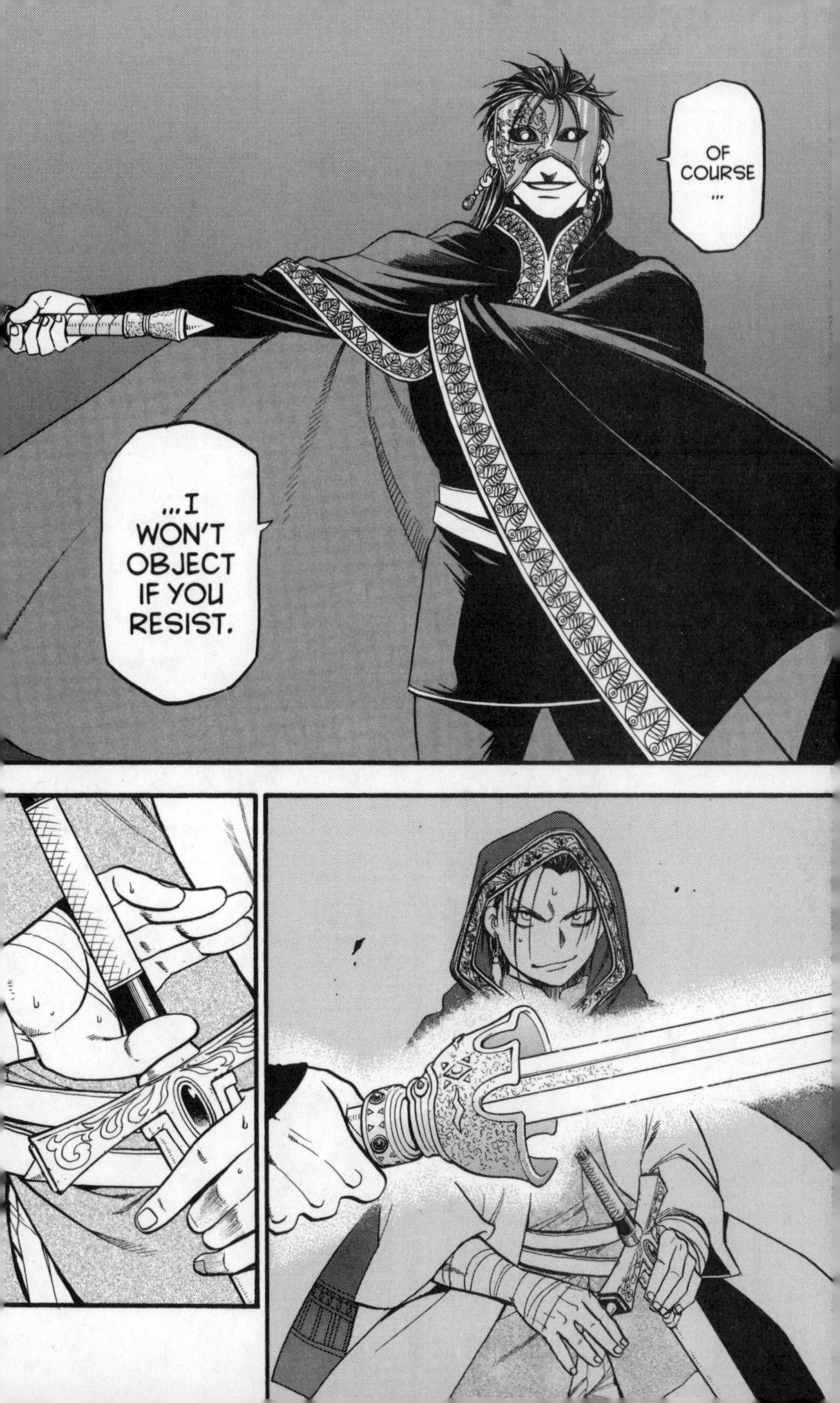
OF COURSE ...
...I WON'T OBJECT IF YOU RESIST.

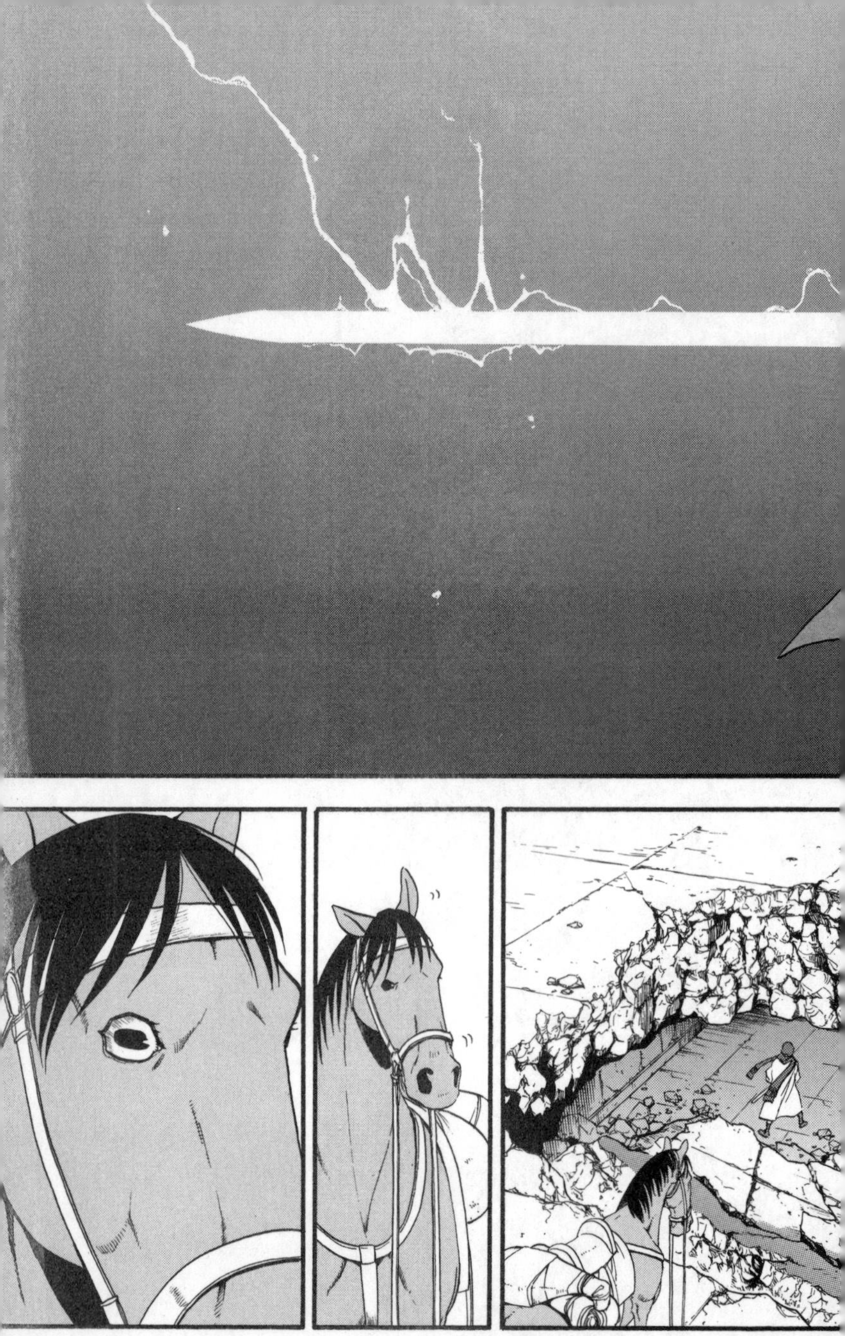

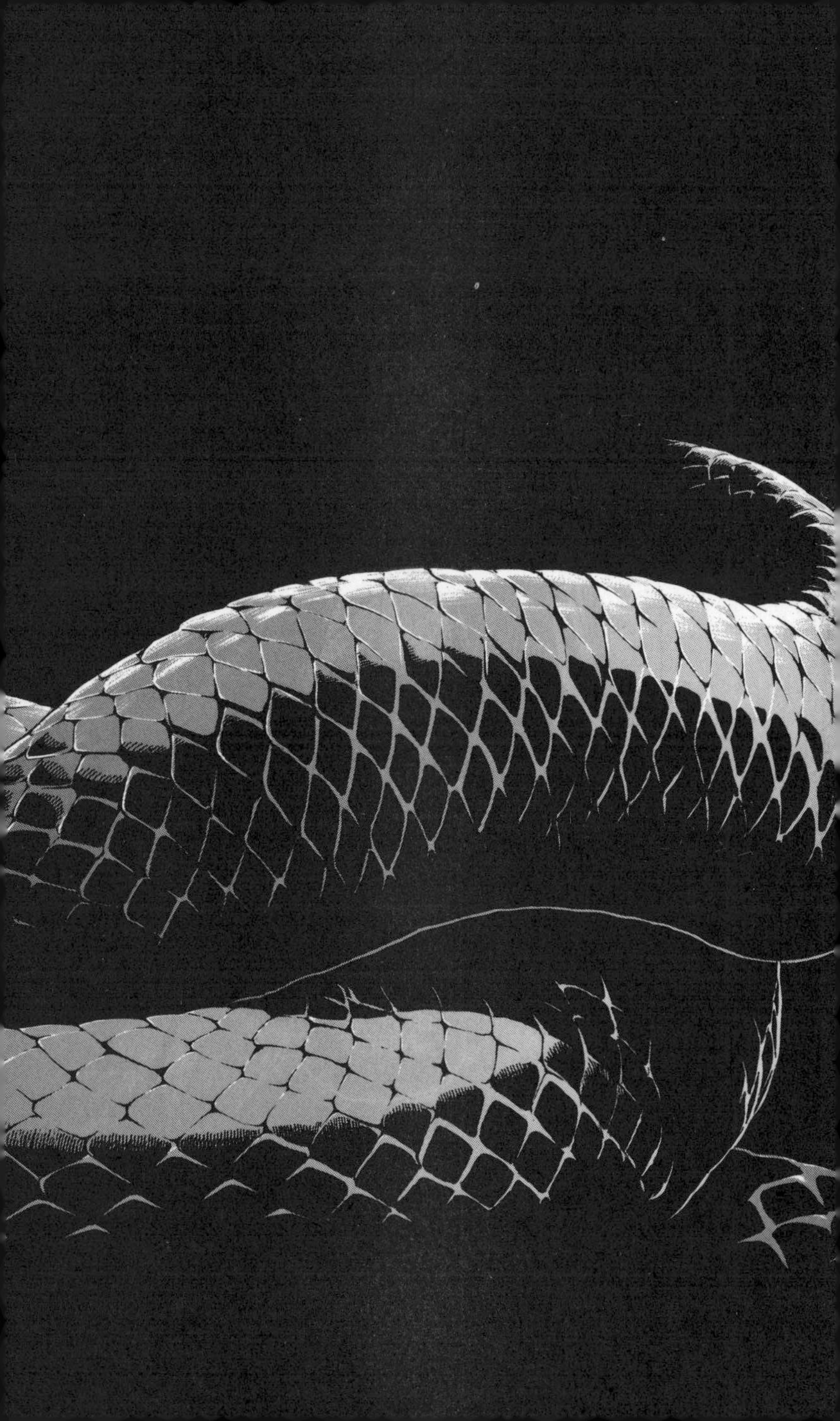

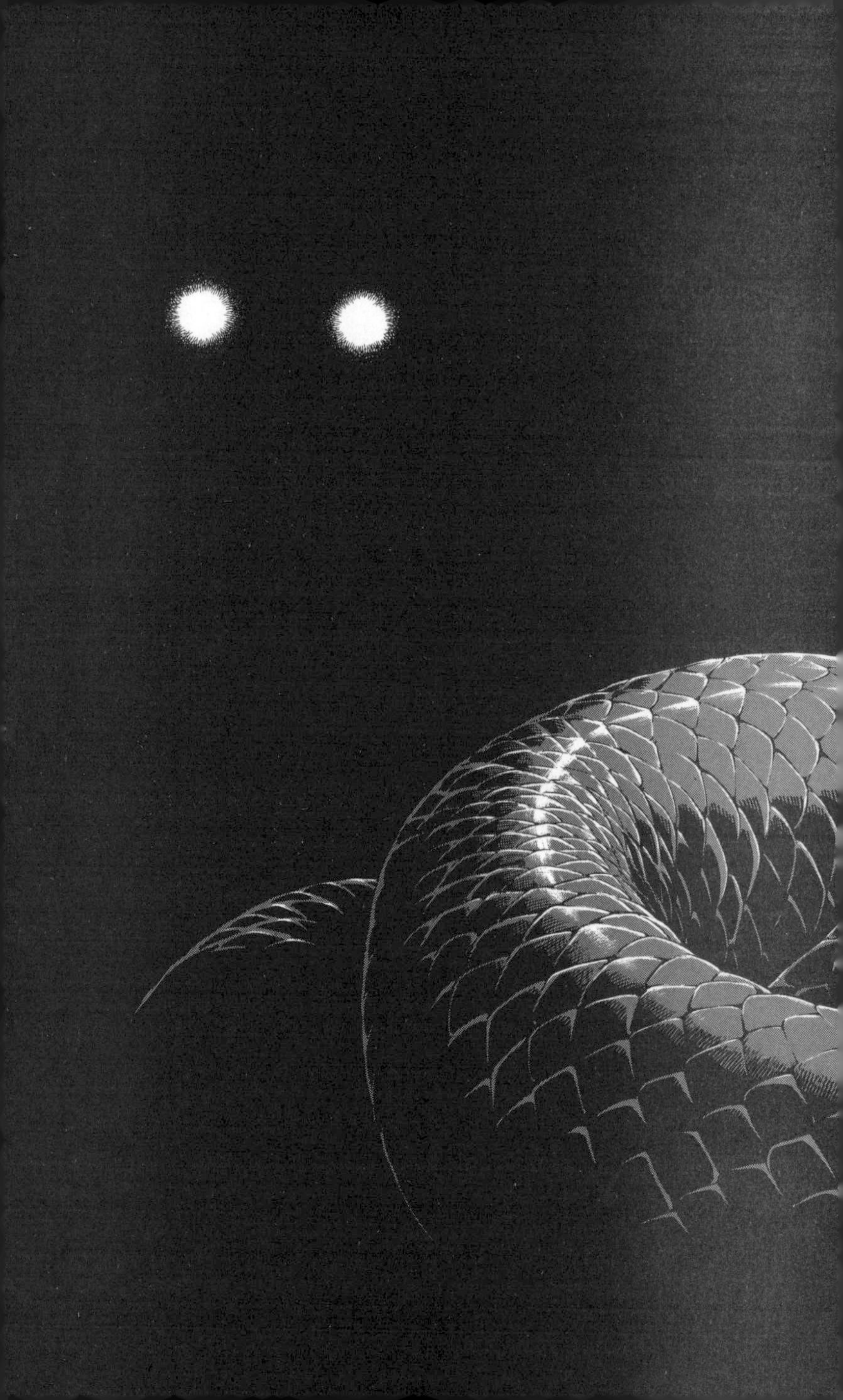

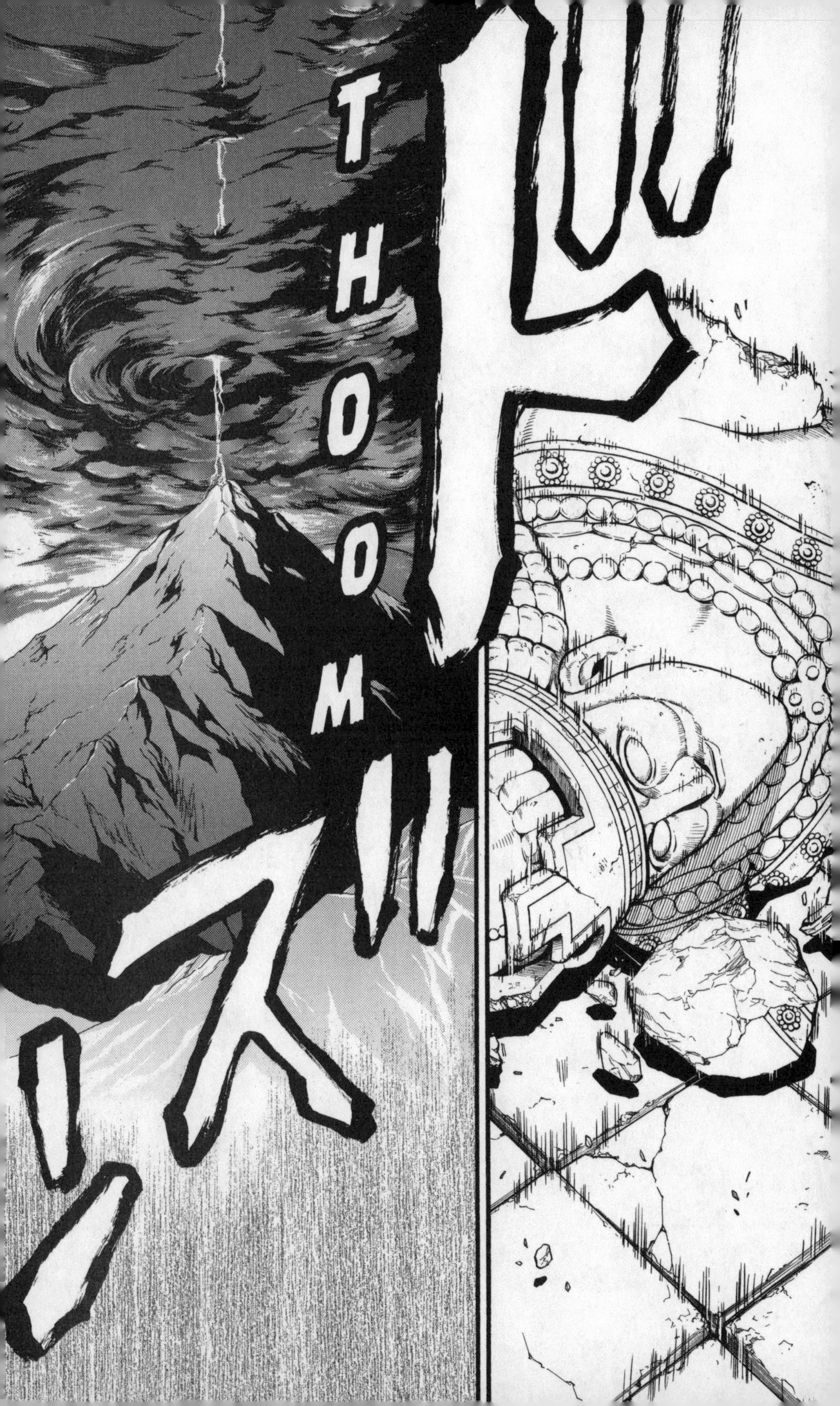
THOOM

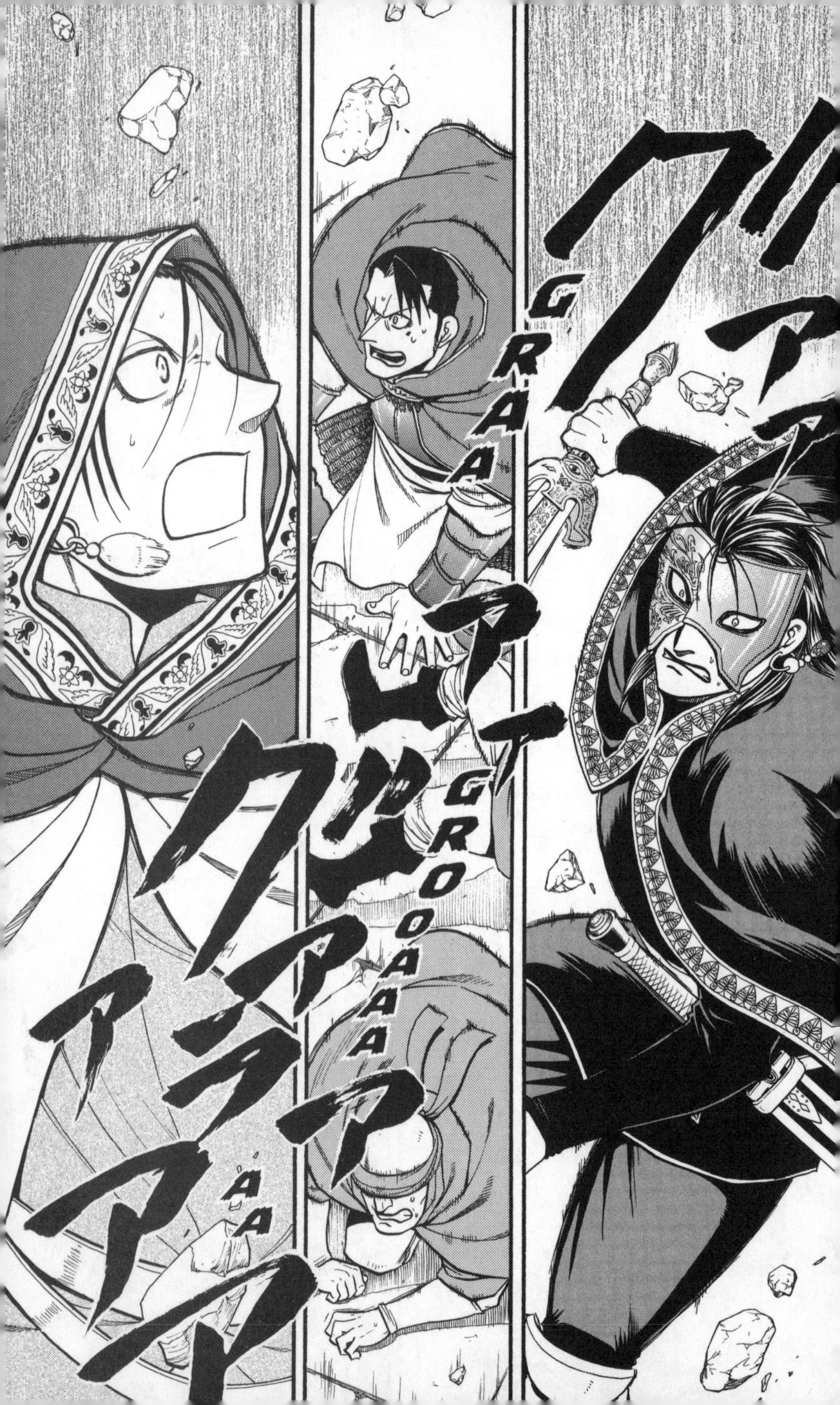
GRAA
GROOAAAA
AA

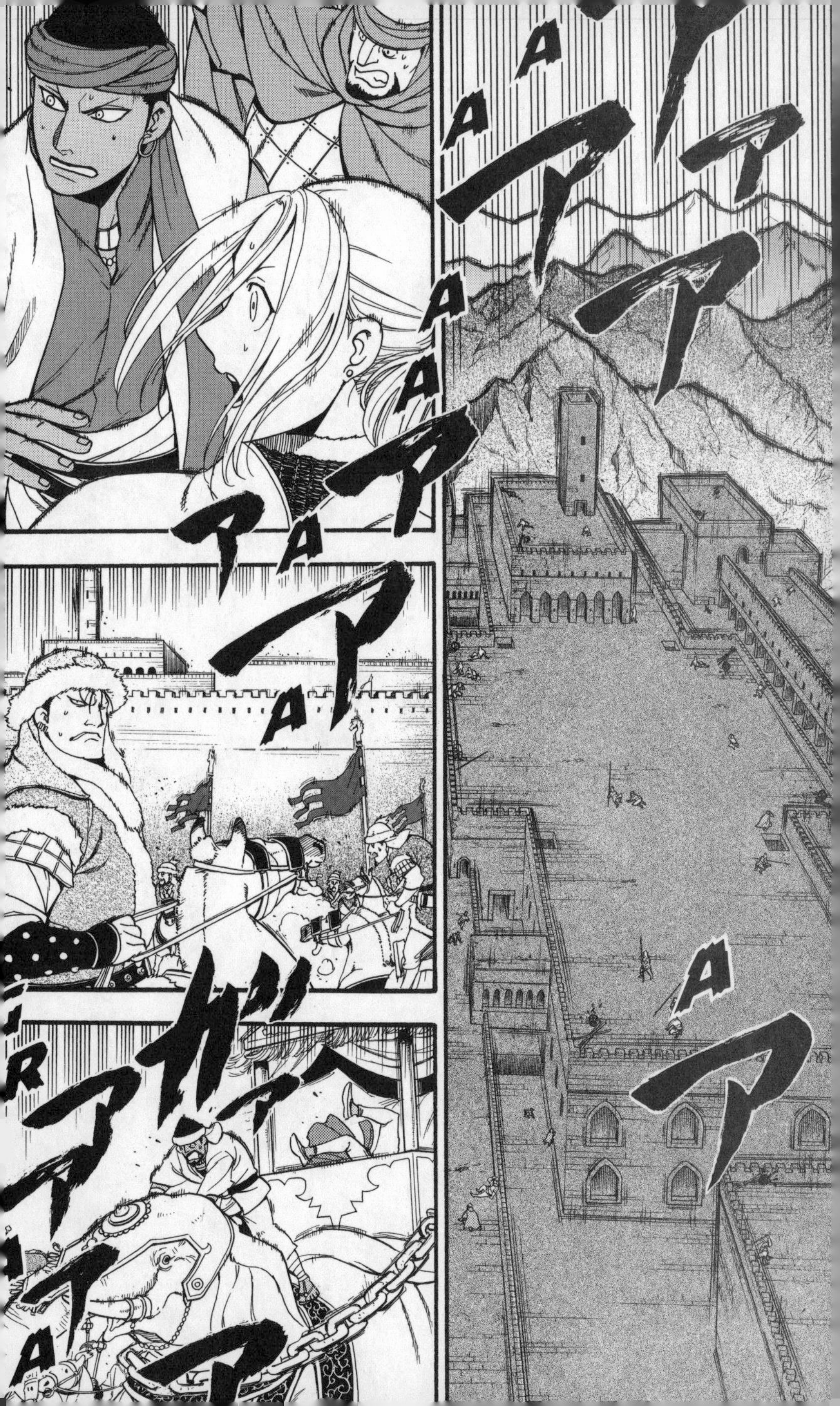

AAAAAA
A
アアアア
ア
AA
アア
RA
アガアアアア

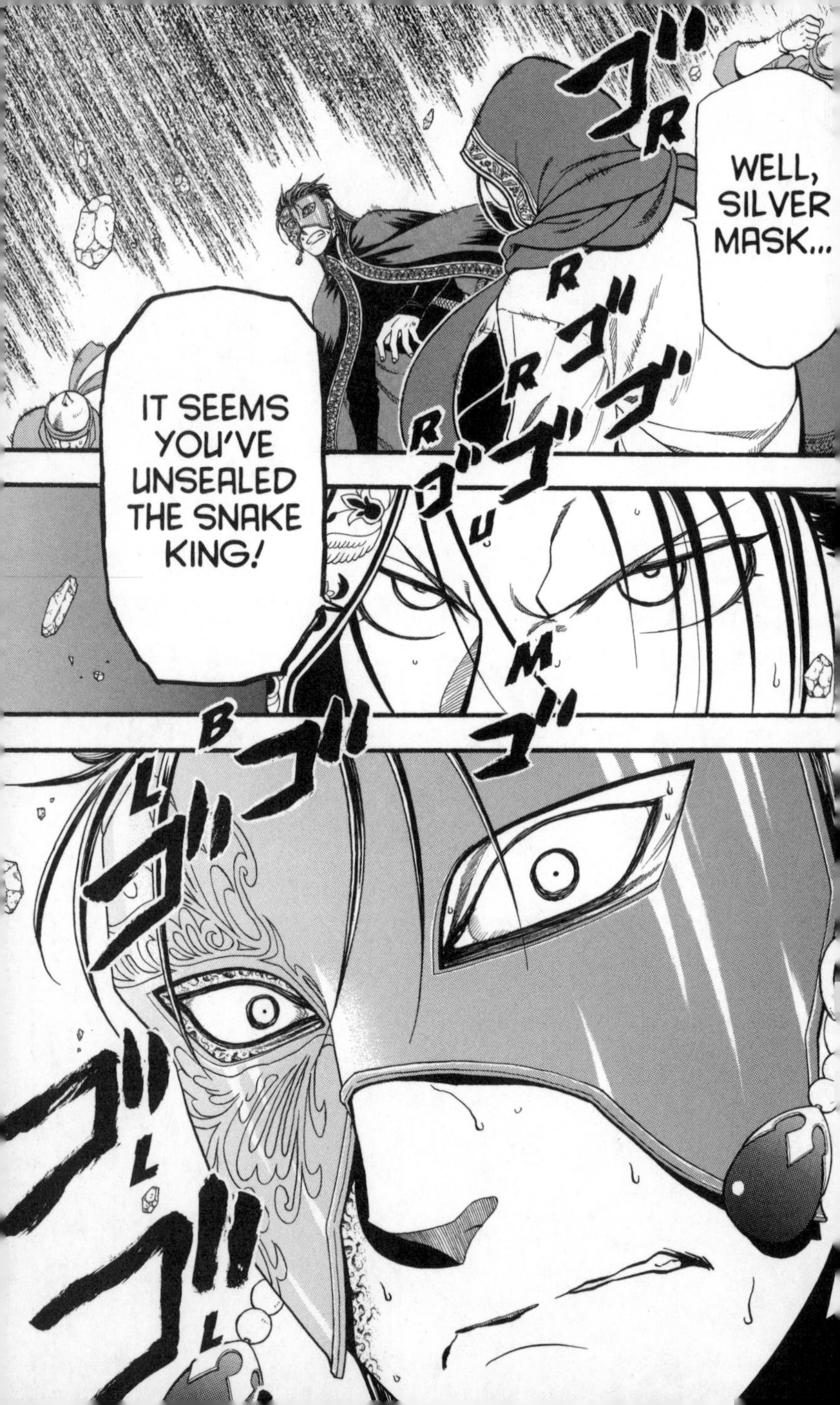
WELL, SILVER MASK...
IT SEEMS YOU'VE UNSEALED THE SNAKE KING!

THE HEROIC LEGEND OF
ARSLAN

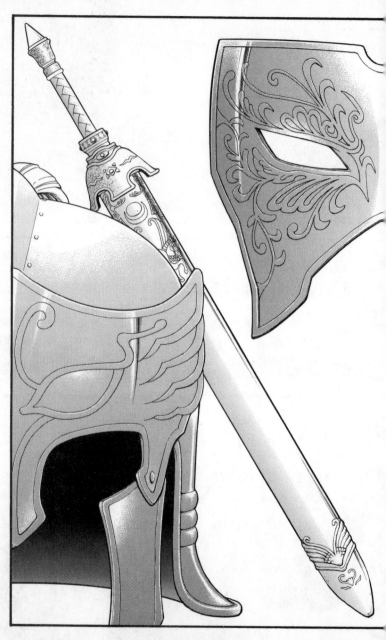

Chapter 79: Spasms of the Earth

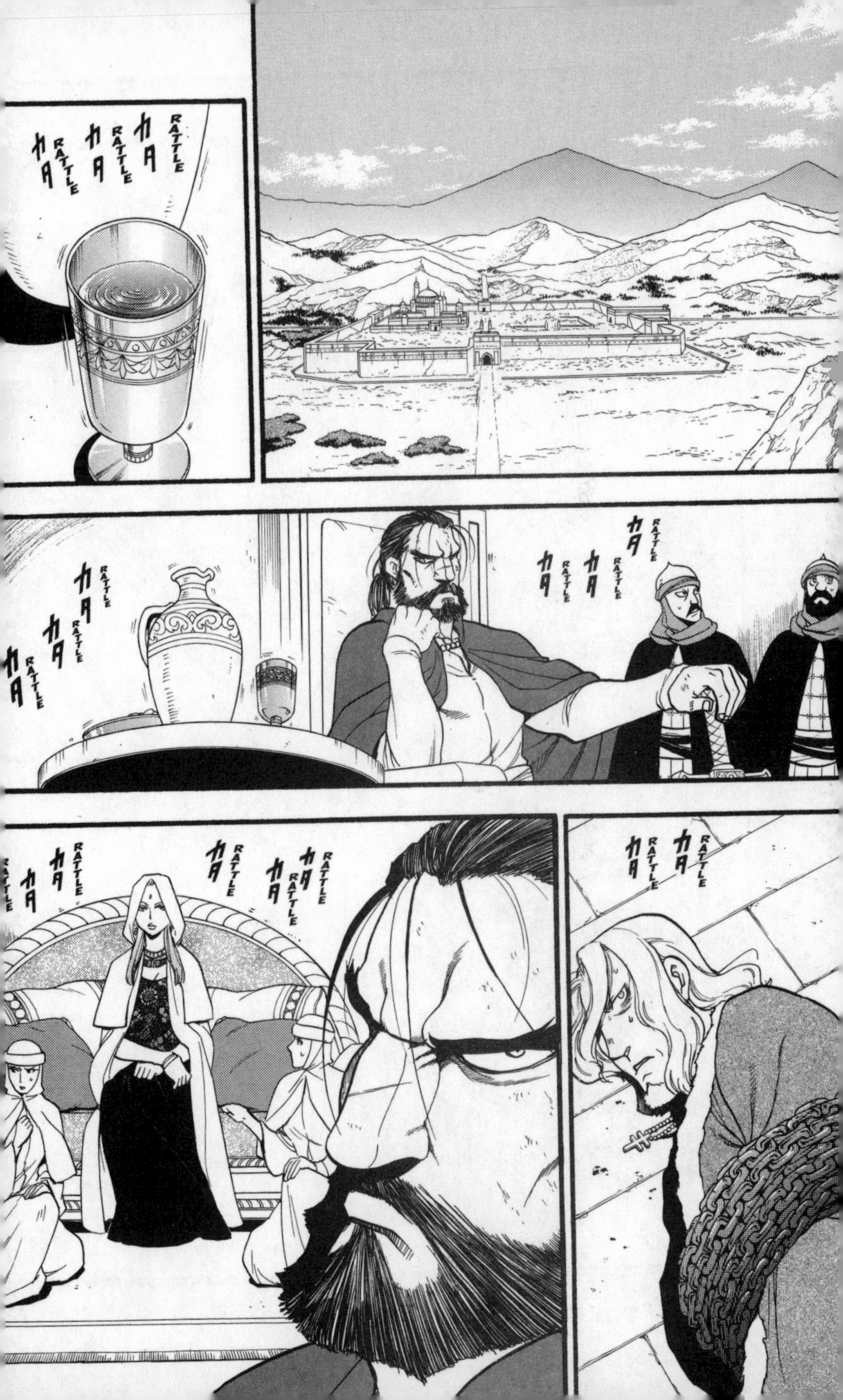
カタ RATTLE
カタ RATTLE
カタ RATTLE
カタ RATTLE
カタ RATTLE
カタ RATTLE
カタ RATTLE
カタ RATTLE
カタ RATTLE
カタ RATTLE
カタ RATTLE
カタ RATTLE
カタ RATTLE
カタ RATTLE
カタ RATTLE
カタ RATTLE

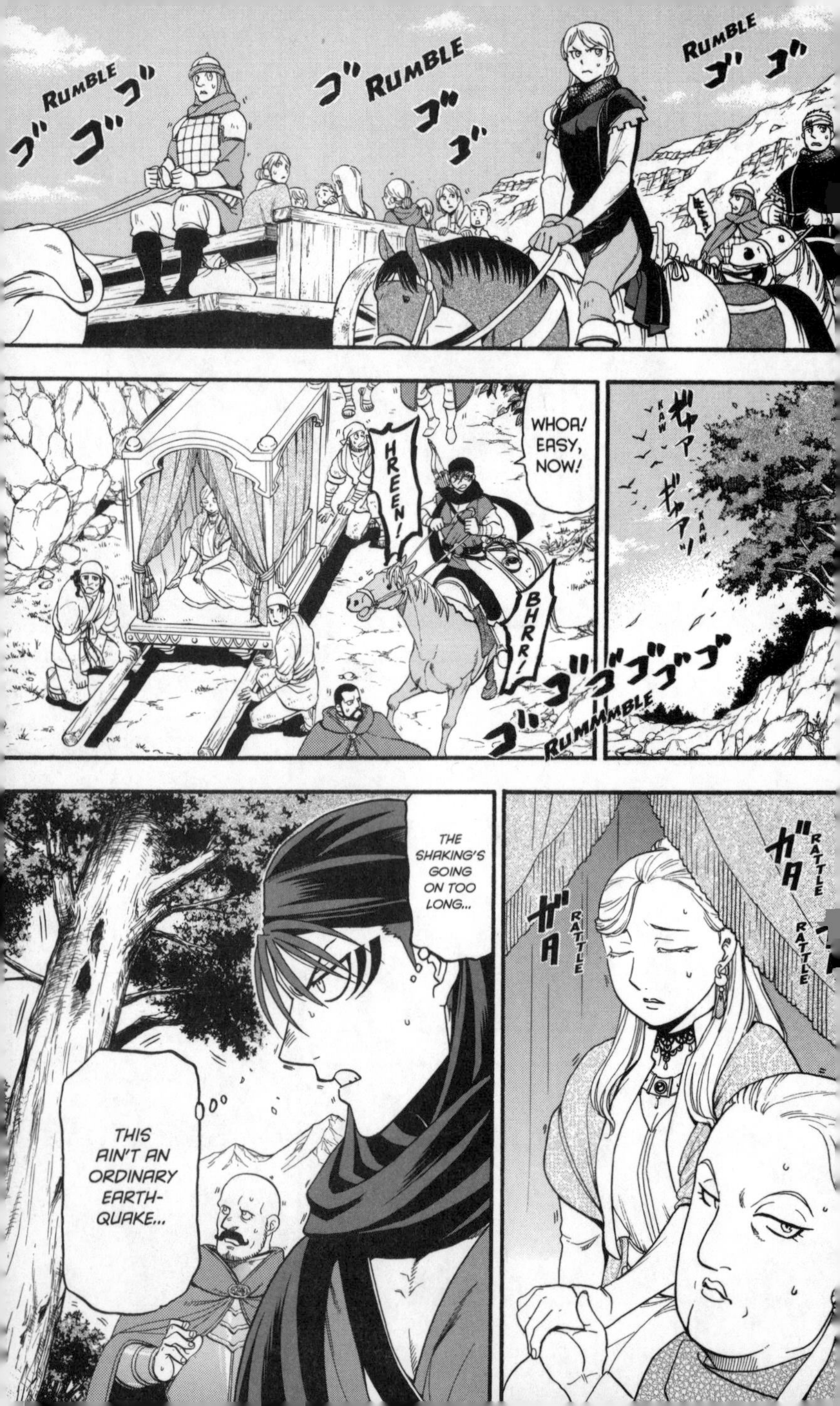
RUMBLE
ゴゴ
ゴ
RUMBLE
ゴゴ
RUMBLE
ゴゴ
ギャア
KAW
ギャア
KAW
WHOA! EASY, NOW!
HREEN!
BHRR!
ゴゴゴゴゴゴ
RUMMMBLE
ガタ
RATTLE
ガタ
RATTLE
RATTLE
THE SHAKING'S GOING ON TOO LONG...
THIS AIN'T AN ORDINARY EARTH-QUAKE...

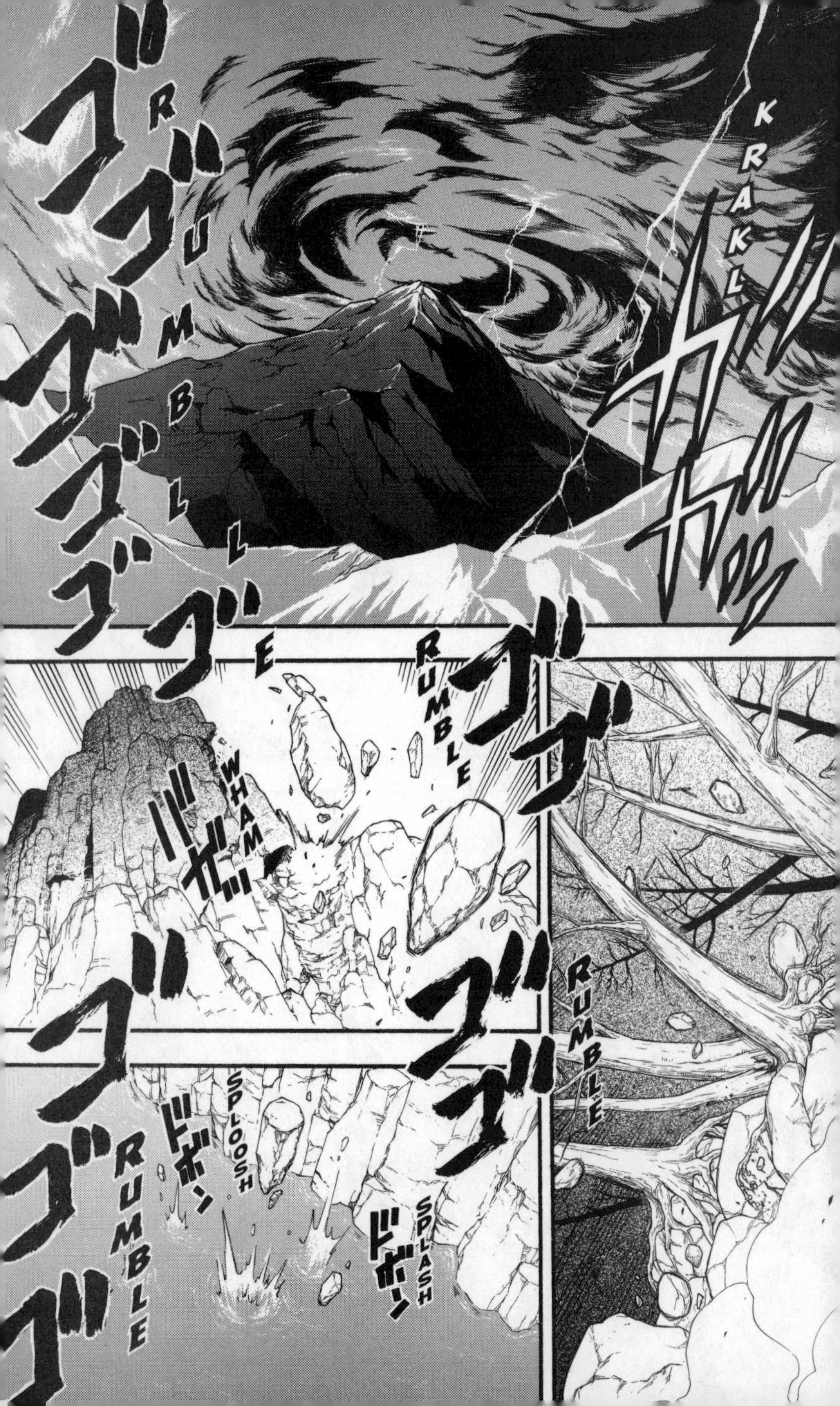
KRAKL
RUMBLLE
RUMBLE
RUMBLE
WHAM
SPLASH
SPLOOSH
RUMBLE

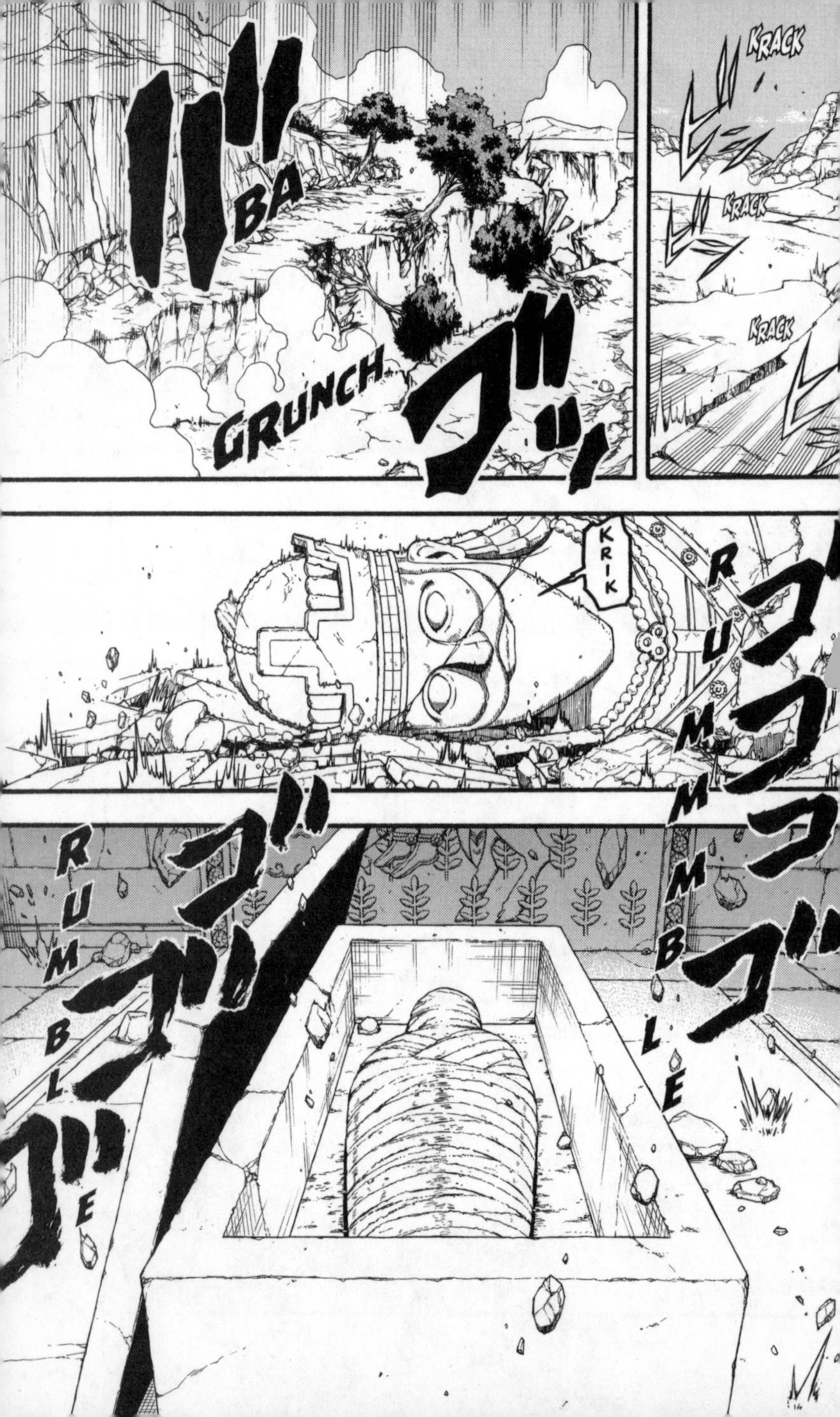
KRACK
KRACK
KRACK
BA
GRUNCH
KRIK
RUMMMBLE
RUMBLE

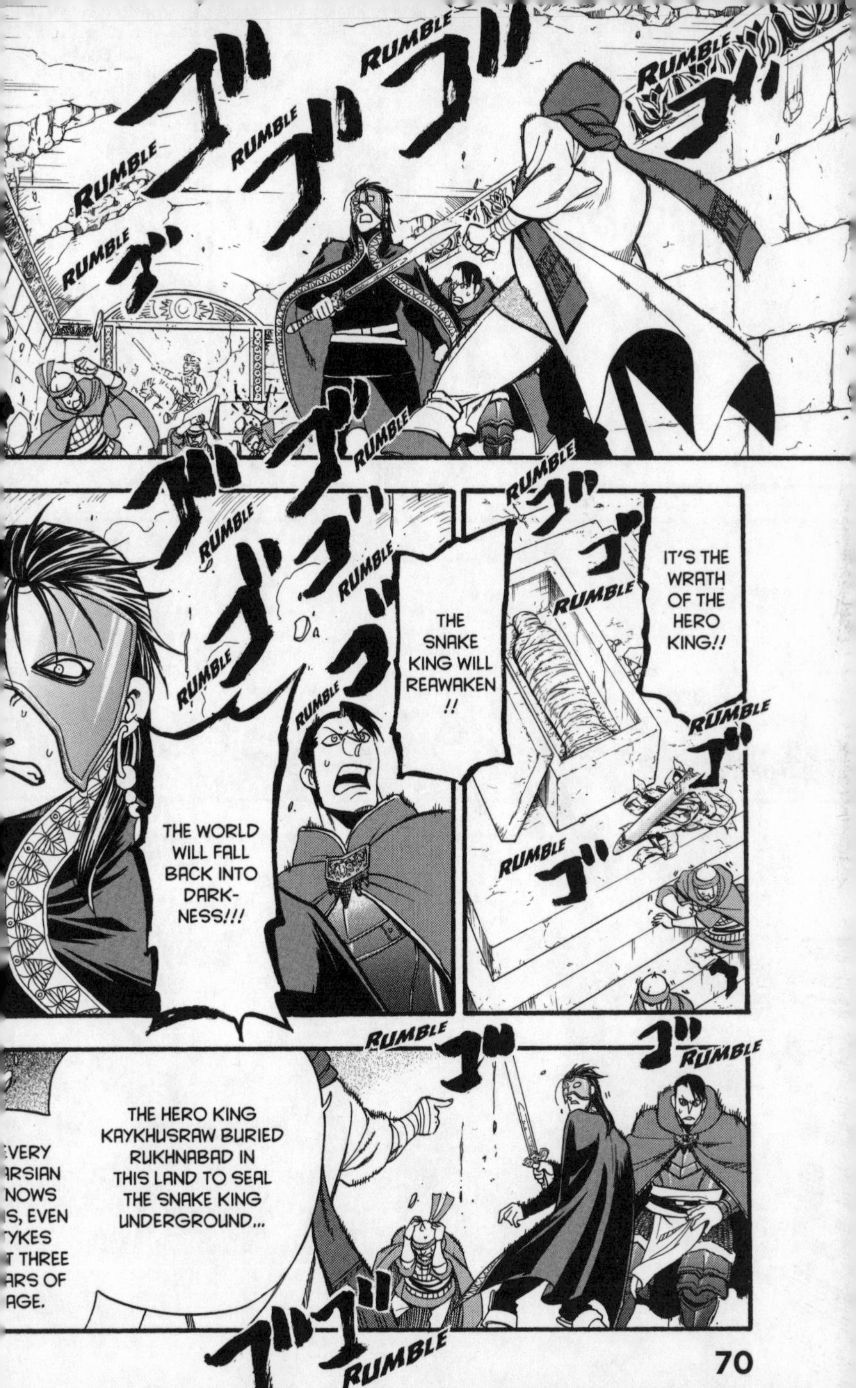
RUMBLE RUMBLE RUMBLE RUMBLE RUMBLE
RUMBLE RUMBLE RUMBLE
RUMBLE
IT'S THE WRATH OF THE HERO KING!!
RUMBLE RUMBLE RUMBLE
THE SNAKE KING WILL REAWAKEN!!
THE WORLD WILL FALL BACK INTO DARK-NESS!!!
RUMBLE RUMBLE
THE HERO KING KAYKHUSRAW BURIED RUKHNABAD IN THIS LAND TO SEAL THE SNAKE KING UNDERGROUND...
EVERY ARSIAN NOWS S, EVEN TYKES T THREE ARS OF AGE.
RUMBLE

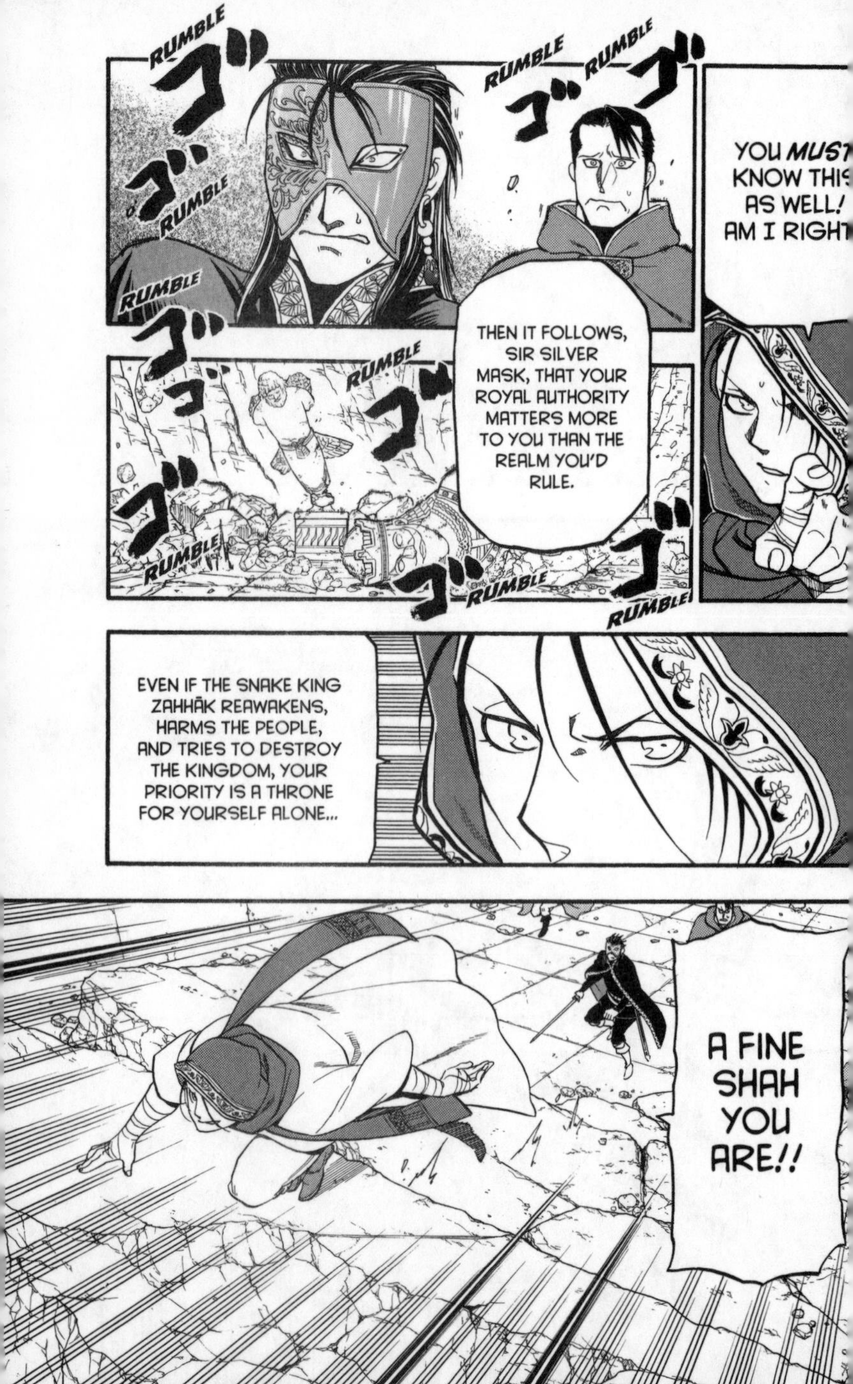
YOU MUST KNOW THIS AS WELL! AM I RIGHT
RUMBLE
RUMBLE
RUMBLE
RUMBLE
RUMBLE
THEN IT FOLLOWS, SIR SILVER MASK, THAT YOUR ROYAL AUTHORITY MATTERS MORE TO YOU THAN THE REALM YOU'D RULE.
RUMBLE
RUMBLE
RUMBLE
RUMBLE
EVEN IF THE SNAKE KING ZAHHĀK REAWAKENS, HARMS THE PEOPLE, AND TRIES TO DESTROY THE KINGDOM, YOUR PRIORITY IS A THRONE FOR YOURSELF ALONE...
A FINE SHAH YOU ARE!!

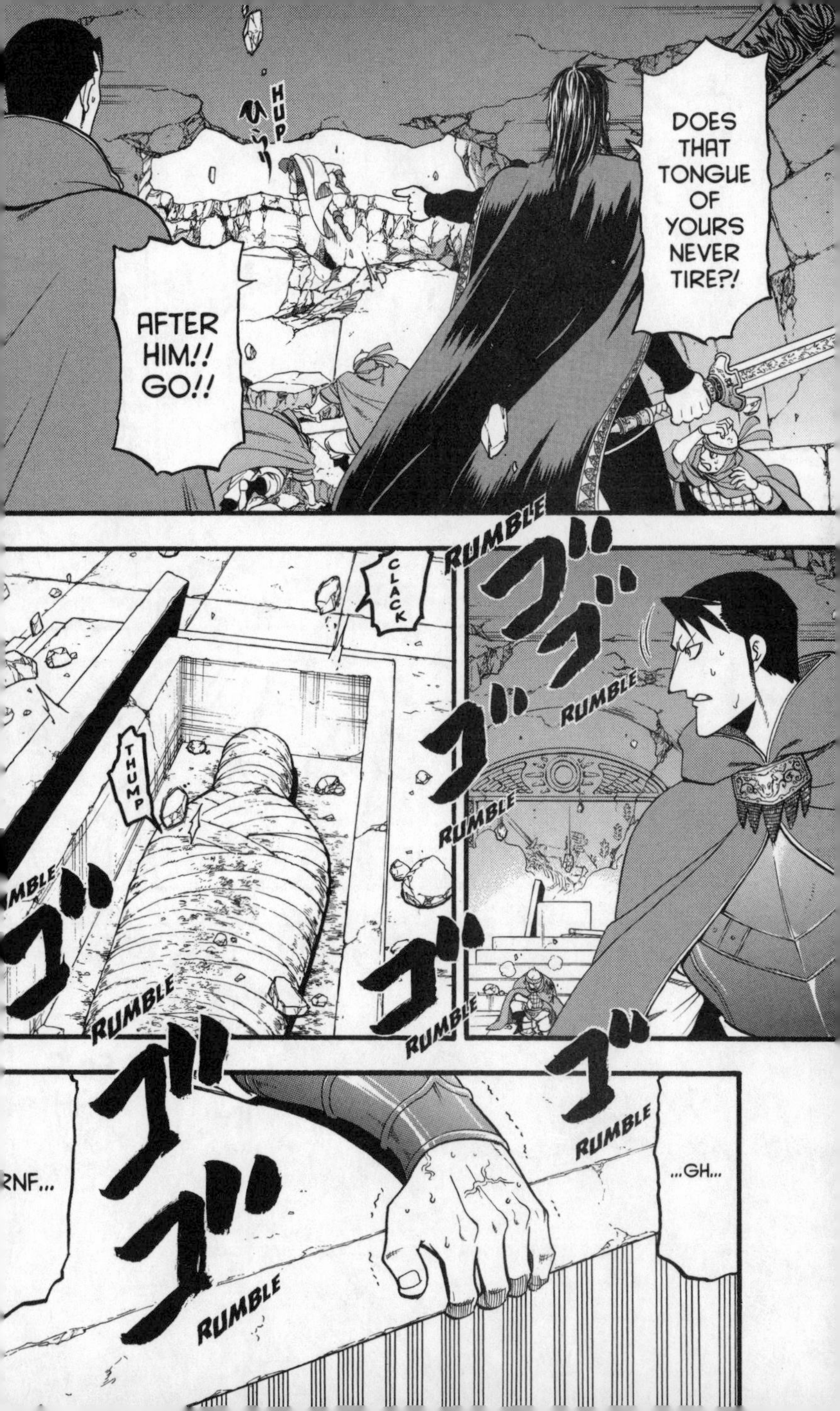

DOES THAT TONGUE OF YOURS NEVER TIRE?!
HUP
AFTER HIM!! GO!!
RUMBLE
RUMBLE
RUMBLE
RUMBLE
CLACK
THUMP
RUMBLE
MBLE
RUMBLE
...GH...
RNF...
RUMBLE

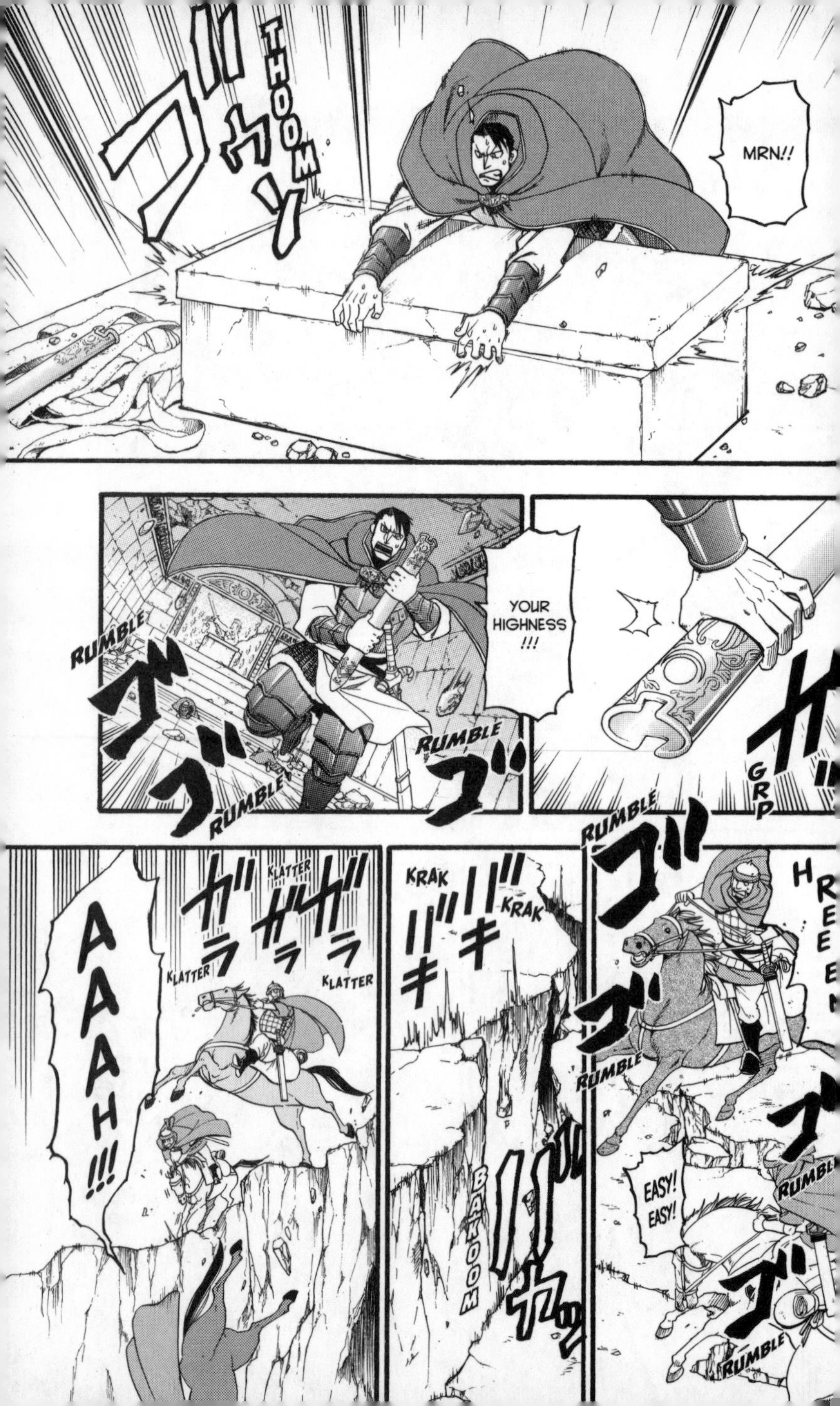
THOOM
MRN!!
GRP
YOUR HIGHNESS !!!
RUMBLE
RUMBLE
RUMBLE
RUMBLE
RUMBLE
HREEE
RUMBLE
EASY! EASY!
RUMBLE
RUMBLE
KRAK
KRAK
BAKOOOM
KLATTER
KLATTER
KLATTER
AAAH!!!

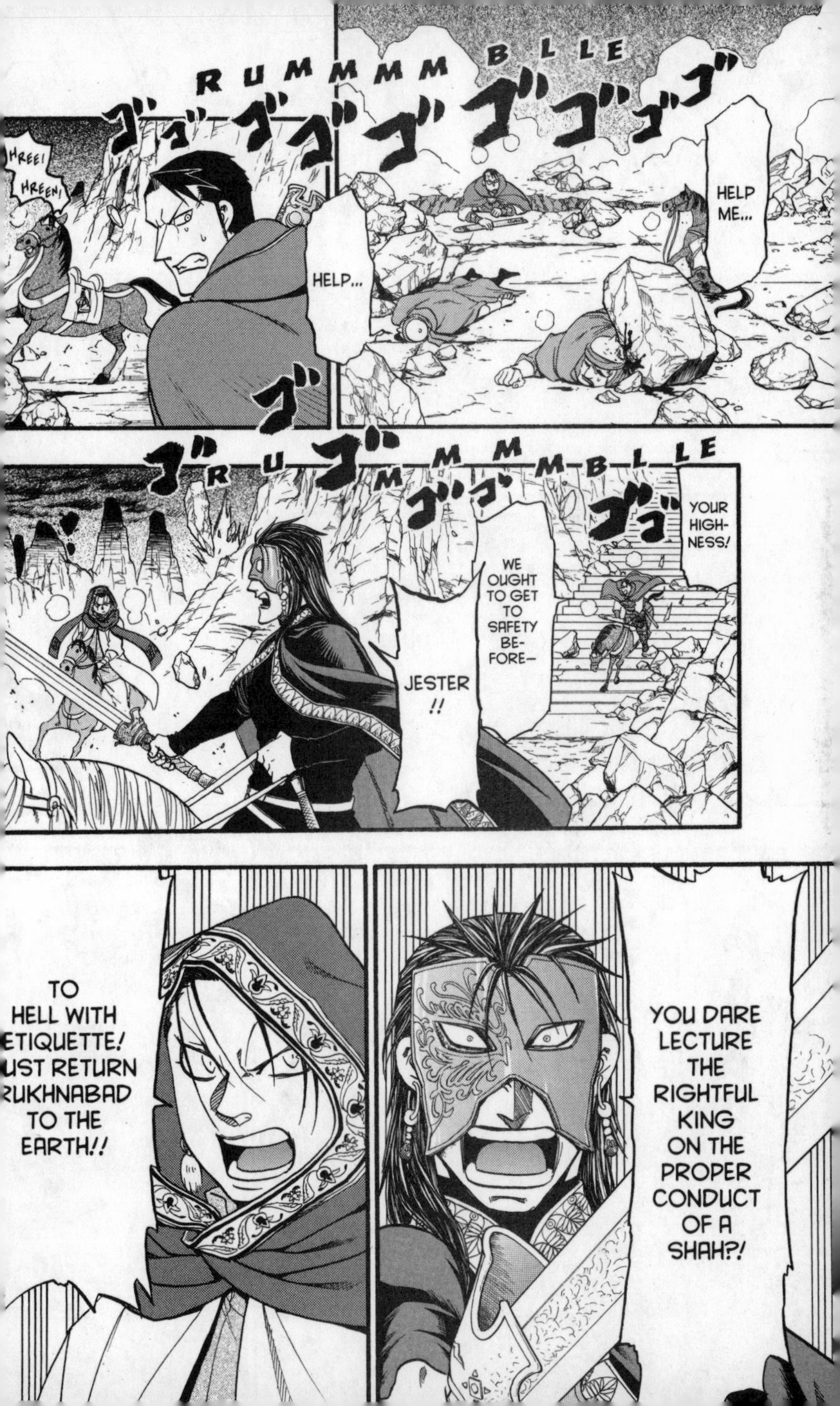
RUMMMMM BLLE
HELP ME...
HELP...
HREE! HREEN!
RUMMMMBLLE
YOUR HIGHNESS!
WE OUGHT TO GET TO SAFETY BEFORE—
JESTER!!
YOU DARE LECTURE THE RIGHTFUL KING ON THE PROPER CONDUCT OF A SHAH?!
TO HELL WITH ETIQUETTE! UST RETURN RUKHNABAD TO THE EARTH!!

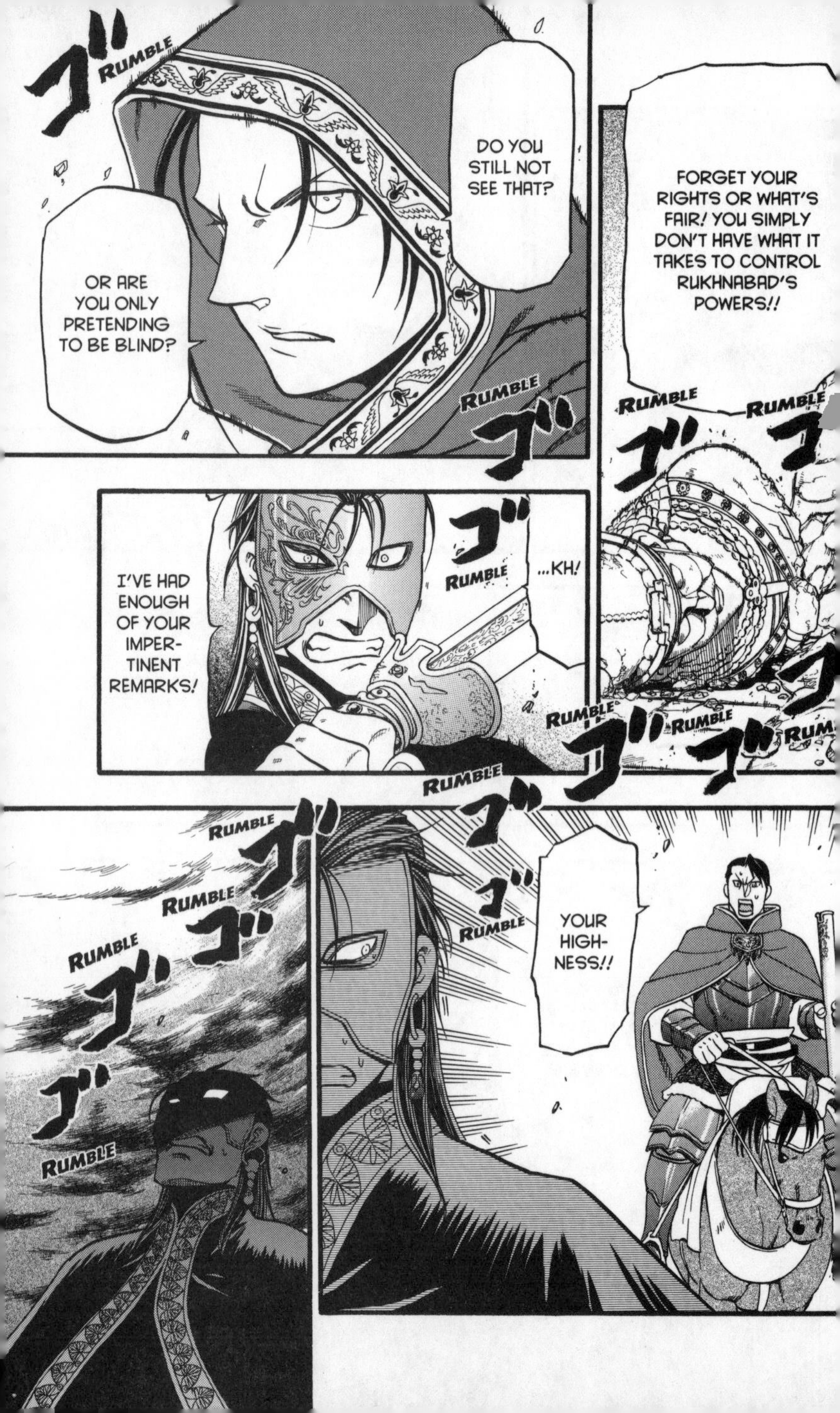
FORGET YOUR RIGHTS OR WHAT'S FAIR! YOU SIMPLY DON'T HAVE WHAT IT TAKES TO CONTROL RUKHNABAD'S POWERS!!
RUMBLE
RUMBLE
RUMBLE
RUMBLE
RUM
RUMBLE
DO YOU STILL NOT SEE THAT?
OR ARE YOU ONLY PRETENDING TO BE BLIND?
RUMBLE
RUMBLE
...KH!
RUMBLE
I'VE HAD ENOUGH OF YOUR IMPERTINENT REMARKS!
RUMBLE
YOUR HIGHNESS!!
RUMBLE
RUMBLE
RUMBLE
RUMBLE
RUMBLE

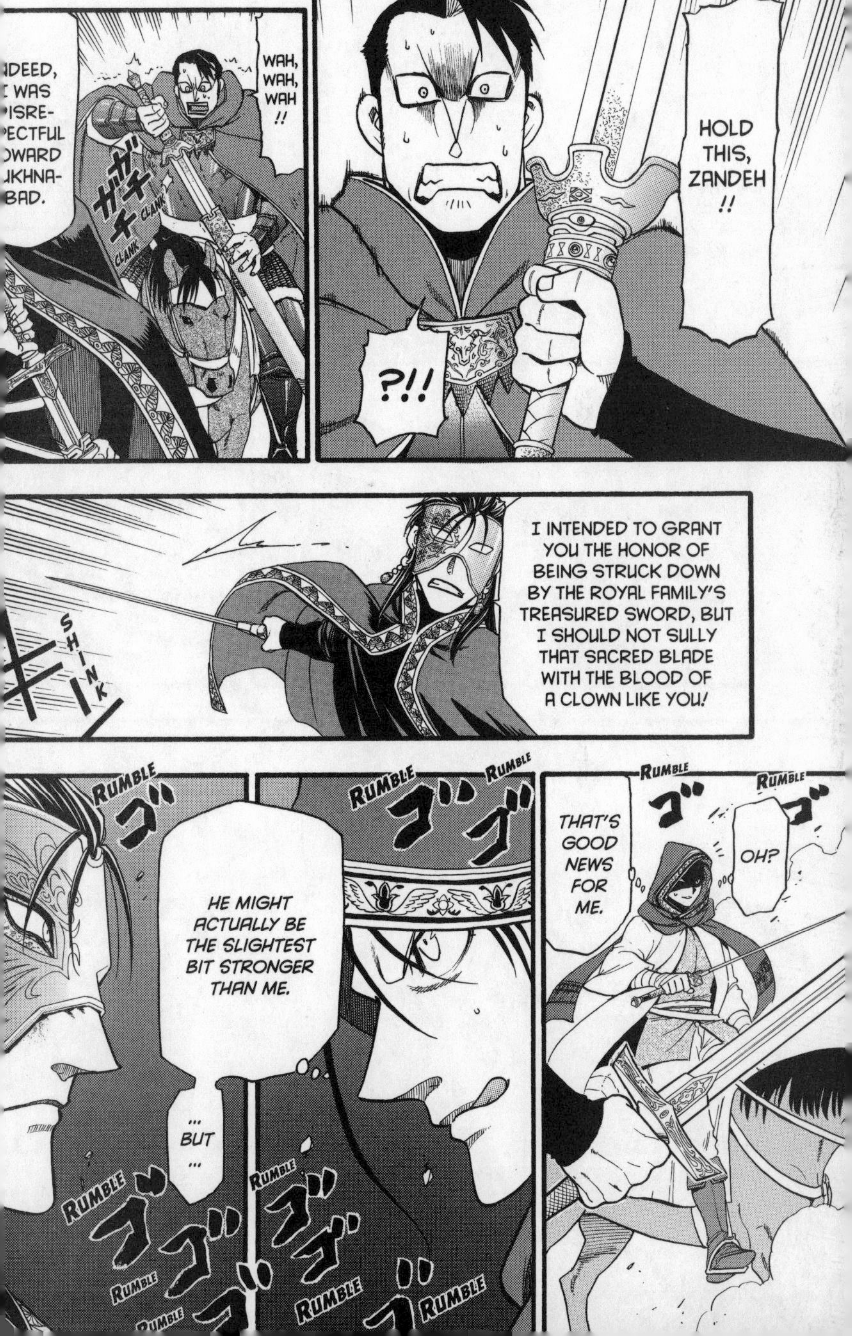
HOLD THIS, ZANDEH!!
?!!
WAH, WAH, WAH!!
NDEED, I WAS ISRE-PECTFUL OWARD UKHNA-BAD.
CLANK CLANK
I INTENDED TO GRANT YOU THE HONOR OF BEING STRUCK DOWN BY THE ROYAL FAMILY'S TREASURED SWORD, BUT I SHOULD NOT SULLY THAT SACRED BLADE WITH THE BLOOD OF A CLOWN LIKE YOU!
SHINK
RUMBLE RUMBLE
OH?
THAT'S GOOD NEWS FOR ME.
RUMBLE RUMBLE
HE MIGHT ACTUALLY BE THE SLIGHTEST BIT STRONGER THAN ME.
RUMBLE RUMBLE
RUMBLE
... BUT ...
RUMBLE RUMBLE RUMBLE

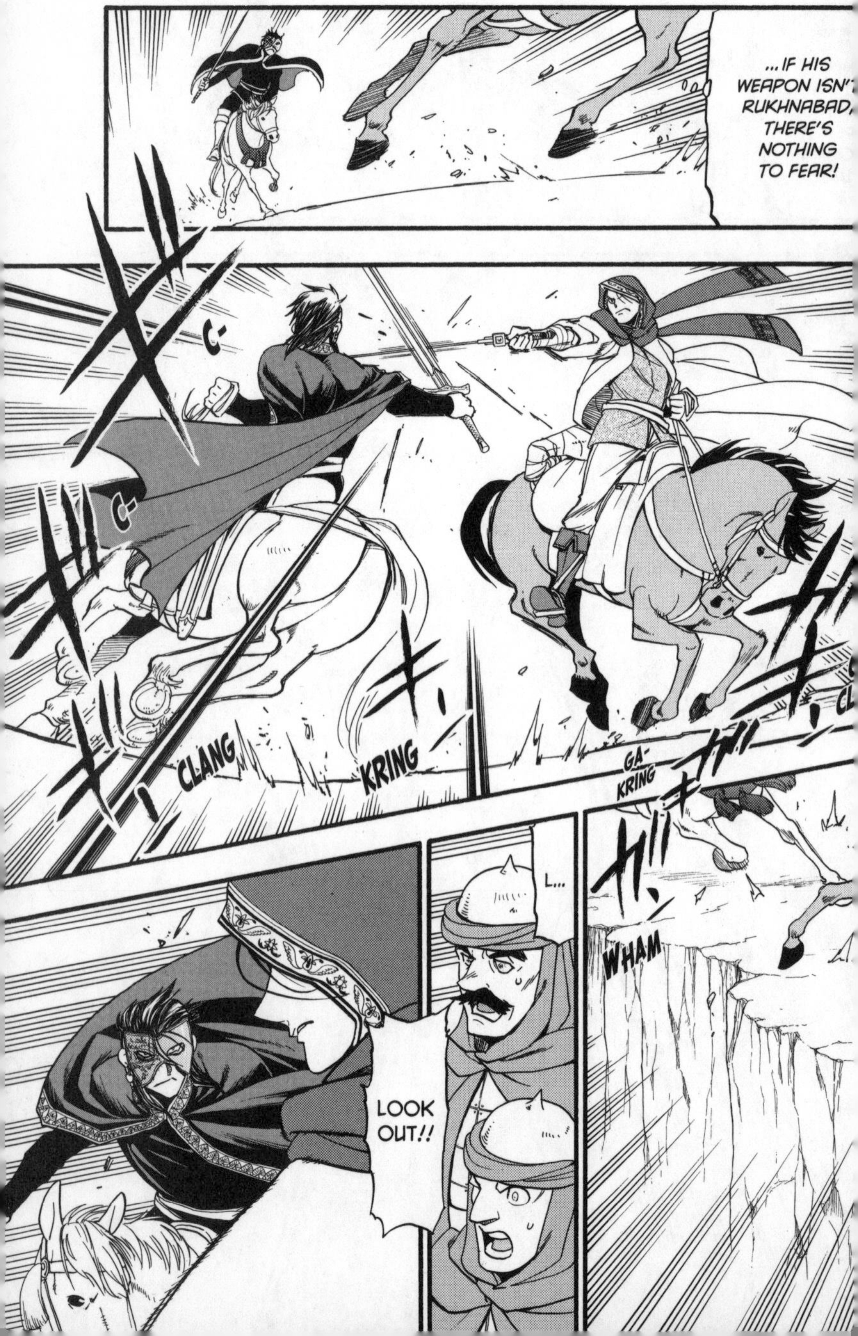
...IF HIS WEAPON ISN'T RUKHNABAD, THERE'S NOTHING TO FEAR!
GA-KRING
KRING
CLANG
WHAM
L...
LOOK OUT!!

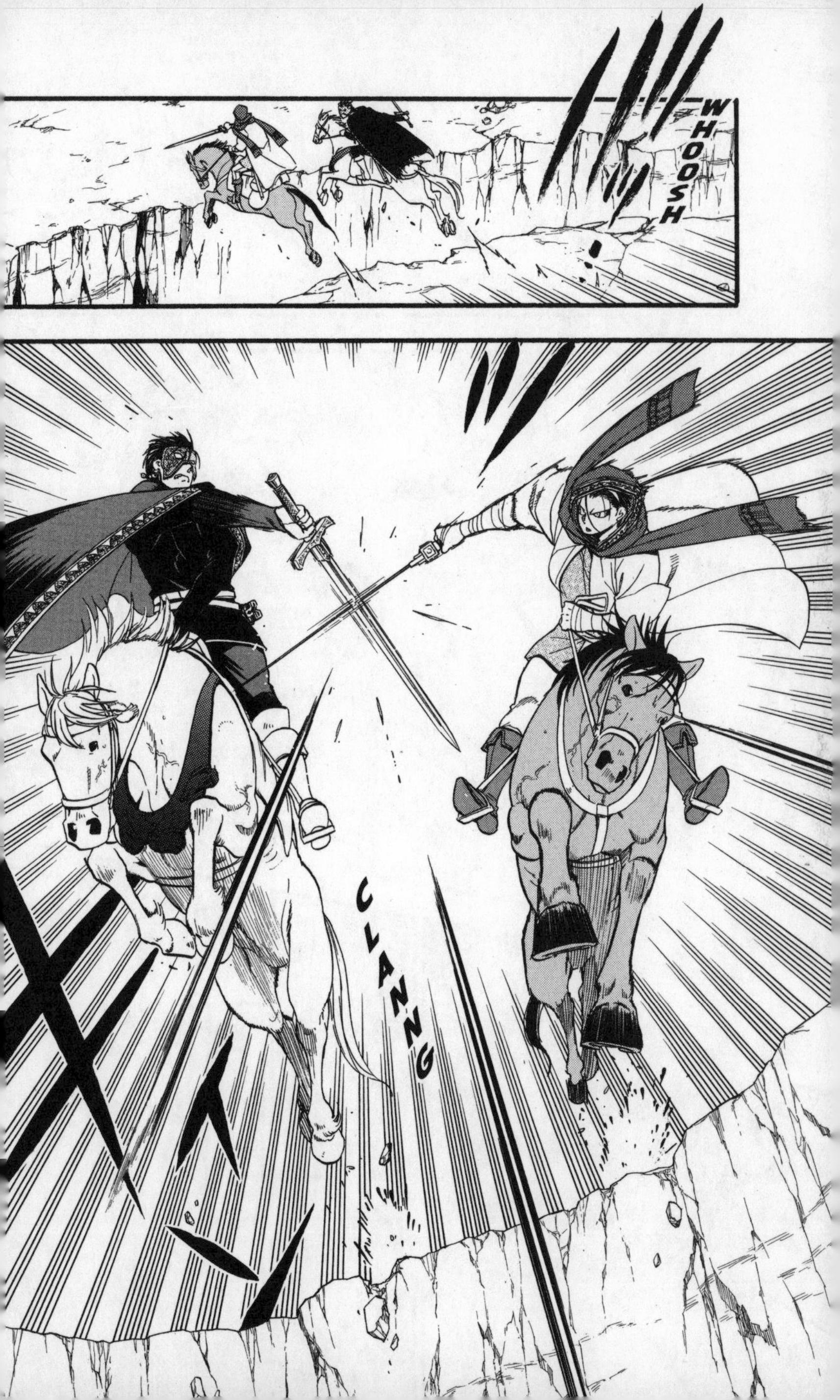
WHOOSH
!
CLANNG

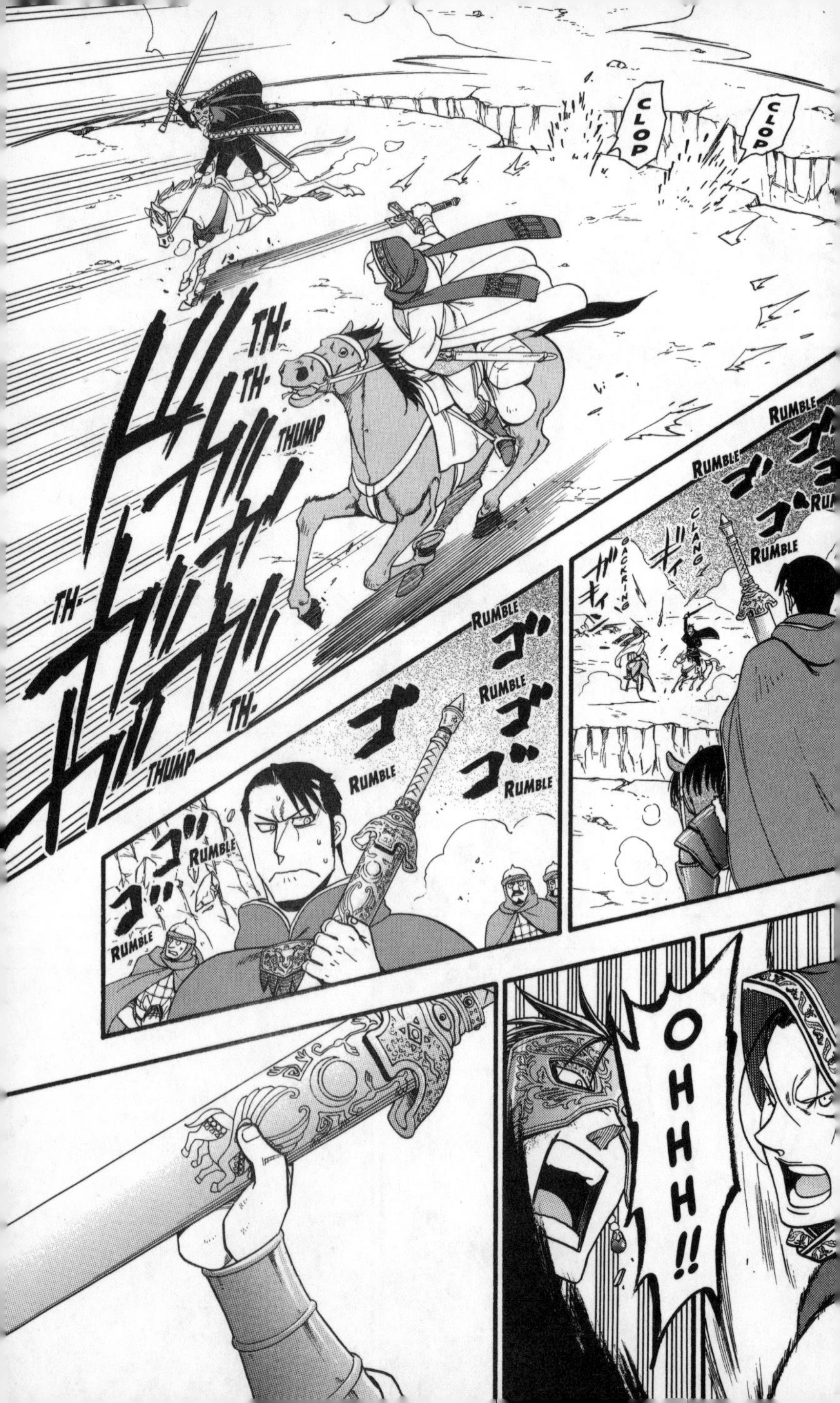
CLOP
CLOP
TH-
TH-
THUMP
TH-
TH-
THUMP
RUMBLE
RUMBLE
RUMBLE
CLANG
GACKRING
RUMBLE
RUMBLE
RUMBLE
RUMBLE
RUMBLE
RUMBLE
OHHH!!

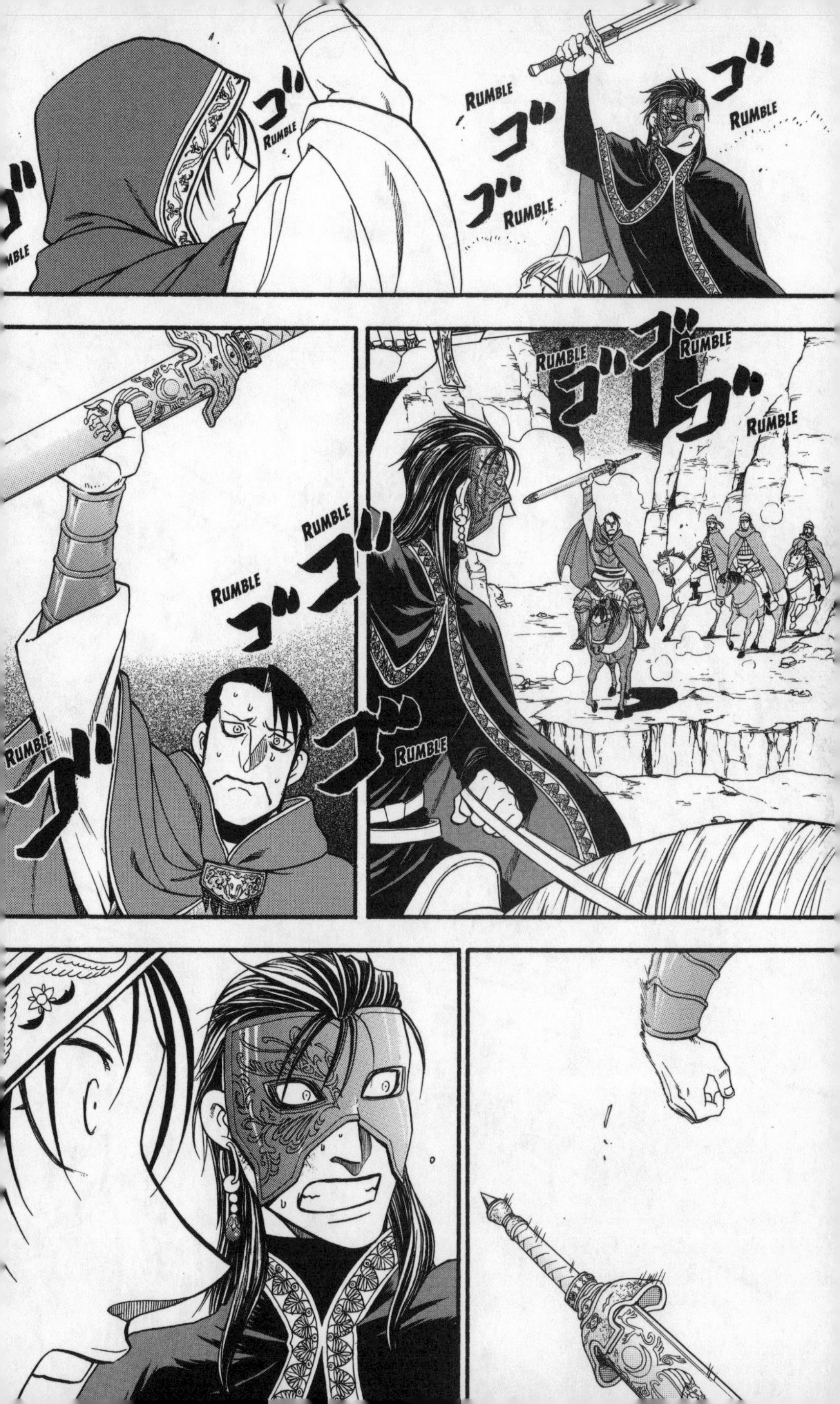

ゴ
RUMBLE
ゴ
RUMBLE
ゴ
RUMBLE
ゴ
RUMBLE
ゴ
RUMBLE
ゴ
RUMBLE
ゴ
RUMBLE
ゴ
RUMBLE
ゴ
RUMBLE
ゴ
RUMBLE
ゴ
RUMBLE
ゴ
RUMBLE
ゴ
RUMBLE

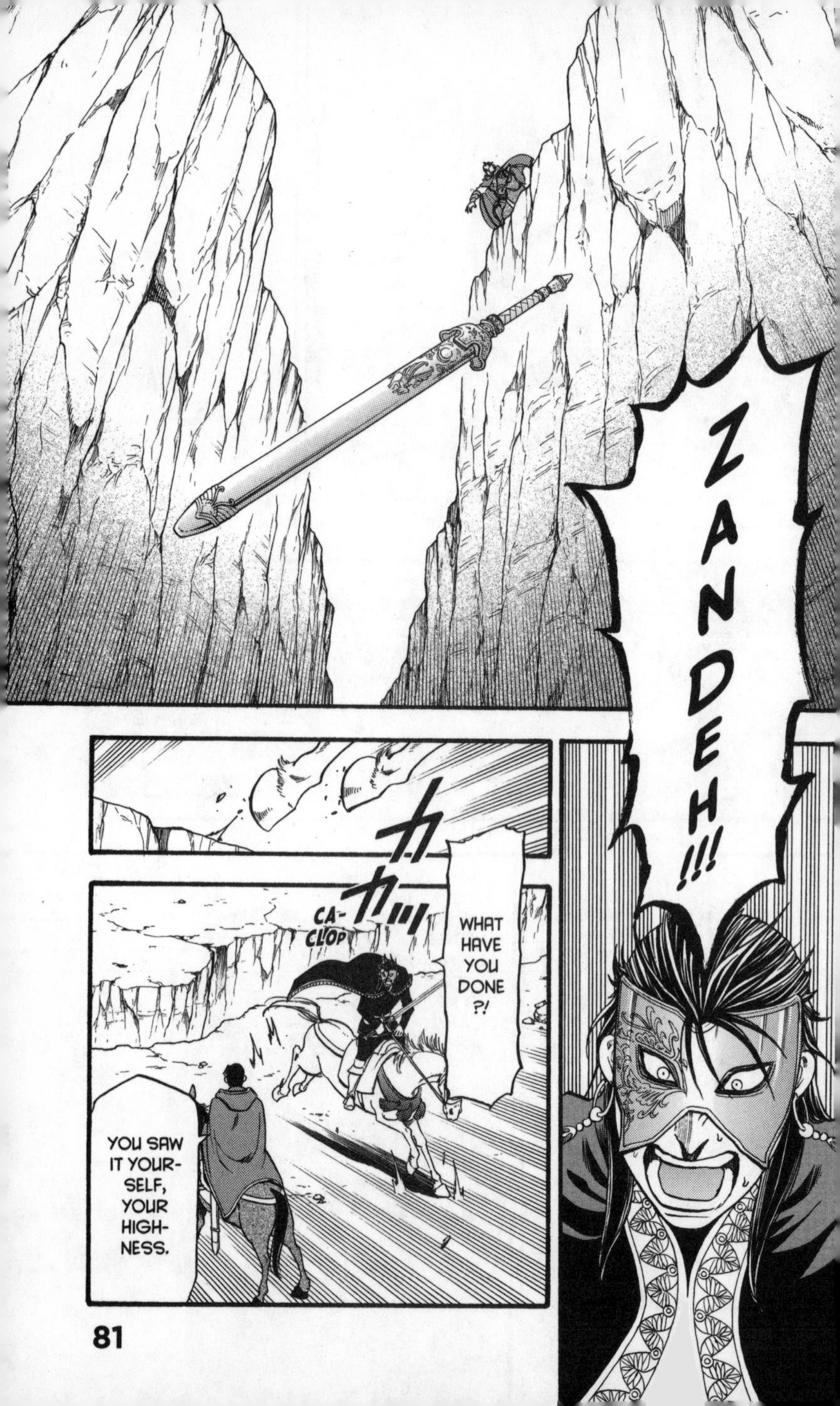
ZANDEH!!!
WHAT HAVE YOU DONE?!
CA-CLOP
カカッ
YOU SAW IT YOURSELF, YOUR HIGHNESS.

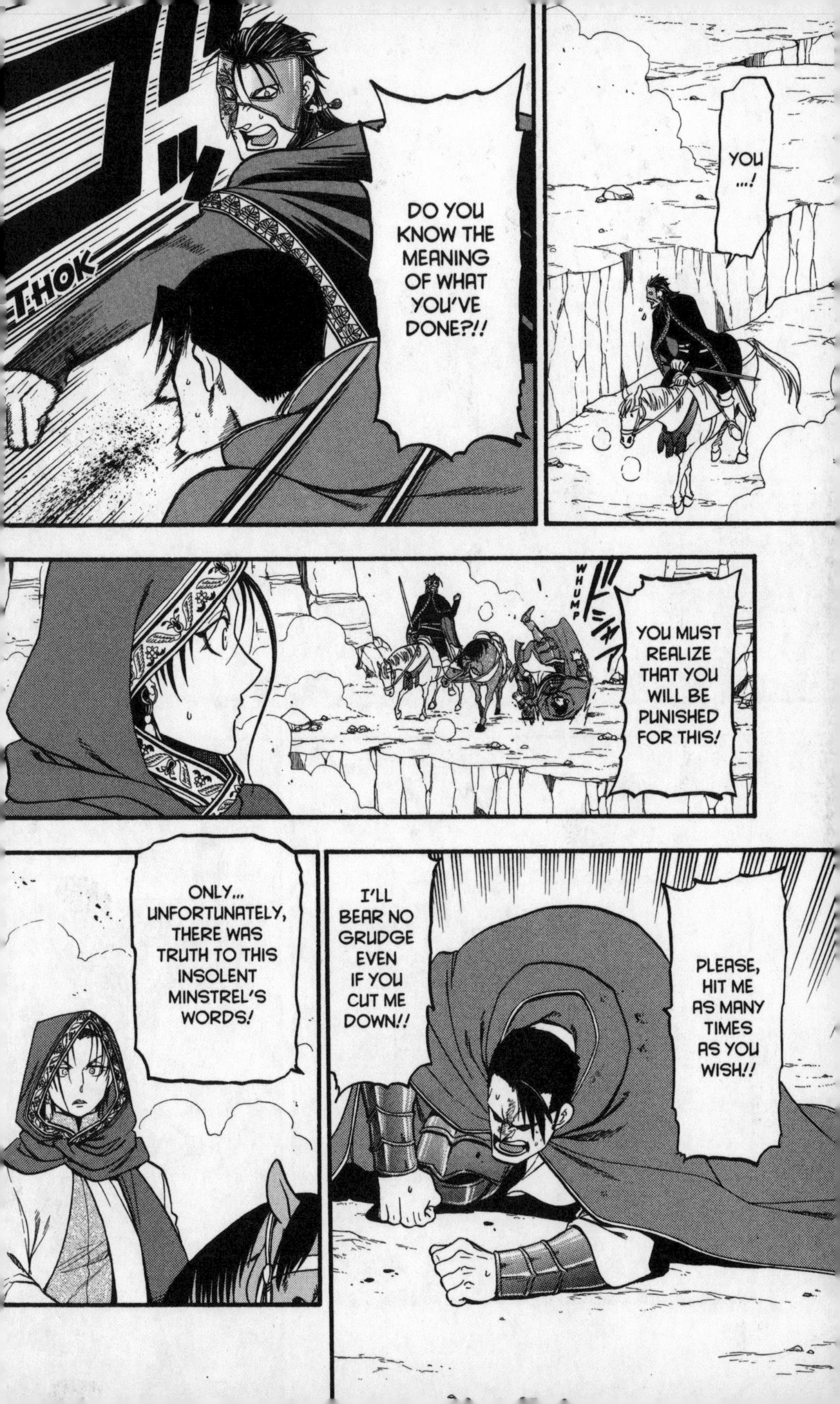
YOU ...!
DO YOU KNOW THE MEANING OF WHAT YOU'VE DONE?!!
THOK
WHUMP
YOU MUST REALIZE THAT YOU WILL BE PUNISHED FOR THIS!
PLEASE, HIT ME AS MANY TIMES AS YOU WISH!!
I'LL BEAR NO GRUDGE EVEN IF YOU CUT ME DOWN!!
ONLY... UNFORTUNATELY, THERE WAS TRUTH TO THIS INSOLENT MINSTREL'S WORDS!

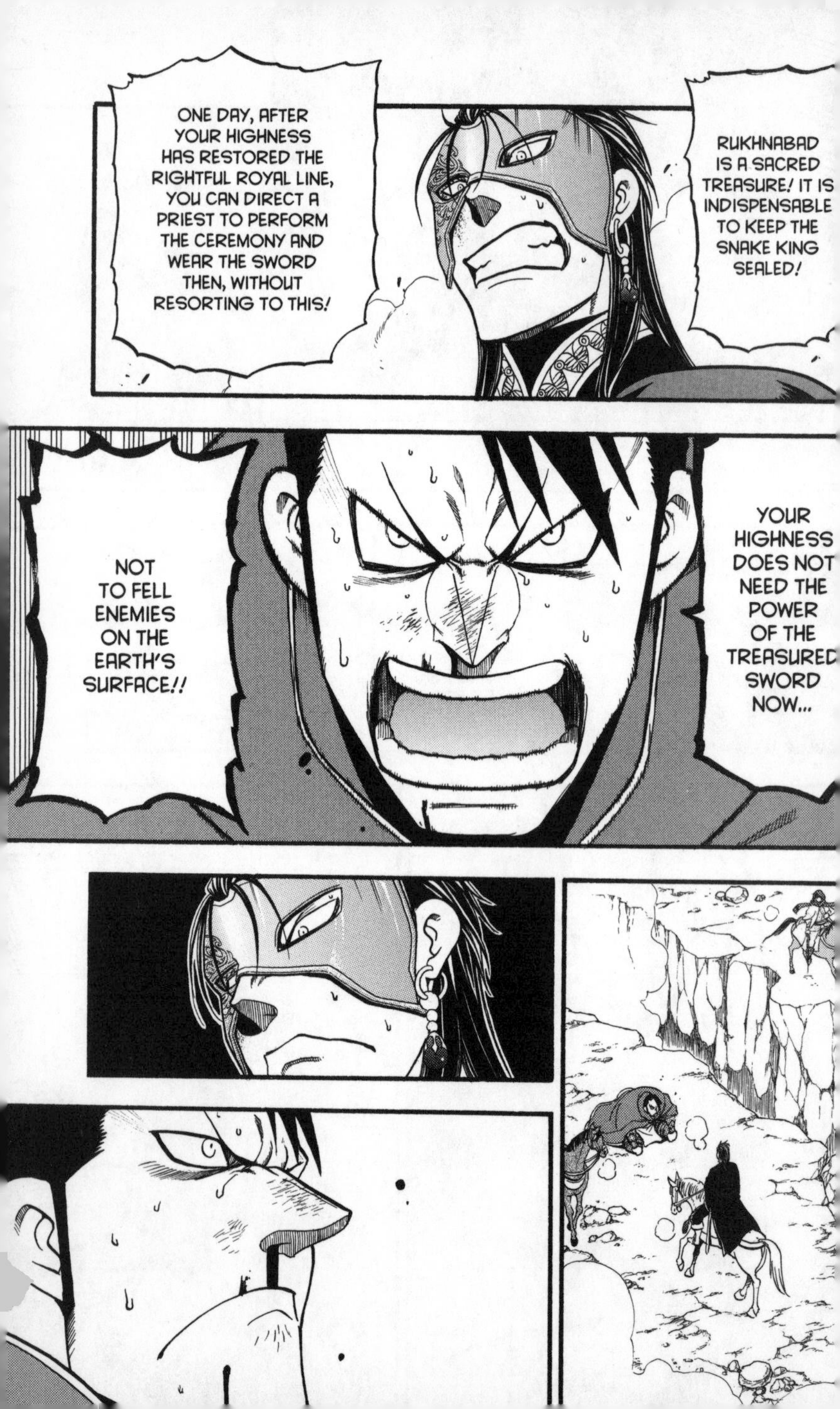
RUKHNABAD IS A SACRED TREASURE! IT IS INDISPENSABLE TO KEEP THE SNAKE KING SEALED!
ONE DAY, AFTER YOUR HIGHNESS HAS RESTORED THE RIGHTFUL ROYAL LINE, YOU CAN DIRECT A PRIEST TO PERFORM THE CEREMONY AND WEAR THE SWORD THEN, WITHOUT RESORTING TO THIS!
YOUR HIGHNESS DOES NOT NEED THE POWER OF THE TREASURED SWORD NOW...
NOT TO FELL ENEMIES ON THE EARTH'S SURFACE!!

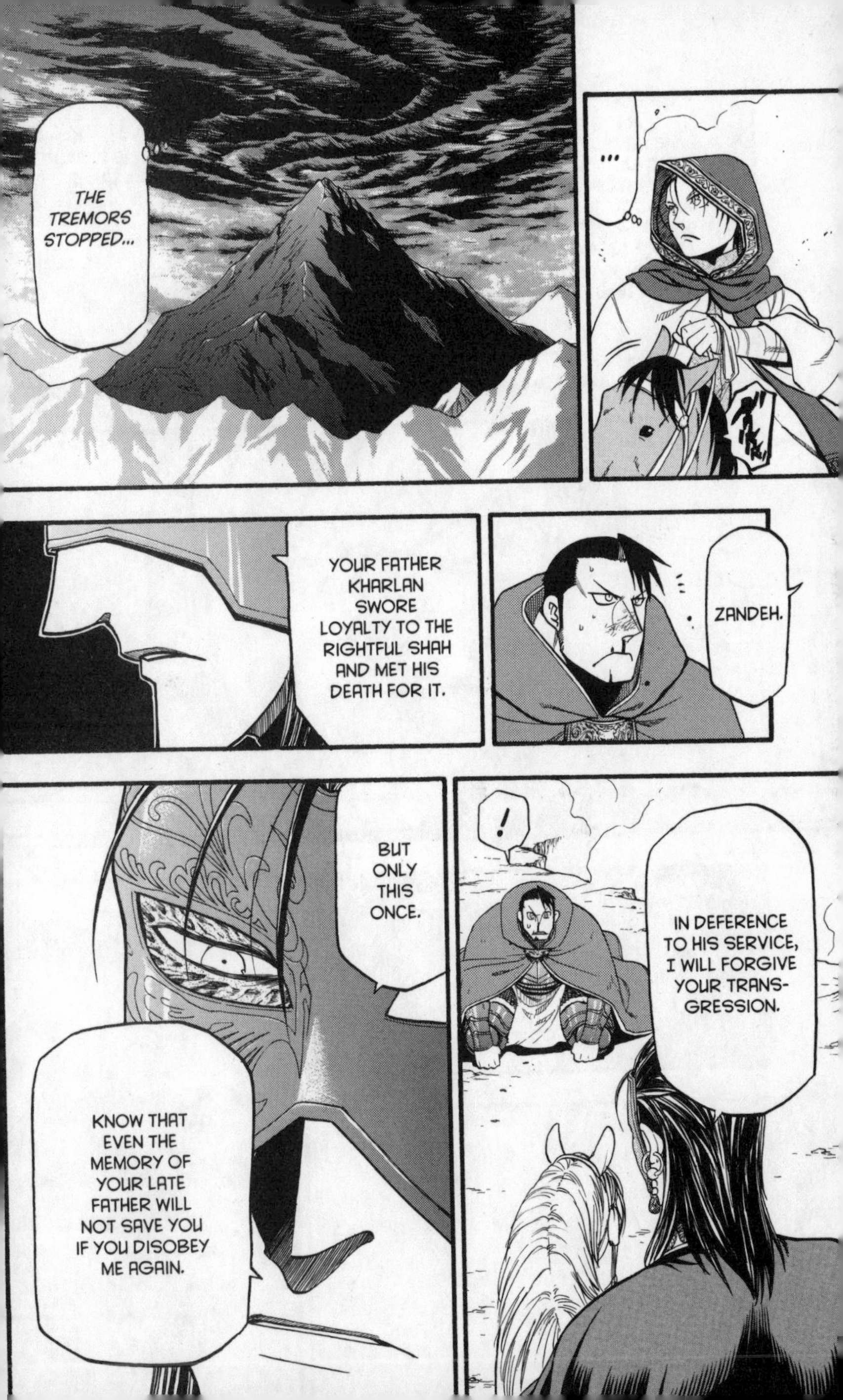
...
THE TREMORS STOPPED...
ZANDEH.
YOUR FATHER KHARLAN SWORE LOYALTY TO THE RIGHTFUL SHAH AND MET HIS DEATH FOR IT.
!
IN DEFERENCE TO HIS SERVICE, I WILL FORGIVE YOUR TRANS-GRESSION.
BUT ONLY THIS ONCE.
KNOW THAT EVEN THE MEMORY OF YOUR LATE FATHER WILL NOT SAVE YOU IF YOU DISOBEY ME AGAIN.

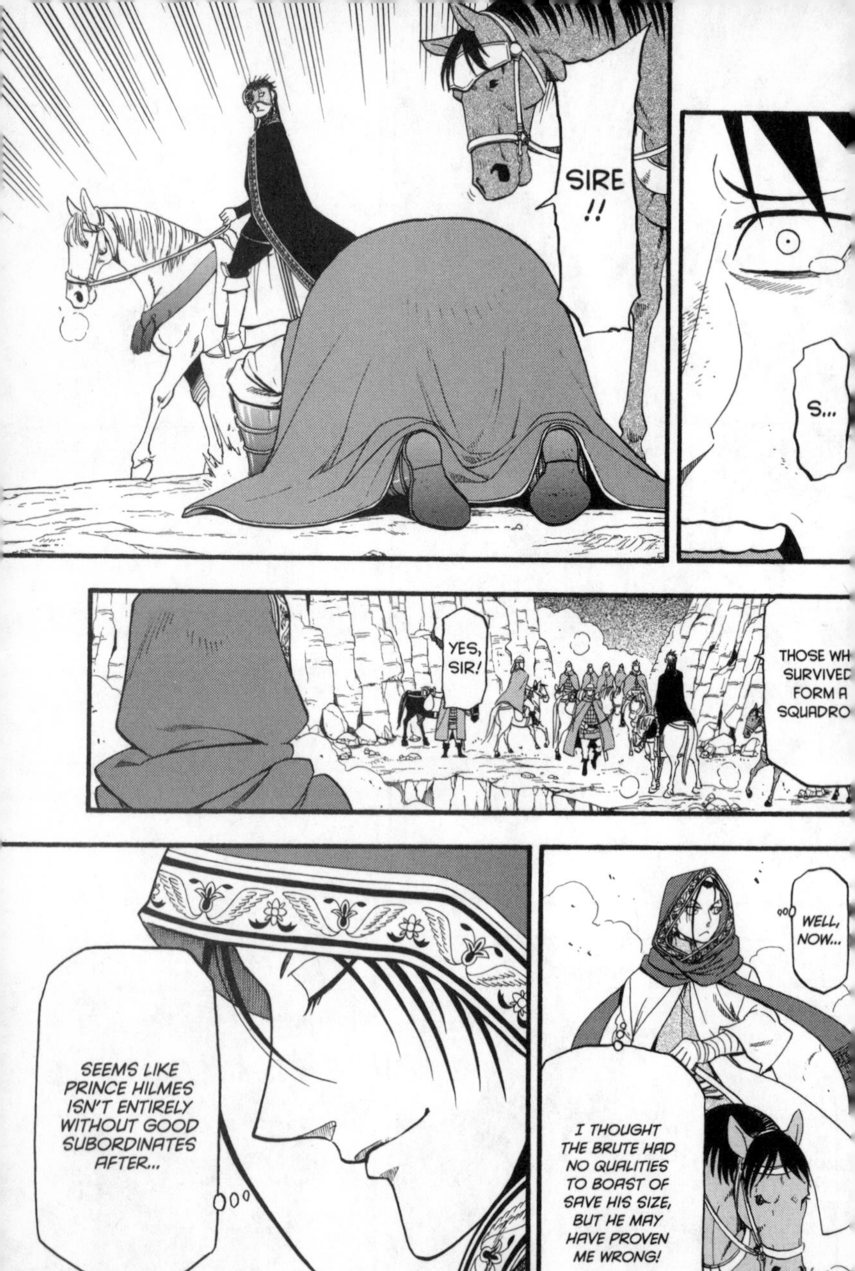
S...
SIRE !!
THOSE WH SURVIVED FORM A SQUADRO
YES, SIR!
WELL, NOW...
I THOUGHT THE BRUTE HAD NO QUALITIES TO BOAST OF SAVE HIS SIZE, BUT HE MAY HAVE PROVEN ME WRONG!
SEEMS LIKE PRINCE HILMES ISN'T ENTIRELY WITHOUT GOOD SUBORDINATES AFTER...

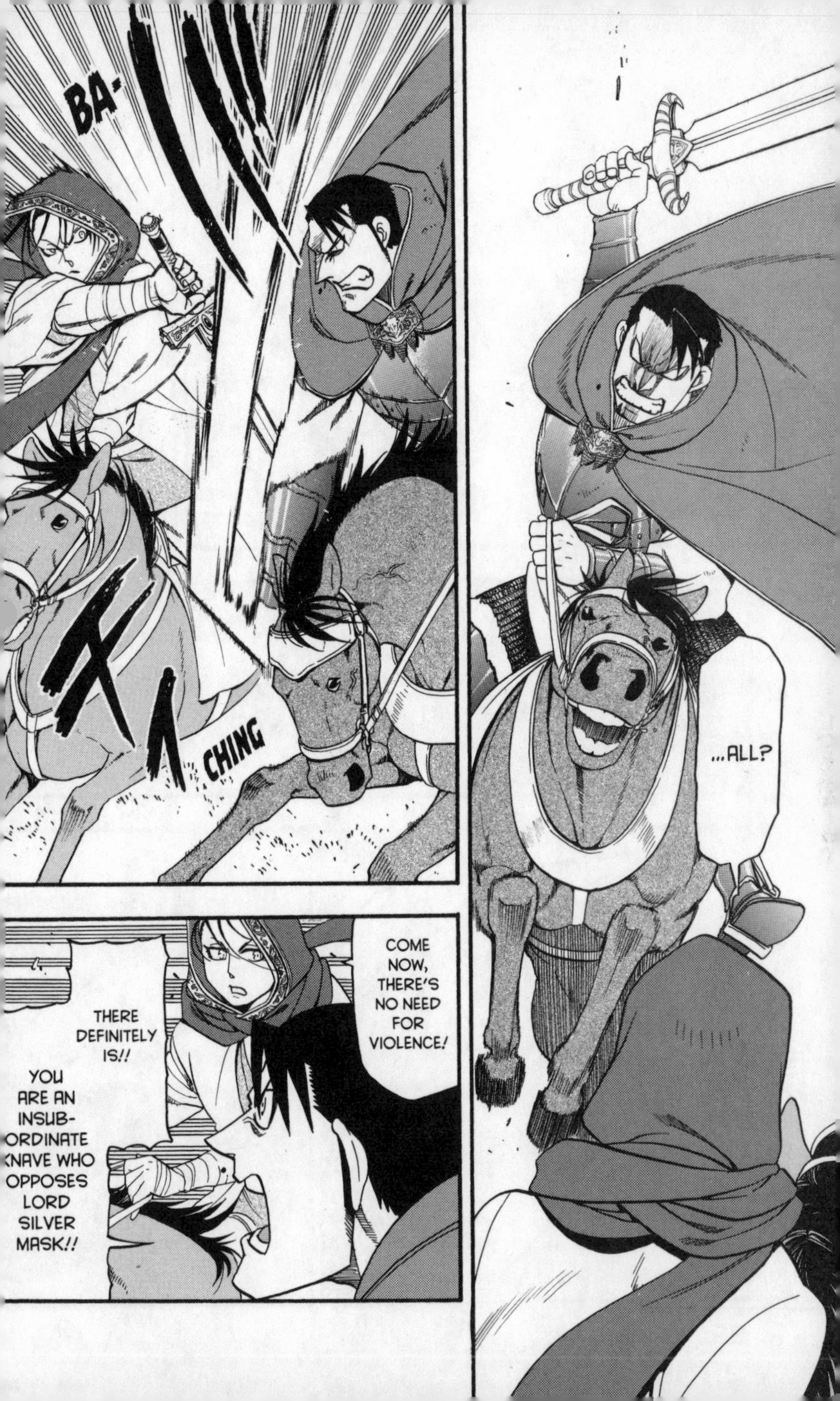
...ALL?
BA-
CHING
COME NOW, THERE'S NO NEED FOR VIOLENCE!
THERE DEFINITELY IS!!
YOU ARE AN INSUB-ORDINATE KNAVE WHO OPPOSES LORD SILVER MASK!!

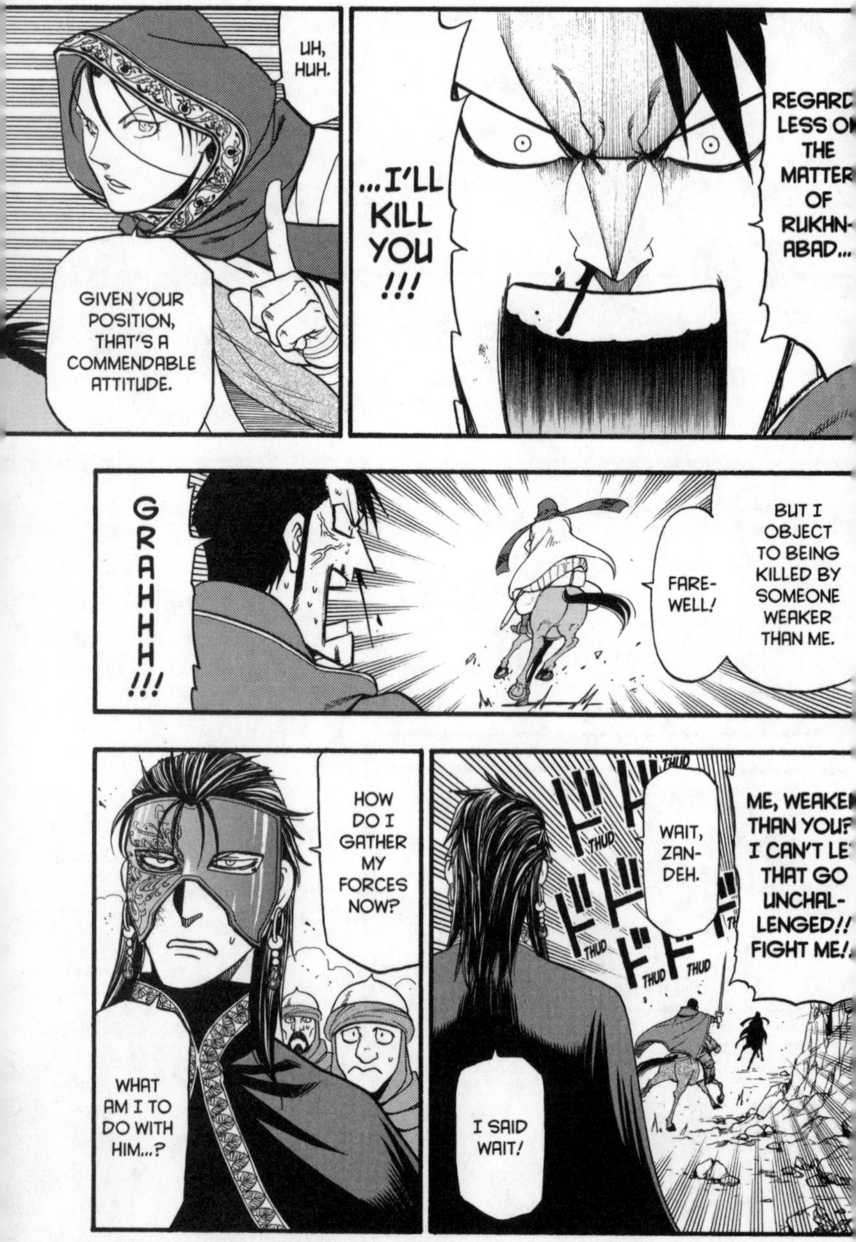

REGARDLESS OF THE MATTER OF RUKHN-ABAD...
...I'LL KILL YOU!!!
UH, HUH.
GIVEN YOUR POSITION, THAT'S A COMMENDABLE ATTITUDE.
BUT I OBJECT TO BEING KILLED BY SOMEONE WEAKER THAN ME.
FARE-WELL!
GRAHHHH!!!
ME, WEAKER THAN YOU? I CAN'T LET THAT GO UNCHAL-LENGED!! FIGHT ME!.
THUD
WAIT, ZAN-DEH.
THUD THUD THUD THUD
I SAID WAIT!
HOW DO I GATHER MY FORCES NOW?
WHAT AM I TO DO WITH HIM...?

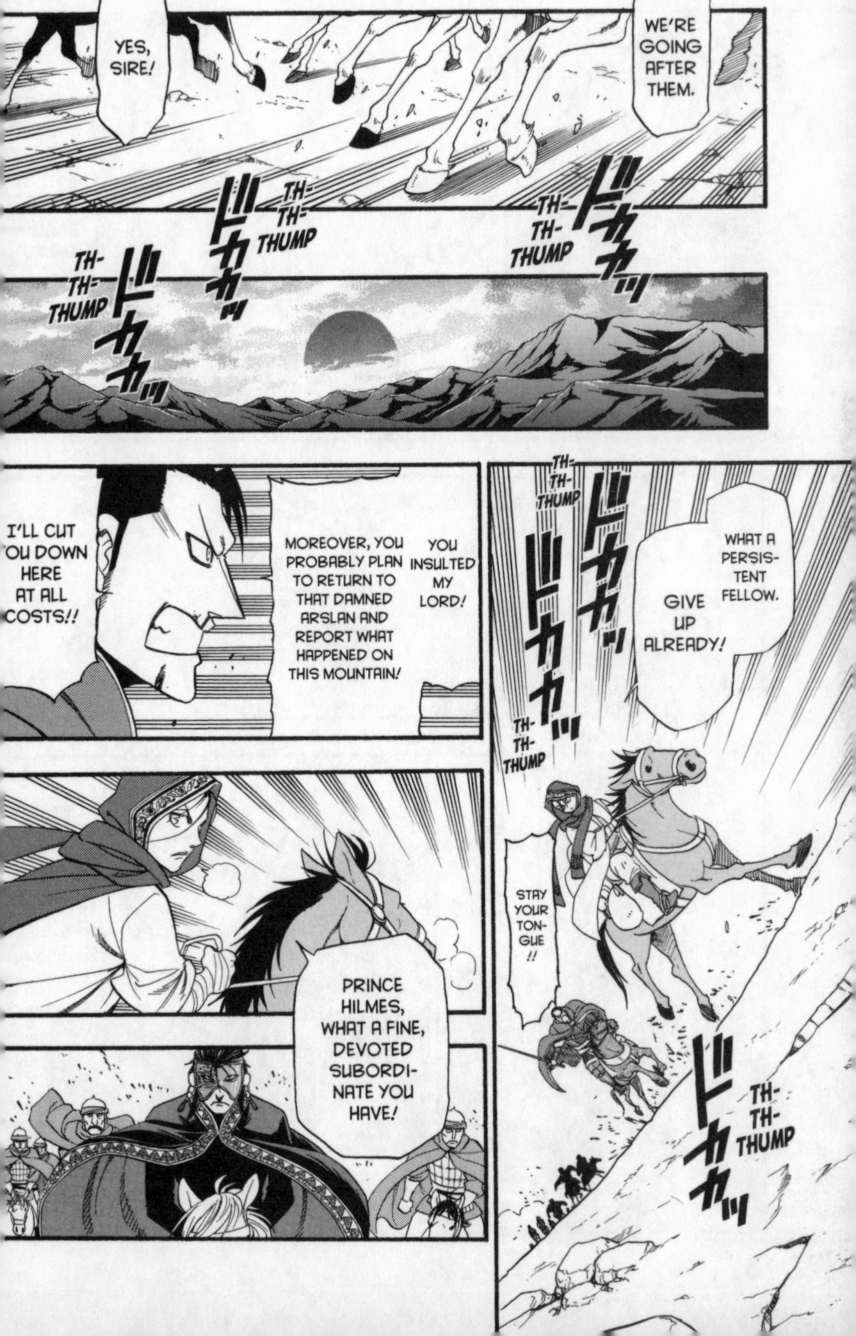
WE'RE GOING AFTER THEM.
YES, SIRE!
TH-TH-THUMP
ドカカッ
TH-TH-THUMP
ドカカッ
TH-TH-THUMP
ドカカッ
TH-TH-THUMP
ドカカッ
WHAT A PERSISTENT FELLOW.
GIVE UP ALREADY!
TH-TH-THUMP
ドカカッ
STAY YOUR TONGUE!!
TH-TH-THUMP
ドカカッ
YOU INSULTED MY LORD!
MOREOVER, YOU PROBABLY PLAN TO RETURN TO THAT DAMNED ARSLAN AND REPORT WHAT HAPPENED ON THIS MOUNTAIN!
I'LL CUT YOU DOWN HERE AT ALL COSTS!!
PRINCE HILMES, WHAT A FINE, DEVOTED SUBORDINATE YOU HAVE!

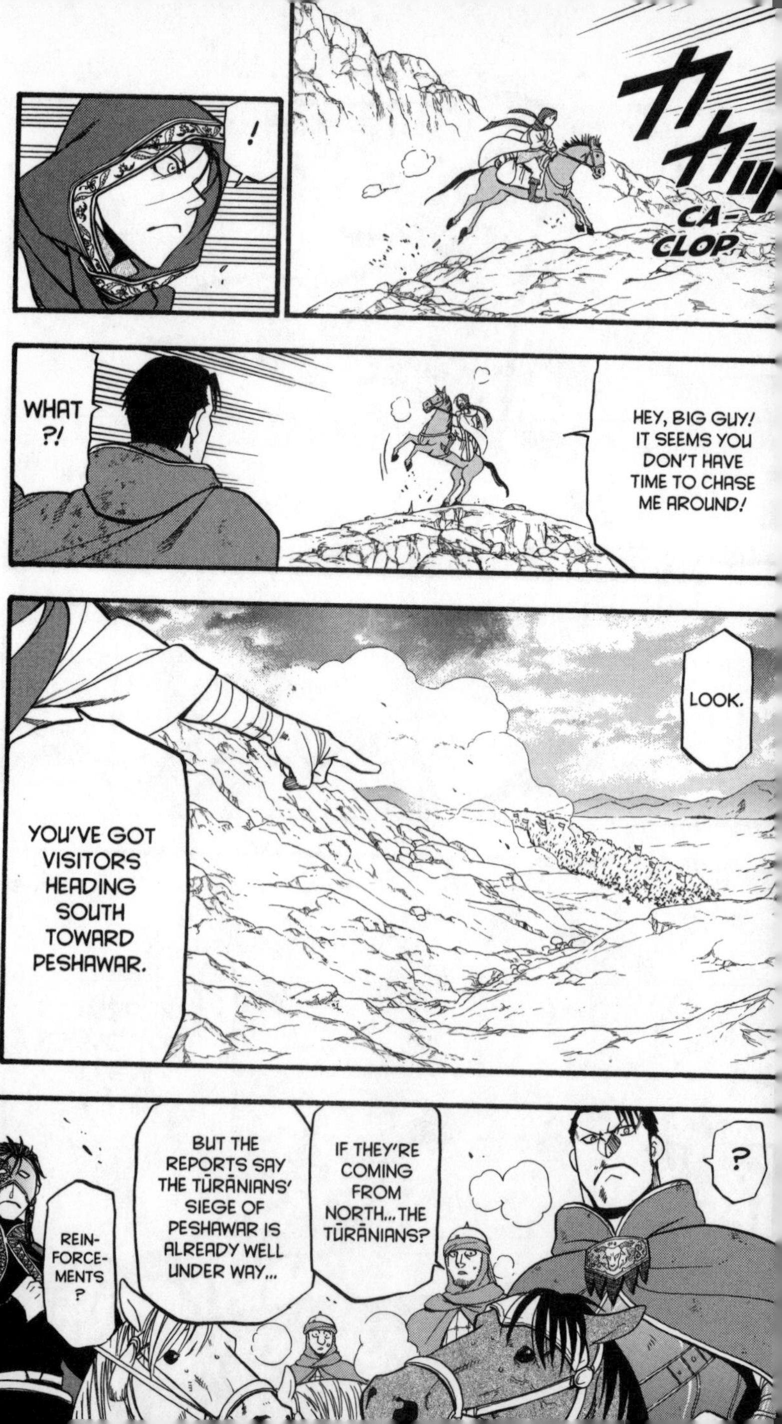
CA-CLOP
!
HEY, BIG GUY! IT SEEMS YOU DON'T HAVE TIME TO CHASE ME AROUND!
WHAT ?!
LOOK.
YOU'VE GOT VISITORS HEADING SOUTH TOWARD PESHAWAR.
?
IF THEY'RE COMING FROM NORTH... THE TŪRĀNIANS?
BUT THE REPORTS SAY THE TŪRĀNIANS' SIEGE OF PESHAWAR IS ALREADY WELL UNDER WAY...
REIN-FORCE-MENTS ?

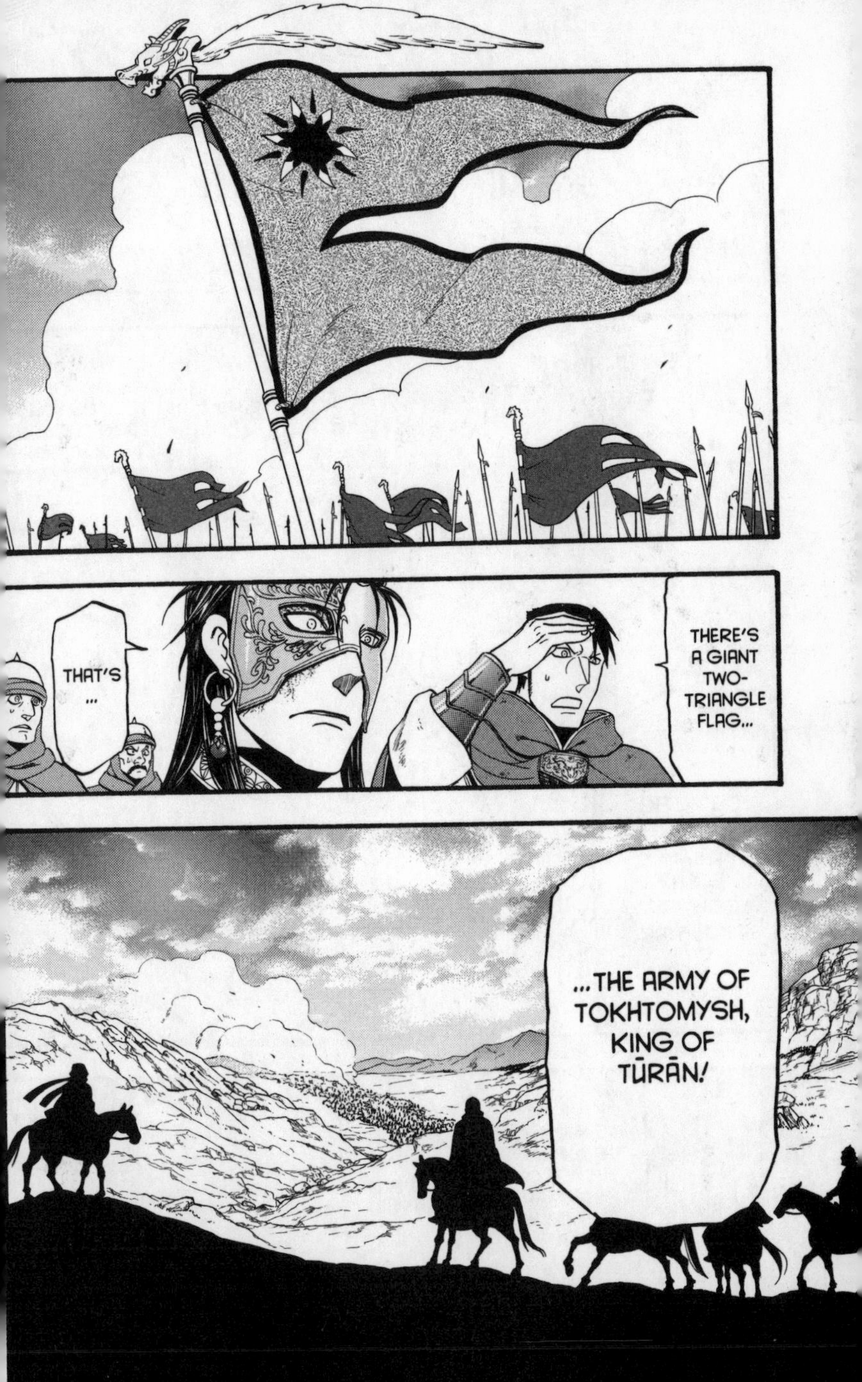
THERE'S A GIANT TWO-TRIANGLE FLAG...
THAT'S ...
...THE ARMY OF TOKHTOMYSH, KING OF TŪRĀN!

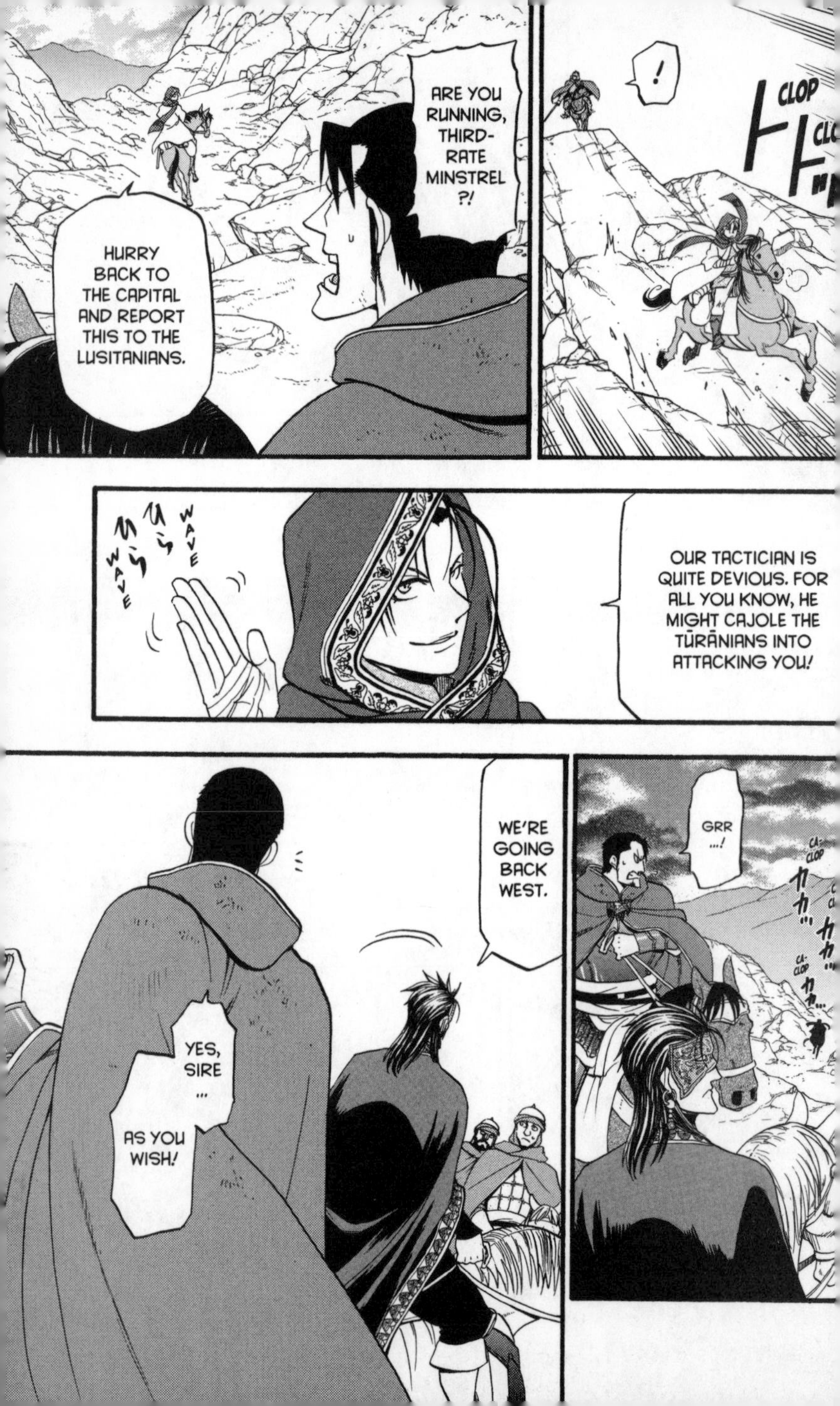
!
CLOP
ARE YOU RUNNING, THIRD-RATE MINSTREL?!
HURRY BACK TO THE CAPITAL AND REPORT THIS TO THE LUSITANIANS.
OUR TACTICIAN IS QUITE DEVIOUS. FOR ALL YOU KNOW, HE MIGHT CAJOLE THE TŪRĀNIANS INTO ATTACKING YOU!
WAVE
WAVE
GRR...!
CA-CLOP
CA-CLOP
WE'RE GOING BACK WEST.
YES, SIRE...
AS YOU WISH!

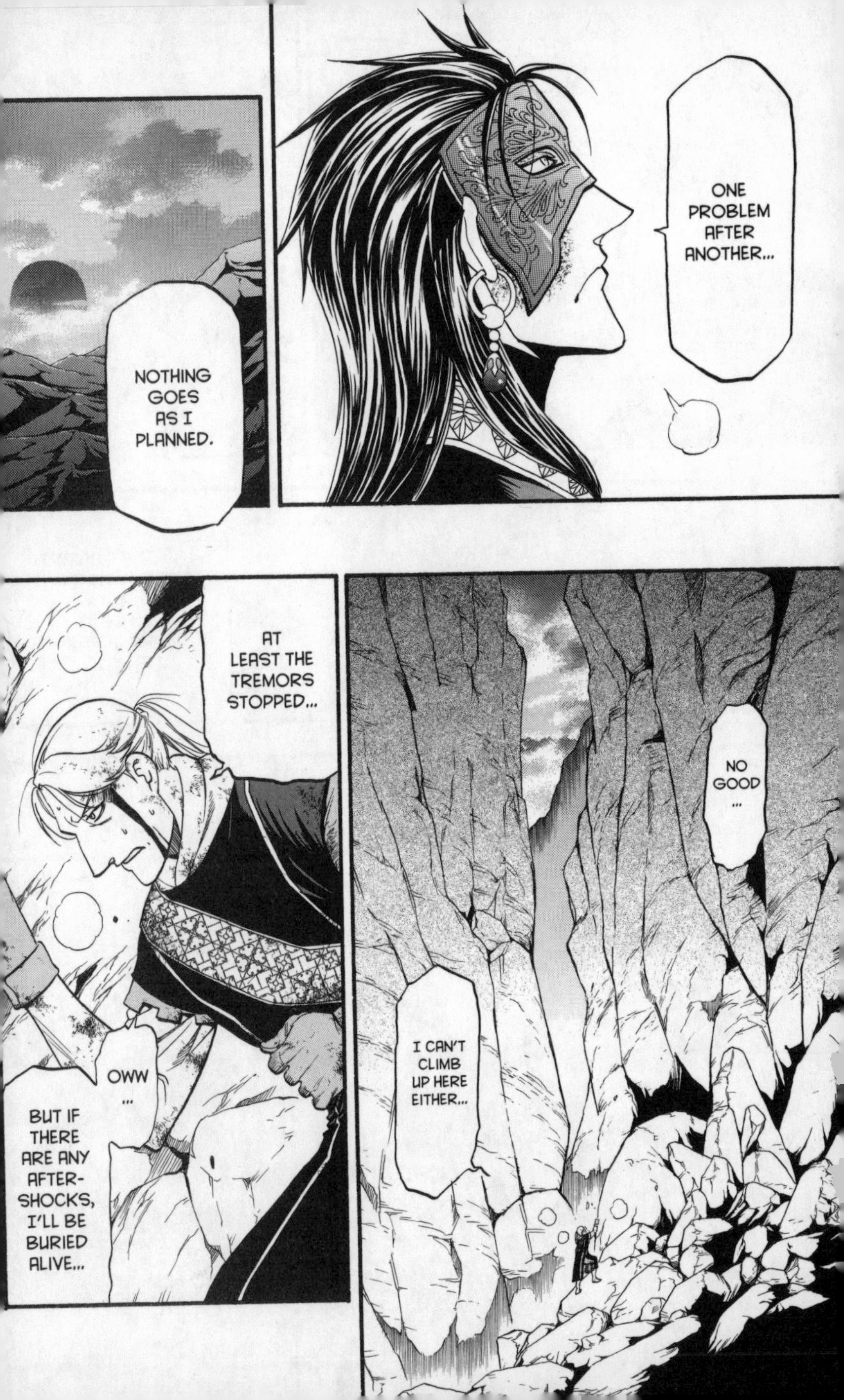
ONE PROBLEM AFTER ANOTHER...
NOTHING GOES AS I PLANNED.
NO GOOD...
I CAN'T CLIMB UP HERE EITHER...
AT LEAST THE TREMORS STOPPED...
OWW...
BUT IF THERE ARE ANY AFTER-SHOCKS, I'LL BE BURIED ALIVE...

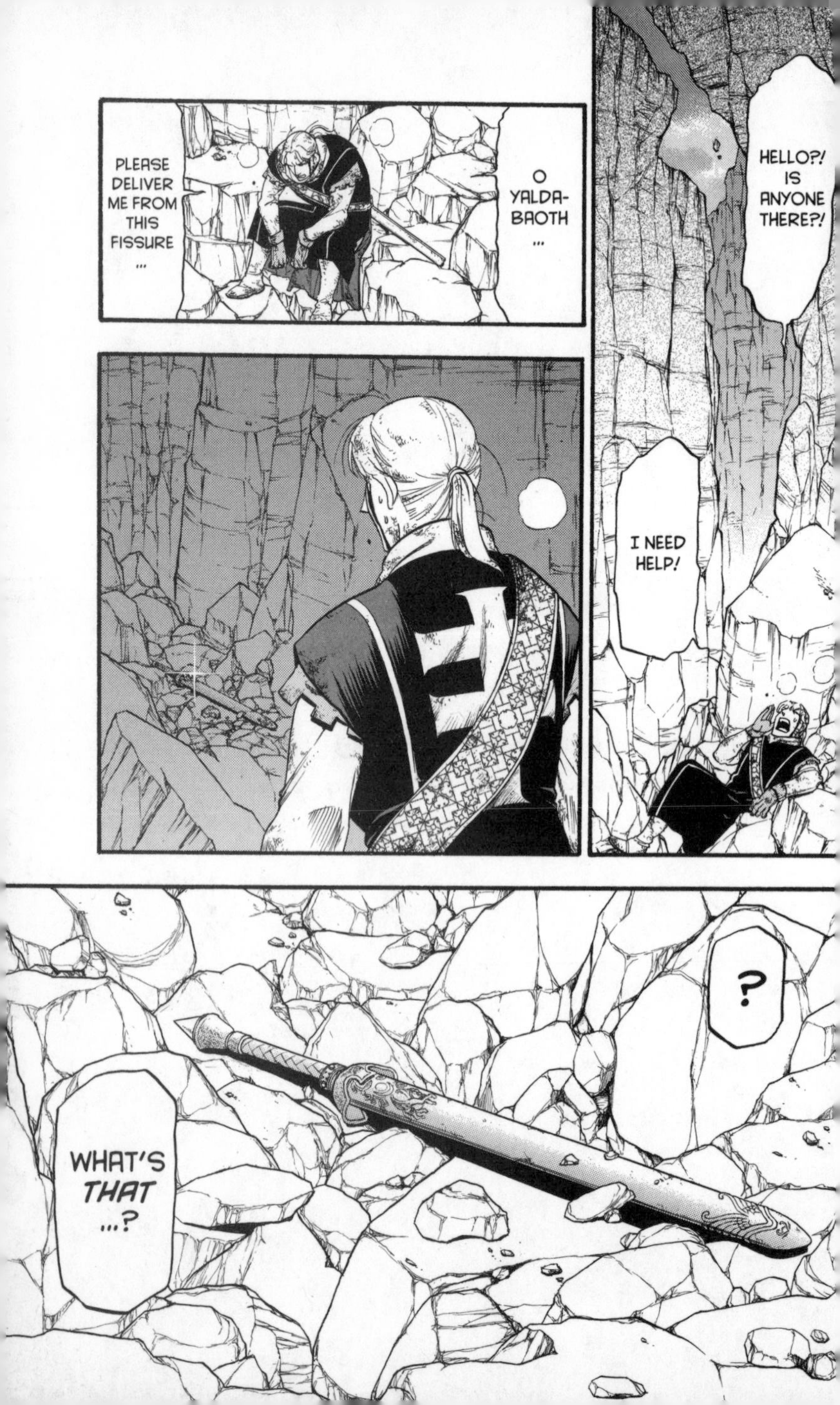
HELLO?! IS ANYONE THERE?!
I NEED HELP!
O YALDA-BAOTH ...
PLEASE DELIVER ME FROM THIS FISSURE ...
?
WHAT'S *THAT* ...?

THE HEROIC LEGEND OF
ARSLAN

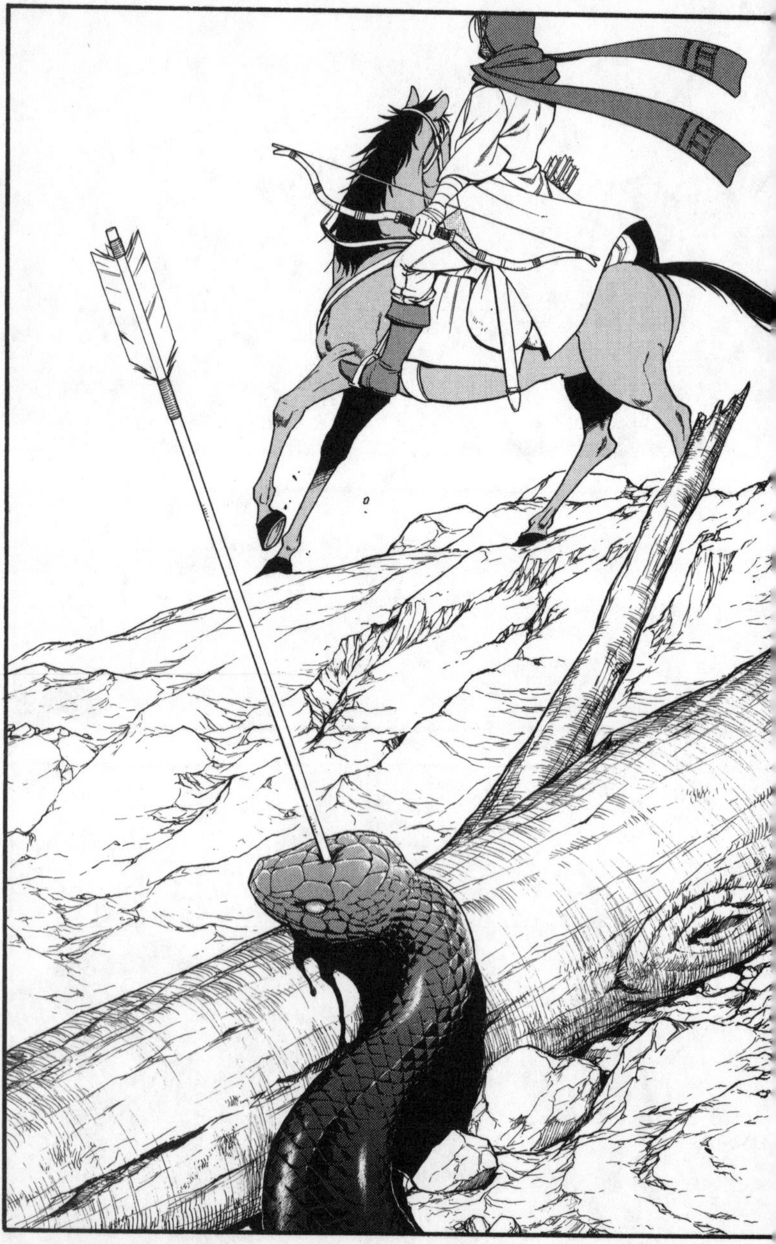

Chapter 80: The Snake King Stirs

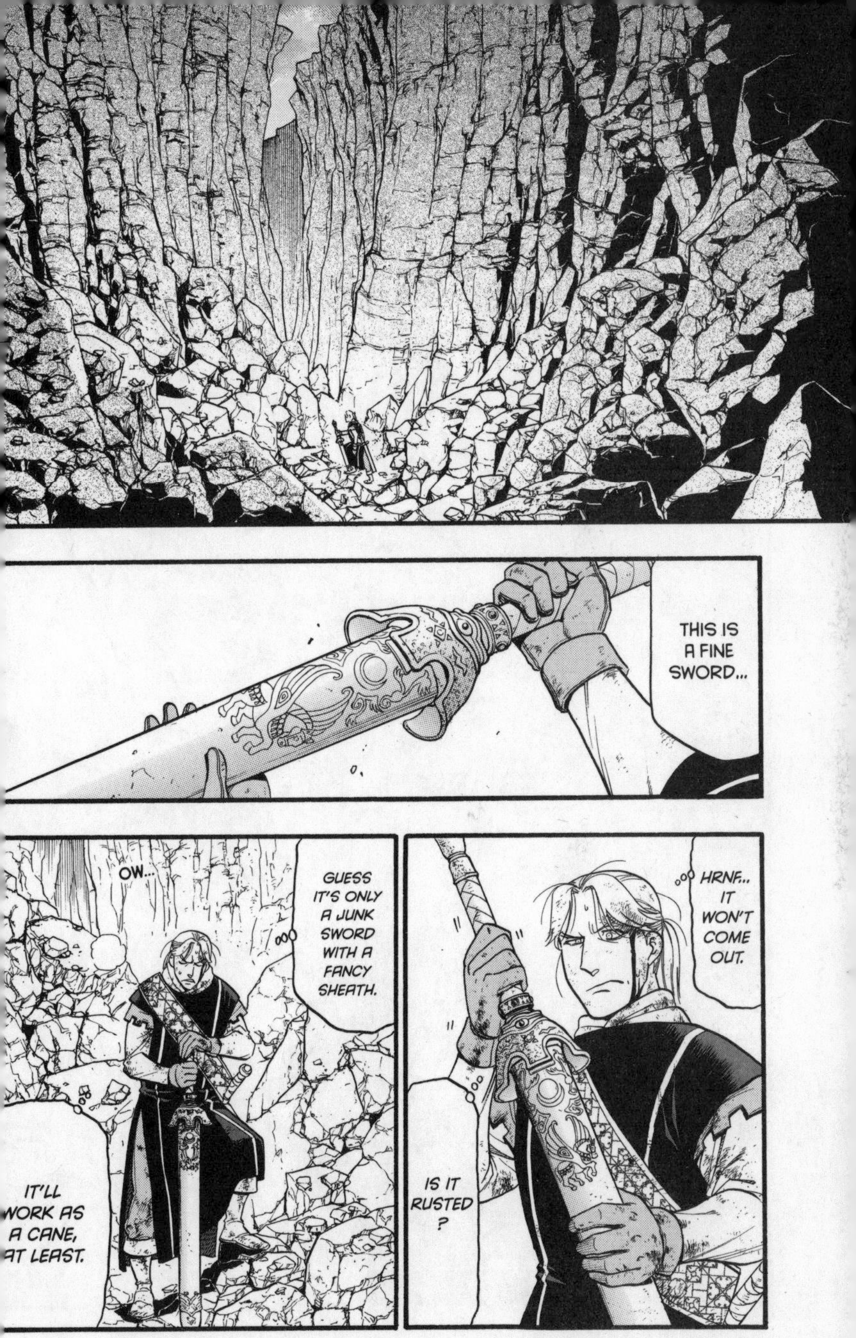
THIS IS A FINE SWORD...
HRNF... IT WON'T COME OUT.
IS IT RUSTED?
GUESS IT'S ONLY A JUNK SWORD WITH A FANCY SHEATH.
OW...
IT'LL WORK AS A CANE, AT LEAST.

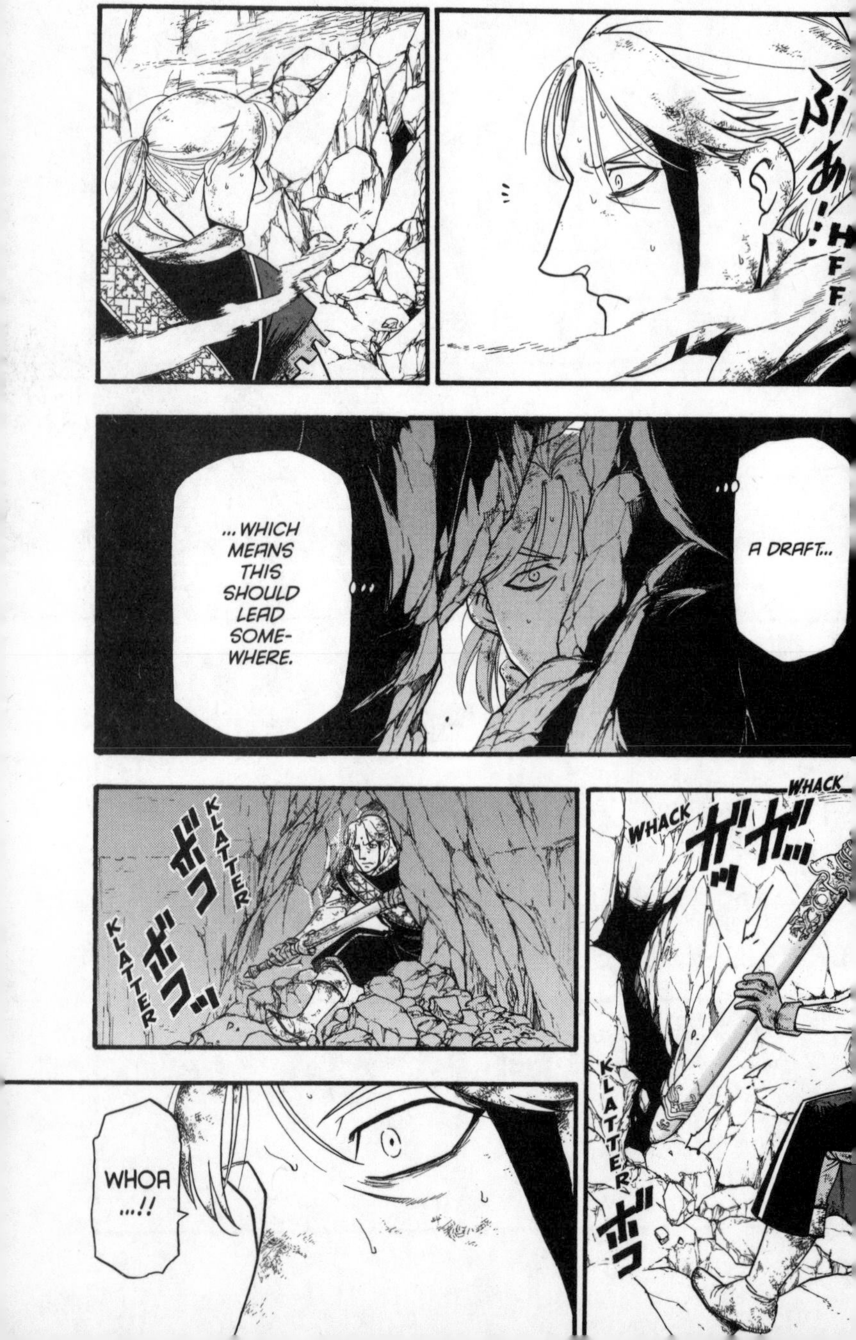

ふあ!!
HFF
...
A DRAFT...
...WHICH MEANS THIS SHOULD LEAD SOME-WHERE.
WHACK
ガッ
ガッ
WHACK
KLATTER
ボフ
KLATTER
ボフ
KLATTER
ボフッ
WHOA ...!!

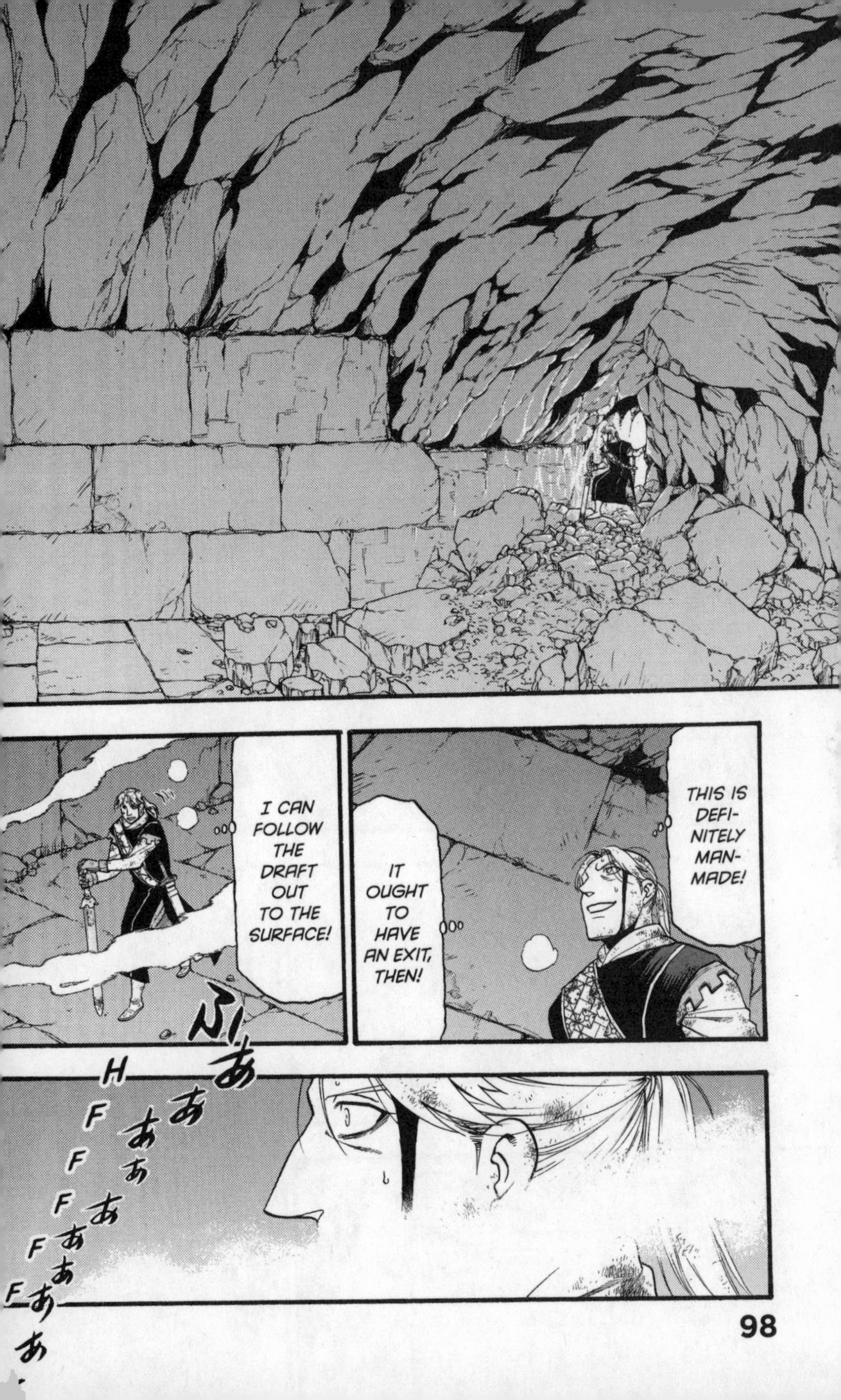
THIS IS DEFINITELY MAN-MADE!
IT OUGHT TO HAVE AN EXIT, THEN!
I CAN FOLLOW THE DRAFT OUT TO THE SURFACE!
HFFFFF

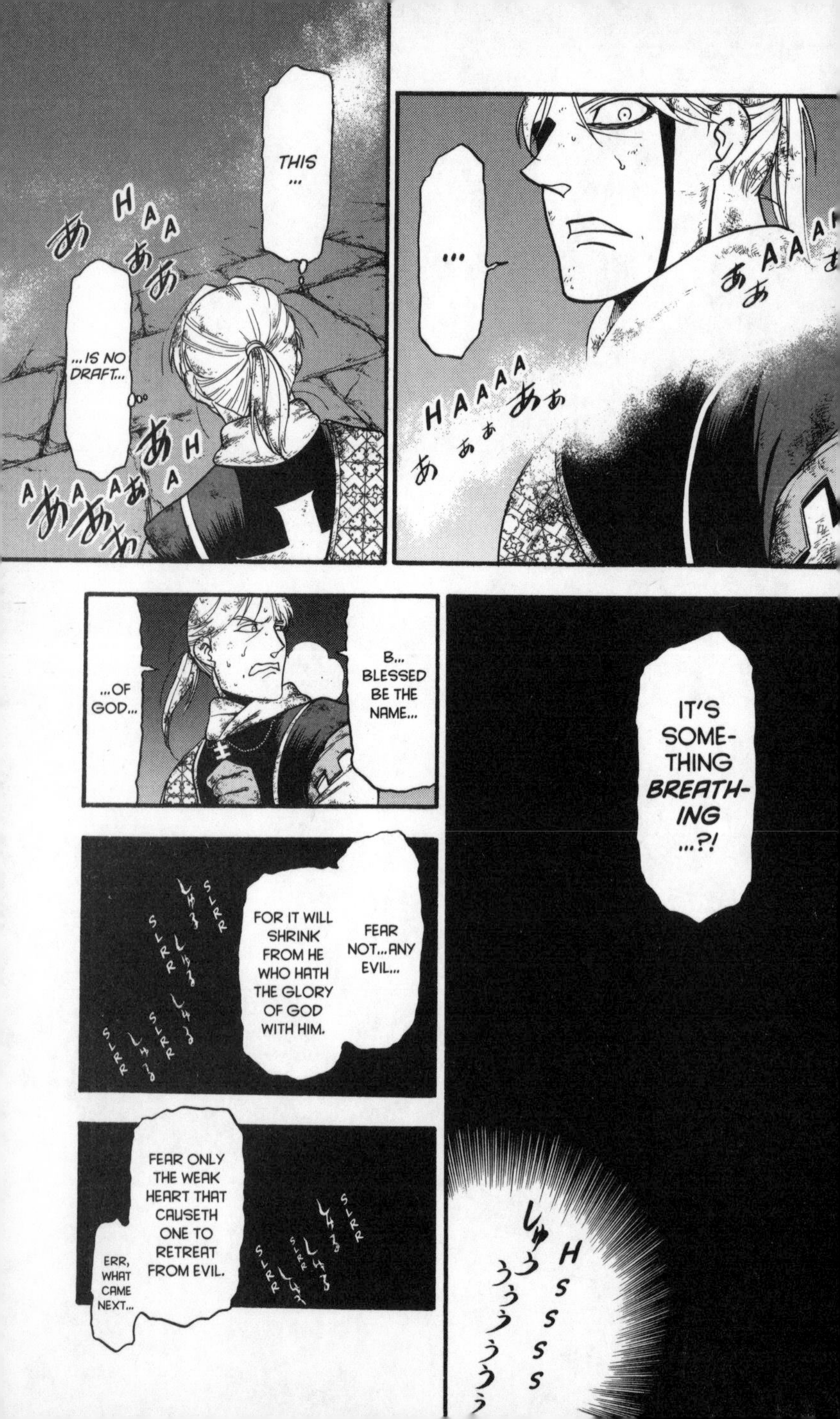
...
HAAAA
HAAAAA
THIS ...
...IS NO DRAFT...
HAAAAAH
IT'S SOMETHING *BREATHING* ...?!
HSSSSS
B... BLESSED BE THE NAME...
...OF GOD...
FEAR NOT...ANY EVIL...
FOR IT WILL SHRINK FROM HE WHO HATH THE GLORY OF GOD WITH HIM.
SLRR SLRR SLRR SLRR
FEAR ONLY THE WEAK HEART THAT CAUSETH ONE TO RETREAT FROM EVIL.
ERR, WHAT CAME NEXT...
SLRR SLRR SLRR

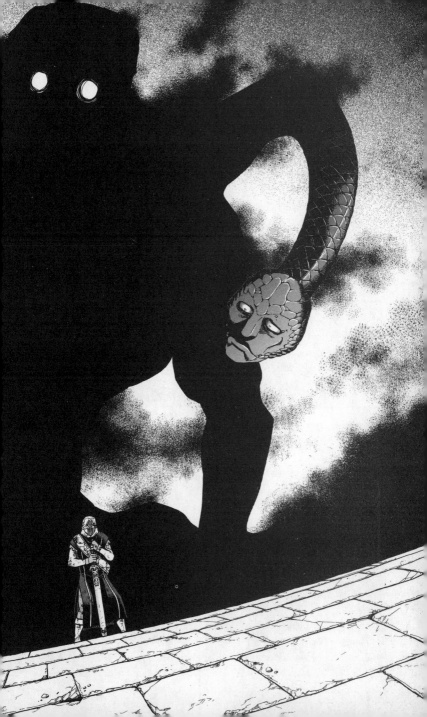

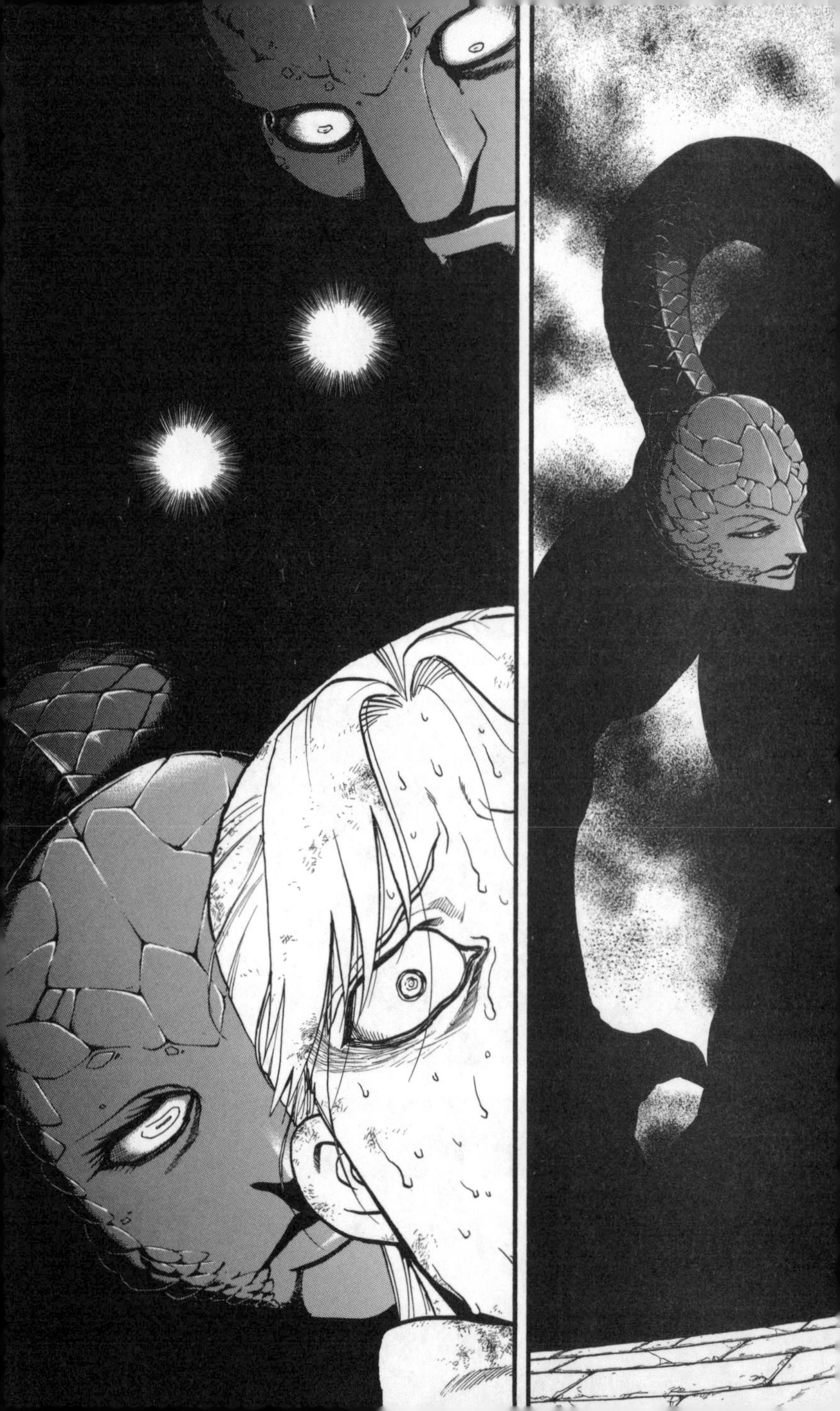

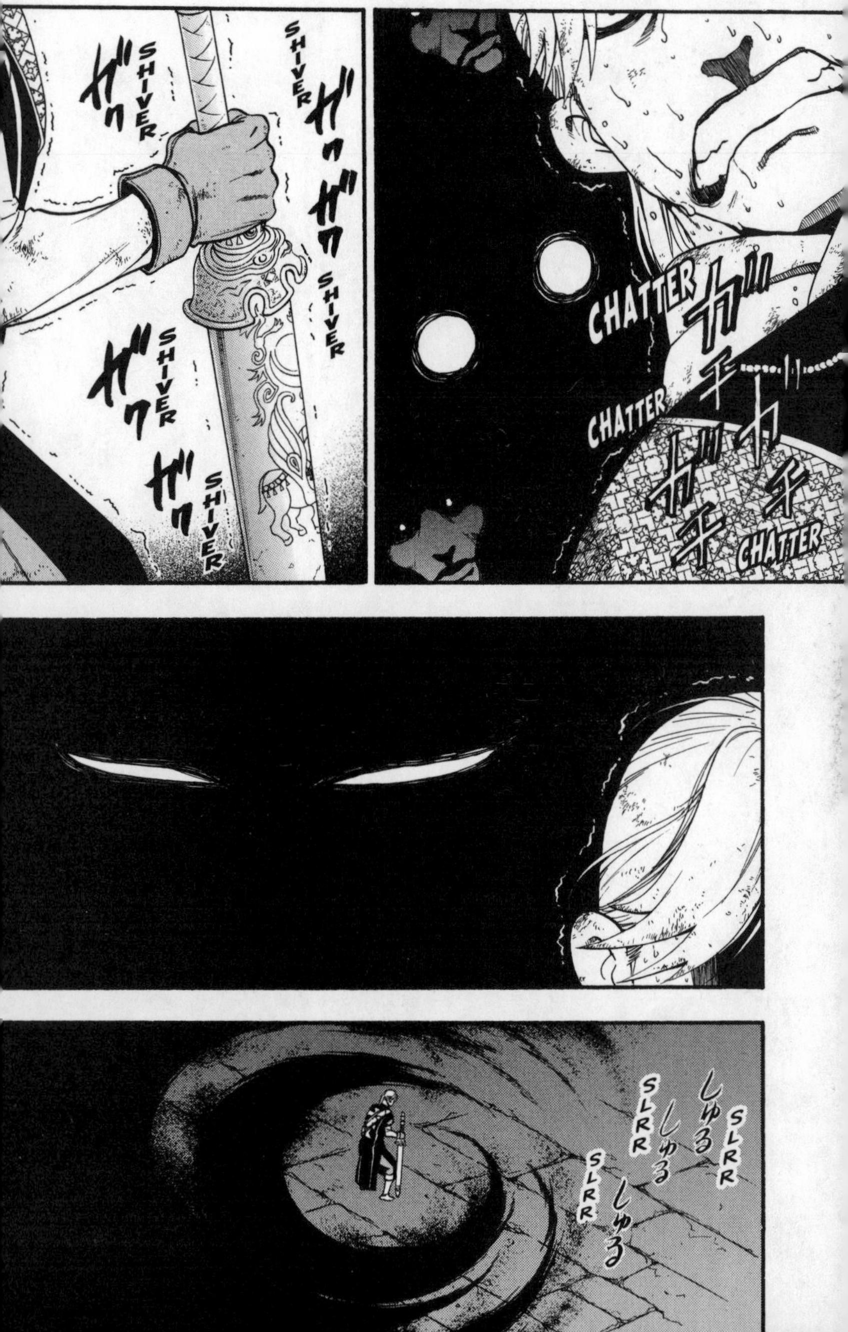
CHATTER
CHATTER
CHATTER
SHIVER
SHIVER
SHIVER
SHIVER
SHIVER
しゅる SLRR
しゅる SLRR
しゅる SLRR

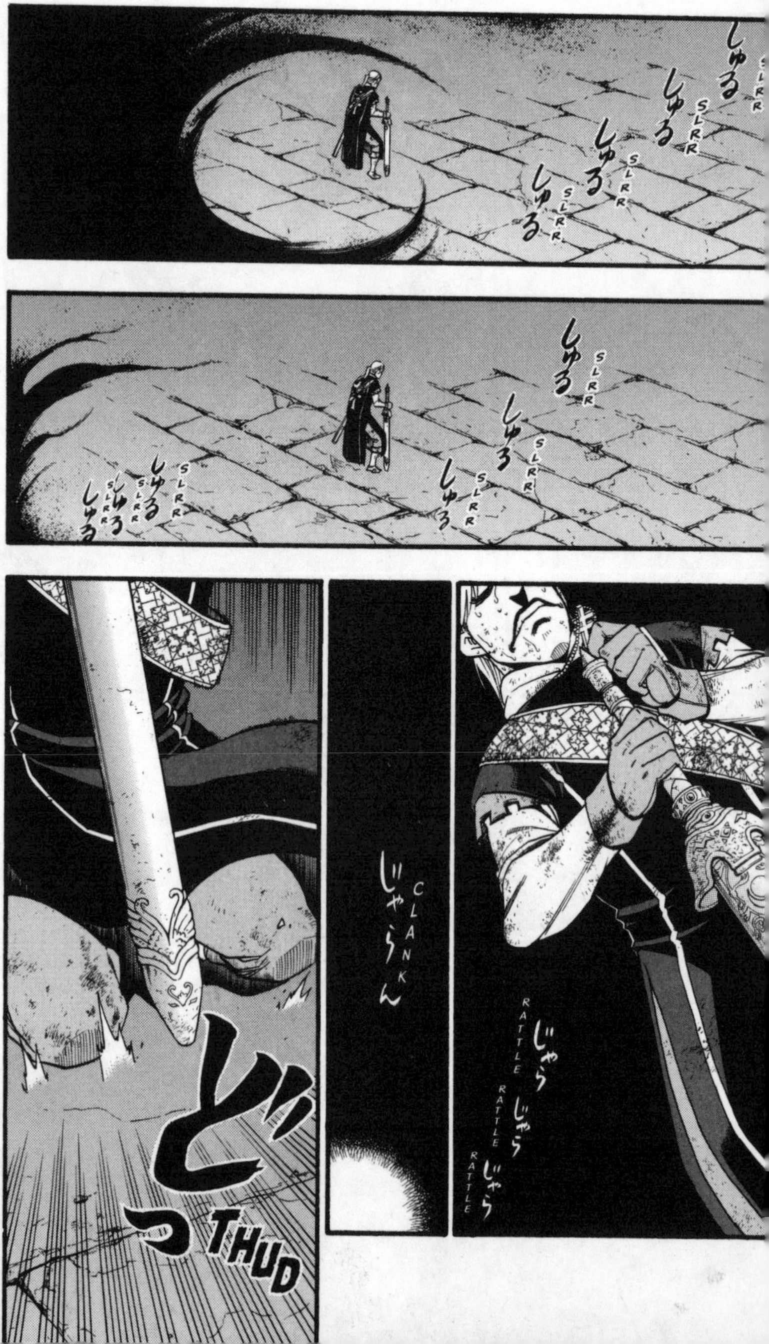

しゅる
SLRR
しゅる
SLRR
しゅる
SLRR
しゅる
SLRR
しゅる
SLRR
しゅる
SLRR
しゅる
SLRR
しゅる
SLRR
しゅる
SLRR
しゅる
じゃら
RATTLE
じゃら
RATTLE
じゃら
RATTLE
じゃらん
CLANK
どっ
THUD

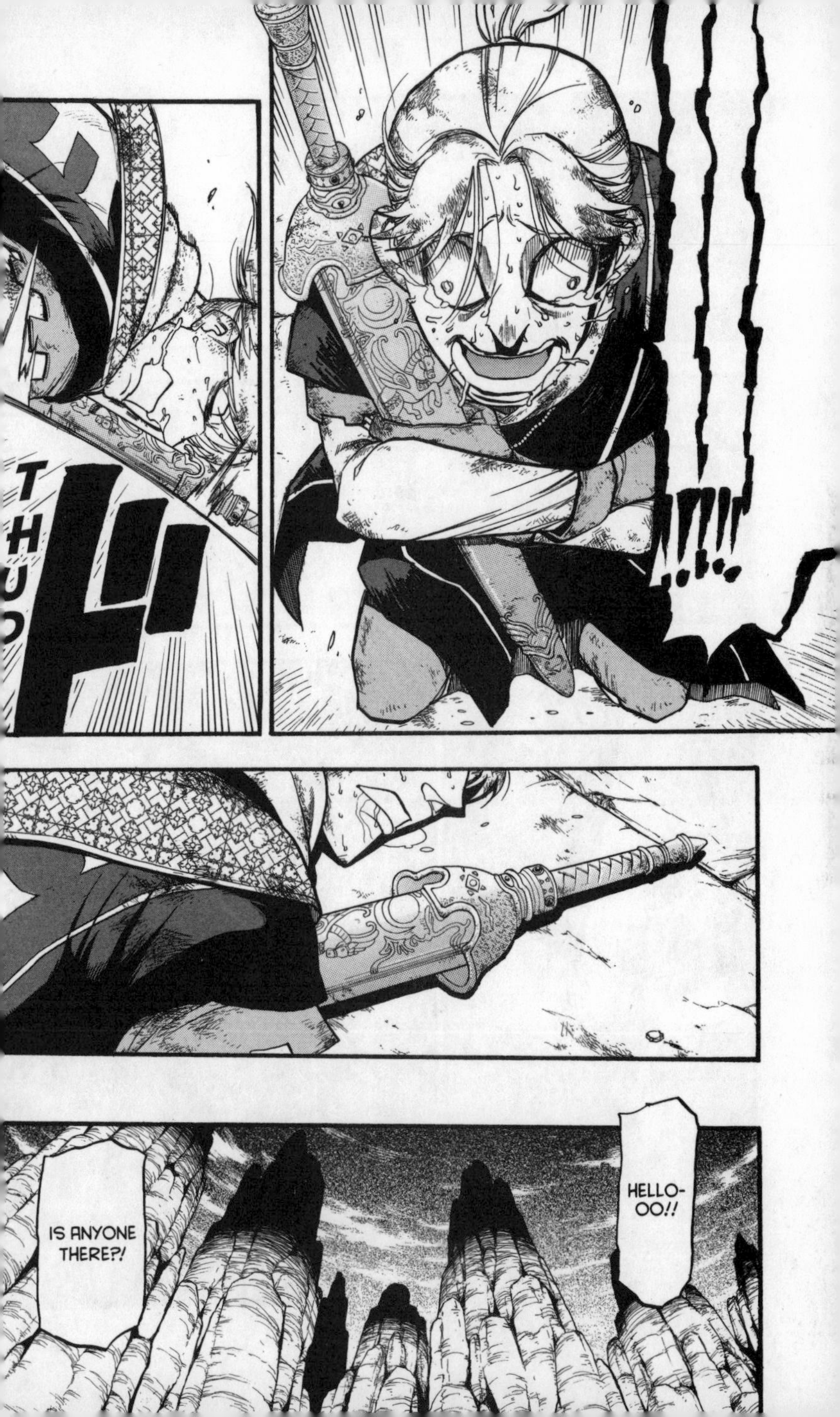
THUD
HELLO-OO!!
IS ANYONE THERE?!

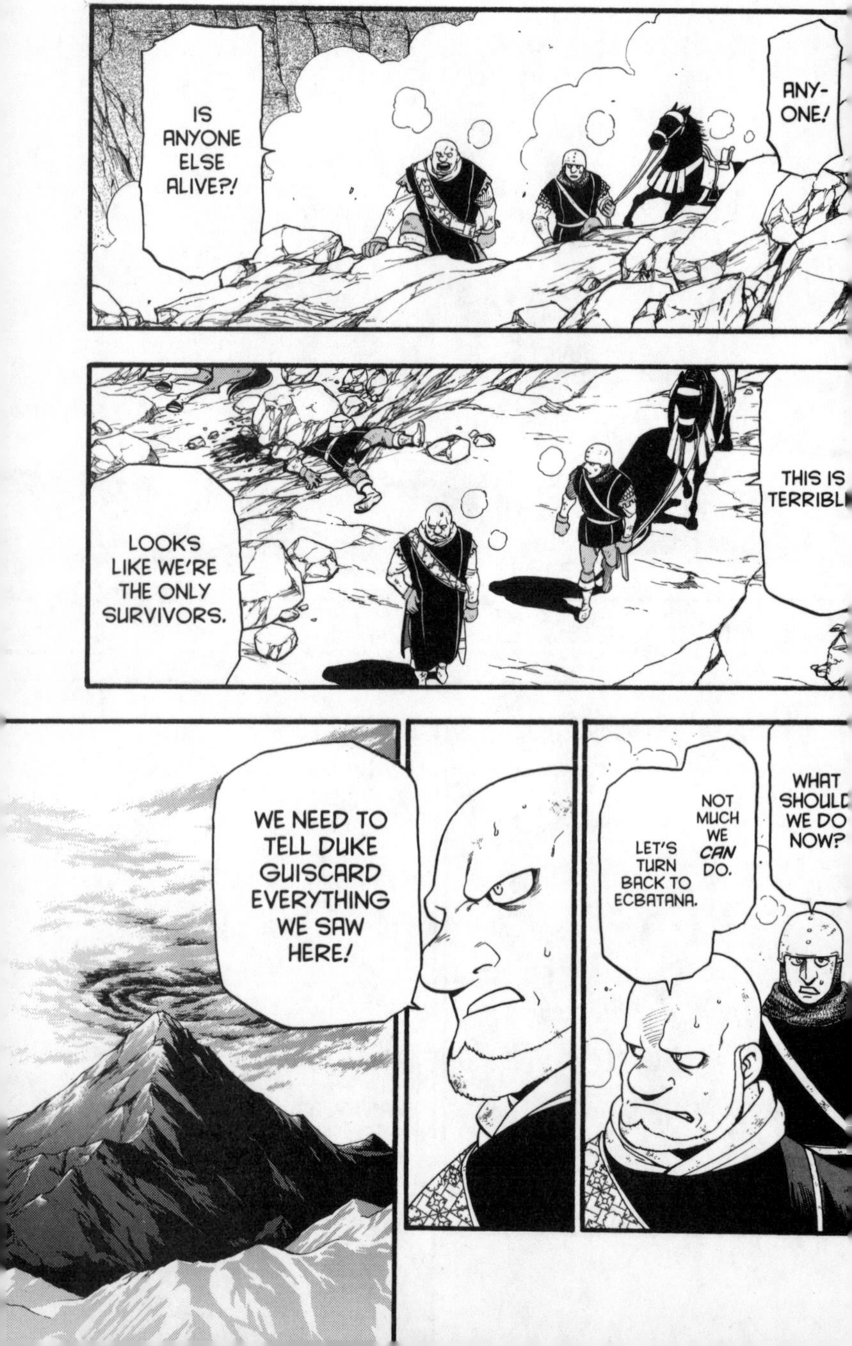
ANY-ONE!
IS ANYONE ELSE ALIVE?!
THIS IS TERRIBL
LOOKS LIKE WE'RE THE ONLY SURVIVORS.
WHAT SHOULD WE DO NOW?
NOT MUCH WE *CAN* DO.
LET'S TURN BACK TO ECBATANA.
WE NEED TO TELL DUKE GUISCARD EVERYTHING WE SAW HERE!

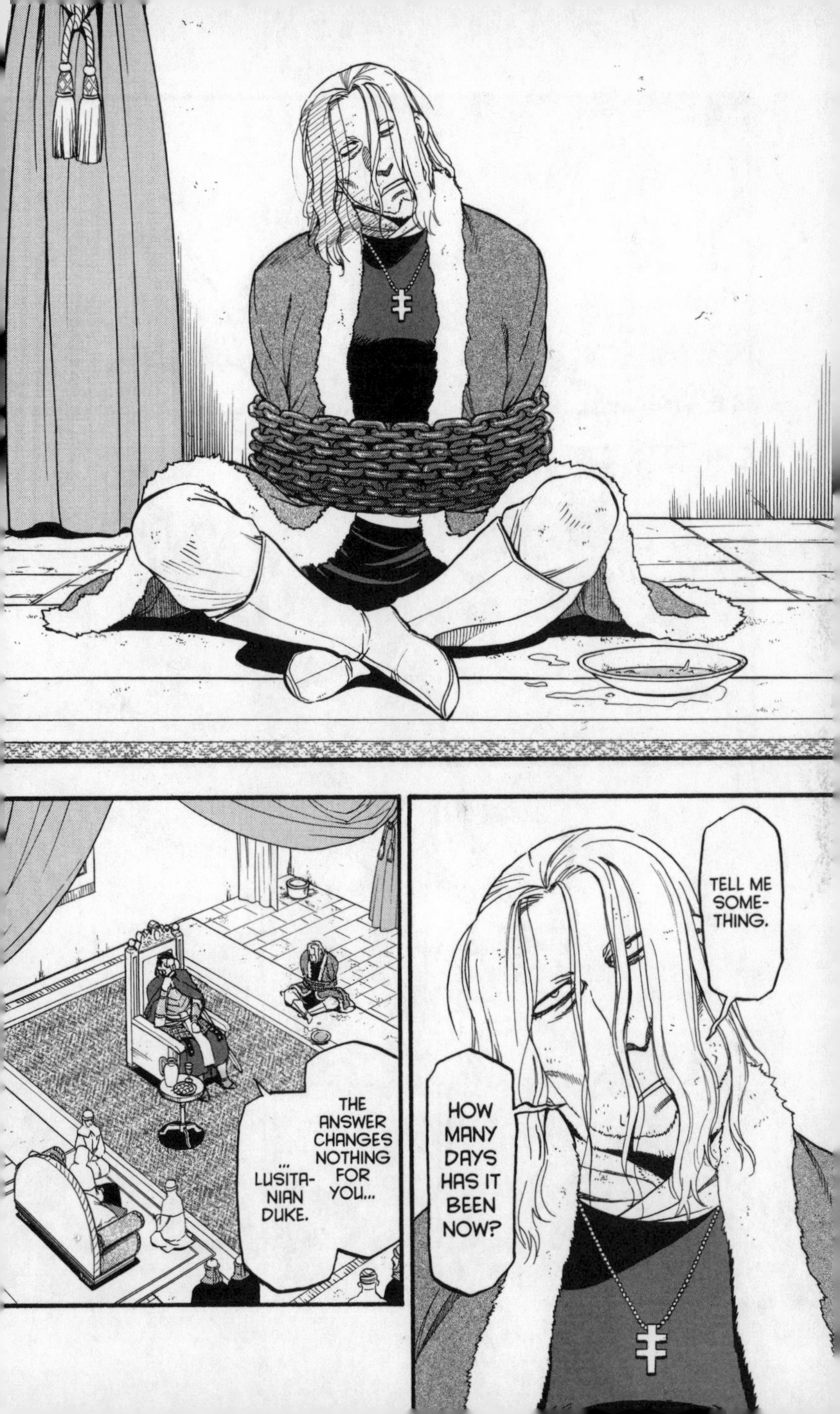
TELL ME SOME-THING.
HOW MANY DAYS HAS IT BEEN NOW?
THE ANSWER CHANGES NOTHING FOR YOU...
... LUSITA-NIAN DUKE.

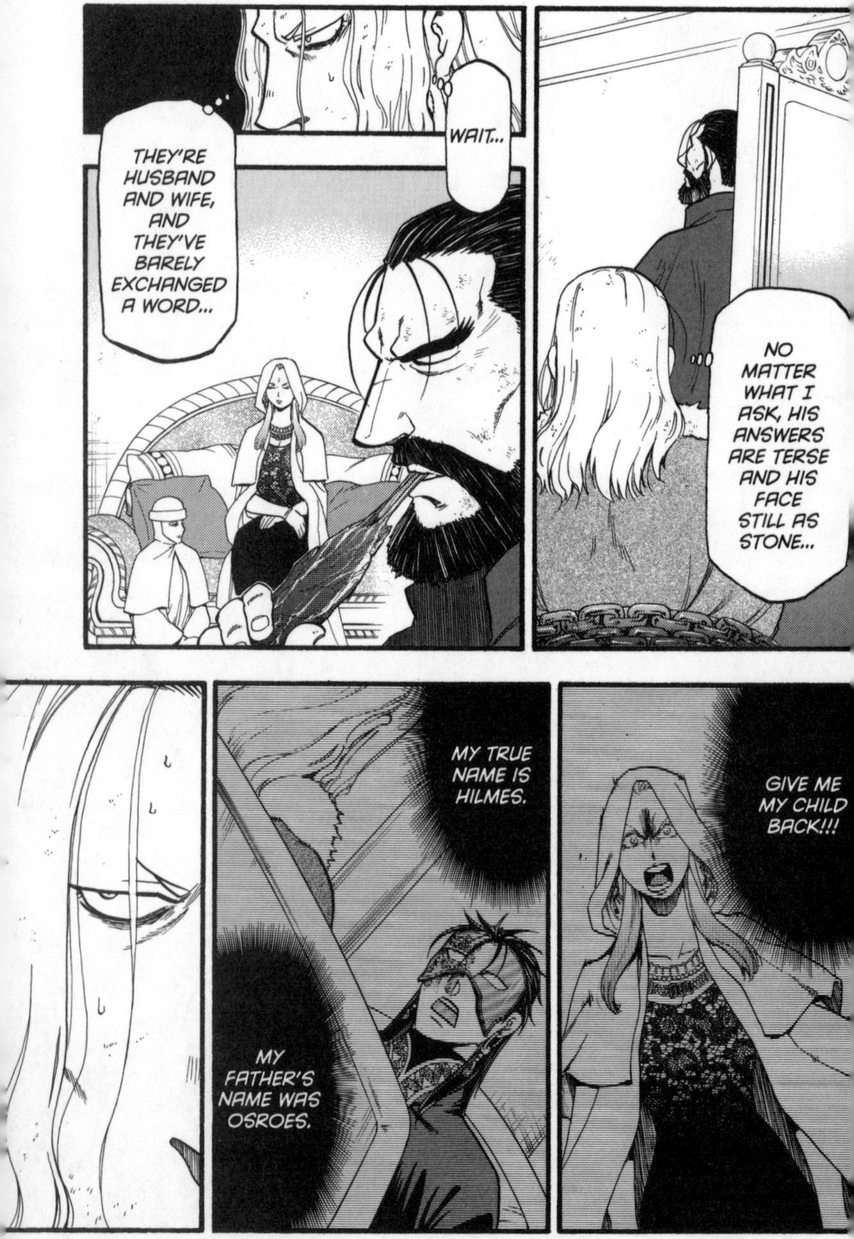
NO MATTER WHAT I ASK, HIS ANSWERS ARE TERSE AND HIS FACE STILL AS STONE...
WAIT...
THEY'RE HUSBAND AND WIFE, AND THEY'VE BARELY EXCHANGED A WORD...
GIVE ME MY CHILD BACK!!!
MY TRUE NAME IS HILMES.
MY FATHER'S NAME WAS OSROES.

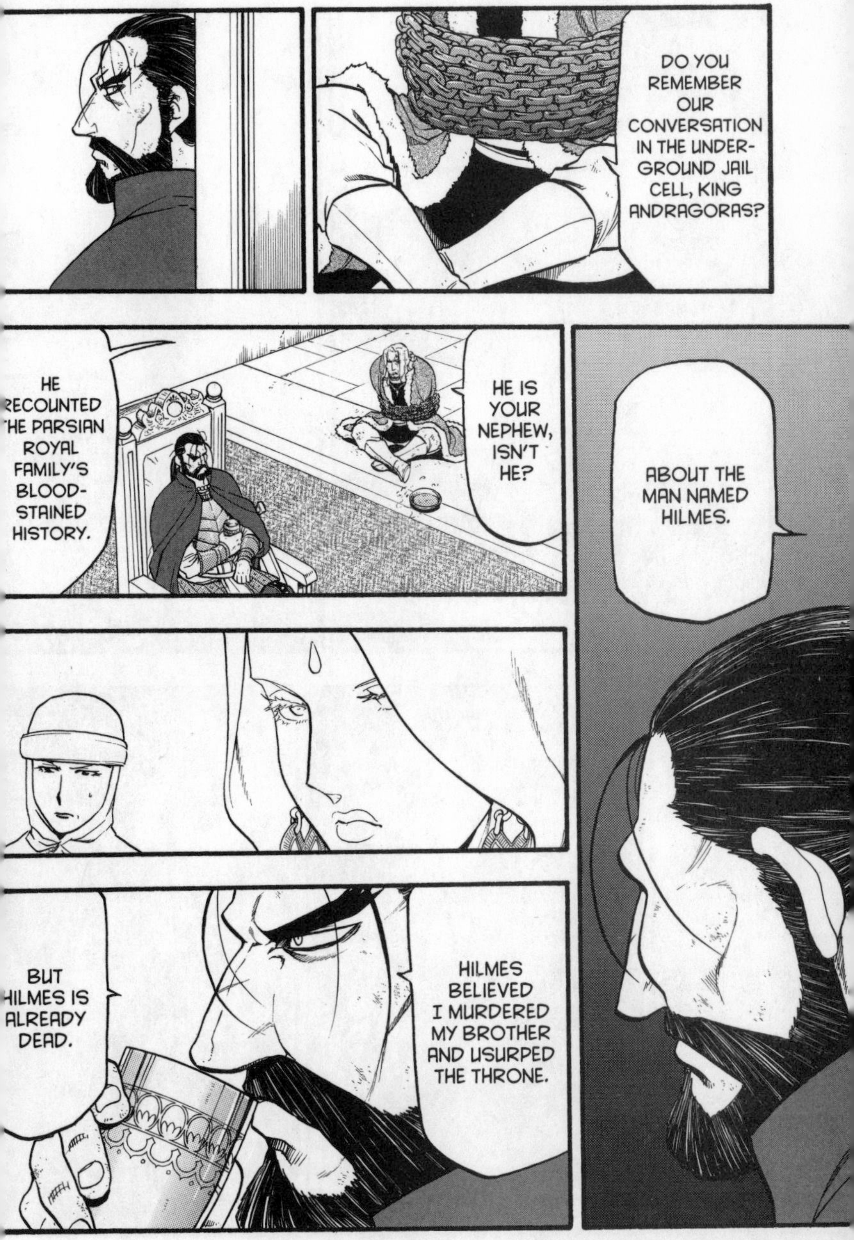
DO YOU REMEMBER OUR CONVERSATION IN THE UNDER-GROUND JAIL CELL, KING ANDRAGORAS?
ABOUT THE MAN NAMED HILMES.
HE IS YOUR NEPHEW, ISN'T HE?
HE RECOUNTED THE PARSIAN ROYAL FAMILY'S BLOOD-STAINED HISTORY.
HILMES BELIEVED I MURDERED MY BROTHER AND USURPED THE THRONE.
BUT HILMES IS ALREADY DEAD.

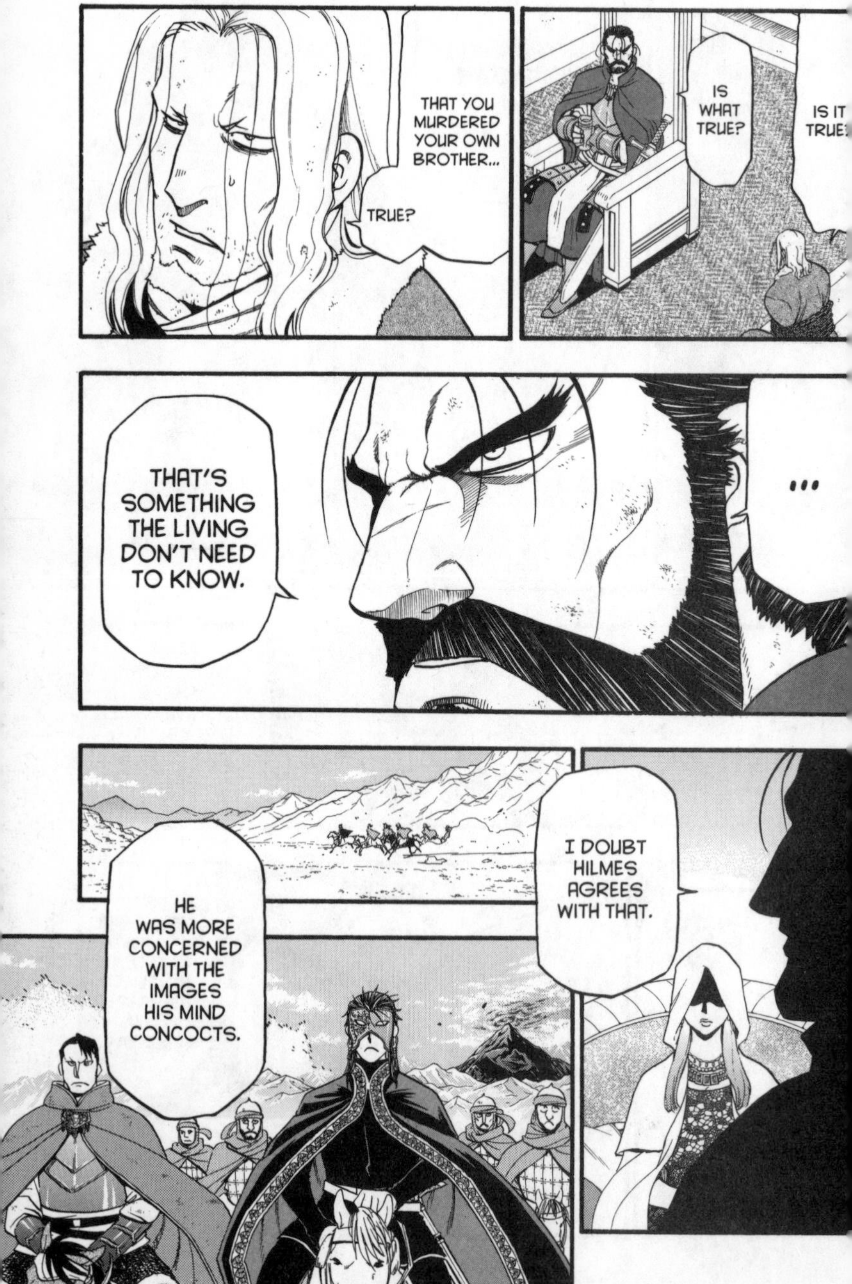
IS IT TRUE
IS WHAT TRUE?
THAT YOU MURDERED YOUR OWN BROTHER...
TRUE?
...
THAT'S SOMETHING THE LIVING DON'T NEED TO KNOW.
I DOUBT HILMES AGREES WITH THAT.
HE WAS MORE CONCERNED WITH THE IMAGES HIS MIND CONCOCTS.

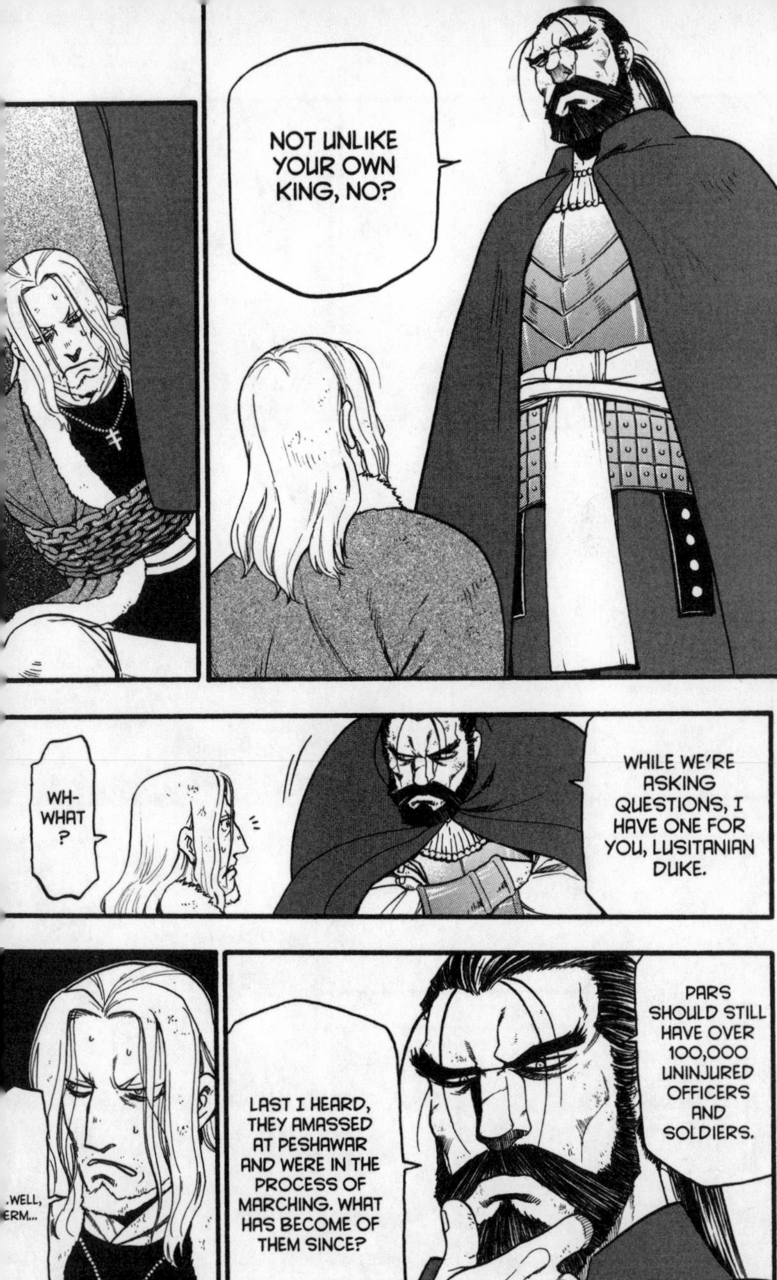
NOT UNLIKE YOUR OWN KING, NO?
WHILE WE'RE ASKING QUESTIONS, I HAVE ONE FOR YOU, LUSITANIAN DUKE.
WH-WHAT?
PARS SHOULD STILL HAVE OVER 100,000 UNINJURED OFFICERS AND SOLDIERS.
LAST I HEARD, THEY AMASSED AT PESHAWAR AND WERE IN THE PROCESS OF MARCHING. WHAT HAS BECOME OF THEM SINCE?
.WELL, ERM...

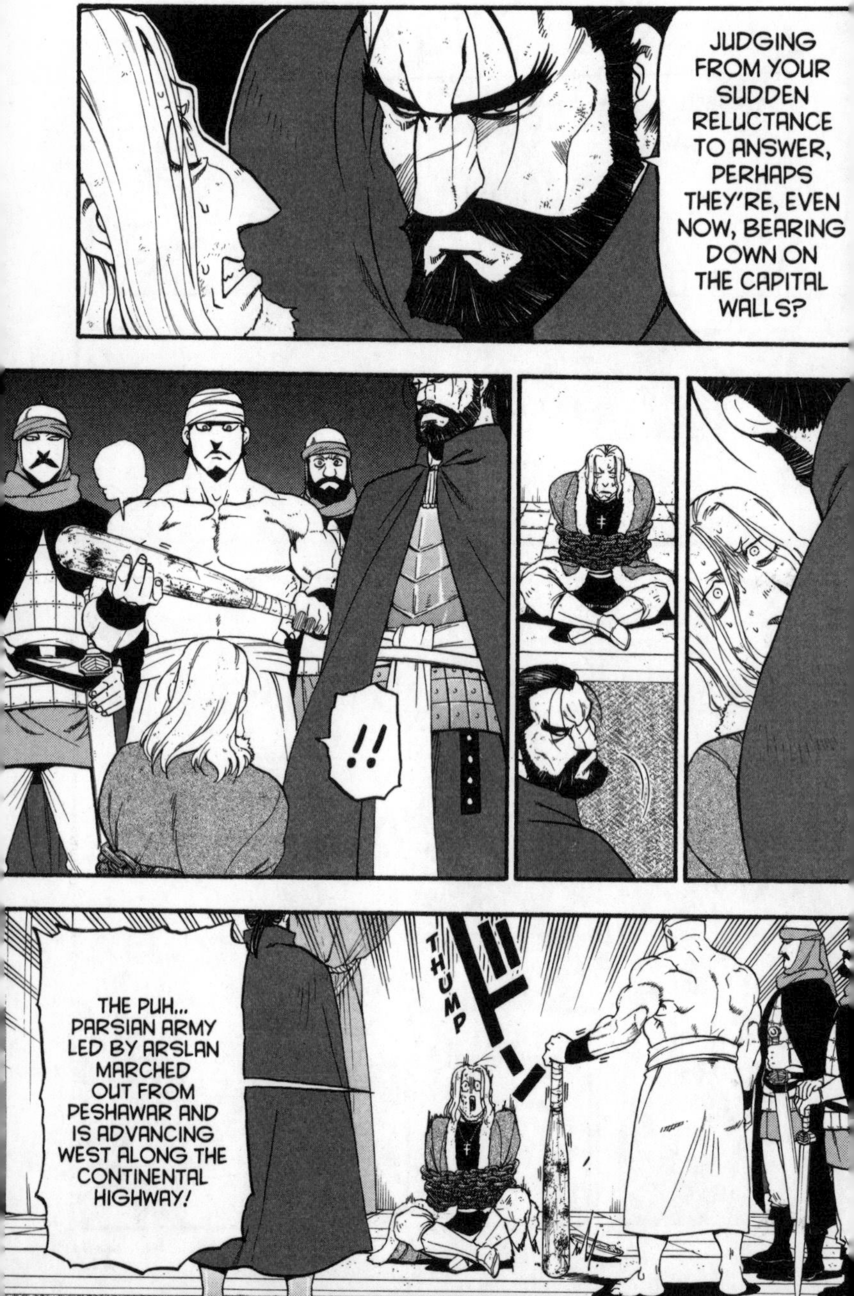
JUDGING FROM YOUR SUDDEN RELUCTANCE TO ANSWER, PERHAPS THEY'RE, EVEN NOW, BEARING DOWN ON THE CAPITAL WALLS?
!!
THUMP
THE PUH... PARSIAN ARMY LED BY ARSLAN MARCHED OUT FROM PESHAWAR AND IS ADVANCING WEST ALONG THE CONTINENTAL HIGHWAY!

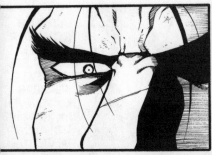

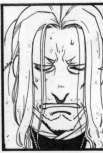

THEY FELLED BOTH CHASOOM FORTRESS AND THE KEEP OF SAINT EMMANUEL ALONG THE WAY.

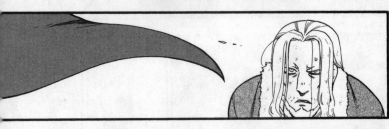

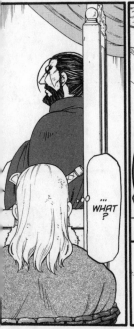

...WHAT?

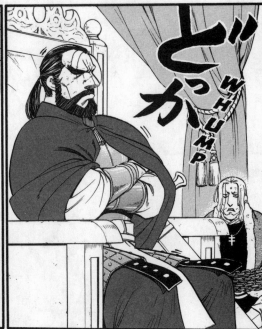

WHUMP

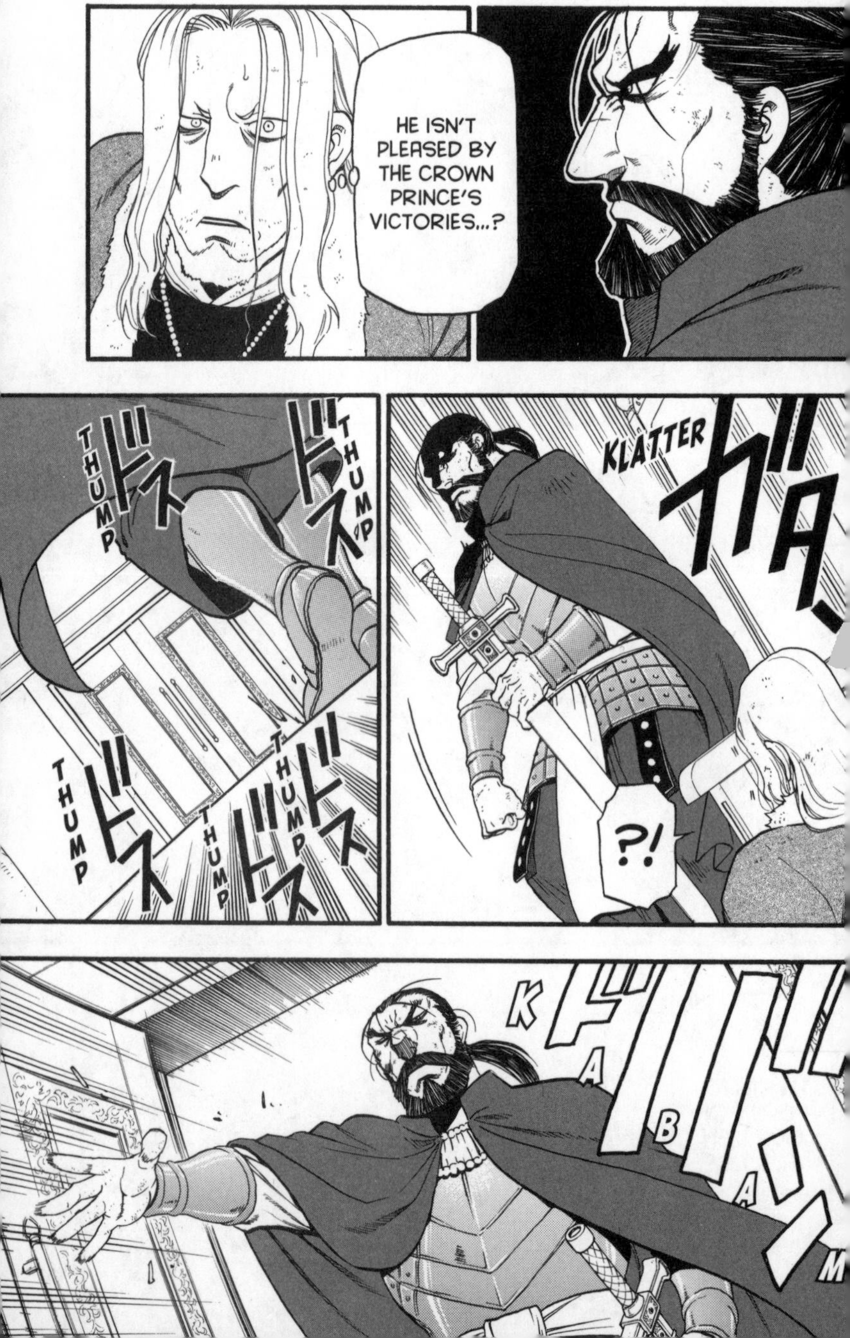
HE ISN'T PLEASED BY THE CROWN PRINCE'S VICTORIES...?
KLATTER
?!
THUMP
THUMP
THUMP
THUMP
KABAM
!...

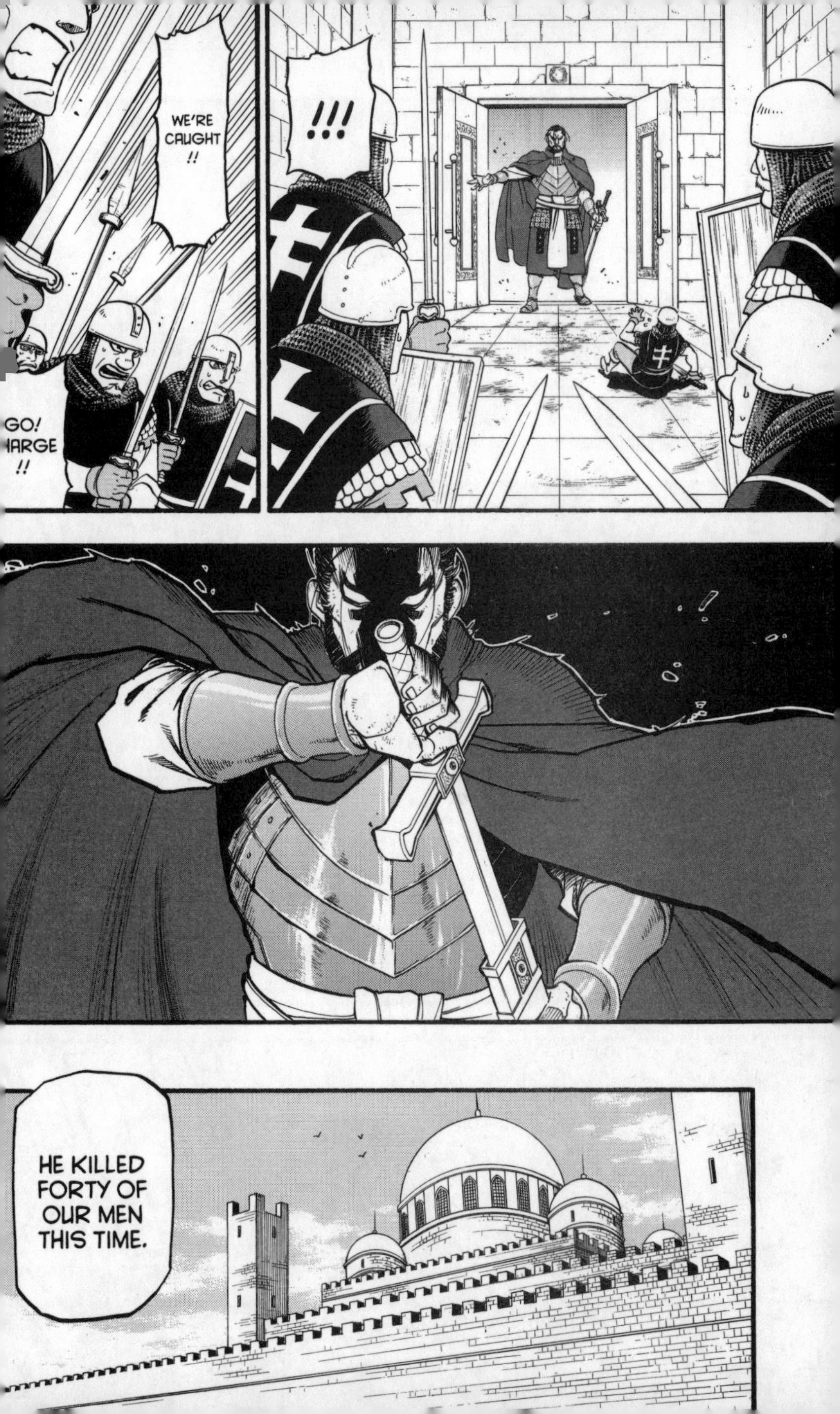
!!!
WE'RE CAUGHT !!
GO!
HARGE !!
HE KILLED FORTY OF OUR MEN THIS TIME.

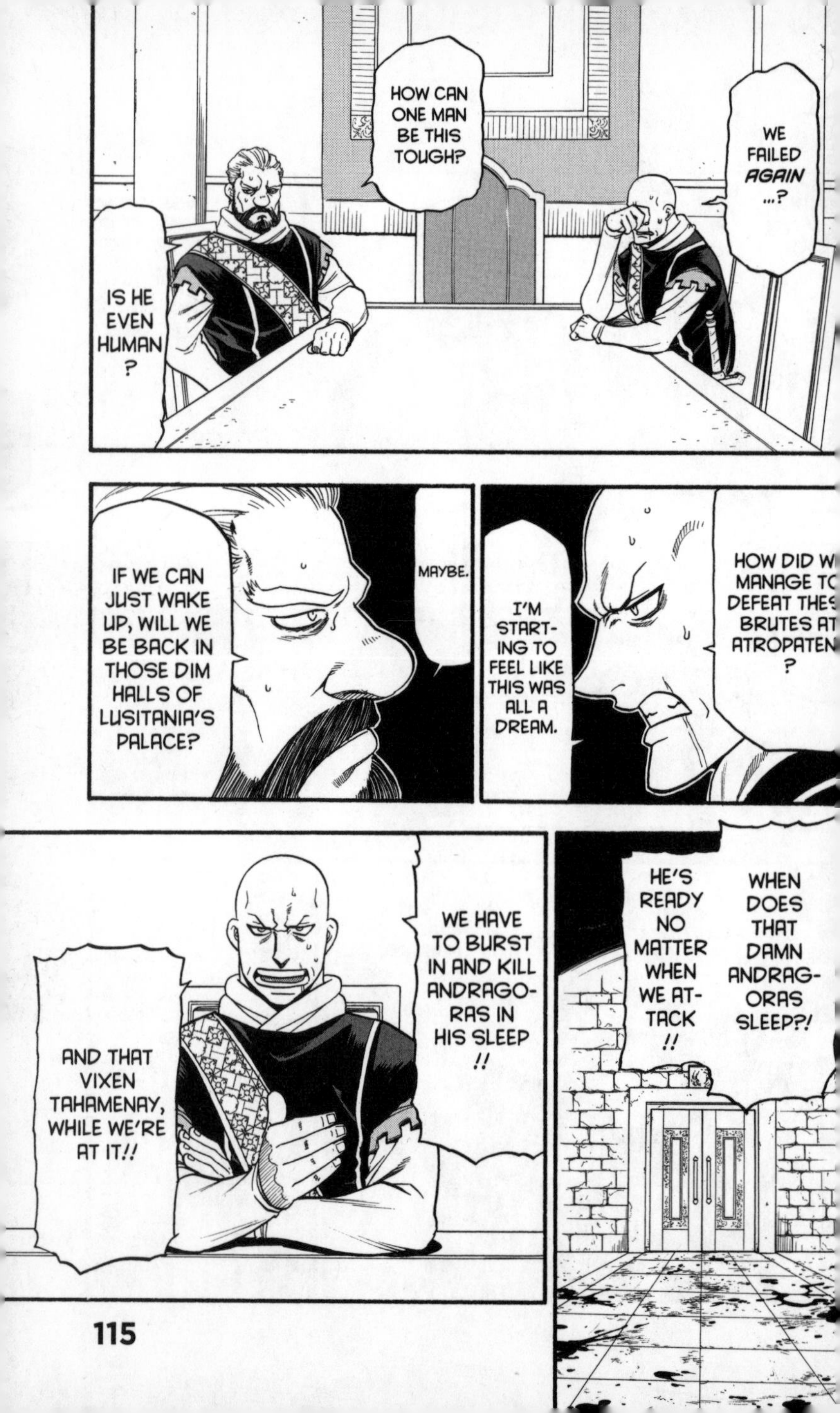

WE FAILED AGAIN ...?
HOW CAN ONE MAN BE THIS TOUGH?
IS HE EVEN HUMAN?
HOW DID W MANAGE TO DEFEAT THES BRUTES AT ATROPATEN ?
I'M STARTING TO FEEL LIKE THIS WAS ALL A DREAM.
MAYBE.
IF WE CAN JUST WAKE UP, WILL WE BE BACK IN THOSE DIM HALLS OF LUSITANIA'S PALACE?
WHEN DOES THAT DAMN ANDRAGORAS SLEEP?!
HE'S READY NO MATTER WHEN WE ATTACK!!
WE HAVE TO BURST IN AND KILL ANDRAGORAS IN HIS SLEEP!!
AND THAT VIXEN TAHAMENAY, WHILE WE'RE AT IT!!

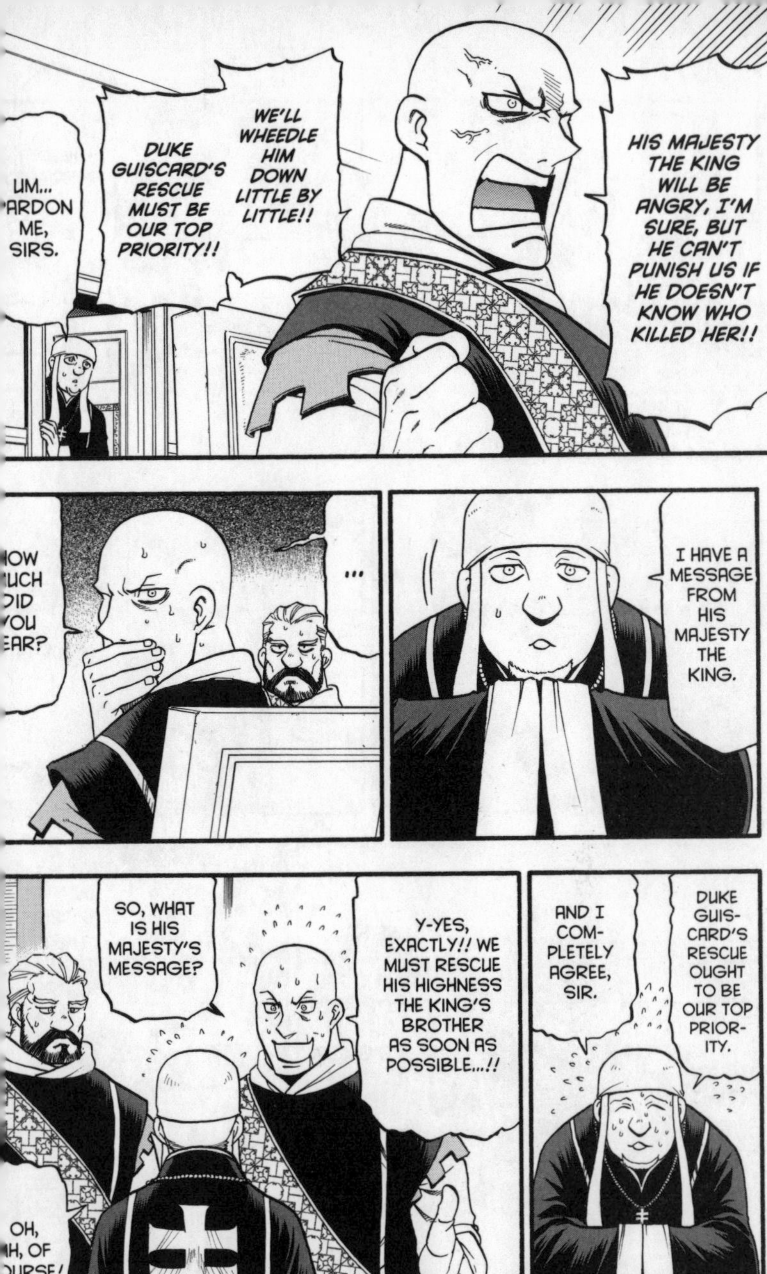
HIS MAJESTY THE KING WILL BE ANGRY, I'M SURE, BUT HE CAN'T PUNISH US IF HE DOESN'T KNOW WHO KILLED HER!!
WE'LL WHEEDLE HIM DOWN LITTLE BY LITTLE!!
DUKE GUISCARD'S RESCUE MUST BE OUR TOP PRIORITY!!
UM... ARDON ME, SIRS.
I HAVE A MESSAGE FROM HIS MAJESTY THE KING.
...
OW UCH DID YOU EAR?
DUKE GUISCARD'S RESCUE OUGHT TO BE OUR TOP PRIORITY.
AND I COMPLETELY AGREE, SIR.
Y-YES, EXACTLY!! WE MUST RESCUE HIS HIGHNESS THE KING'S BROTHER AS SOON AS POSSIBLE...!!
SO, WHAT IS HIS MAJESTY'S MESSAGE?
OH, H, OF OURSE!

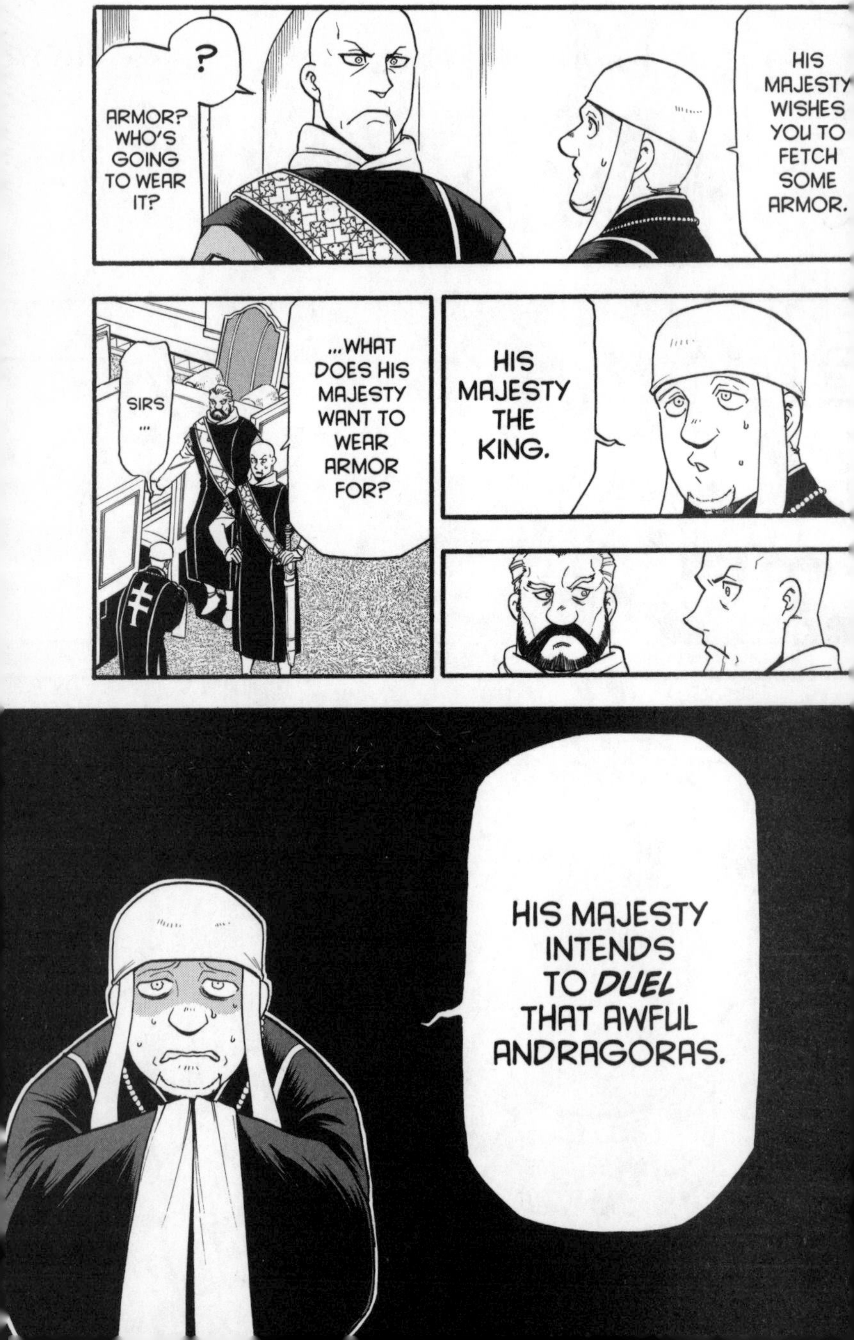
HIS MAJESTY WISHES YOU TO FETCH SOME ARMOR.
?
ARMOR? WHO'S GOING TO WEAR IT?
HIS MAJESTY THE KING.
...WHAT DOES HIS MAJESTY WANT TO WEAR ARMOR FOR?
SIRS ...
HIS MAJESTY INTENDS TO *DUEL* THAT AWFUL ANDRAGORAS.

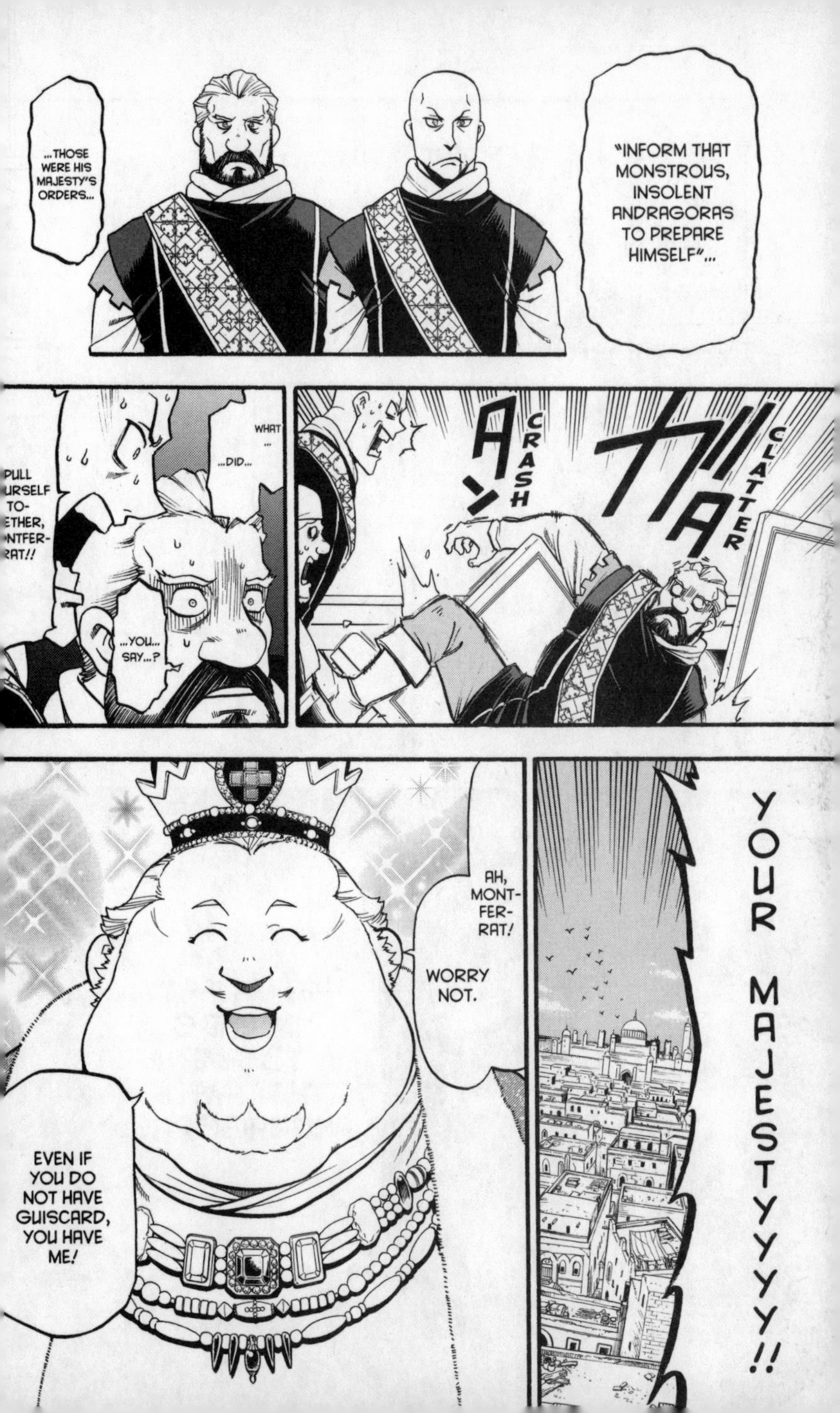
"INFORM THAT MONSTROUS, INSOLENT ANDRAGORAS TO PREPARE HIMSELF"...
...THOSE WERE HIS MAJESTY'S ORDERS...
CLATTER
CRASH
WHAT...
...DID...
...YOU... SAY...?
PULL URSELF TO-ETHER, NTFER-RAT!!
YOUR MAJESTYYYYY!!
AH, MONT-FER-RAT!
WORRY NOT.
EVEN IF YOU DO NOT HAVE GUISCARD, YOU HAVE ME!

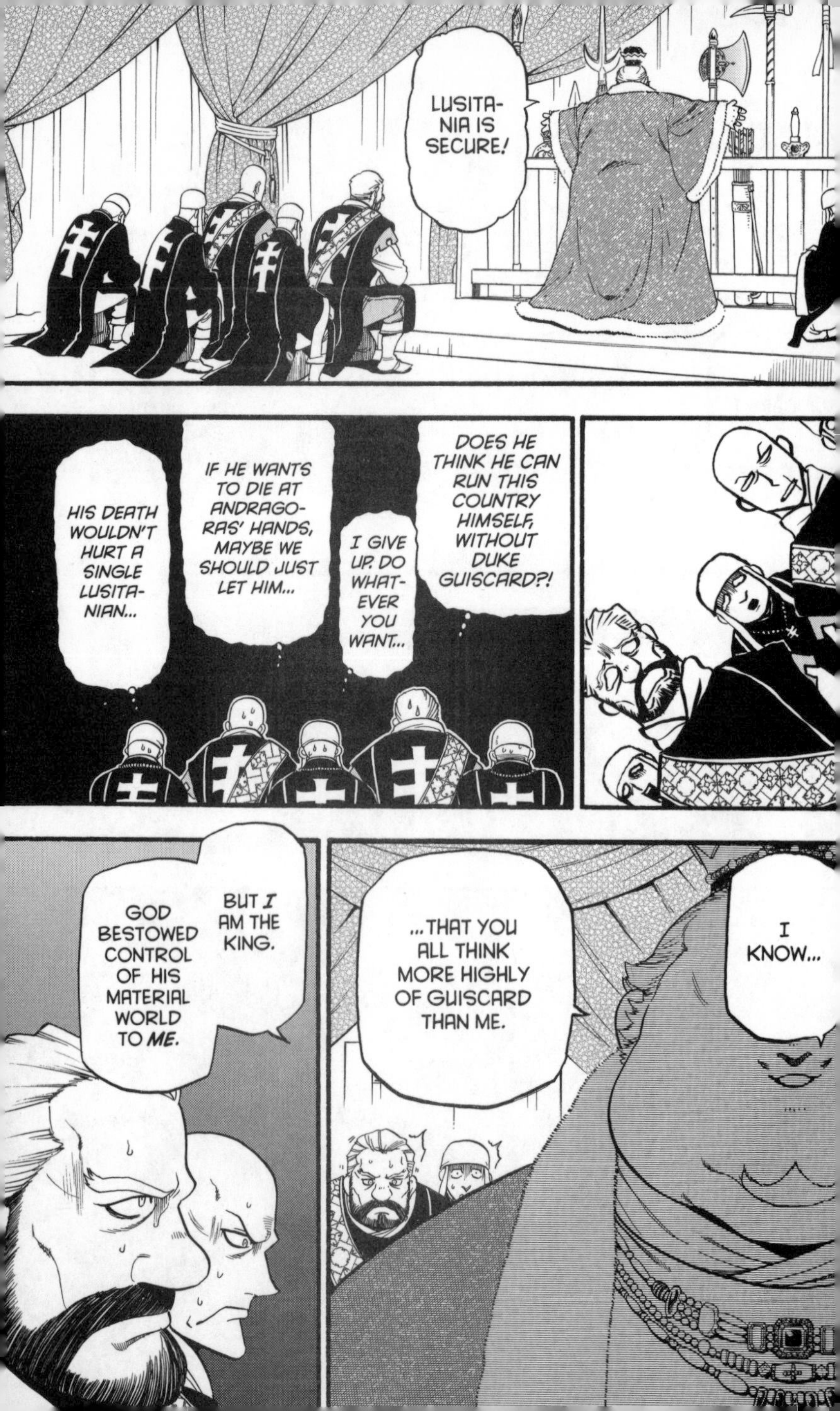
LUSITA-NIA IS SECURE!
DOES HE THINK HE CAN RUN THIS COUNTRY HIMSELF, WITHOUT DUKE GUISCARD?!
I GIVE UP. DO WHAT-EVER YOU WANT...
IF HE WANTS TO DIE AT ANDRAGO-RAS' HANDS, MAYBE WE SHOULD JUST LET HIM...
HIS DEATH WOULDN'T HURT A SINGLE LUSITA-NIAN...
I KNOW...
...THAT YOU ALL THINK MORE HIGHLY OF GUISCARD THAN ME.
BUT *I* AM THE KING.
GOD BESTOWED CONTROL OF HIS MATERIAL WORLD TO ***ME***.

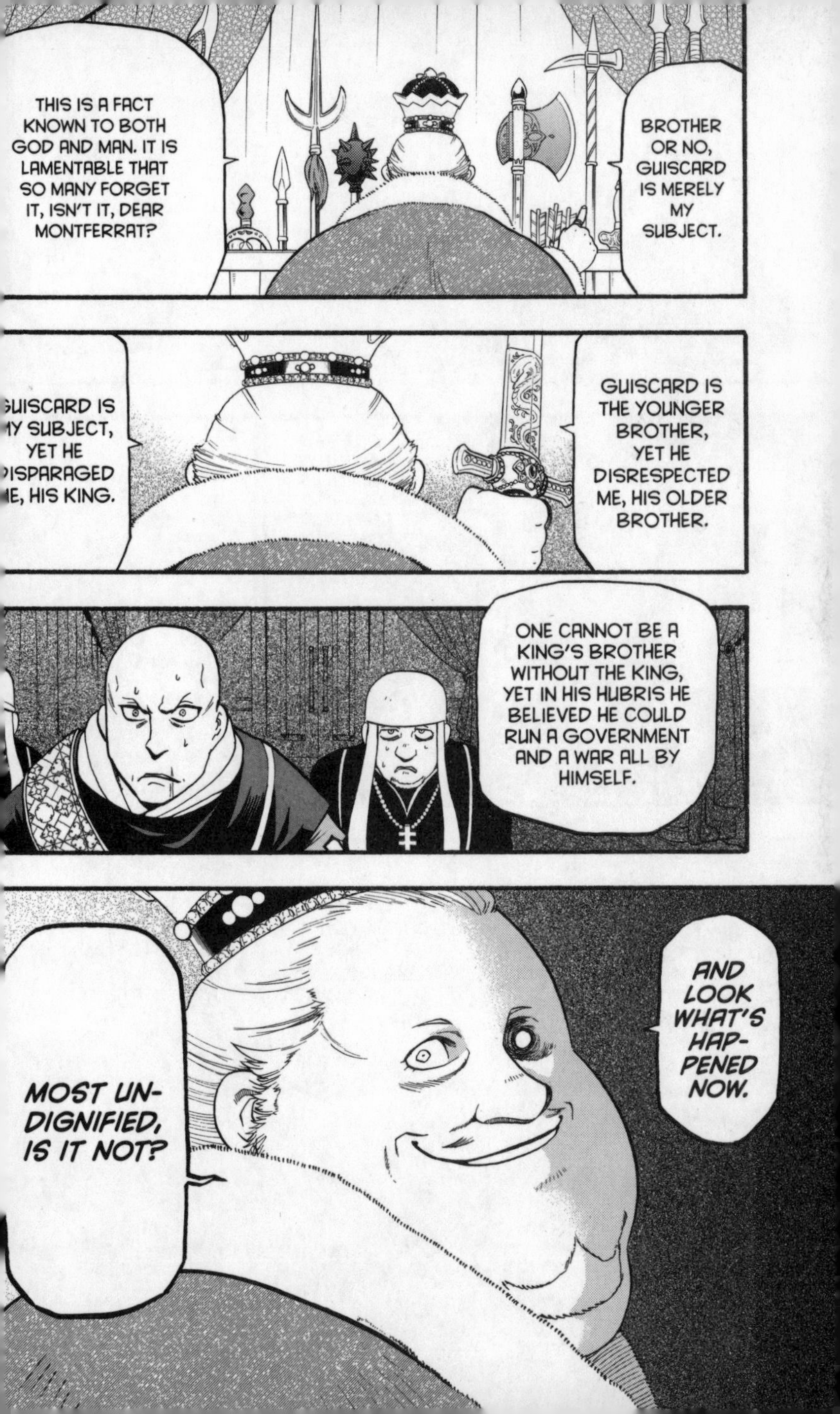
BROTHER OR NO, GUISCARD IS MERELY MY SUBJECT.
THIS IS A FACT KNOWN TO BOTH GOD AND MAN. IT IS LAMENTABLE THAT SO MANY FORGET IT, ISN'T IT, DEAR MONTFERRAT?
GUISCARD IS THE YOUNGER BROTHER, YET HE DISRESPECTED ME, HIS OLDER BROTHER.
GUISCARD IS MY SUBJECT, YET HE DISPARAGED ME, HIS KING.
ONE CANNOT BE A KING'S BROTHER WITHOUT THE KING, YET IN HIS HUBRIS HE BELIEVED HE COULD RUN A GOVERNMENT AND A WAR ALL BY HIMSELF.
AND LOOK WHAT'S HAP-PENED NOW.
MOST UN-DIGNIFIED, IS IT NOT?

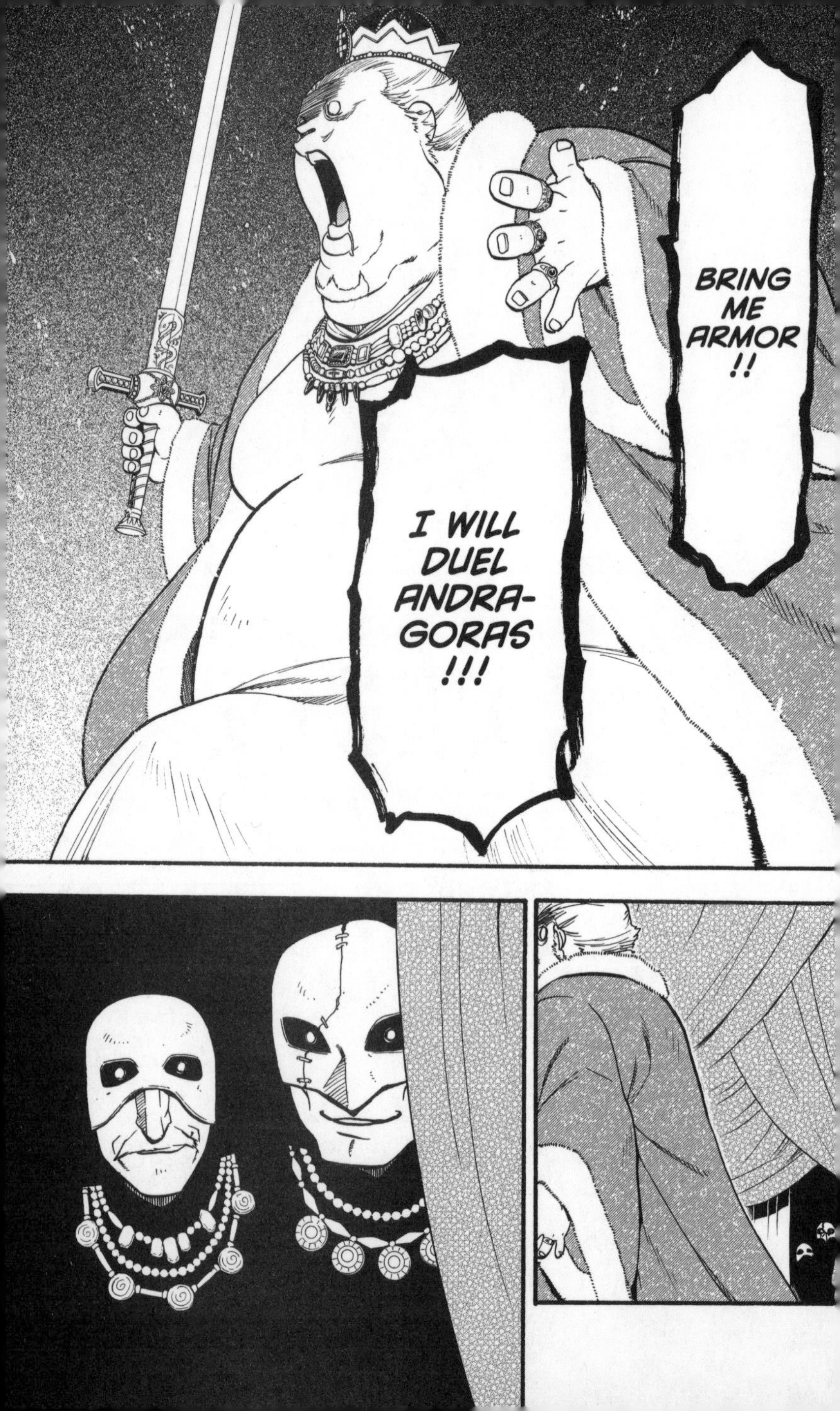
BRING ME ARMOR !!
I WILL DUEL ANDRAGORAS !!!

THE HEROIC LEGEND OF
ARSLAN

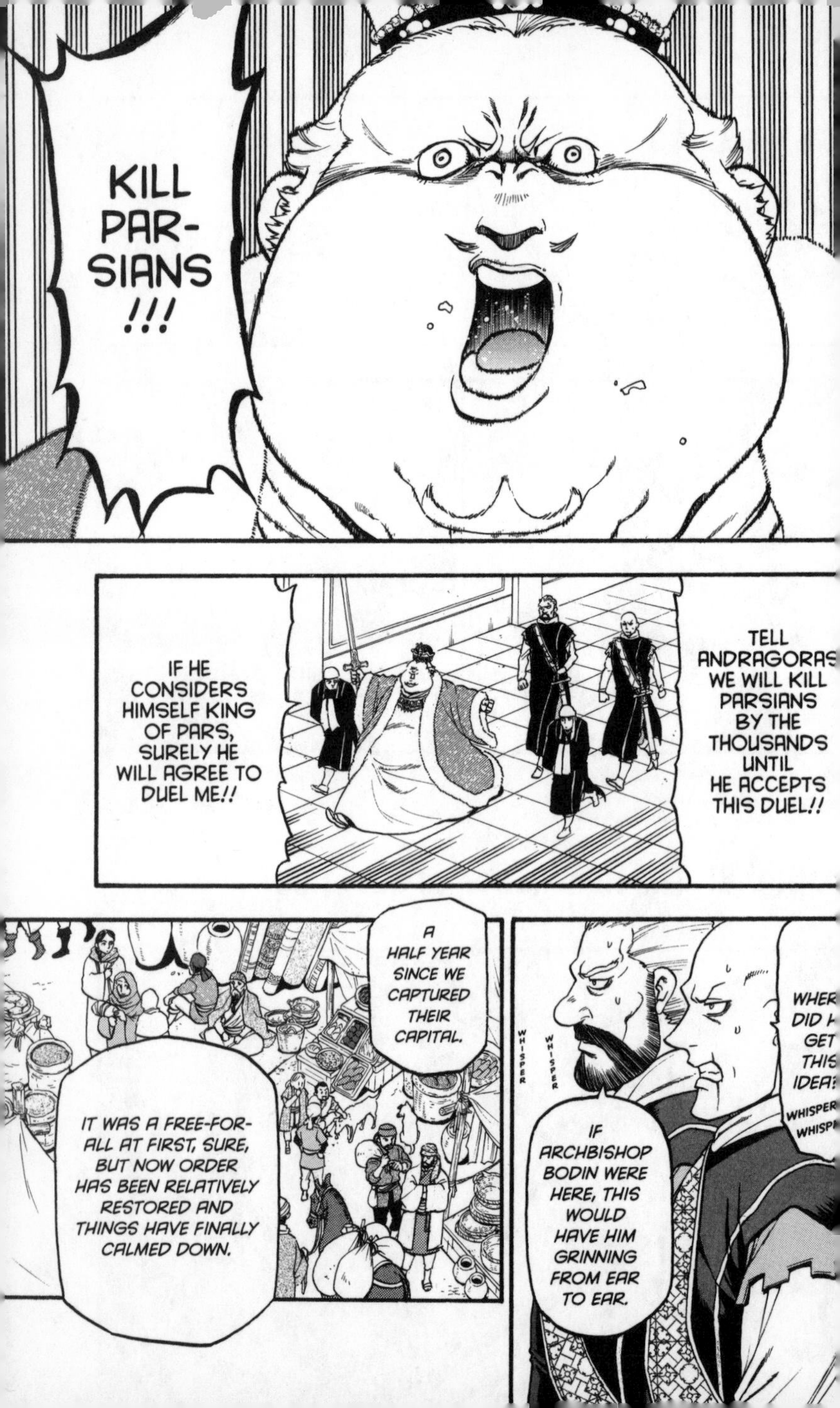
KILL PAR-SIANS!!!
TELL ANDRAGORAS WE WILL KILL PARSIANS BY THE THOUSANDS UNTIL HE ACCEPTS THIS DUEL!!
IF HE CONSIDERS HIMSELF KING OF PARS, SURELY HE WILL AGREE TO DUEL ME!!
WHER DID H GET THIS IDEA?
WHISPER WHISP
IF ARCHBISHOP BODIN WERE HERE, THIS WOULD HAVE HIM GRINNING FROM EAR TO EAR.
WHISPER WHISPER
A HALF YEAR SINCE WE CAPTURED THEIR CAPITAL.
IT WAS A FREE-FOR-ALL AT FIRST, SURE, BUT NOW ORDER HAS BEEN RELATIVELY RESTORED AND THINGS HAVE FINALLY CALMED DOWN.

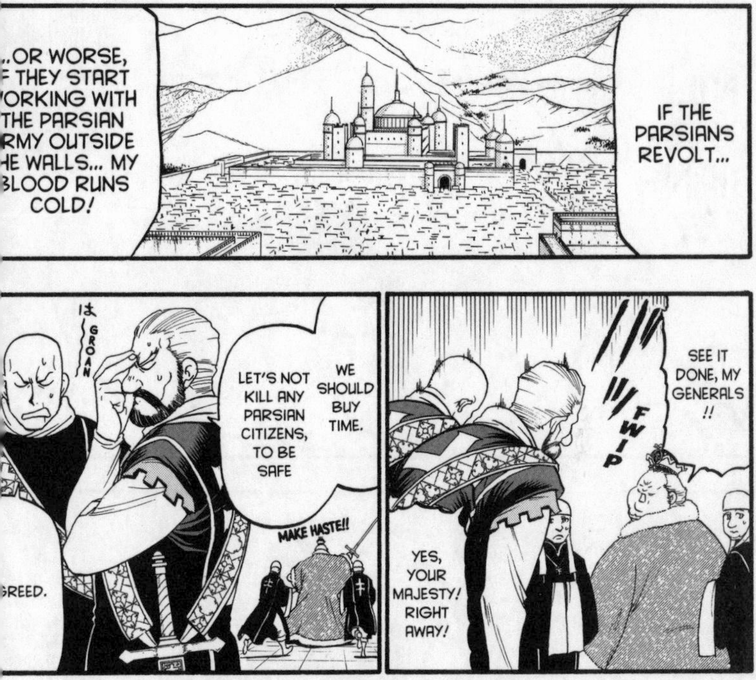
IF THE PARSIANS REVOLT...
..OR WORSE, F THEY START ORKING WITH THE PARSIAN RMY OUTSIDE HE WALLS... MY BLOOD RUNS COLD!
SEE IT DONE, MY GENERALS !!
FWIP
YES, YOUR MAJESTY! RIGHT AWAY!
WE SHOULD BUY TIME.
LET'S NOT KILL ANY PARSIAN CITIZENS, TO BE SAFE
は— GROAN
MAKE HASTE!!
GREED.

hapter 81: The Humiliation of Lusitania

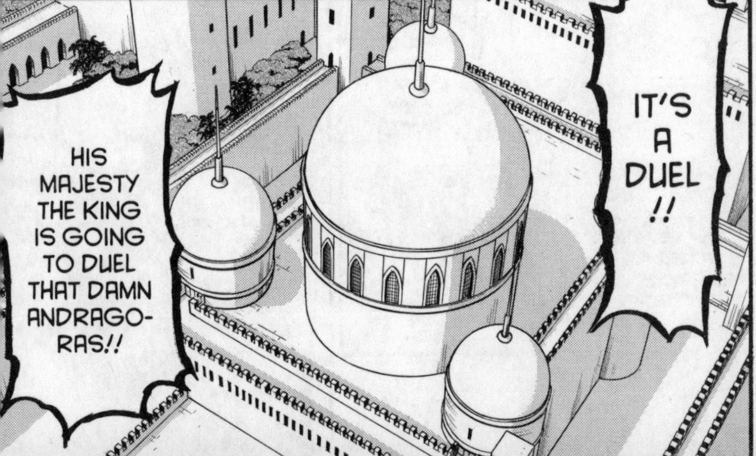
IT'S A DUEL !!
HIS MAJESTY THE KING IS GOING TO DUEL THAT DAMN ANDRAGO-RAS!!

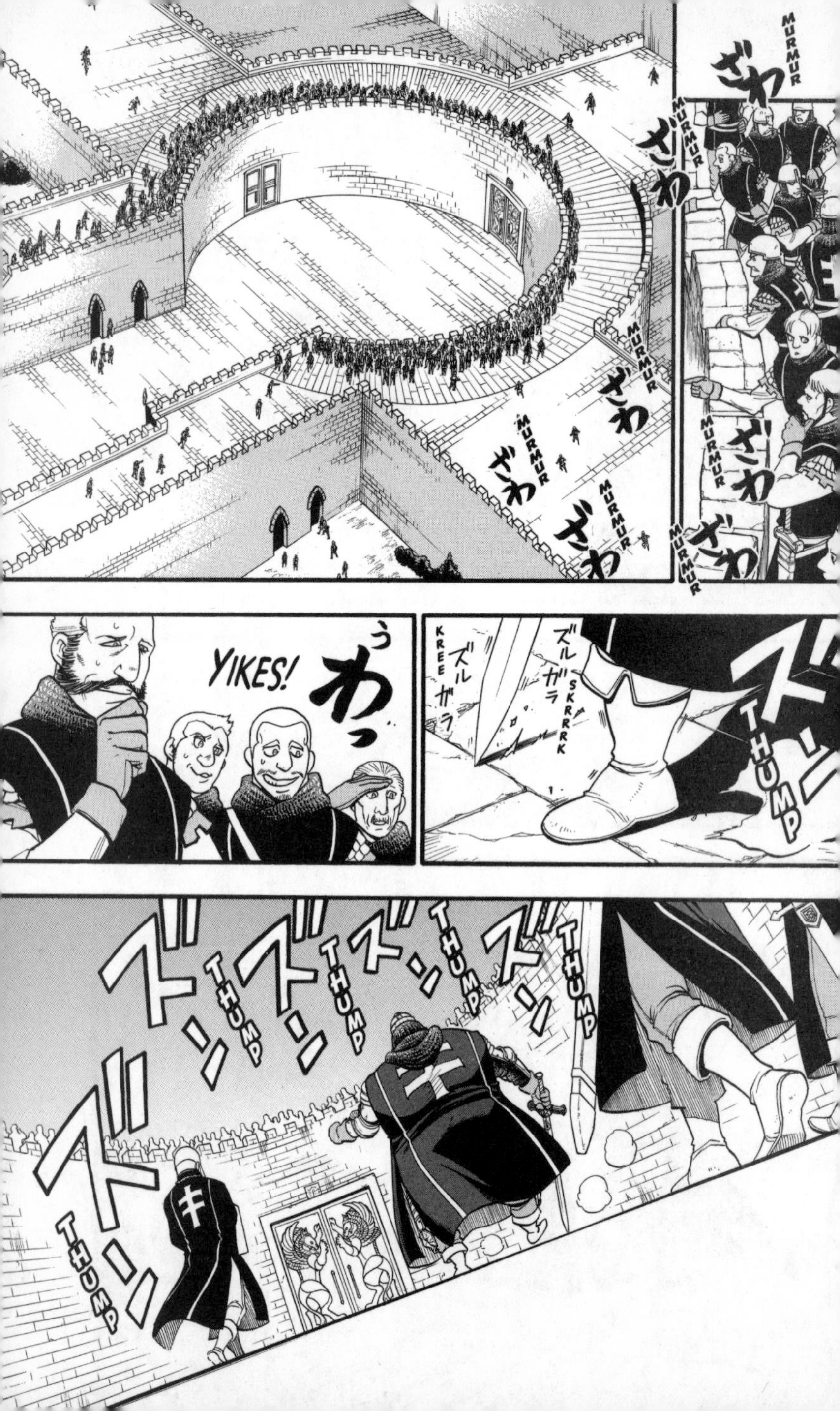
MURMUR
ざわ
MURMUR
ざわ
MURMUR
ざわ
MURMUR
ざわ
MURMUR
ざわ
MURMUR
ざわ
MURMUR
ざわ
ズーン
THUMP
ズルガラ
SKRRRK
ズルガラ
KREE
うわっ
YIKES!
ズーン
THUMP
ズーン
THUMP
ズーン
THUMP
ズーン
THUMP
ズーン
THUMP

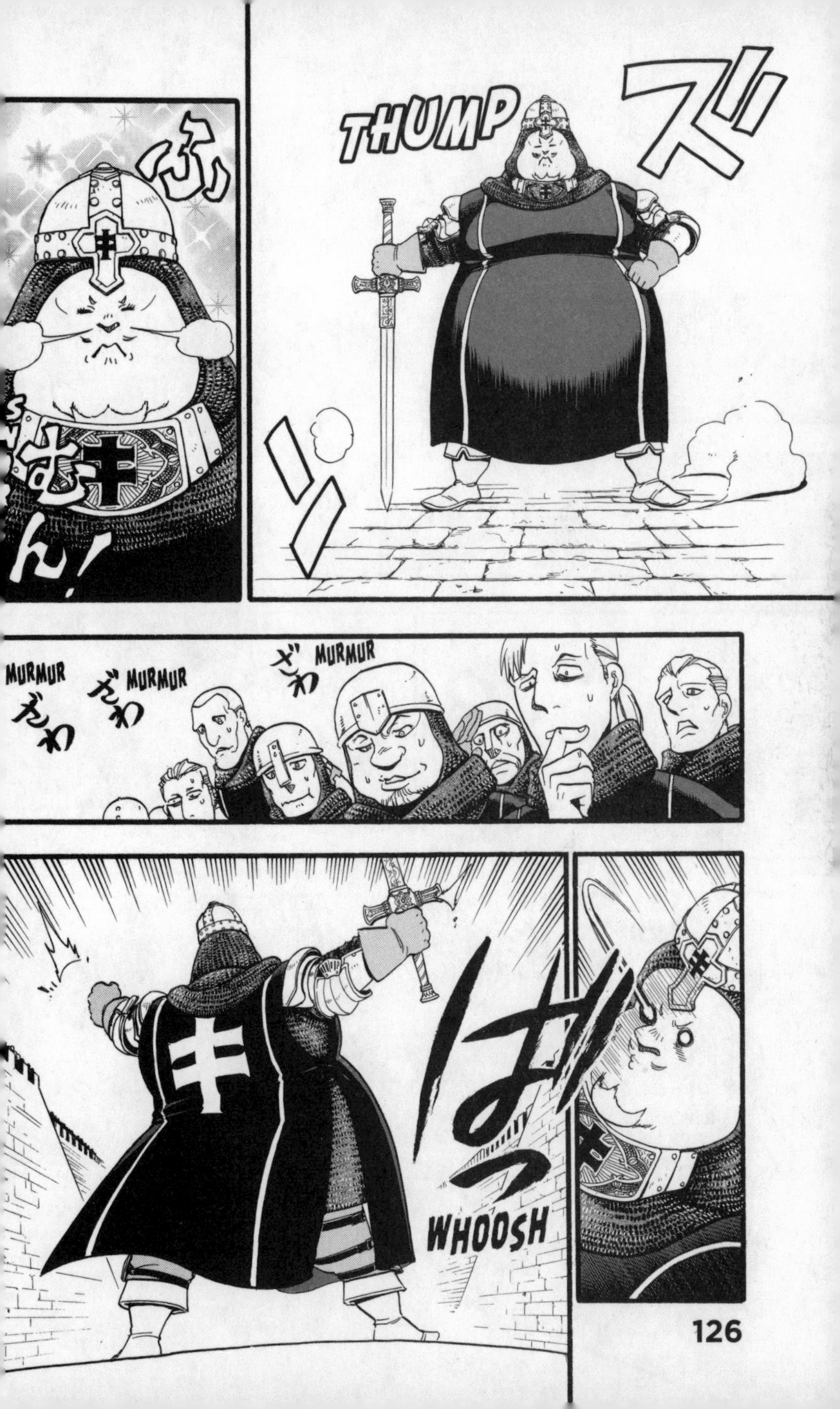
THUMP
ズン
ふんっ
むん!
ざわ MURMUR
だわ MURMUR
だわ MURMUR
はっ
WHOOSH

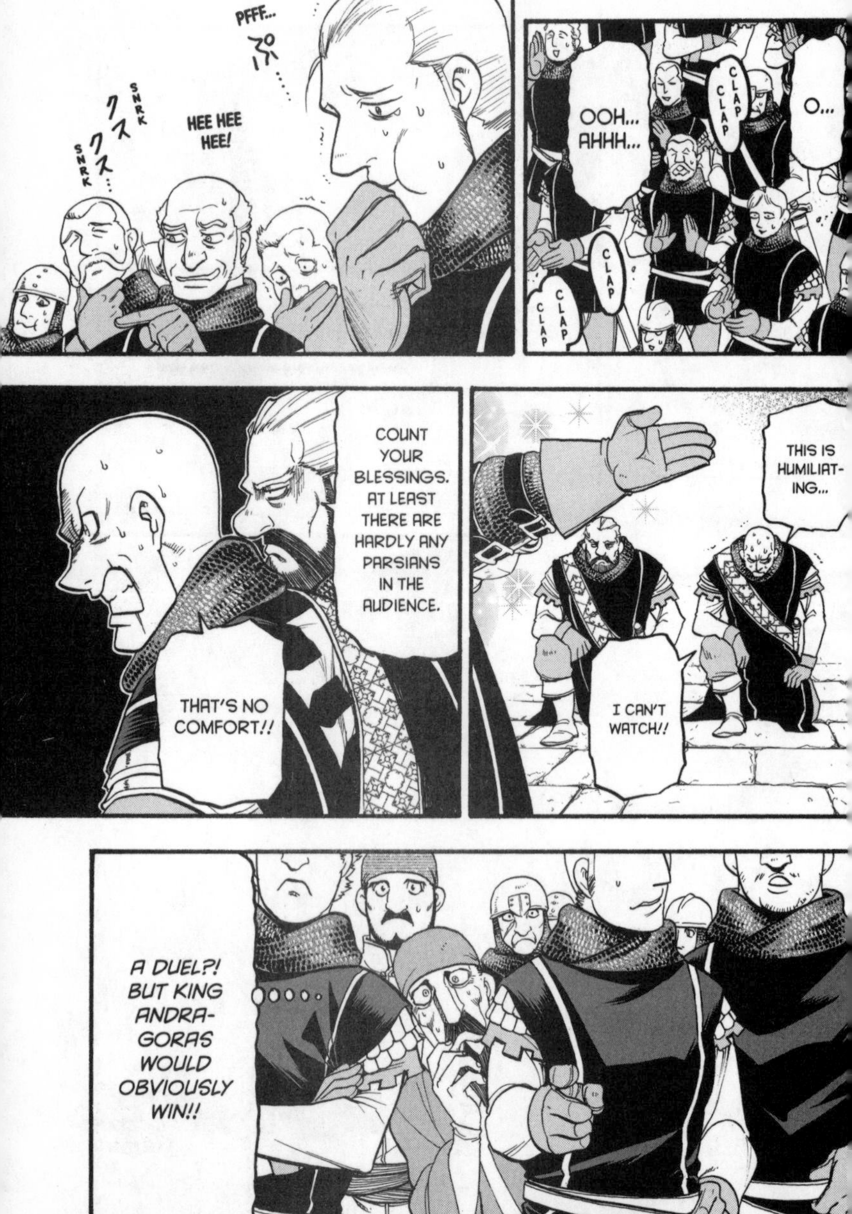
O...
CLAP CLAP
OOH... AHHH...
CLAP CLAP
CLAP
PFFF...
ぷ...
HEE HEE HEE!
SNRK
クス
SNRK
クス...
THIS IS HUMILIATING...
I CAN'T WATCH!!
COUNT YOUR BLESSINGS. AT LEAST THERE ARE HARDLY ANY PARSIANS IN THE AUDIENCE.
THAT'S NO COMFORT!!
A DUEL?! BUT KING ANDRAGORAS WOULD OBVIOUSLY WIN!!

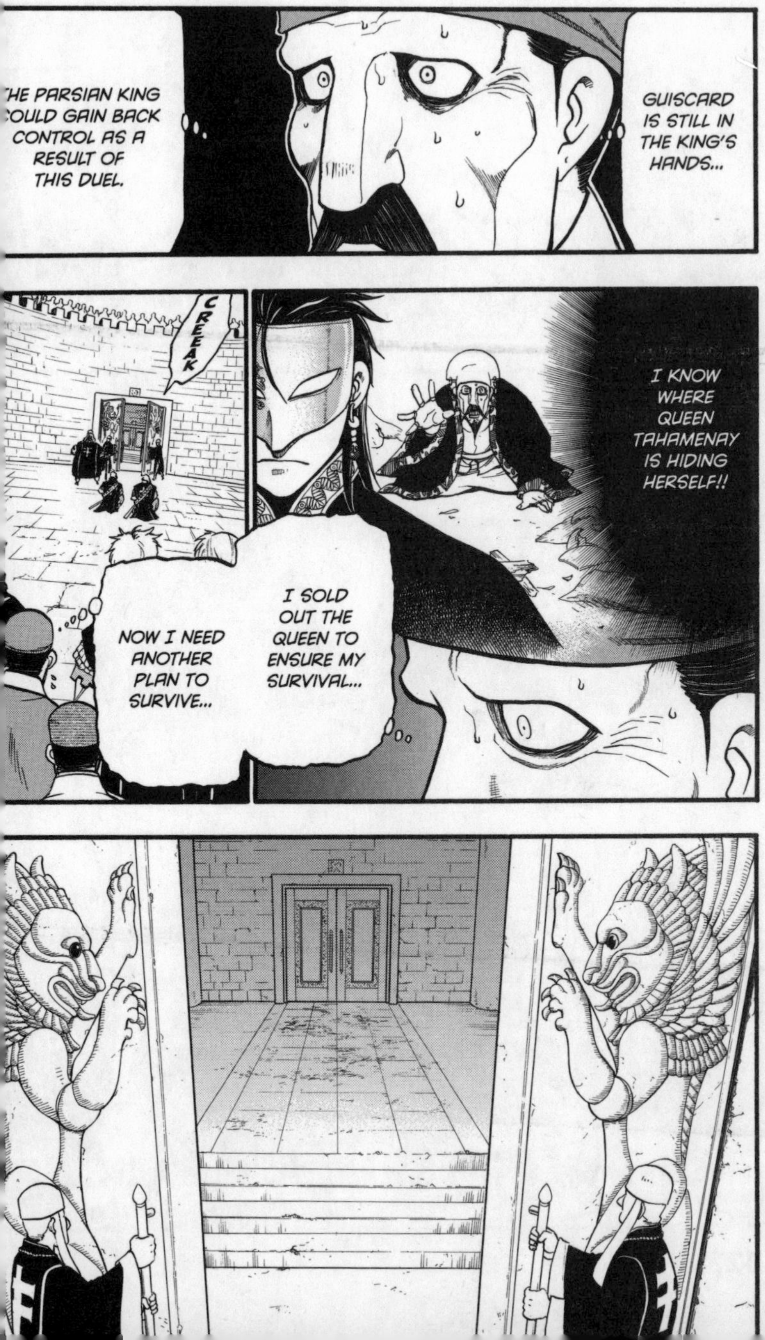
GUISCARD IS STILL IN THE KING'S HANDS...
THE PARSIAN KING COULD GAIN BACK CONTROL AS A RESULT OF THIS DUEL.
I KNOW WHERE QUEEN TAHAMENAY IS HIDING HERSELF!!
I SOLD OUT THE QUEEN TO ENSURE MY SURVIVAL...
NOW I NEED ANOTHER PLAN TO SURVIVE...
CREEAK

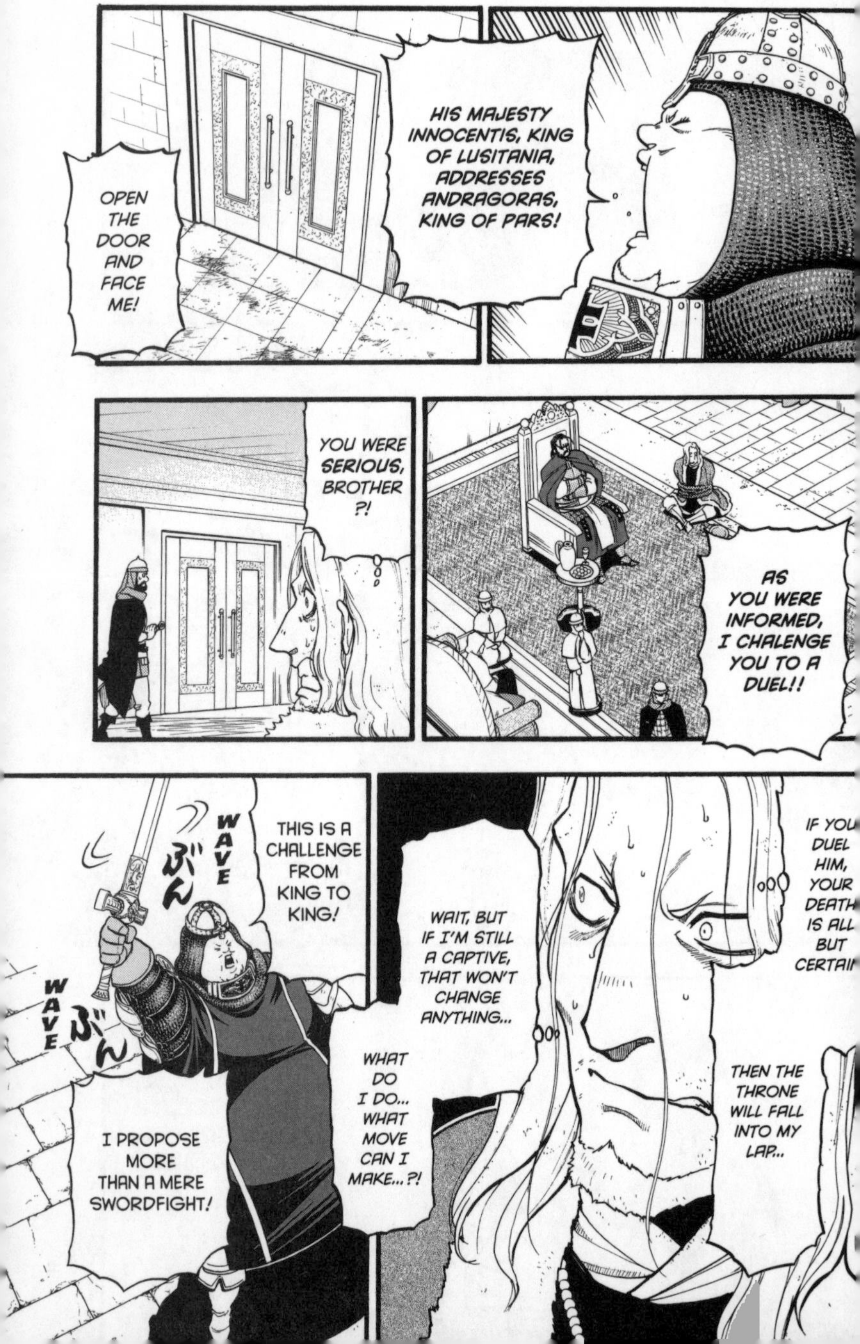
HIS MAJESTY INNOCENTIS, KING OF LUSITANIA, ADDRESSES ANDRAGORAS, KING OF PARS!
OPEN THE DOOR AND FACE ME!
AS YOU WERE INFORMED, I CHALENGE YOU TO A DUEL!!
YOU WERE SERIOUS, BROTHER?!
IF YOU DUEL HIM, YOUR DEATH IS ALL BUT CERTAI
THEN THE THRONE WILL FALL INTO MY LAP...
WAIT, BUT IF I'M STILL A CAPTIVE, THAT WON'T CHANGE ANYTHING...
WHAT DO I DO... WHAT MOVE CAN I MAKE...?!
THIS IS A CHALLENGE FROM KING TO KING!
WAVE ぶん
WAVE ぶん
I PROPOSE MORE THAN A MERE SWORDFIGHT!

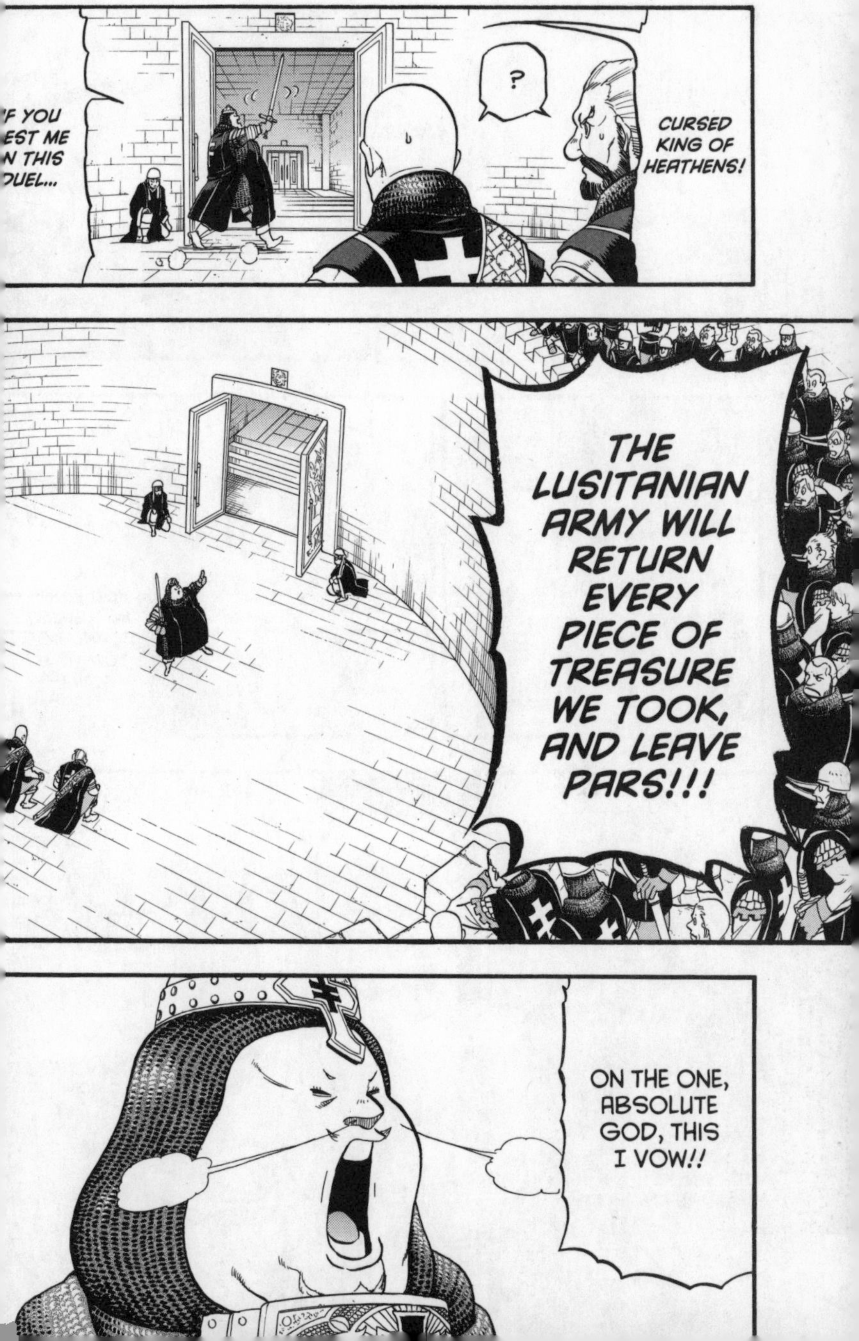
CURSED KING OF HEATHENS!
?
THE LUSITANIAN ARMY WILL RETURN EVERY PIECE OF TREASURE WE TOOK, AND LEAVE PARS!!!
ON THE ONE, ABSOLUTE GOD, THIS I VOW!!

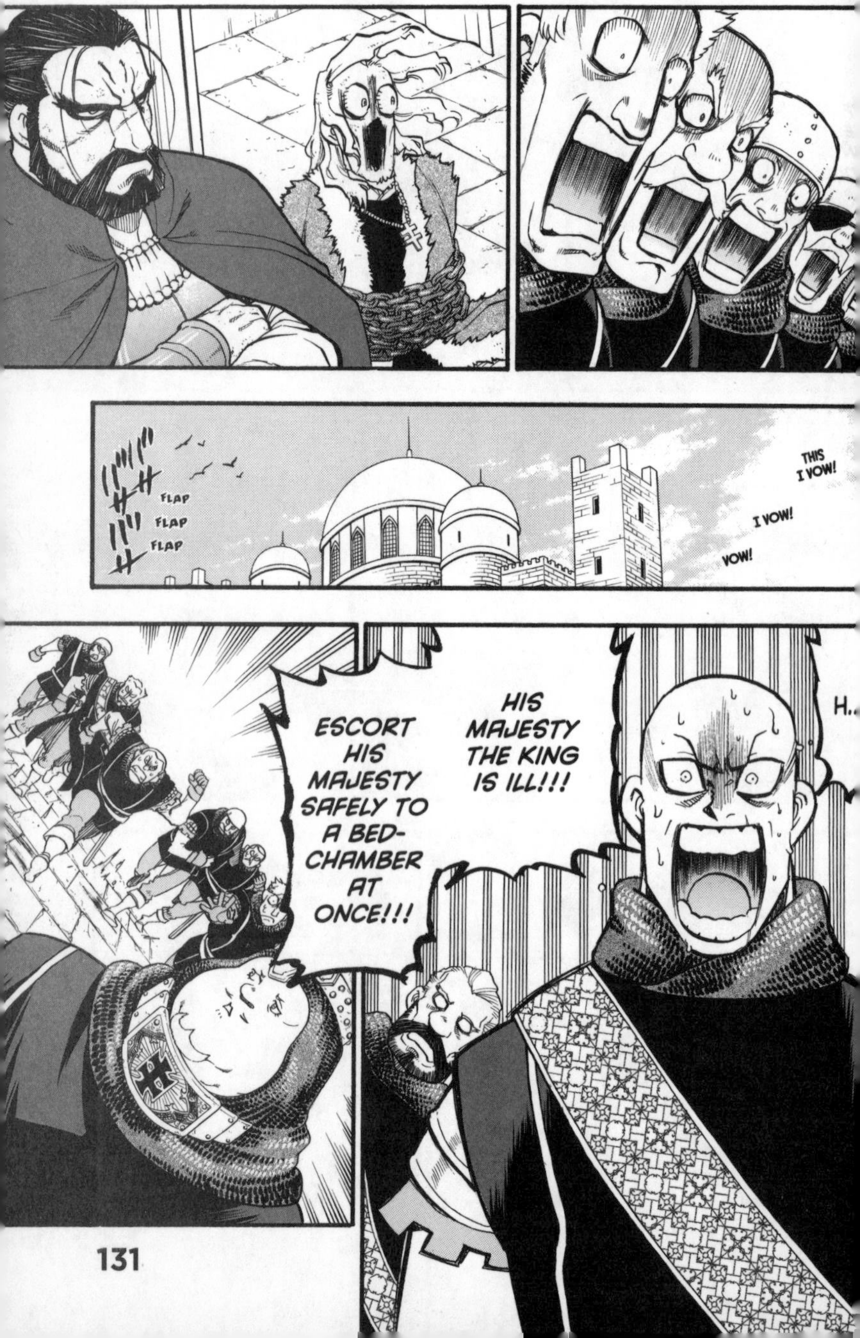
THIS I VOW!
I VOW!
VOW!
FLAP
FLAP
FLAP
H..
HIS MAJESTY THE KING IS ILL!!!
ESCORT HIS MAJESTY SAFELY TO A BED-CHAMBER AT ONCE!!!

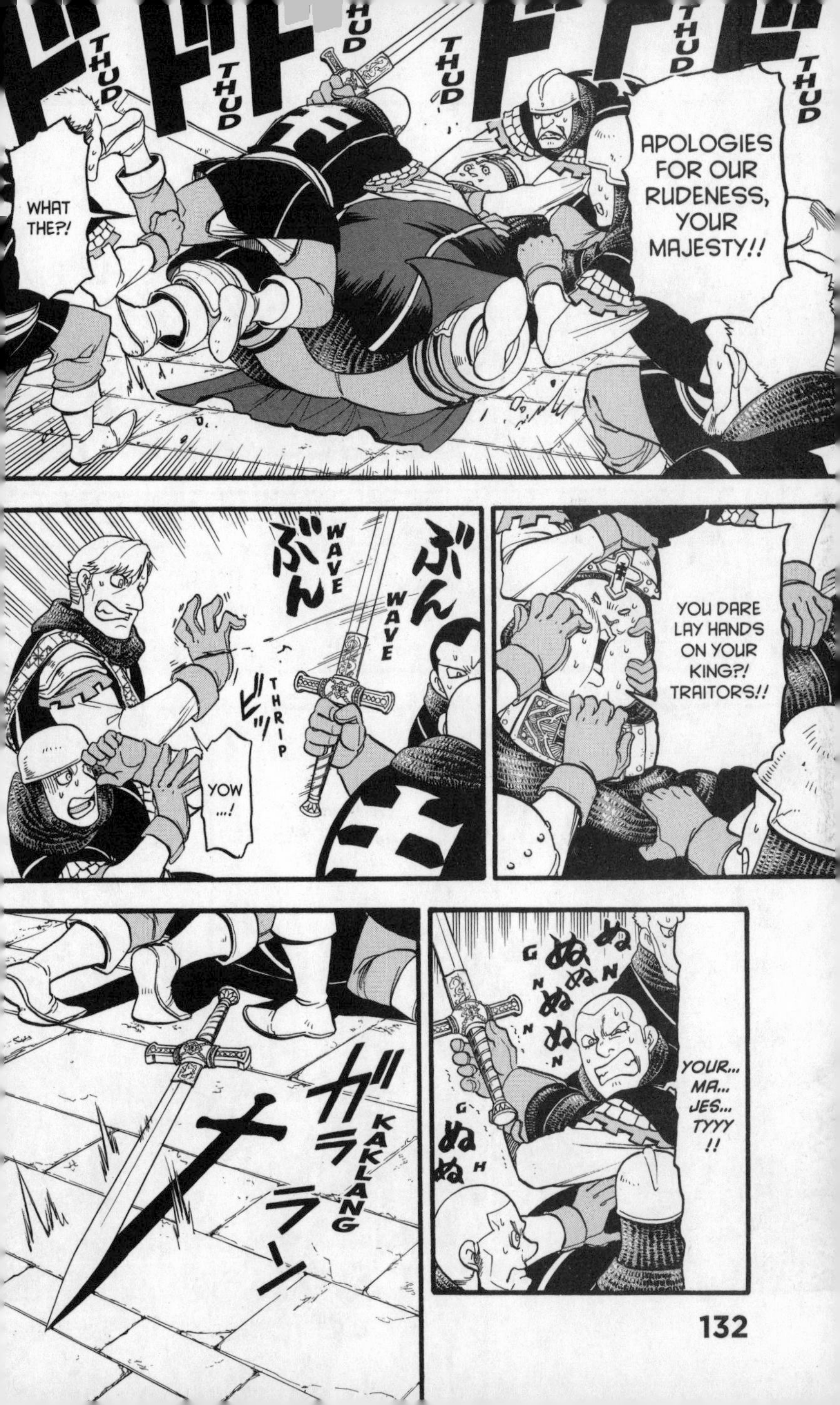

THUD THUD THUD THUD THUD THUD
APOLOGIES FOR OUR RUDENESS, YOUR MAJESTY!!
WHAT THE?!
YOU DARE LAY HANDS ON YOUR KING?! TRAITORS!!
ぶん WAVE
ぶん WAVE
ビッ THRIP
YOW ...!
ぬぬぬぬぬぬ GNNNN
ぬぬ GH
YOUR... MA... JES... TYYY !!
ガラーン KAKLANG

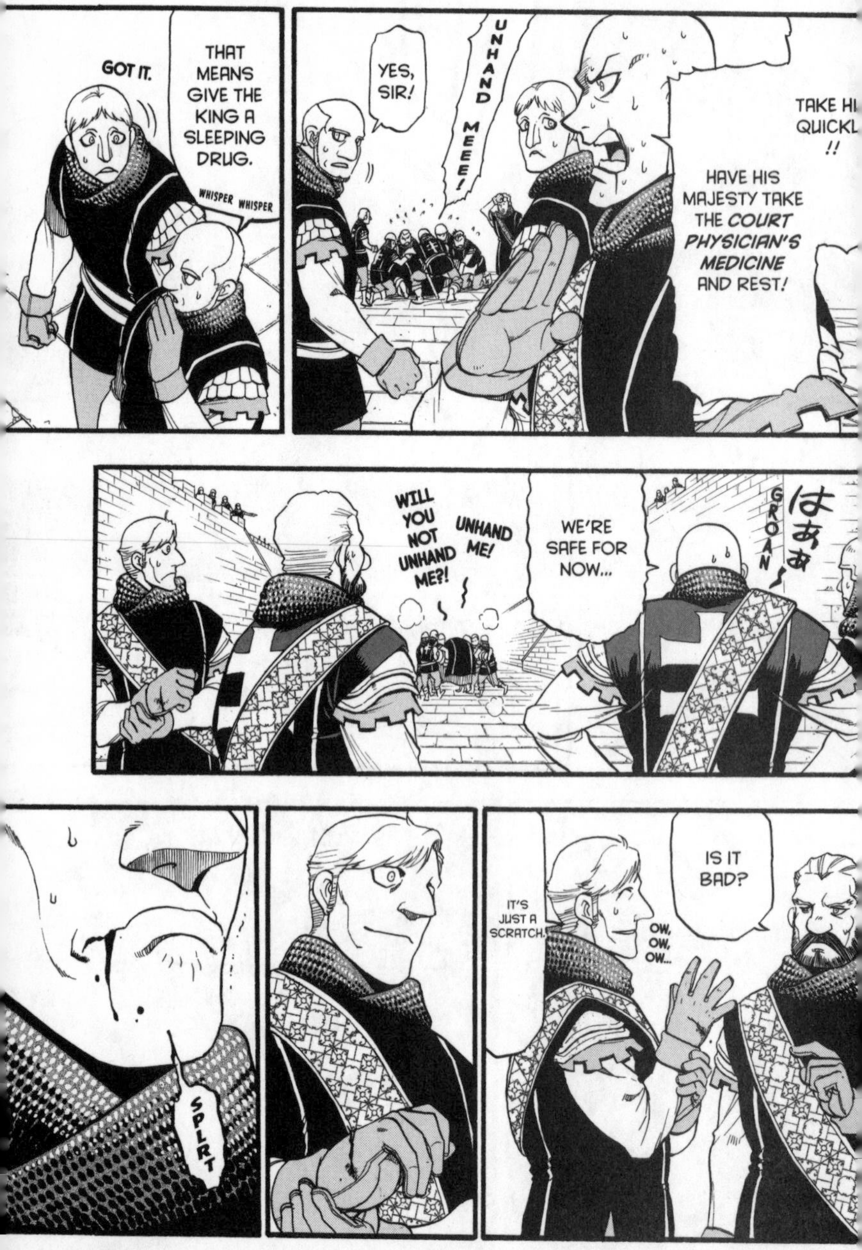
TAKE HI
QUICKL
!!
HAVE HIS MAJESTY TAKE THE *COURT PHYSICIAN'S MEDICINE* AND REST!
UNHAND MEEEE!
YES, SIR!
THAT MEANS GIVE THE KING A SLEEPING DRUG.
WHISPER WHISPER
GOT IT.
はぁぁ~
GROAN
WE'RE SAFE FOR NOW...
UNHAND ME!
WILL YOU NOT UNHAND ME?!
IS IT BAD?
OW, OW, OW...
IT'S JUST A SCRATCH.
SPLRT

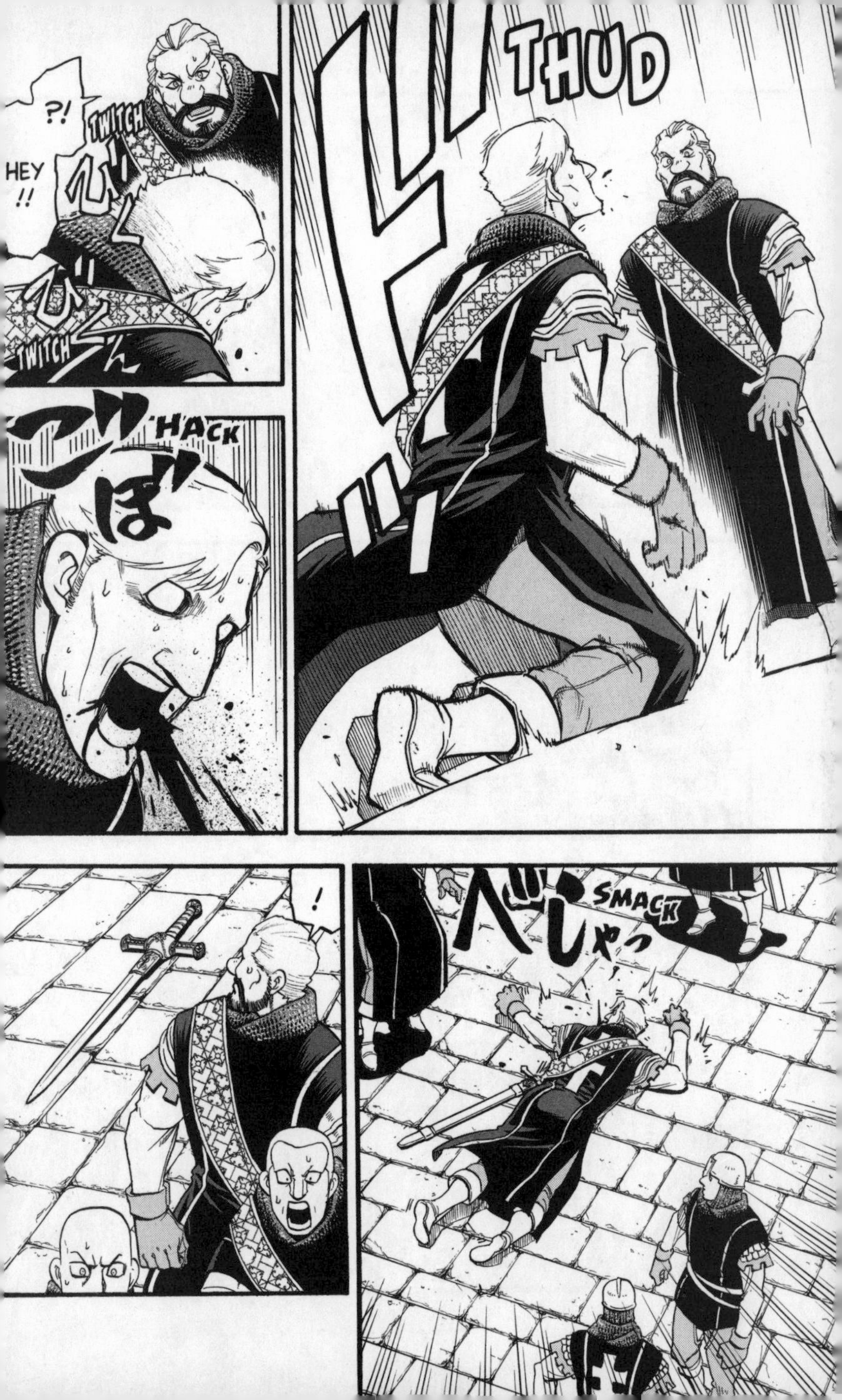
THUD
?!
HEY!!
TWITCH
TWITCH
HACK
SMACK
!

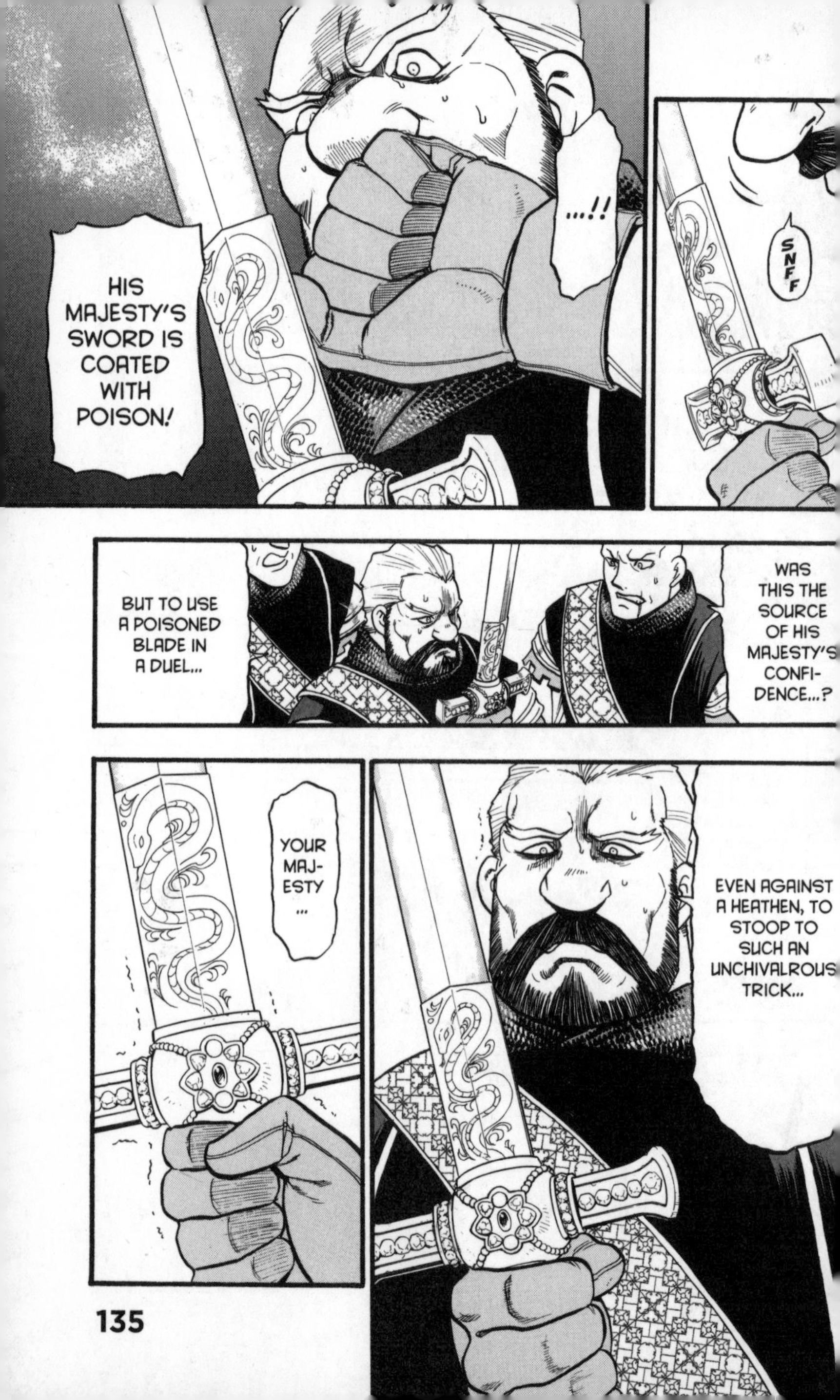
SNFF
...!!
HIS MAJESTY'S SWORD IS COATED WITH POISON!
WAS THIS THE SOURCE OF HIS MAJESTY'S CONFI-DENCE...?
BUT TO USE A POISONED BLADE IN A DUEL...
EVEN AGAINST A HEATHEN, TO STOOP TO SUCH AN UNCHIVALROUS TRICK...
YOUR MAJ-ESTY ...

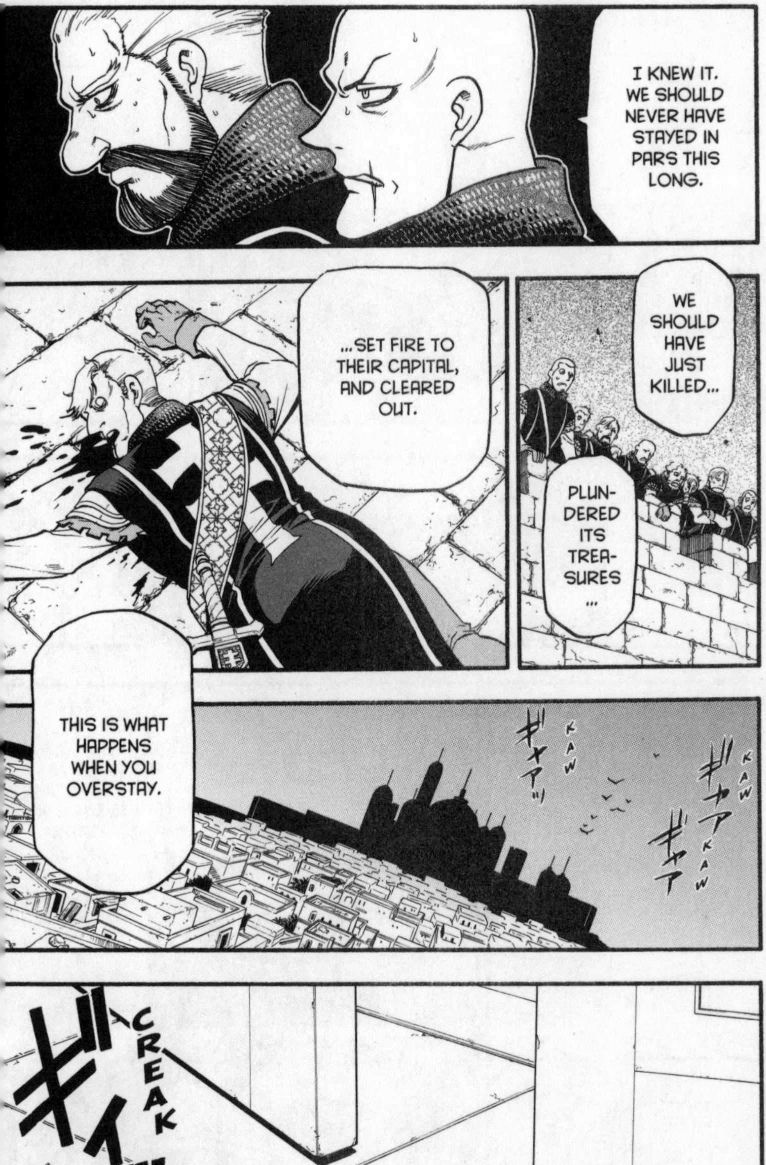
I KNEW IT. WE SHOULD NEVER HAVE STAYED IN PARS THIS LONG.
WE SHOULD HAVE JUST KILLED...
PLUNDERED ITS TREASURES ...
...SET FIRE TO THEIR CAPITAL, AND CLEARED OUT.
THIS IS WHAT HAPPENS WHEN YOU OVERSTAY.
KAW
KAW
KAW
CREAK

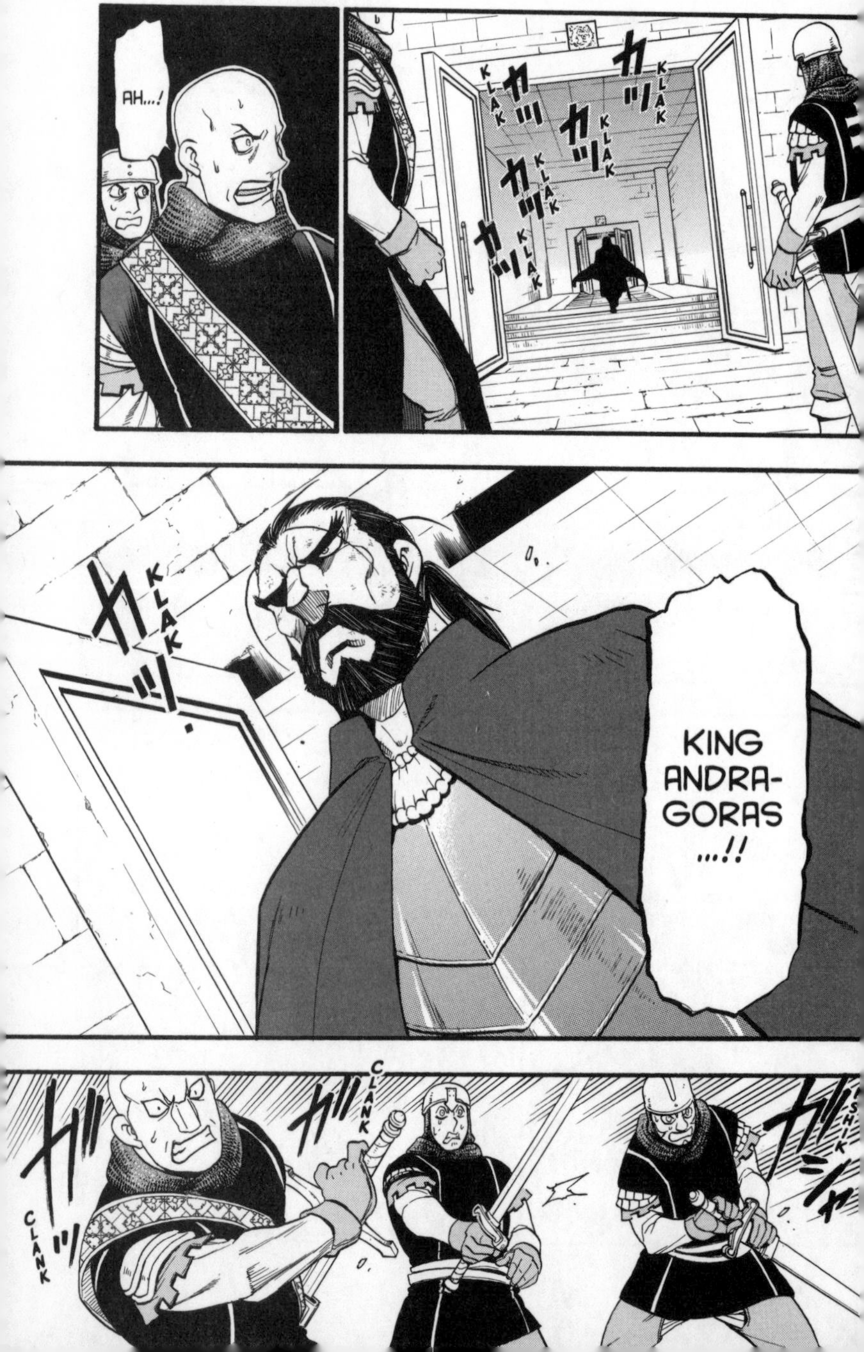
KLAK
KLAK
KLAK
KLAK
KLAK
AH...!
KLAK
KING ANDRA-GORAS ...!!
SHIK
CLANK
CLANK

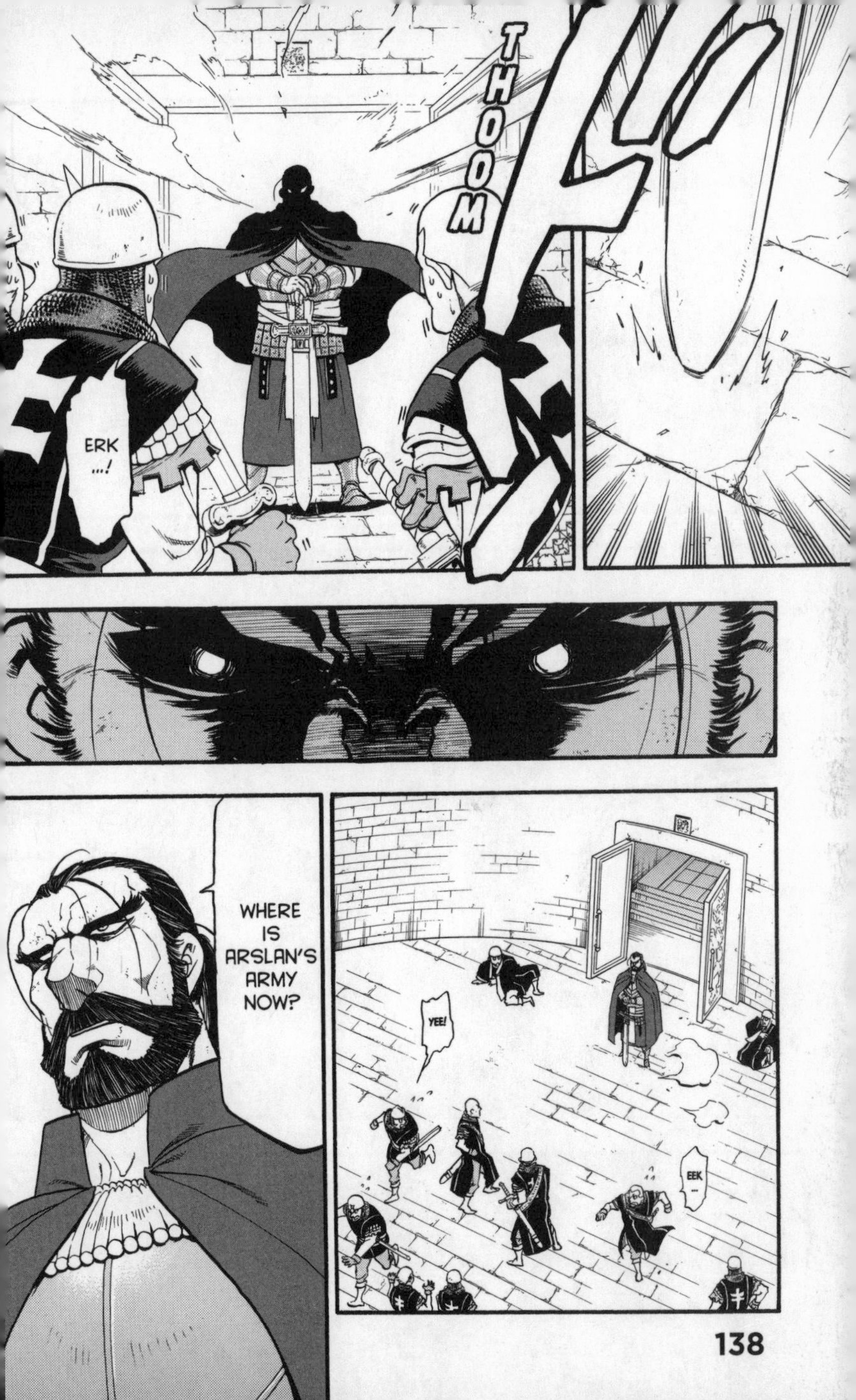
THOOM
ERK ...!
YEE!
EEK ...
WHERE IS ARSLAN'S ARMY NOW?

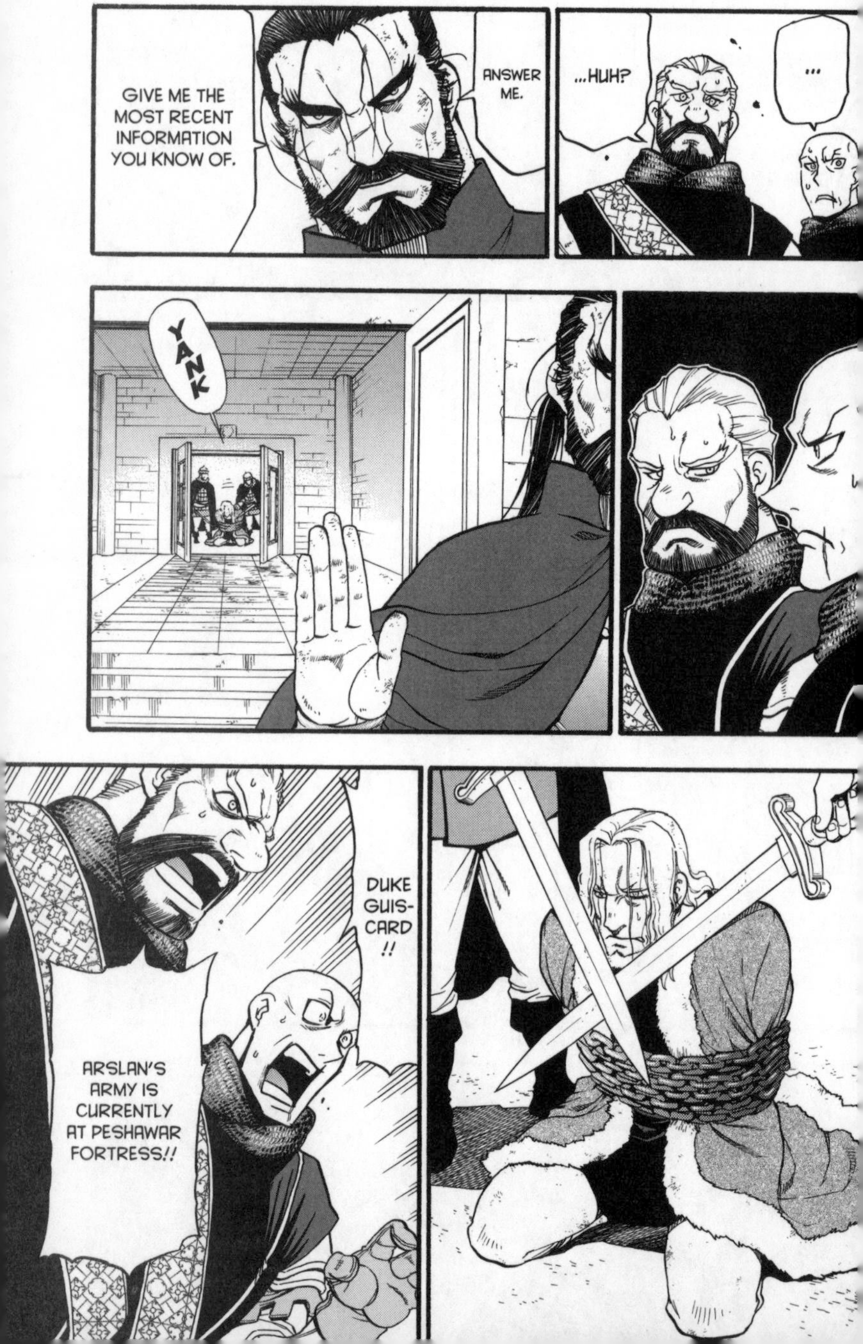

...HUH?
...
ANSWER ME.
GIVE ME THE MOST RECENT INFORMATION YOU KNOW OF.
YANK
DUKE GUIS-CARD!!
ARSLAN'S ARMY IS CURRENTLY AT PESHAWAR FORTRESS!!

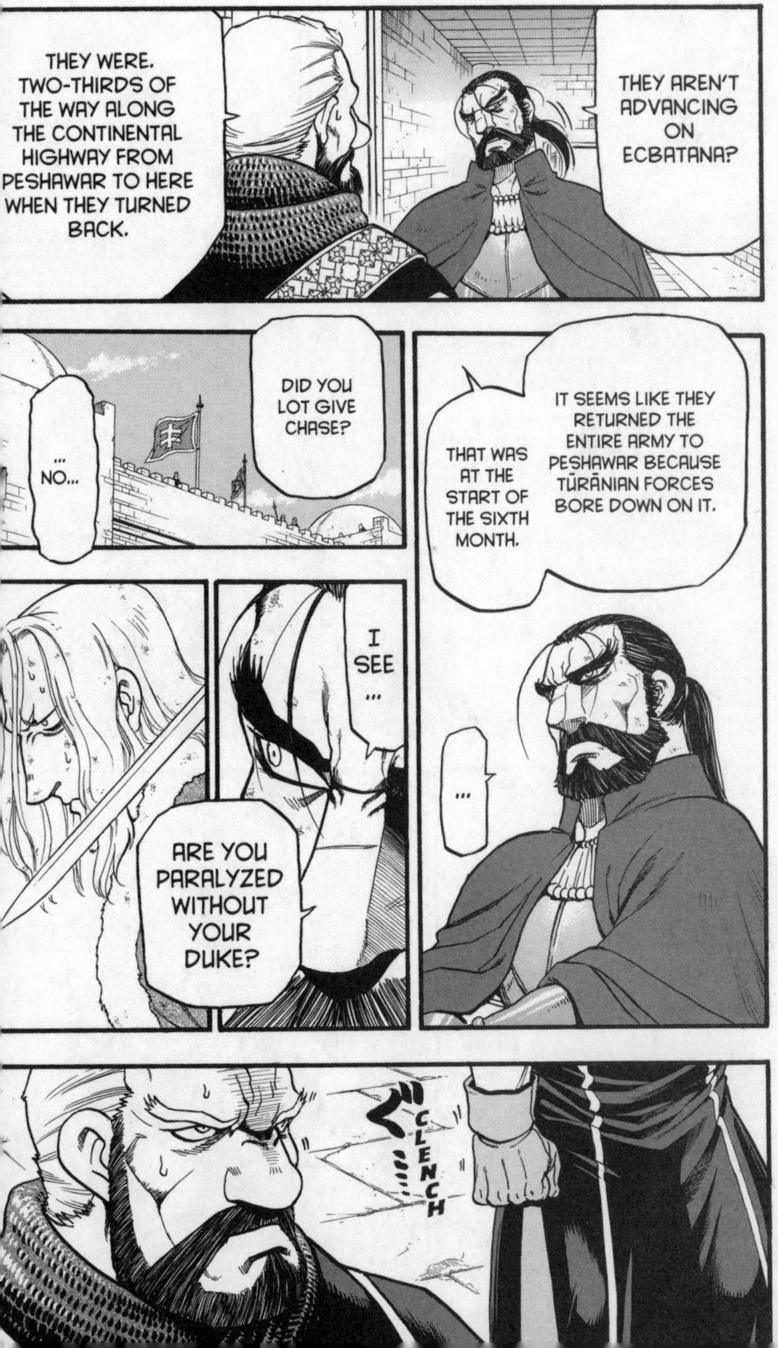
THEY AREN'T ADVANCING ON ECBATANA?
THEY WERE. TWO-THIRDS OF THE WAY ALONG THE CONTINENTAL HIGHWAY FROM PESHAWAR TO HERE WHEN THEY TURNED BACK.
IT SEEMS LIKE THEY RETURNED THE ENTIRE ARMY TO PESHAWAR BECAUSE TŪRĀNIAN FORCES BORE DOWN ON IT.
THAT WAS AT THE START OF THE SIXTH MONTH.
...
DID YOU LOT GIVE CHASE?
... NO...
I SEE ...
ARE YOU PARALYZED WITHOUT YOUR DUKE?
CLENCH

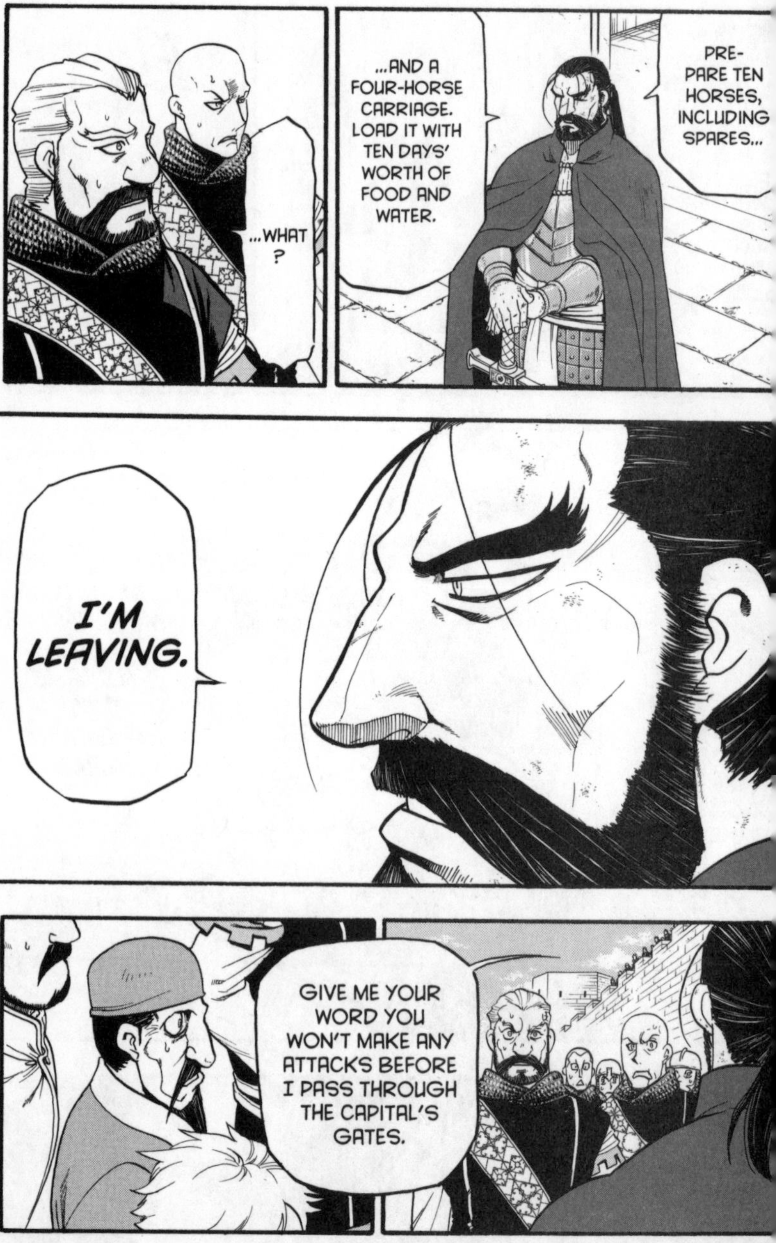
PRE-PARE TEN HORSES, INCLUDING SPARES...
...AND A FOUR-HORSE CARRIAGE. LOAD IT WITH TEN DAYS' WORTH OF FOOD AND WATER.
...WHAT ?
I'M LEAVING.
GIVE ME YOUR WORD YOU WON'T MAKE ANY ATTACKS BEFORE I PASS THROUGH THE CAPITAL'S GATES.

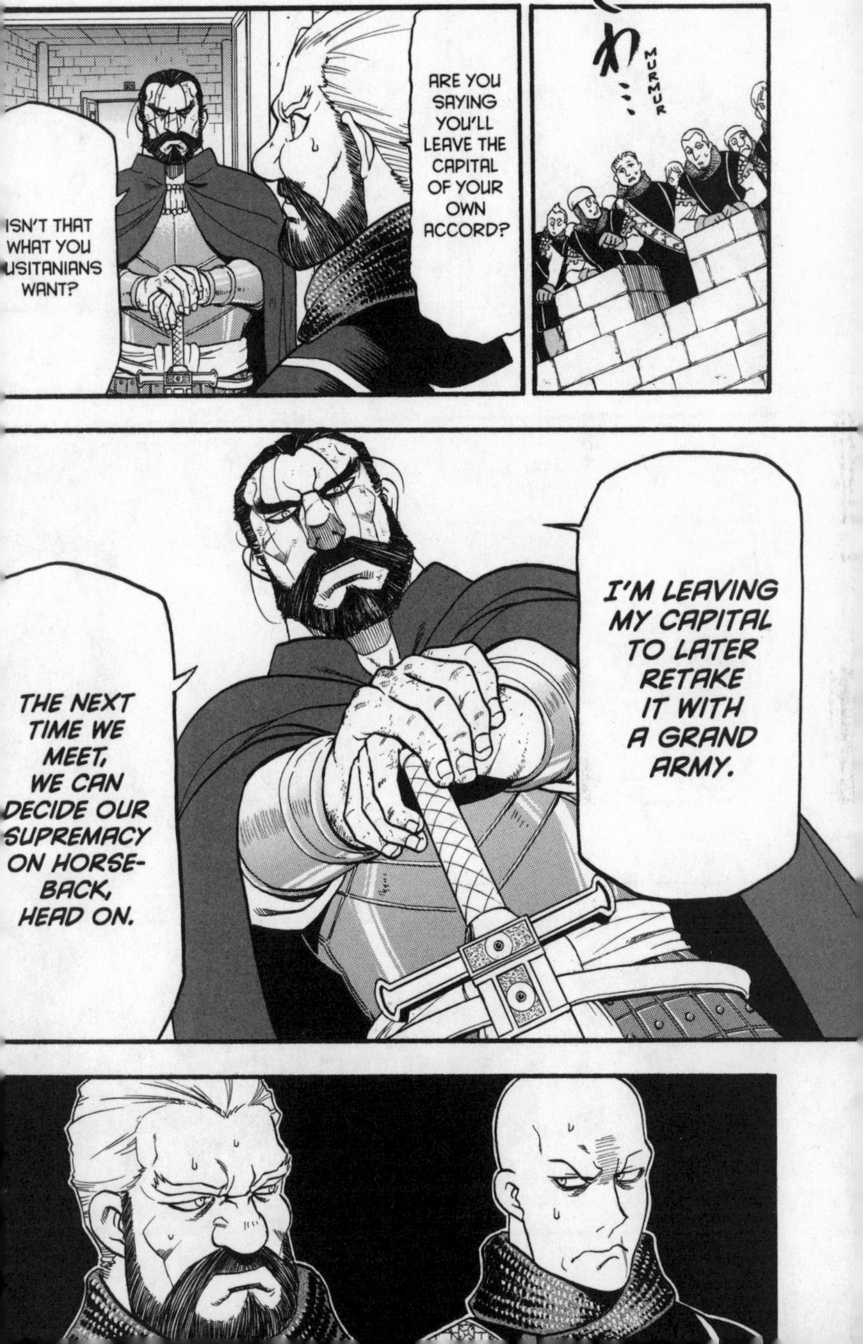
ざわ…
MURMUR
ARE YOU SAYING YOU'LL LEAVE THE CAPITAL OF YOUR OWN ACCORD?
ISN'T THAT WHAT YOU USITANIANS WANT?
I'M LEAVING MY CAPITAL TO LATER RETAKE IT WITH A GRAND ARMY.
THE NEXT TIME WE MEET, WE CAN DECIDE OUR SUPREMACY ON HORSE-BACK, HEAD ON.

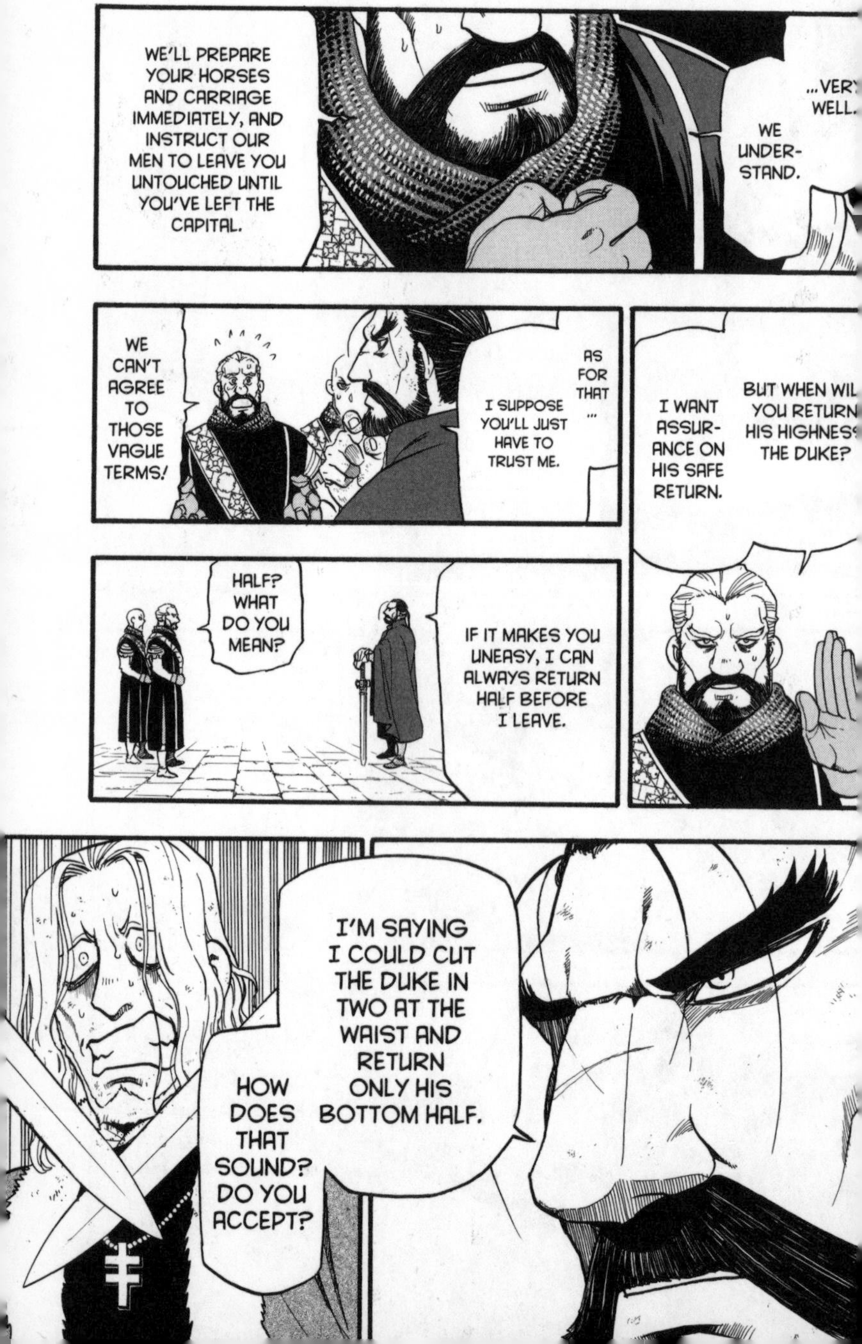
...VERY WELL.
WE UNDERSTAND.
WE'LL PREPARE YOUR HORSES AND CARRIAGE IMMEDIATELY, AND INSTRUCT OUR MEN TO LEAVE YOU UNTOUCHED UNTIL YOU'VE LEFT THE CAPITAL.
BUT WHEN WILL YOU RETURN HIS HIGHNESS THE DUKE?
I WANT ASSURANCE ON HIS SAFE RETURN.
AS FOR THAT ...
I SUPPOSE YOU'LL JUST HAVE TO TRUST ME.
WE CAN'T AGREE TO THOSE VAGUE TERMS!
IF IT MAKES YOU UNEASY, I CAN ALWAYS RETURN HALF BEFORE I LEAVE.
HALF? WHAT DO YOU MEAN?
I'M SAYING I COULD CUT THE DUKE IN TWO AT THE WAIST AND RETURN ONLY HIS BOTTOM HALF.
HOW DOES THAT SOUND? DO YOU ACCEPT?

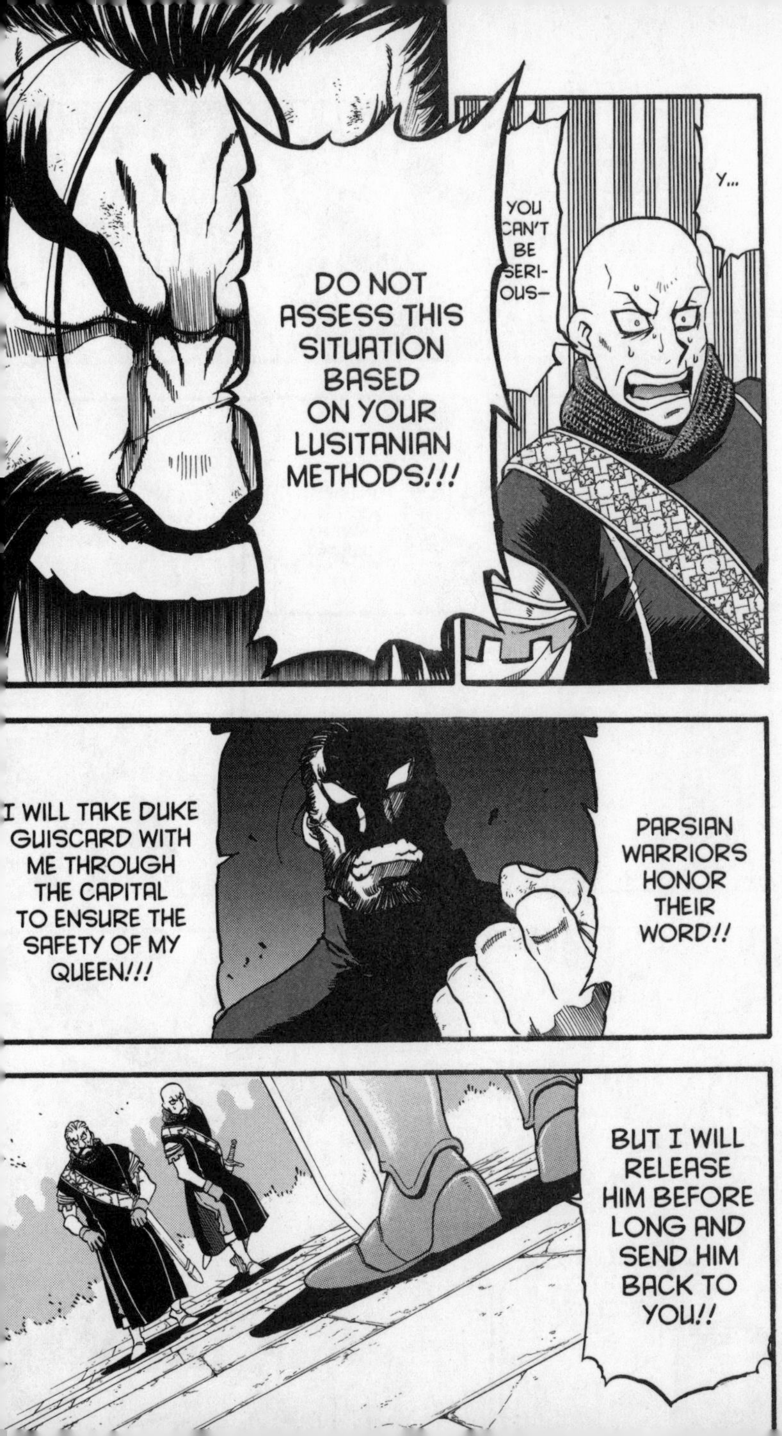
Y...
YOU CAN'T BE SERI-OUS—
DO NOT ASSESS THIS SITUATION BASED ON YOUR LUSITANIAN METHODS!!!
PARSIAN WARRIORS HONOR THEIR WORD!!
I WILL TAKE DUKE GUISCARD WITH ME THROUGH THE CAPITAL TO ENSURE THE SAFETY OF MY QUEEN!!!
BUT I WILL RELEASE HIM BEFORE LONG AND SEND HIM BACK TO YOU!!

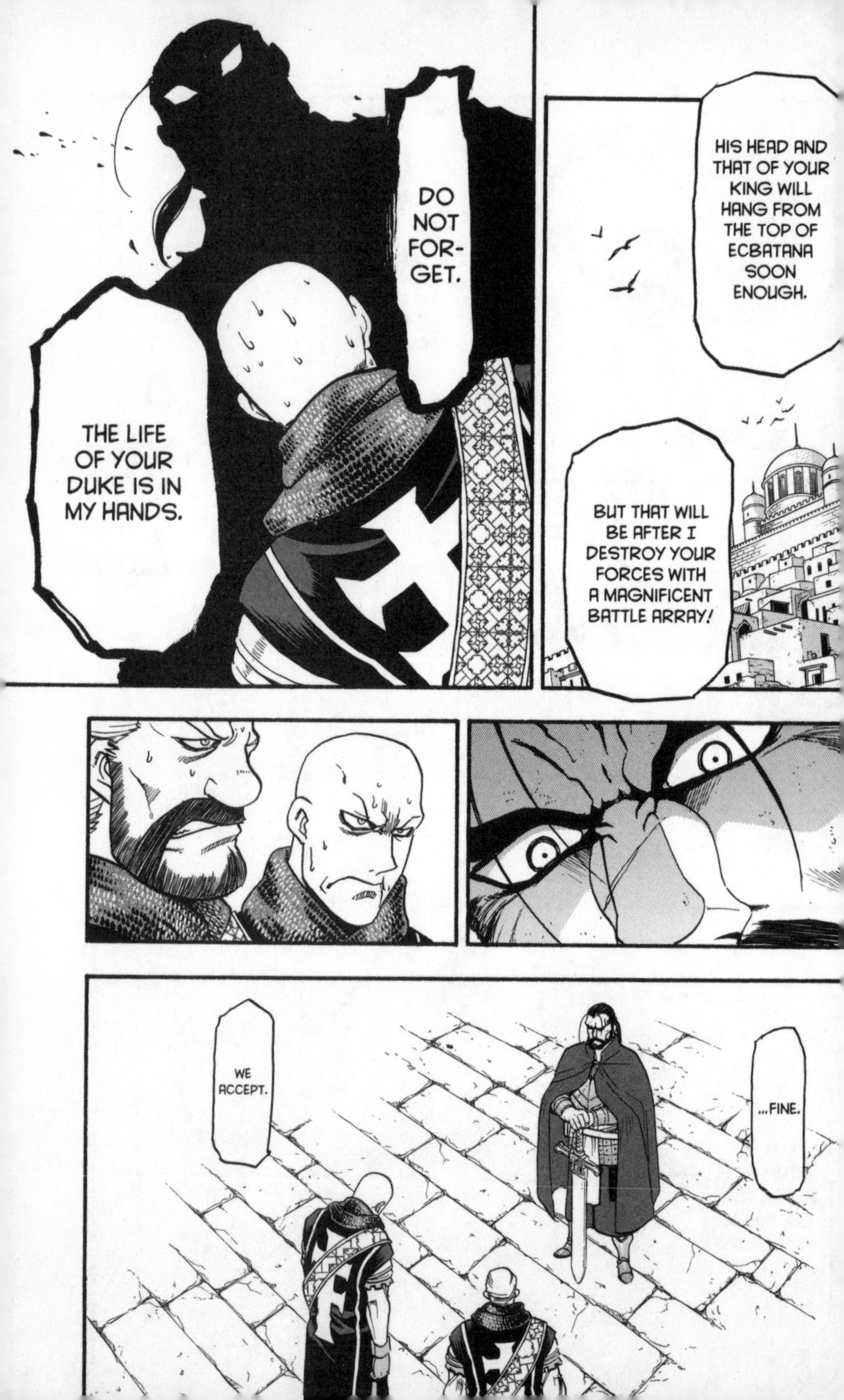
HIS HEAD AND THAT OF YOUR KING WILL HANG FROM THE TOP OF ECBATANA SOON ENOUGH.
BUT THAT WILL BE AFTER I DESTROY YOUR FORCES WITH A MAGNIFICENT BATTLE ARRAY!
DO NOT FOR-GET.
THE LIFE OF YOUR DUKE IS IN MY HANDS.
...FINE.
WE ACCEPT.

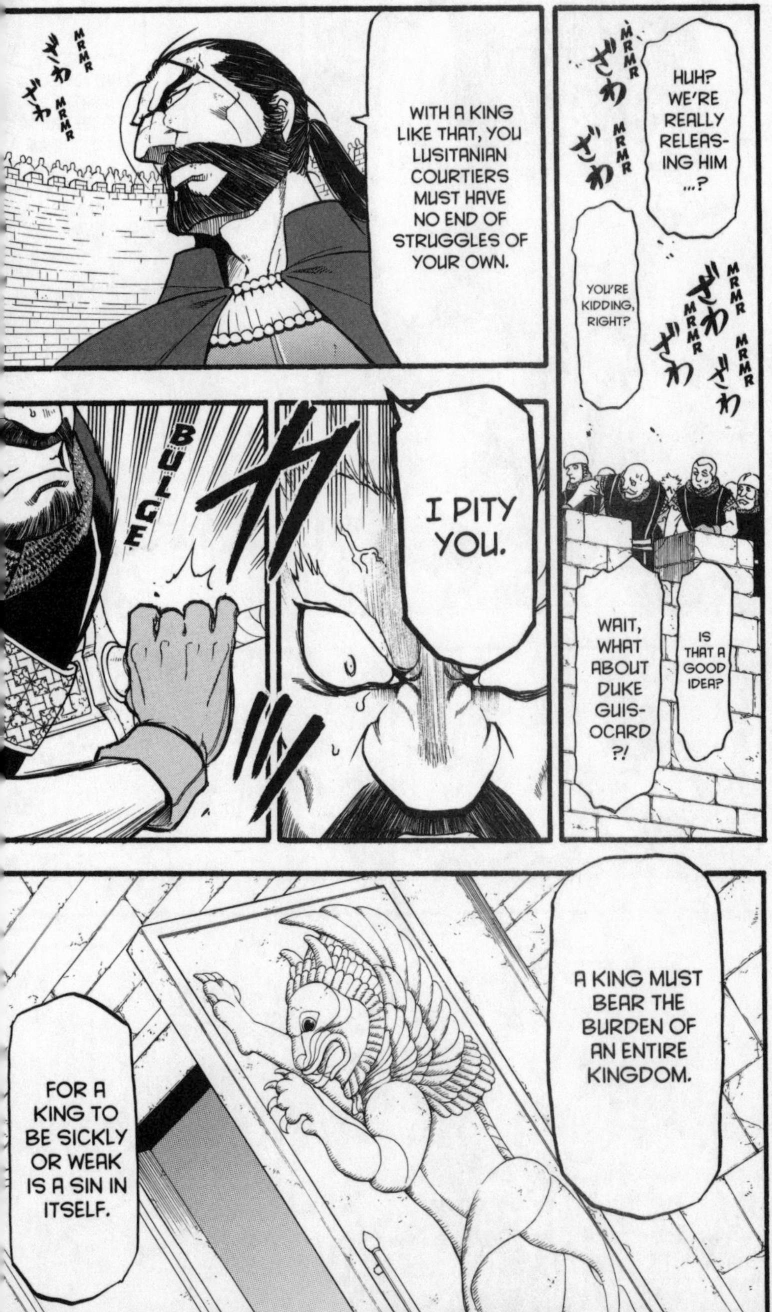

MRMR
ざわ
MRMR
ざわ
HUH? WE'RE REALLY RELEAS-ING HIM ...?
YOU'RE KIDDING, RIGHT?
MRMR
ざわ
MRMR
ざわ
MRMR
ざわ
IS THAT A GOOD IDEA?
WAIT, WHAT ABOUT DUKE GUIS-OCARD ?!
WITH A KING LIKE THAT, YOU LUSITANIAN COURTIERS MUST HAVE NO END OF STRUGGLES OF YOUR OWN.
MRMR
ざわ
MRMR
ざわ
I PITY YOU.
BULGE
A KING MUST BEAR THE BURDEN OF AN ENTIRE KINGDOM.
FOR A KING TO BE SICKLY OR WEAK IS A SIN IN ITSELF.

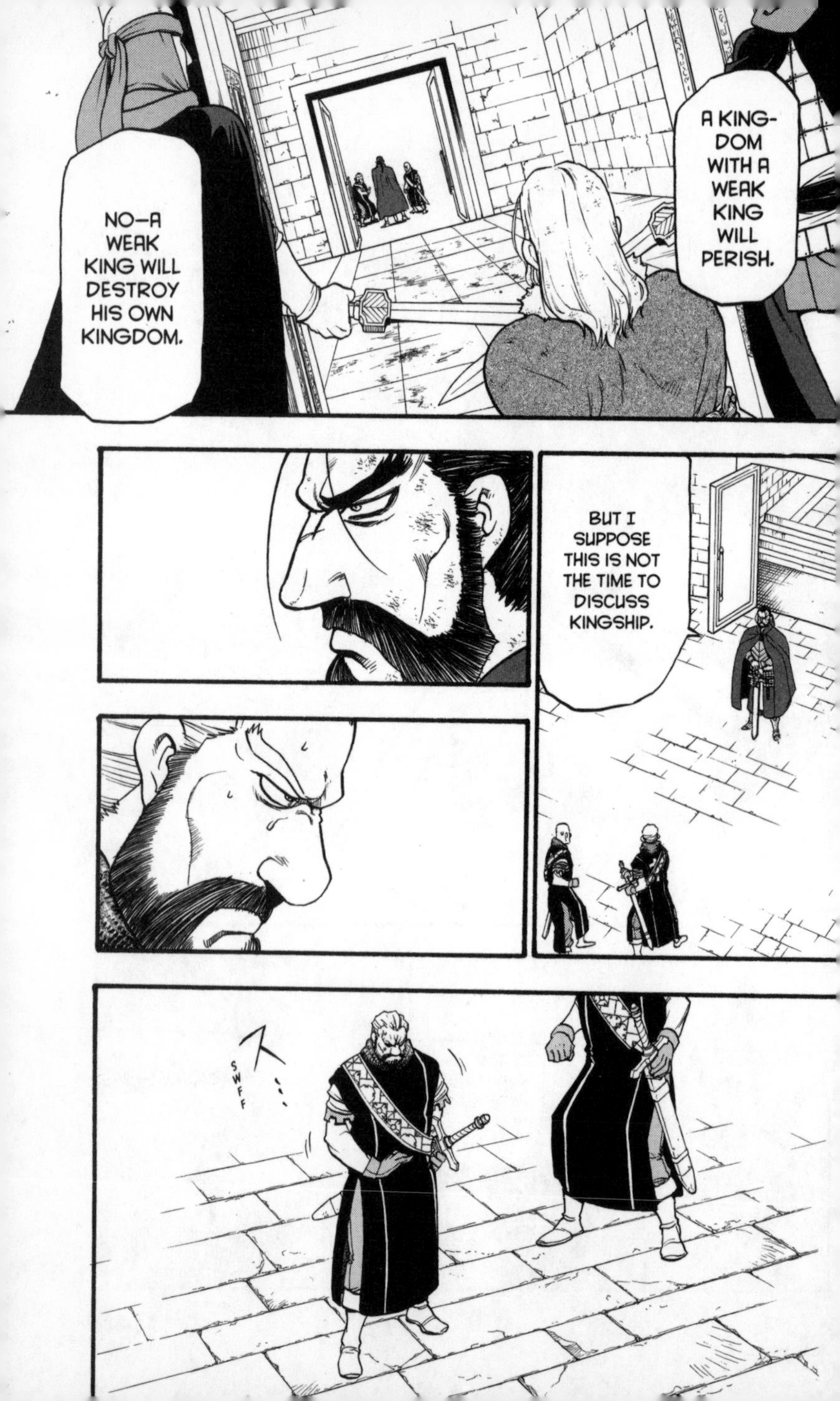

A KING-DOM WITH A WEAK KING WILL PERISH.
NO—A WEAK KING WILL DESTROY HIS OWN KINGDOM.
BUT I SUPPOSE THIS IS NOT THE TIME TO DISCUSS KINGSHIP.
SWFF

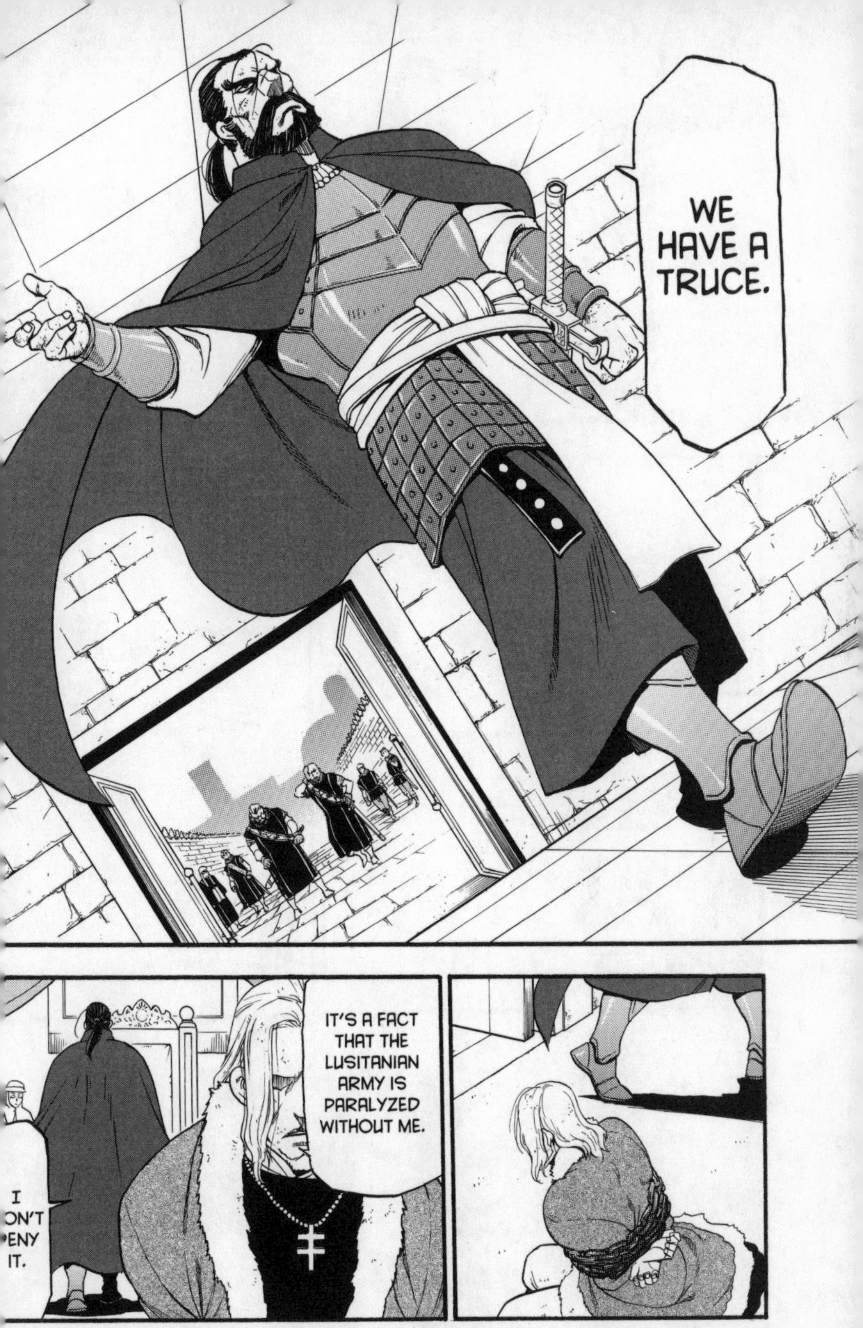
WE HAVE A TRUCE.
IT'S A FACT THAT THE LUSITANIAN ARMY IS PARALYZED WITHOUT ME.
I ON'T ENY IT.

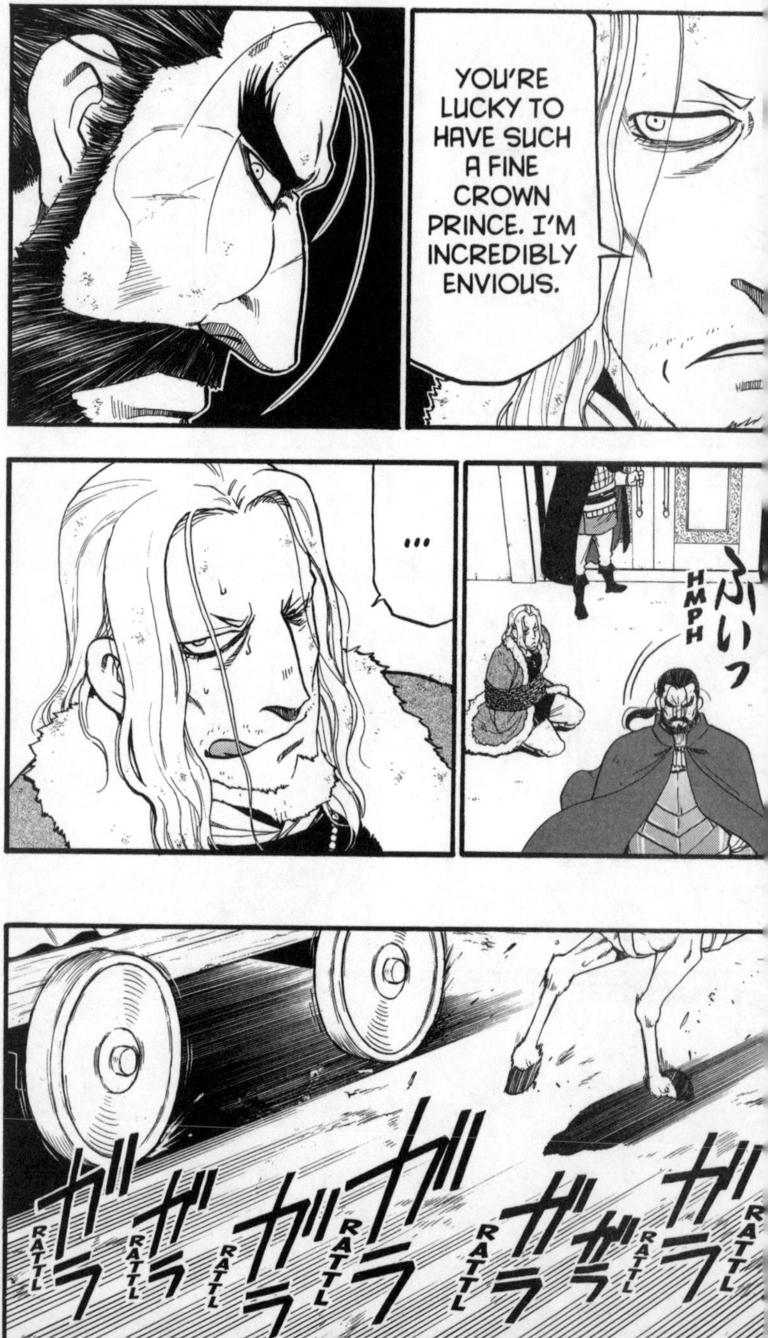
YOU'RE LUCKY TO HAVE SUCH A FINE CROWN PRINCE. I'M INCREDIBLY ENVIOUS.
ふいっ
HMPH
...
ガラ
RATTL
ガラ
RATTL
ガラ
RATTL
ガラ
RATTL
ガラ
RATTL
ガラ
RATTL
ガラ
RATTL

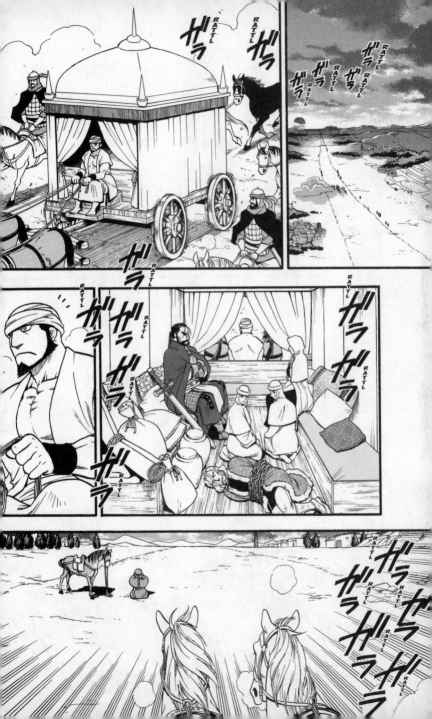

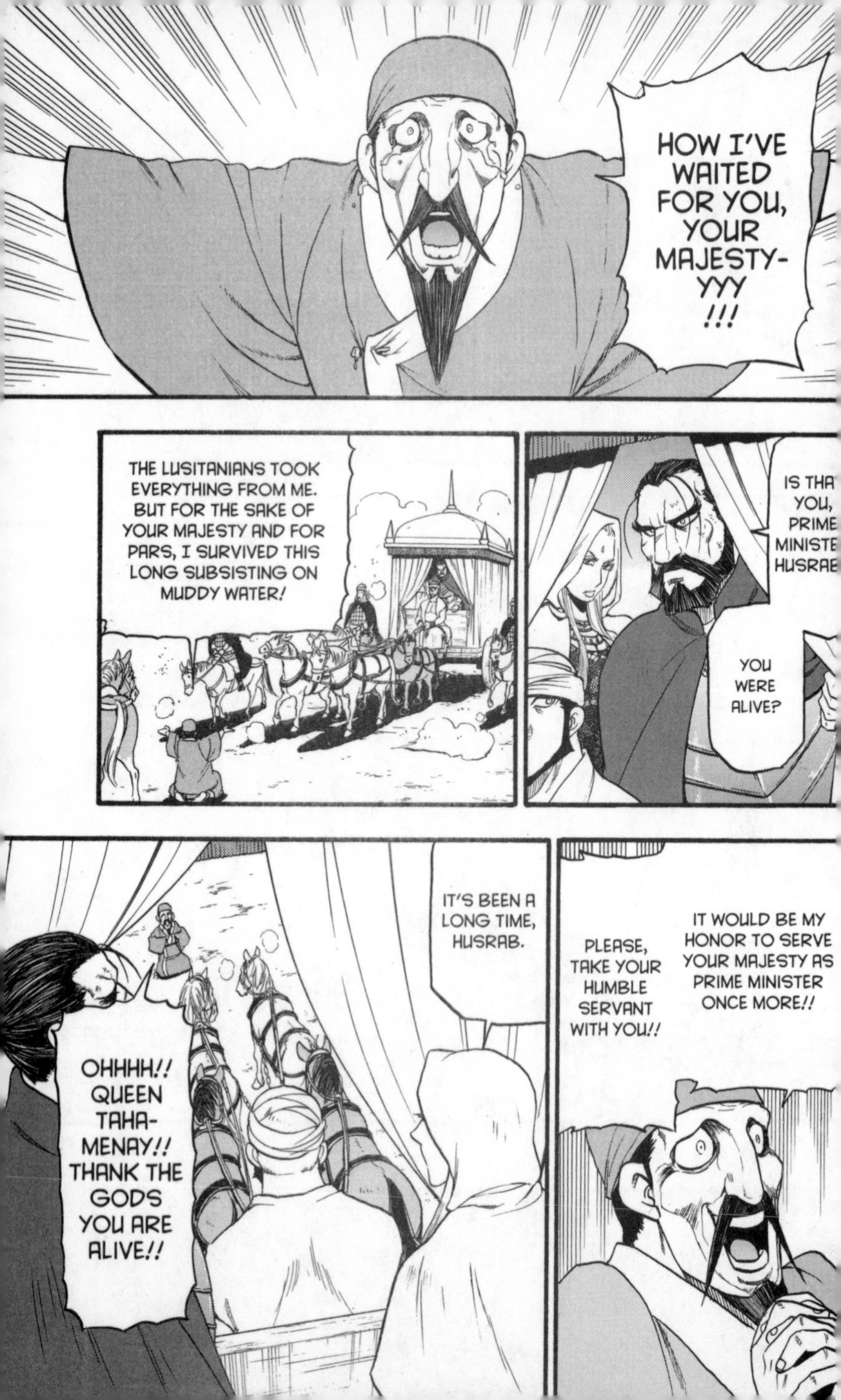
HOW I'VE WAITED FOR YOU, YOUR MAJESTY-YYY!!!
IS THA YOU, PRIME MINISTE HUSRA
YOU WERE ALIVE?
THE LUSITANIANS TOOK EVERYTHING FROM ME. BUT FOR THE SAKE OF YOUR MAJESTY AND FOR PARS, I SURVIVED THIS LONG SUBSISTING ON MUDDY WATER!
IT WOULD BE MY HONOR TO SERVE YOUR MAJESTY AS PRIME MINISTER ONCE MORE!!
PLEASE, TAKE YOUR HUMBLE SERVANT WITH YOU!!
IT'S BEEN A LONG TIME, HUSRAB.
OHHHH!! QUEEN TAHA-MENAY!! THANK THE GODS YOU ARE ALIVE!!

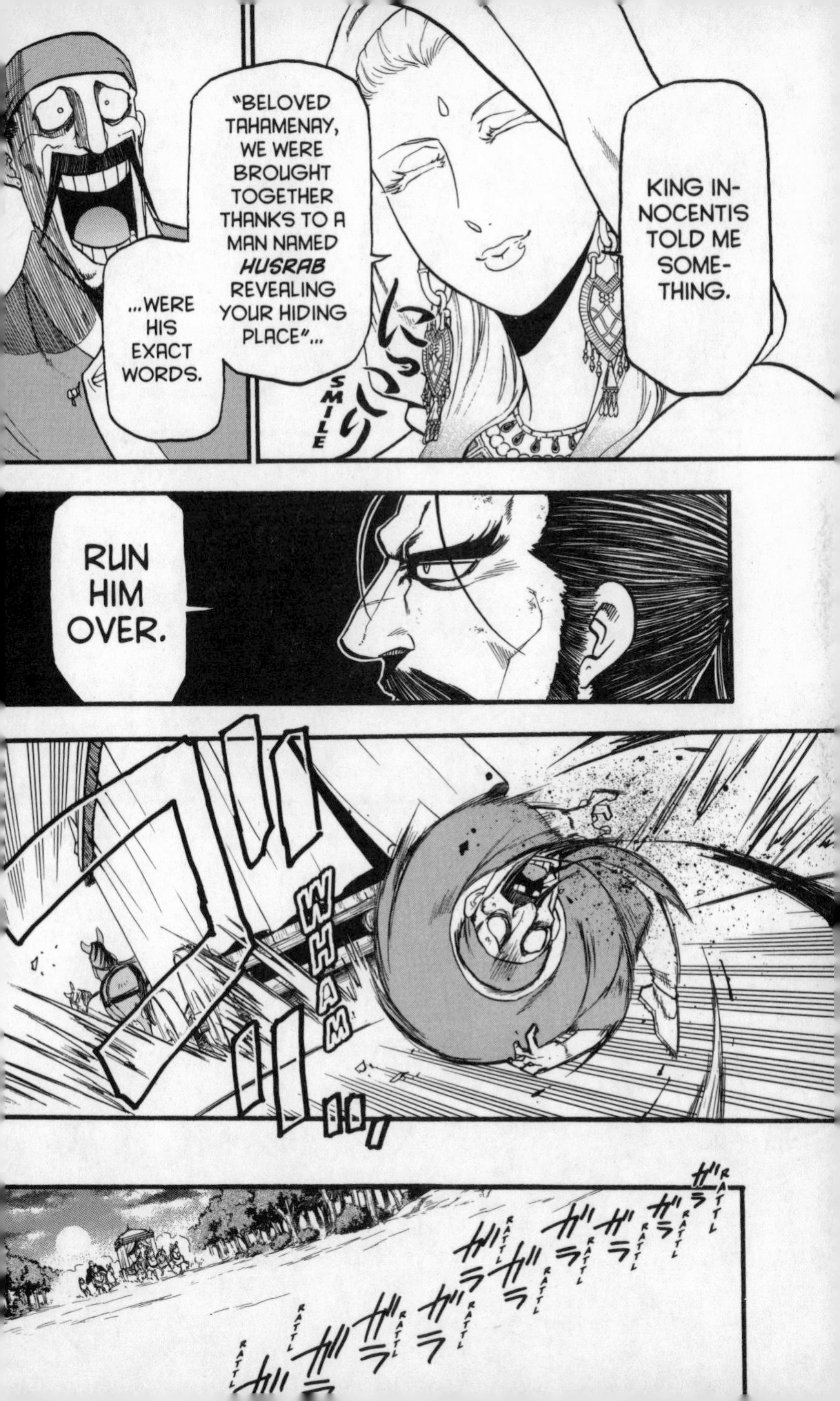
KING IN-
NOCENTIS
TOLD ME
SOME-
THING.
SMILE
"BELOVED TAHAMENAY, WE WERE BROUGHT TOGETHER THANKS TO A MAN NAMED *HUSRAB* REVEALING YOUR HIDING PLACE"...
...WERE HIS EXACT WORDS.
RUN HIM OVER.
WHAM
RATTL
RATTL
RATTL
RATTL
RATTL
RATTL
RATTL
RATTL
RATTL
RATTL

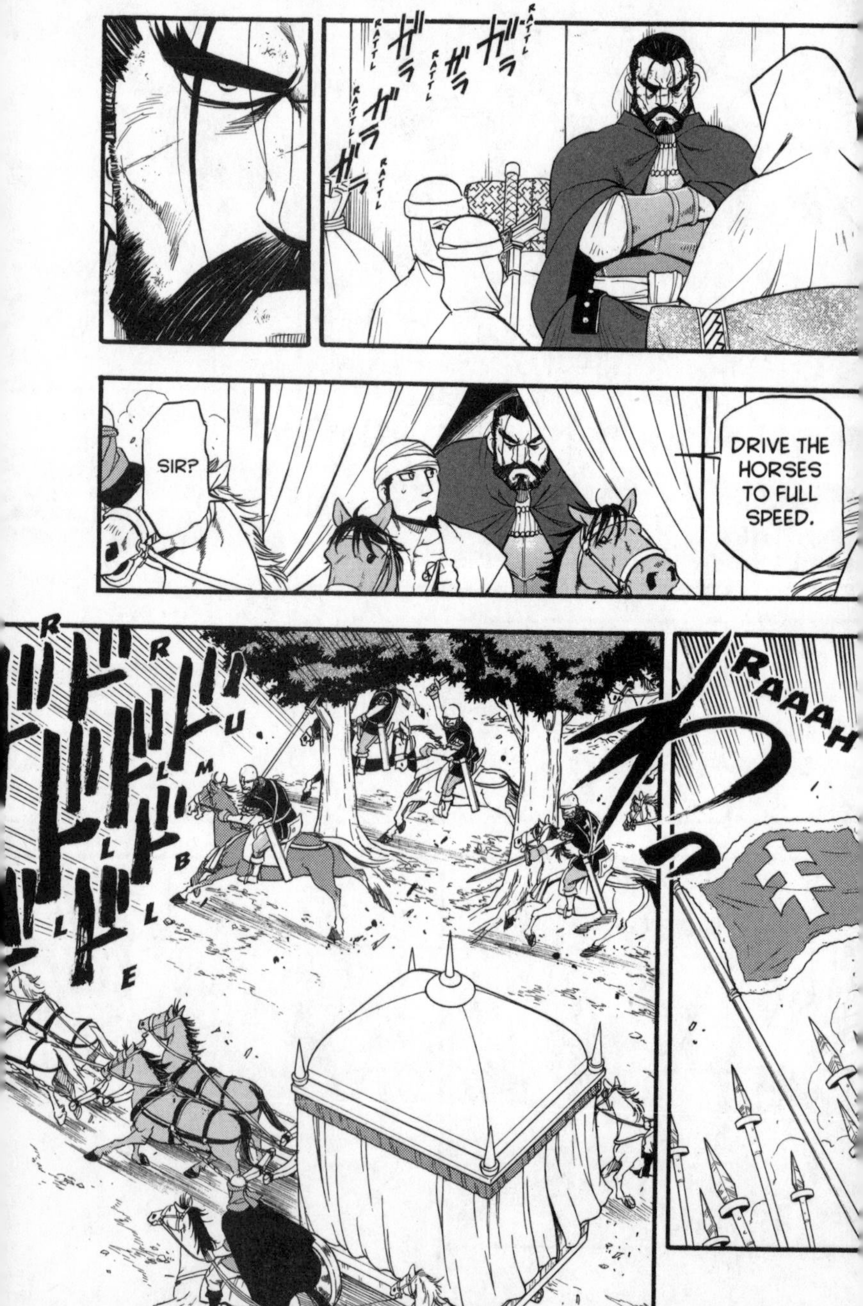
RATTL RATTL RATTL RATTL
DRIVE THE HORSES TO FULL SPEED.
SIR?
RAAAAH
RUMBLE

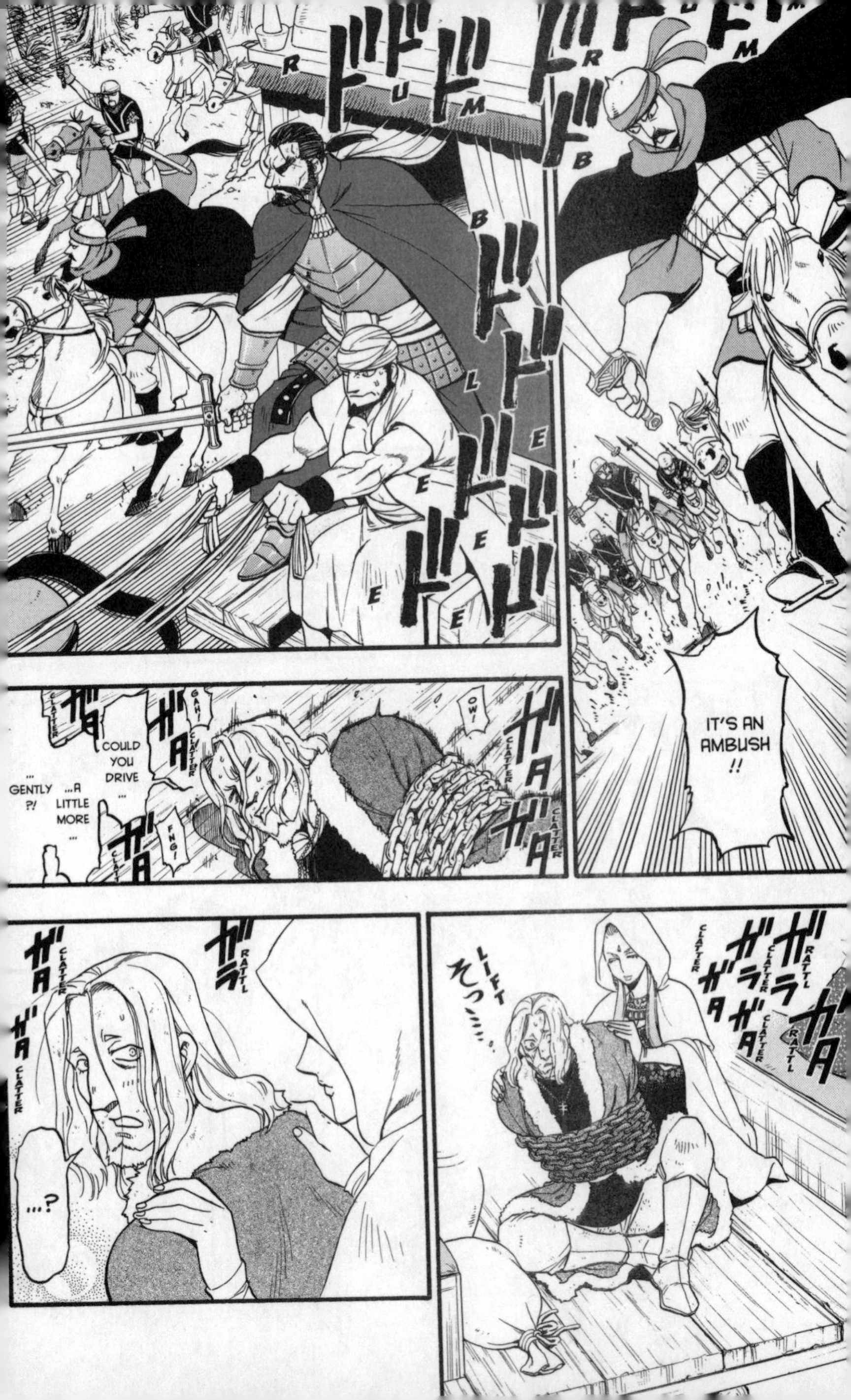
ドドド
RUMB
ドドドド
RUMBLE
ドドドドドド
BLEEEE
IT'S AN AMBUSH !!
ガタ
CLATTER
ガタ
CLATTER
OW!
GAH!
ガタ
CLATTER
COULD YOU DRIVE ...
...A LITTLE MORE ...
... GENTLY ?!
FNG!
ガタ
CLATT
ガラ
RATTL
ガラ
RATTL
ガタ
CLATTER
ガタ
CLATTER
そっ
LIFT
ガラ
RATTL
ガタ
CLATTER
ガタ
CLATTER
...?

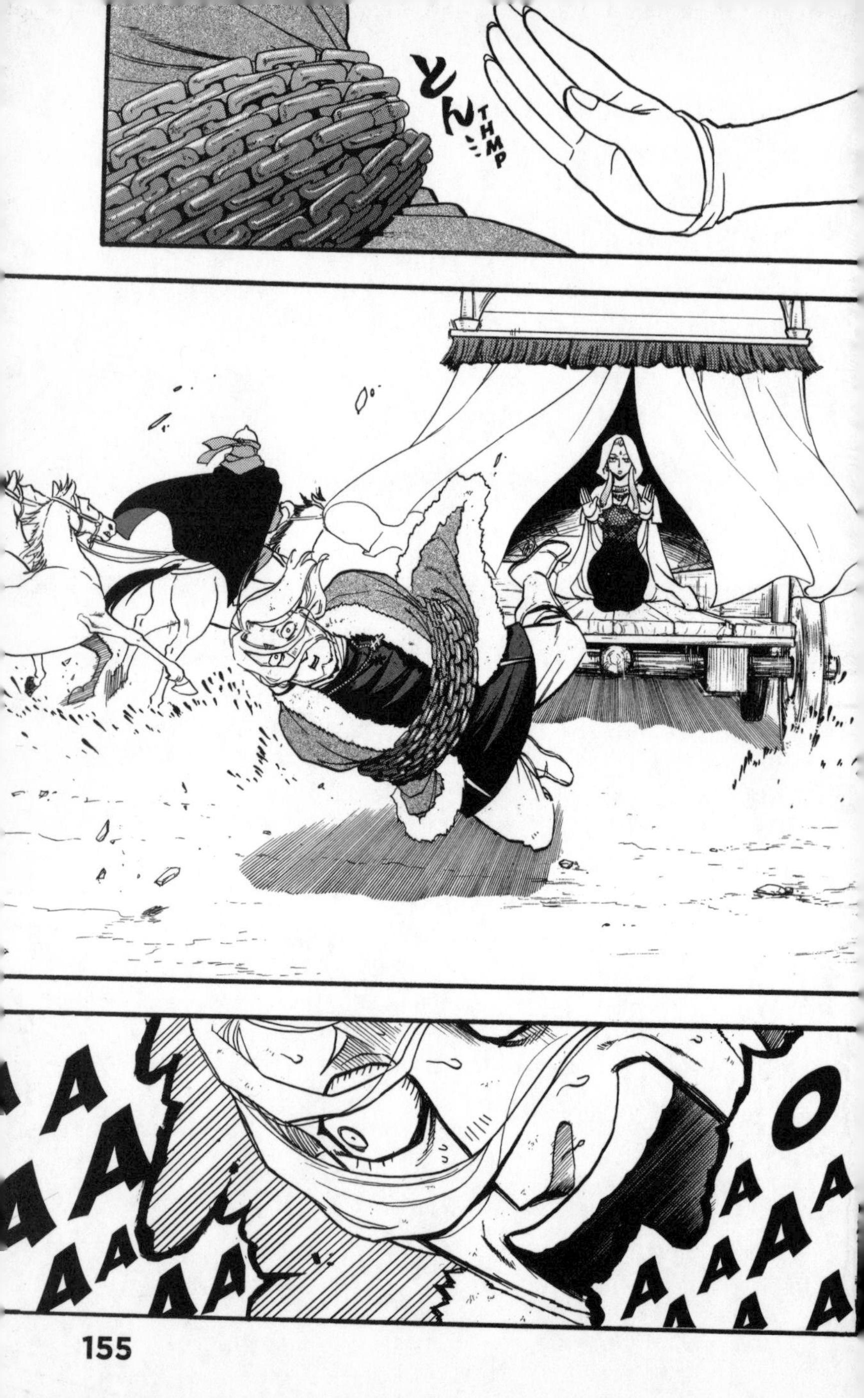
とん
THMP
OAAAAAAAAAA
AAAAAAAAAAA

THE HEROIC LEGEND OF
ARSLAN

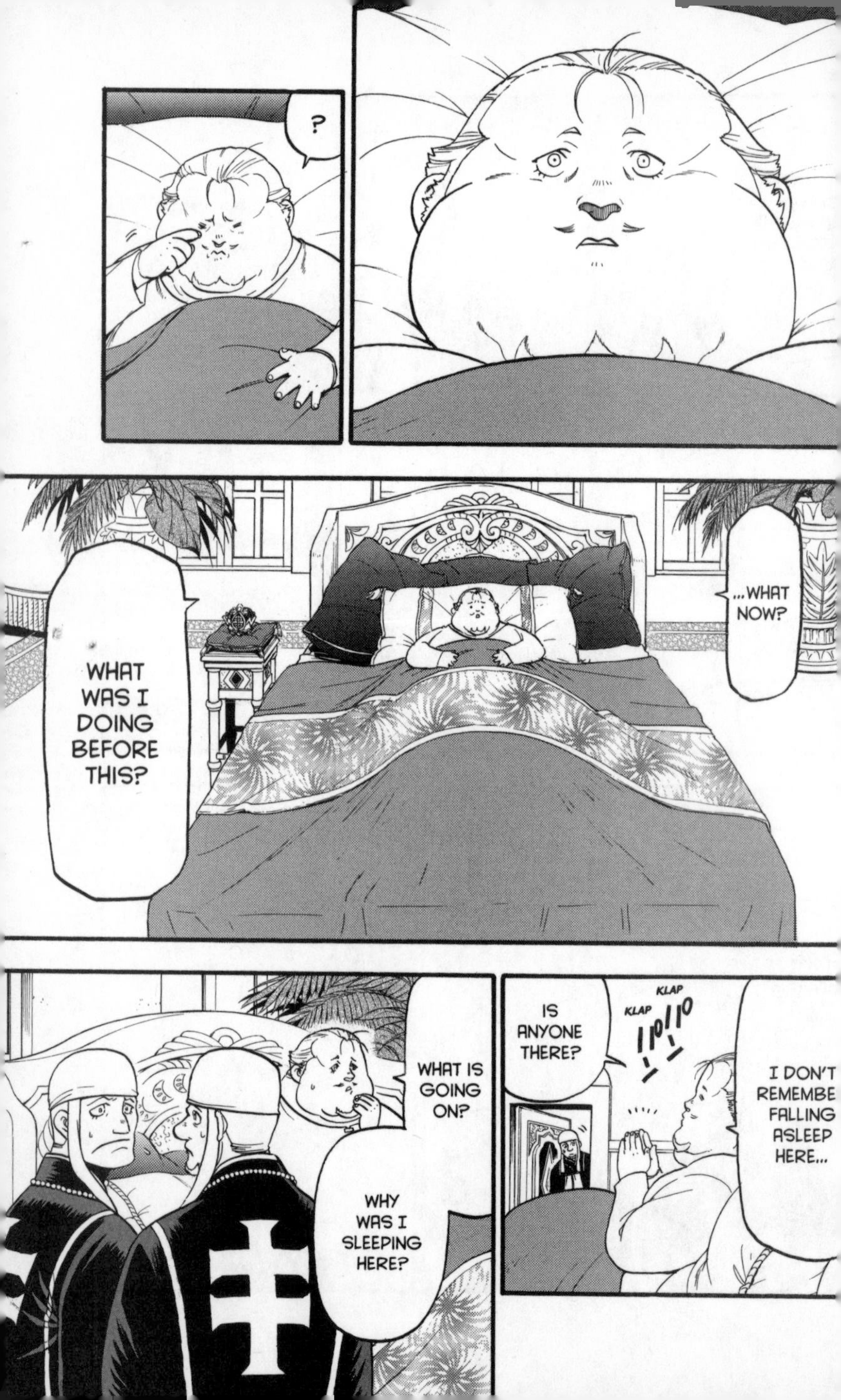
?
...WHAT NOW?
WHAT WAS I DOING BEFORE THIS?
I DON'T REMEMBE FALLING ASLEEP HERE...
KLAP
KLAP
IS ANYONE THERE?
WHAT IS GOING ON?
WHY WAS I SLEEPING HERE?

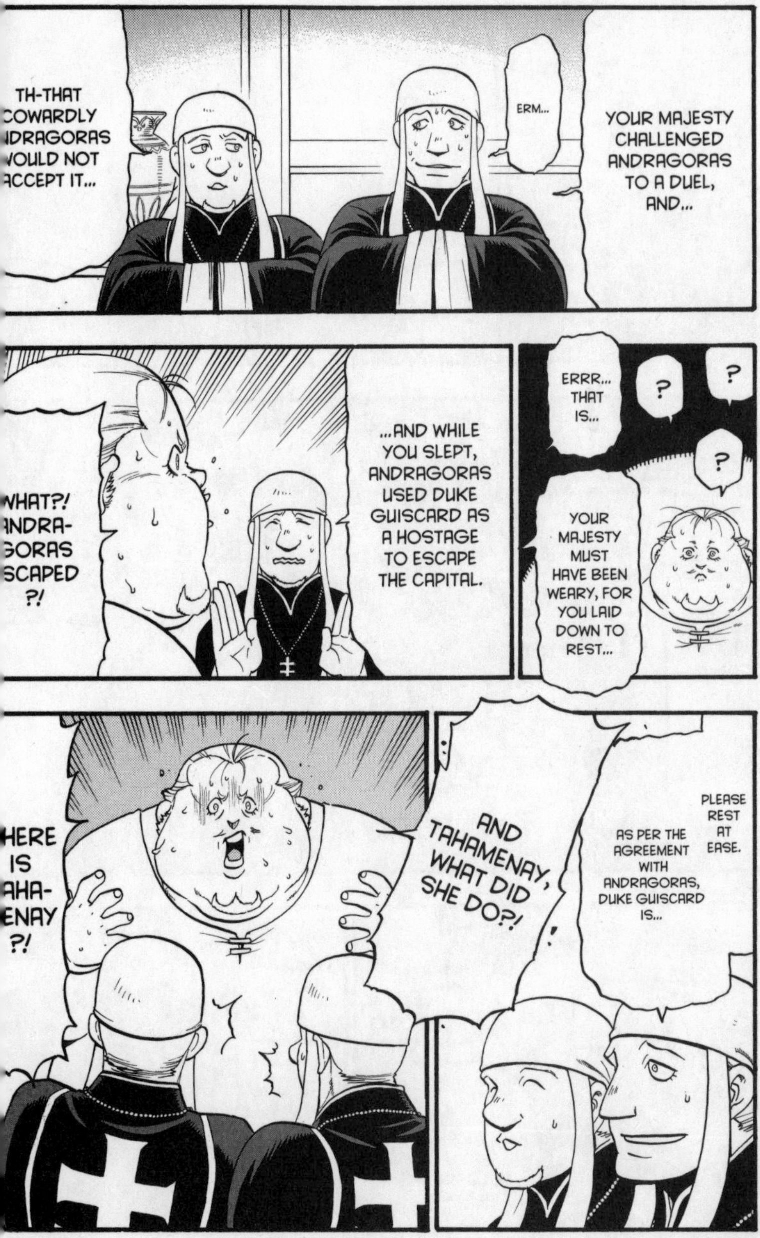
YOUR MAJESTY CHALLENGED ANDRAGORAS TO A DUEL, AND...
ERM...
TH-THAT COWARDLY NDRAGORAS WOULD NOT ACCEPT IT...
?
?
ERRR... THAT IS...
?
YOUR MAJESTY MUST HAVE BEEN WEARY, FOR YOU LAID DOWN TO REST...
...AND WHILE YOU SLEPT, ANDRAGORAS USED DUKE GUISCARD AS A HOSTAGE TO ESCAPE THE CAPITAL.
WHAT?! NDRA-GORAS SCAPED ?!
PLEASE REST AT EASE.
AS PER THE AGREEMENT WITH ANDRAGORAS, DUKE GUISCARD IS...
AND TAHAMENAY, WHAT DID SHE DO?!
HERE IS AHA-ENAY ?!

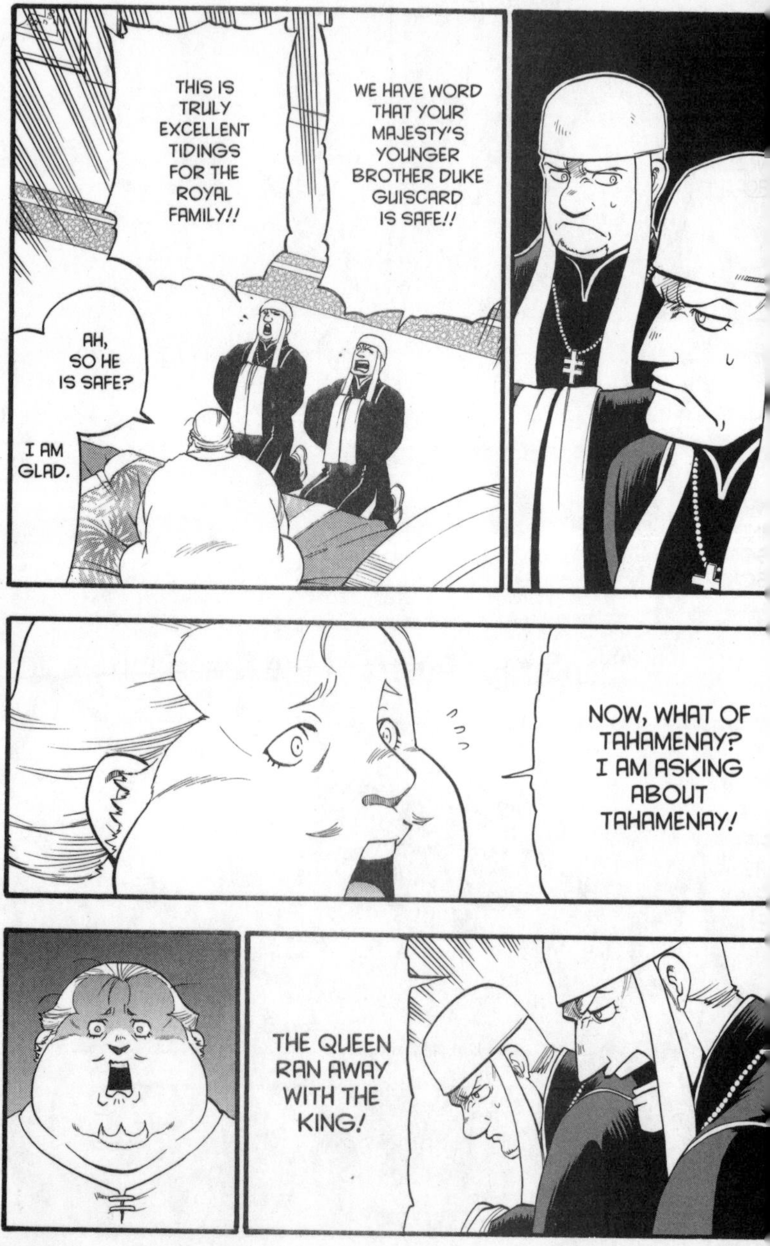
WE HAVE WORD THAT YOUR MAJESTY'S YOUNGER BROTHER DUKE GUISCARD IS SAFE!!
THIS IS TRULY EXCELLENT TIDINGS FOR THE ROYAL FAMILY!!
AH, SO HE IS SAFE?
I AM GLAD.
NOW, WHAT OF TAHAMENAY? I AM ASKING ABOUT TAHAMENAY!
THE QUEEN RAN AWAY WITH THE KING!

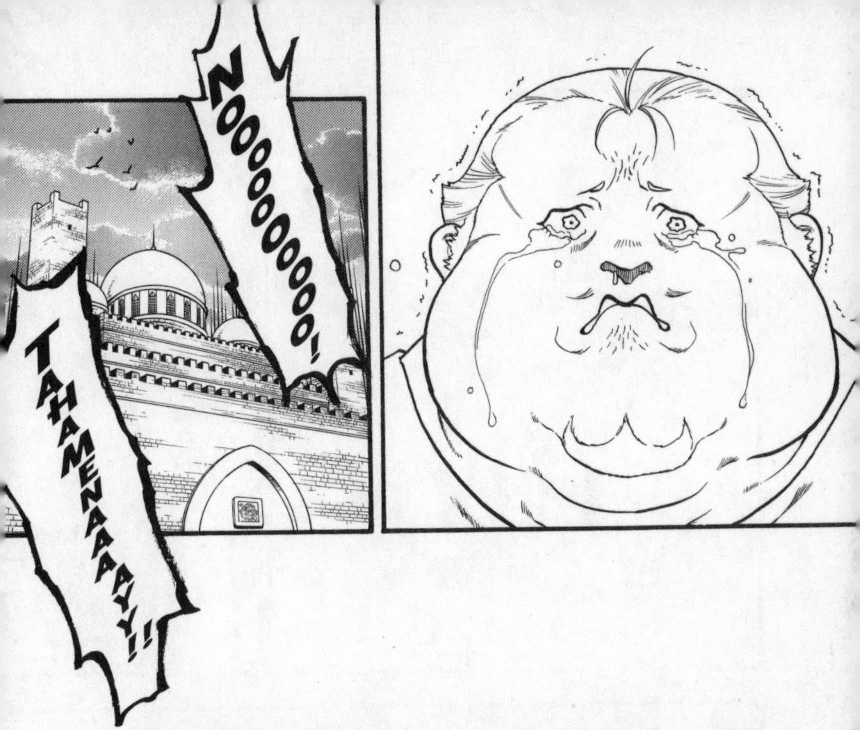
NOOOOOOOOOO!
TAHAMENAAAYY!!

Chapter 82: Rulers of the Grassland

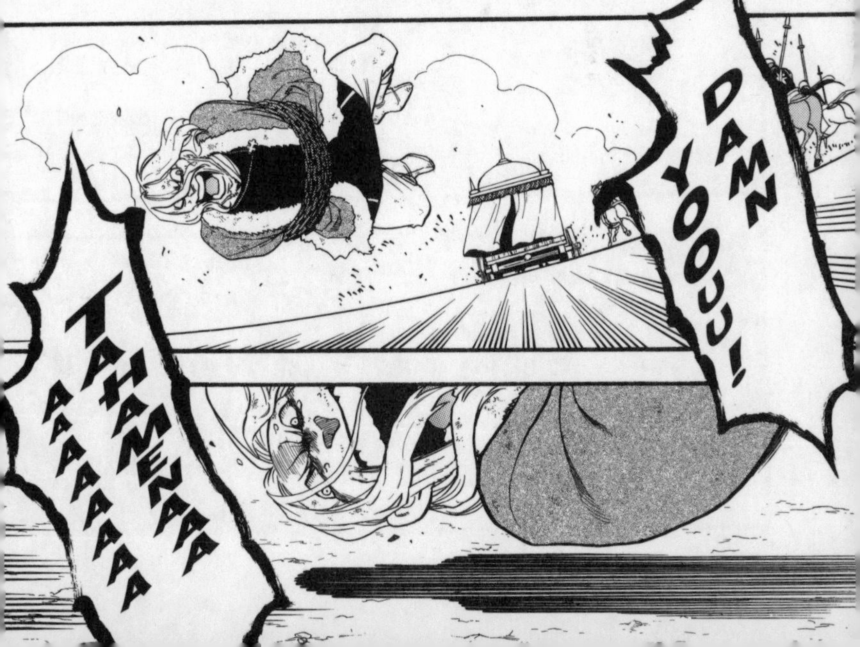
DAMN YOOUUU!
TAHAMENAAA AAAAAAA

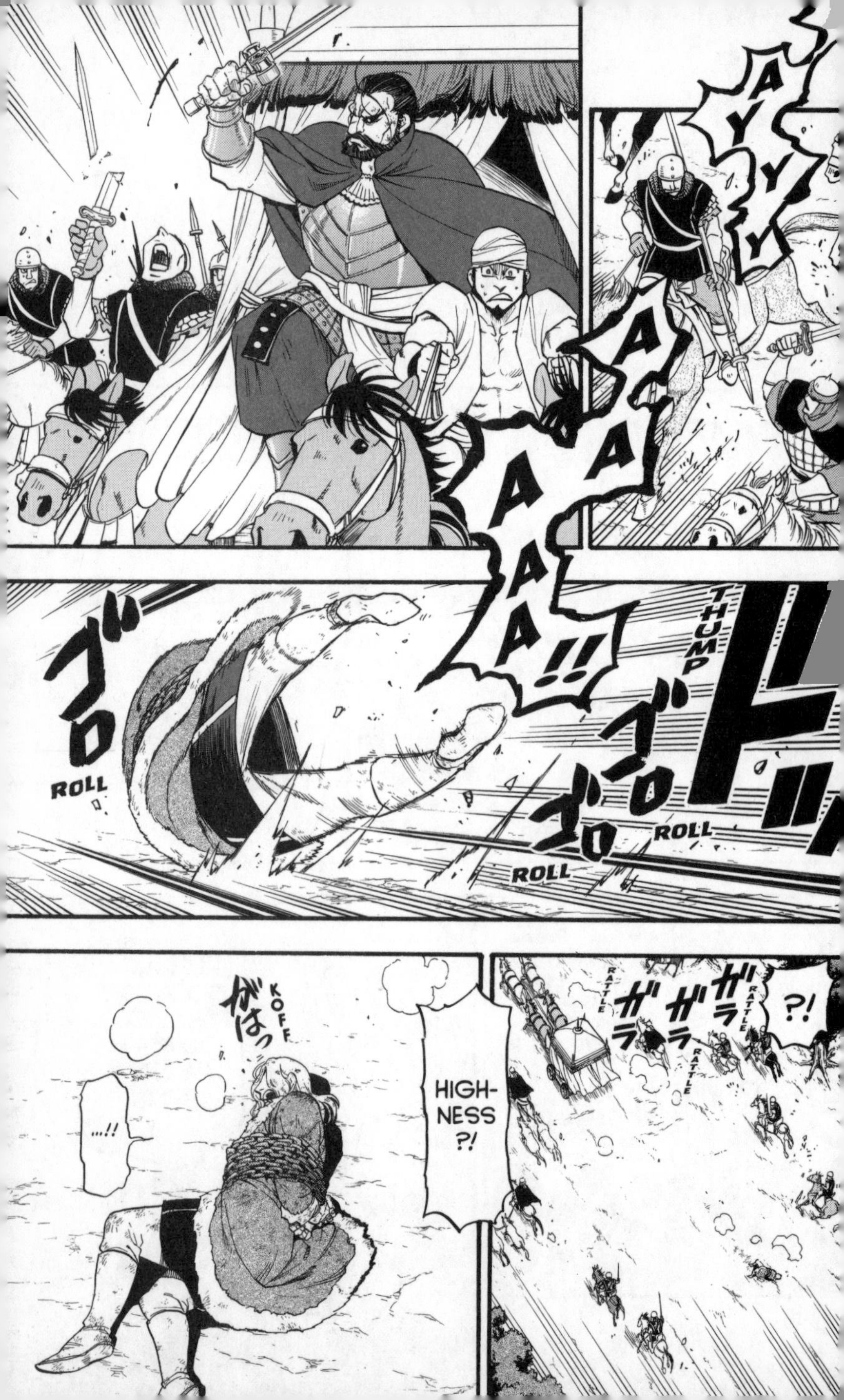
AYYYYAAAAAA!!
ドッ
THUMP
ゴロゴロ
ROLL
ROLL
ゴロ
ROLL
ガラ
RATTLE
ガラ
RATTLE
ガラ
RATTLE
?!
HIGHNESS?!
がはっ
KOFF
...!!

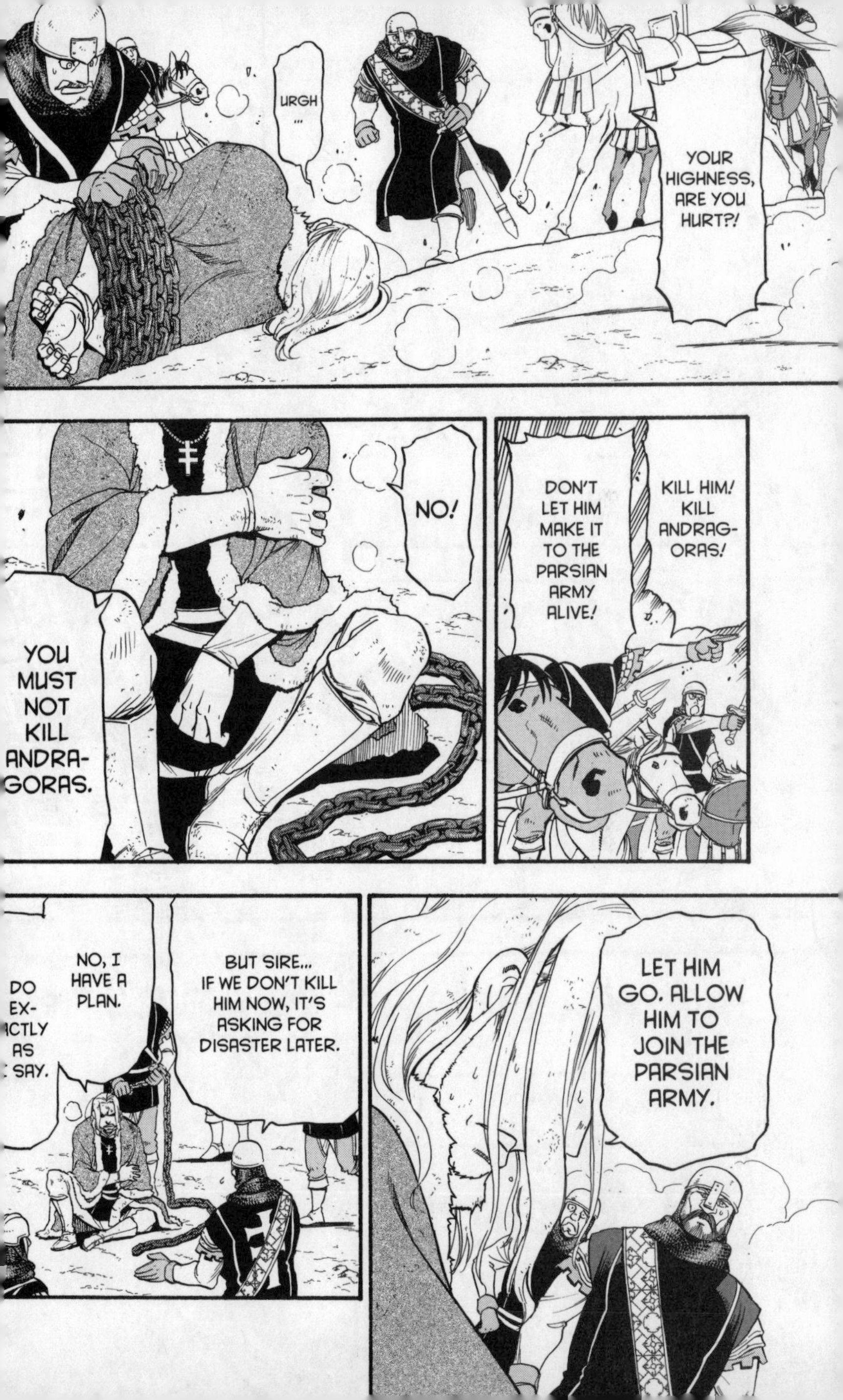
YOUR HIGHNESS, ARE YOU HURT?!
URGH ...
KILL HIM! KILL ANDRAG-ORAS!
DON'T LET HIM MAKE IT TO THE PARSIAN ARMY ALIVE!
NO!
YOU MUST NOT KILL ANDRA-GORAS.
LET HIM GO. ALLOW HIM TO JOIN THE PARSIAN ARMY.
BUT SIRE... IF WE DON'T KILL HIM NOW, IT'S ASKING FOR DISASTER LATER.
NO, I HAVE A PLAN.
DO EX-ACTLY AS SAY.

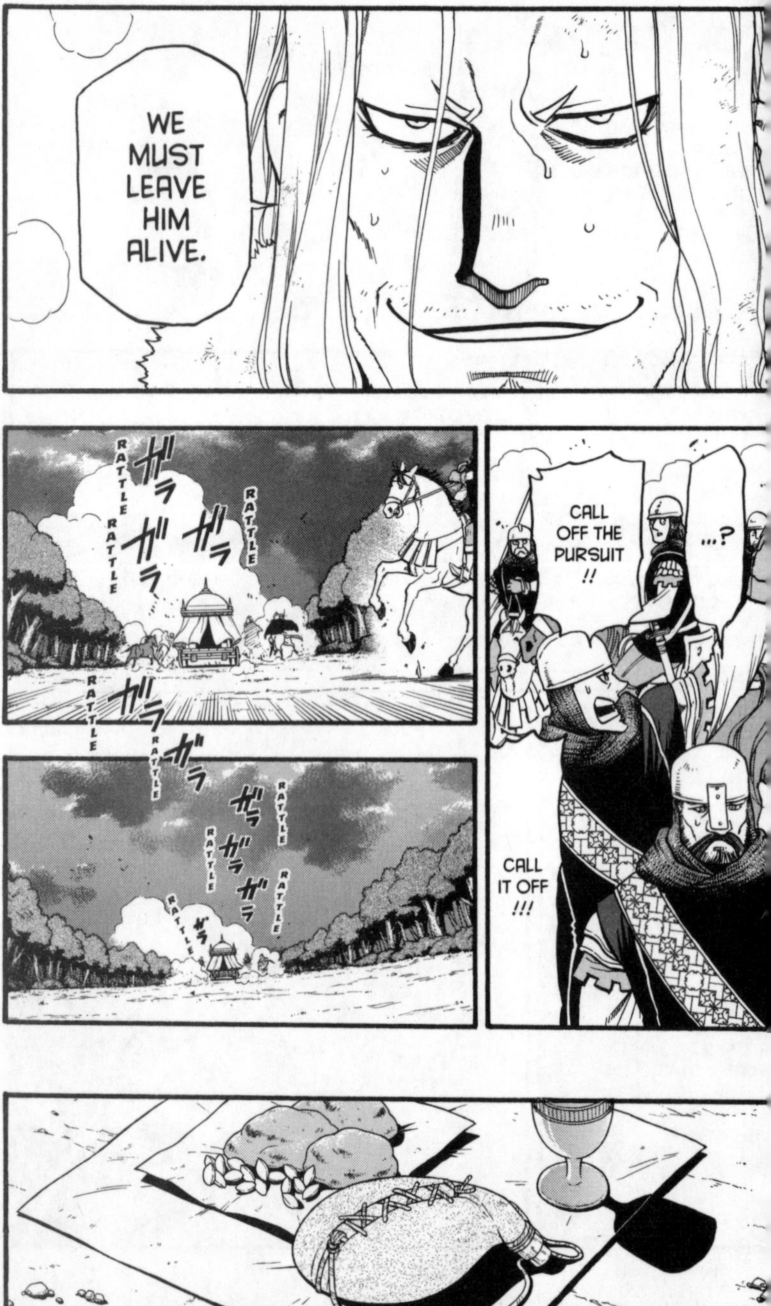
WE MUST LEAVE HIM ALIVE.
CALL OFF THE PURSUIT!!
...?
CALL IT OFF!!!
ガラ RATTLE
ガラ RATTLE
ガラ RATTLE
ガラ RATTLE
ガラ RATTLE
ガラ RATTLE
ガラ RATTLE
ガラ RATTLE
ガラ RATTLE

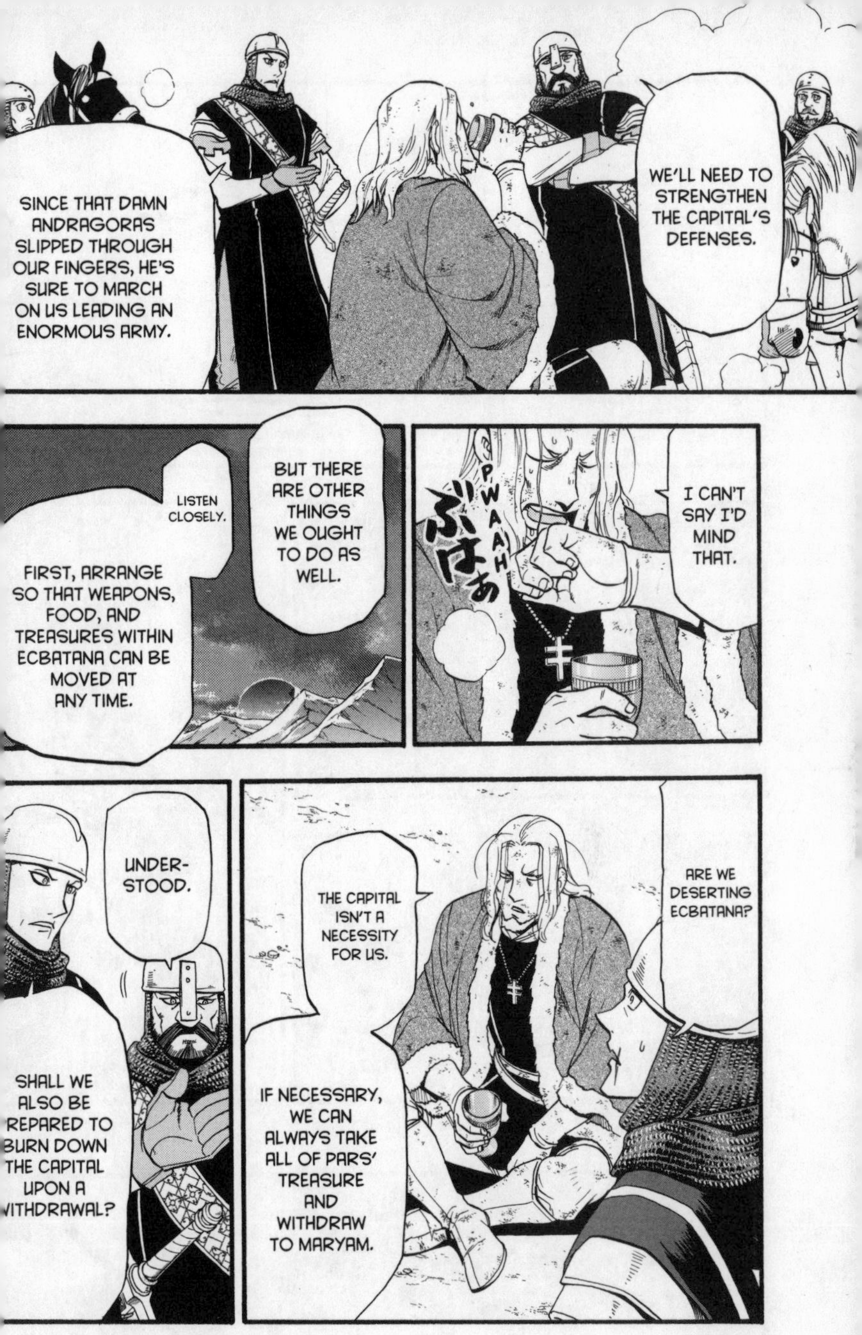
WE'LL NEED TO STRENGTHEN THE CAPITAL'S DEFENSES.
SINCE THAT DAMN ANDRAGORAS SLIPPED THROUGH OUR FINGERS, HE'S SURE TO MARCH ON US LEADING AN ENORMOUS ARMY.
I CAN'T SAY I'D MIND THAT.
PWAAH
ぶはぁ
BUT THERE ARE OTHER THINGS WE OUGHT TO DO AS WELL.
LISTEN CLOSELY.
FIRST, ARRANGE SO THAT WEAPONS, FOOD, AND TREASURES WITHIN ECBATANA CAN BE MOVED AT ANY TIME.
ARE WE DESERTING ECBATANA?
THE CAPITAL ISN'T A NECESSITY FOR US.
IF NECESSARY, WE CAN ALWAYS TAKE ALL OF PARS' TREASURE AND WITHDRAW TO MARYAM.
UNDER-STOOD.
SHALL WE ALSO BE REPARED TO BURN DOWN THE CAPITAL UPON A ITHDRAWAL?

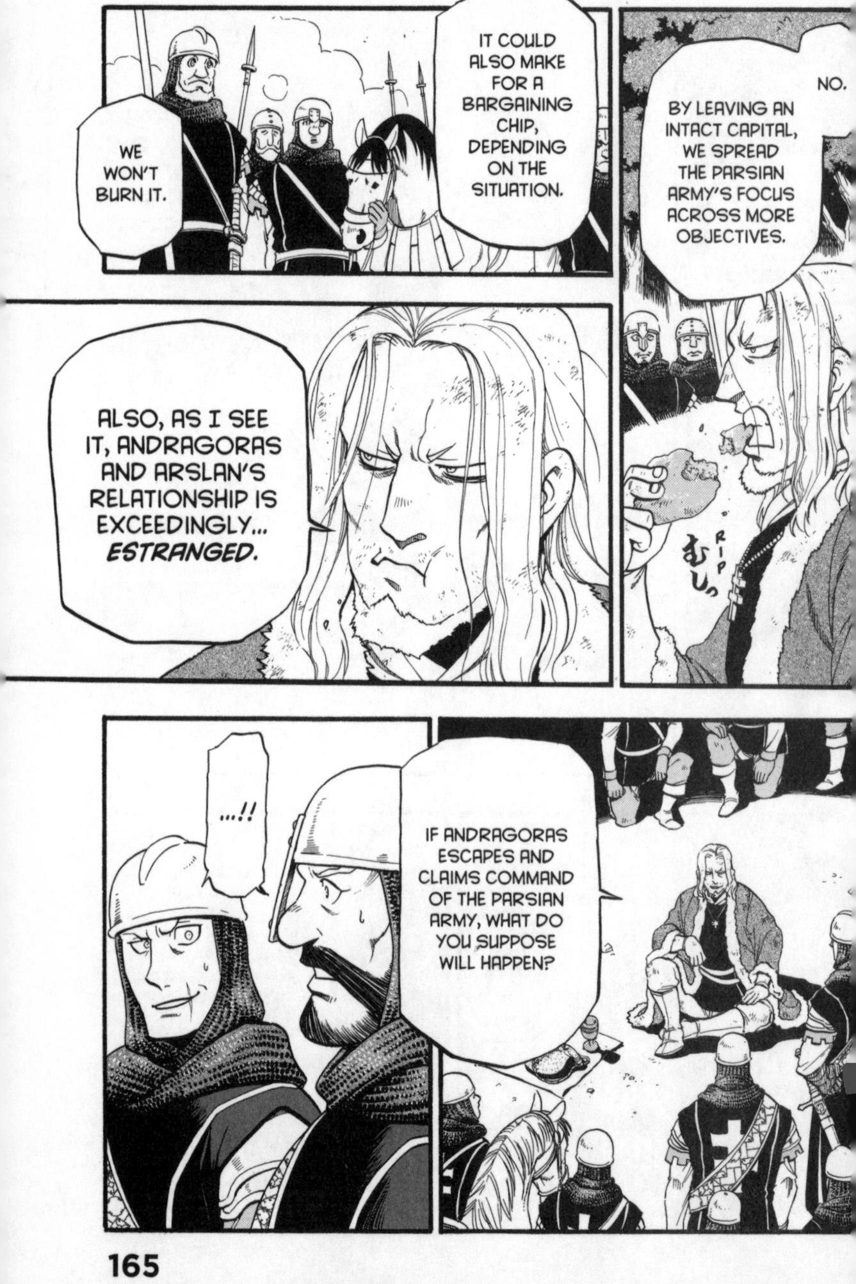
NO.
BY LEAVING AN INTACT CAPITAL, WE SPREAD THE PARSIAN ARMY'S FOCUS ACROSS MORE OBJECTIVES.
RIP
IT COULD ALSO MAKE FOR A BARGAINING CHIP, DEPENDING ON THE SITUATION.
WE WON'T BURN IT.
ALSO, AS I SEE IT, ANDRAGORAS AND ARSLAN'S RELATIONSHIP IS EXCEEDINGLY... *ESTRANGED.*
IF ANDRAGORAS ESCAPES AND CLAIMS COMMAND OF THE PARSIAN ARMY, WHAT DO YOU SUPPOSE WILL HAPPEN?
...!!

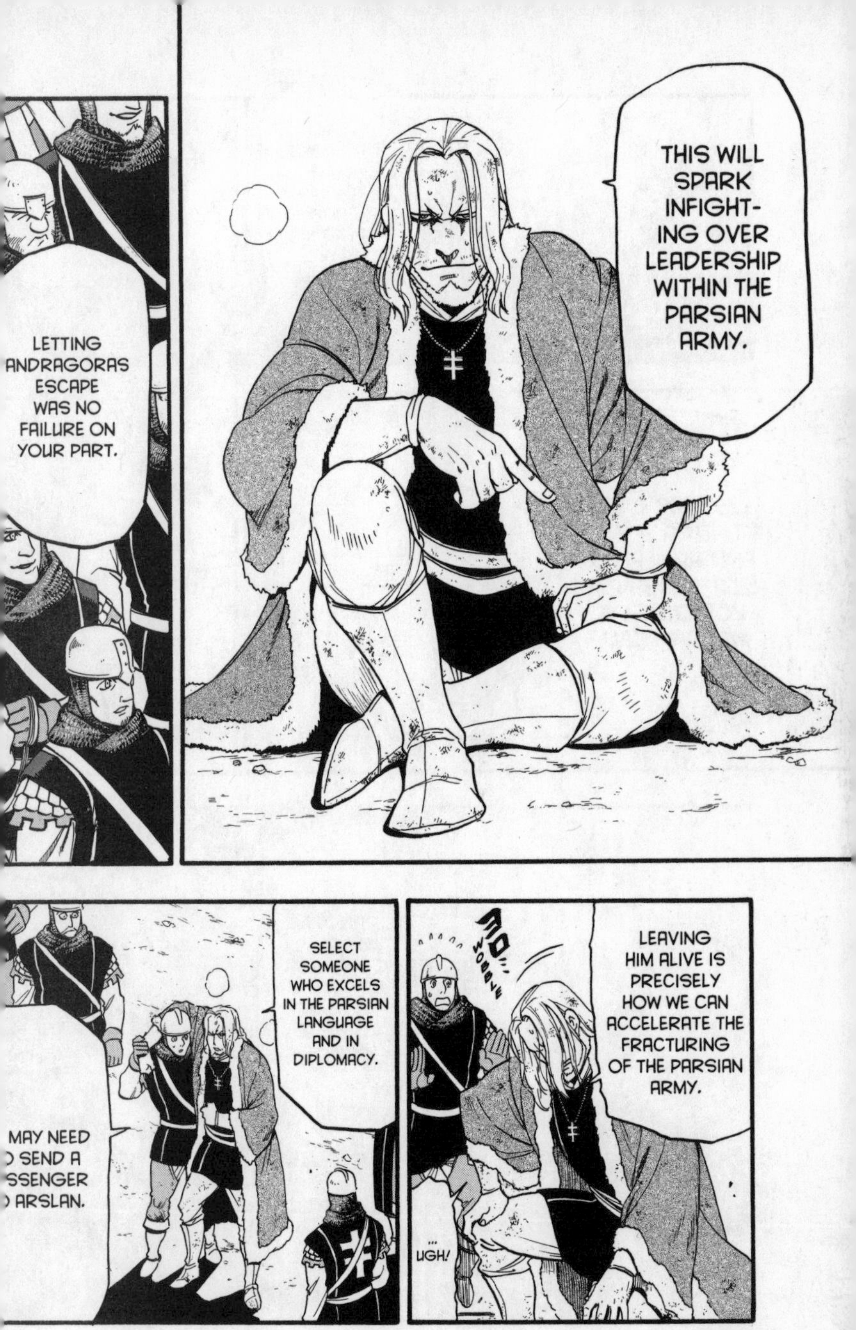
THIS WILL SPARK INFIGHTING OVER LEADERSHIP WITHIN THE PARSIAN ARMY.
LETTING ANDRAGORAS ESCAPE WAS NO FAILURE ON YOUR PART.
WOBBLE
LEAVING HIM ALIVE IS PRECISELY HOW WE CAN ACCELERATE THE FRACTURING OF THE PARSIAN ARMY.
...UGH!
SELECT SOMEONE WHO EXCELS IN THE PARSIAN LANGUAGE AND IN DIPLOMACY.
MAY NEED
SEND A
SSENGER
ARSLAN.

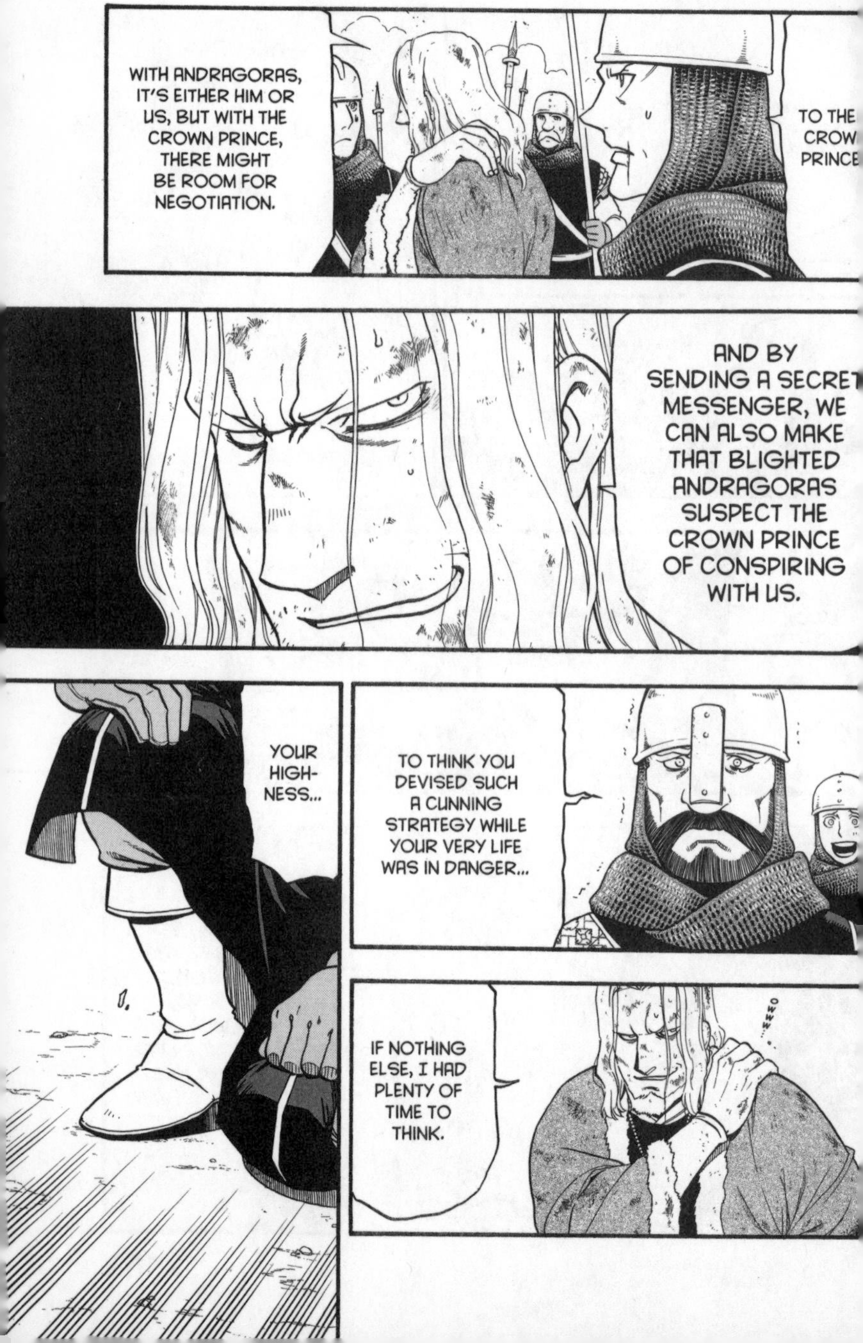

TO THE CROW PRINCE
WITH ANDRAGORAS, IT'S EITHER HIM OR US, BUT WITH THE CROWN PRINCE, THERE MIGHT BE ROOM FOR NEGOTIATION.
AND BY SENDING A SECRET MESSENGER, WE CAN ALSO MAKE THAT BLIGHTED ANDRAGORAS SUSPECT THE CROWN PRINCE OF CONSPIRING WITH US.
TO THINK YOU DEVISED SUCH A CUNNING STRATEGY WHILE YOUR VERY LIFE WAS IN DANGER...
OWWW...
IF NOTHING ELSE, I HAD PLENTY OF TIME TO THINK.
YOUR HIGH-NESS...

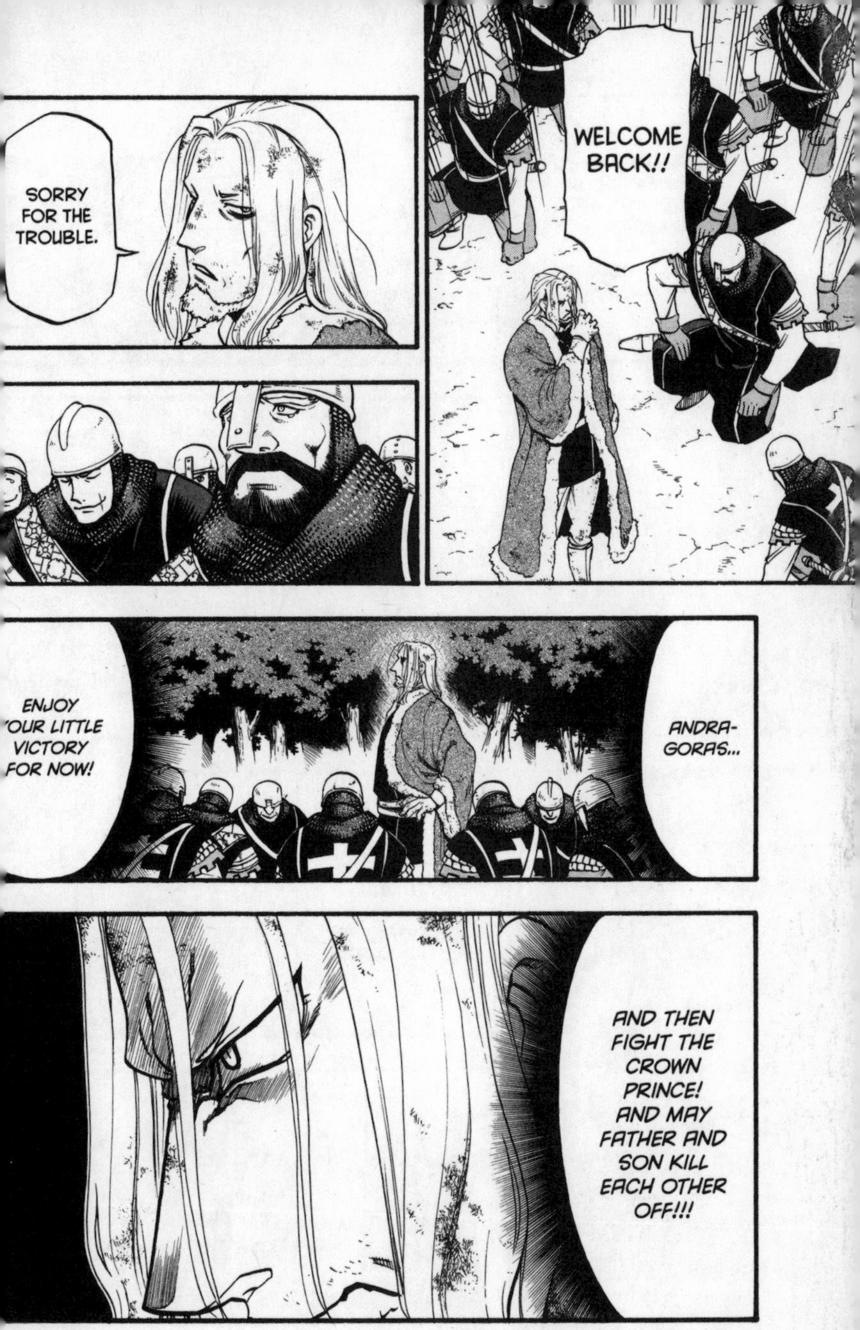
WELCOME BACK!!
SORRY FOR THE TROUBLE.
ANDRA-GORAS...
ENJOY
OUR LITTLE
VICTORY FOR NOW!
AND THEN FIGHT THE CROWN PRINCE! AND MAY FATHER AND SON KILL EACH OTHER OFF!!!

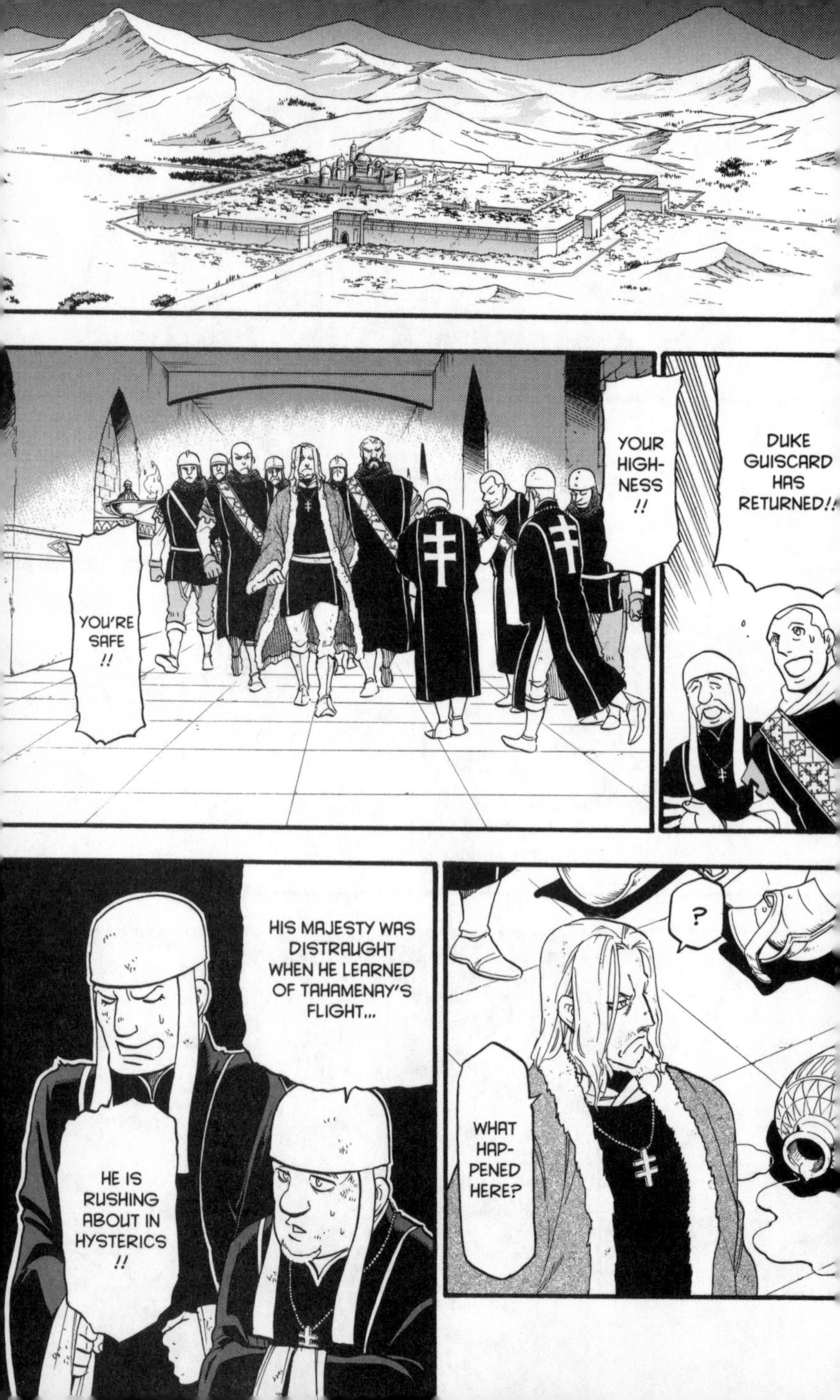
DUKE GUISCARD HAS RETURNED!!
YOUR HIGHNESS!!
YOU'RE SAFE!!
?
WHAT HAPPENED HERE?
HIS MAJESTY WAS DISTRAUGHT WHEN HE LEARNED OF TAHAMENAY'S FLIGHT...
HE IS RUSHING ABOUT IN HYSTERICS!!

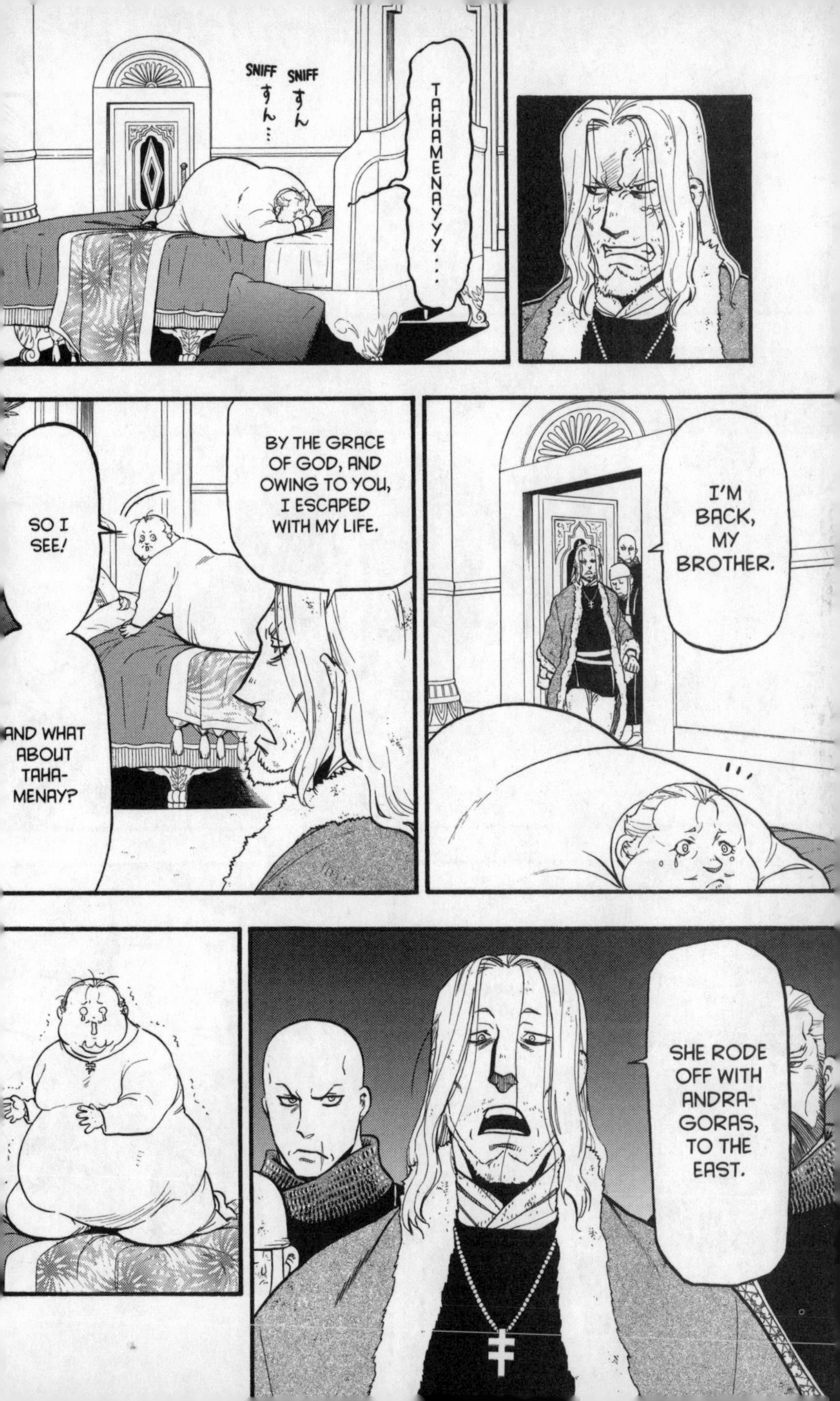
TAHAMENAYYY...
SNIFF SNIFF
すん すん…
I'M BACK, MY BROTHER.
BY THE GRACE OF GOD, AND OWING TO YOU, I ESCAPED WITH MY LIFE.
SO I SEE!
AND WHAT ABOUT TAHA-MENAY?
SHE RODE OFF WITH ANDRA-GORAS, TO THE EAST.

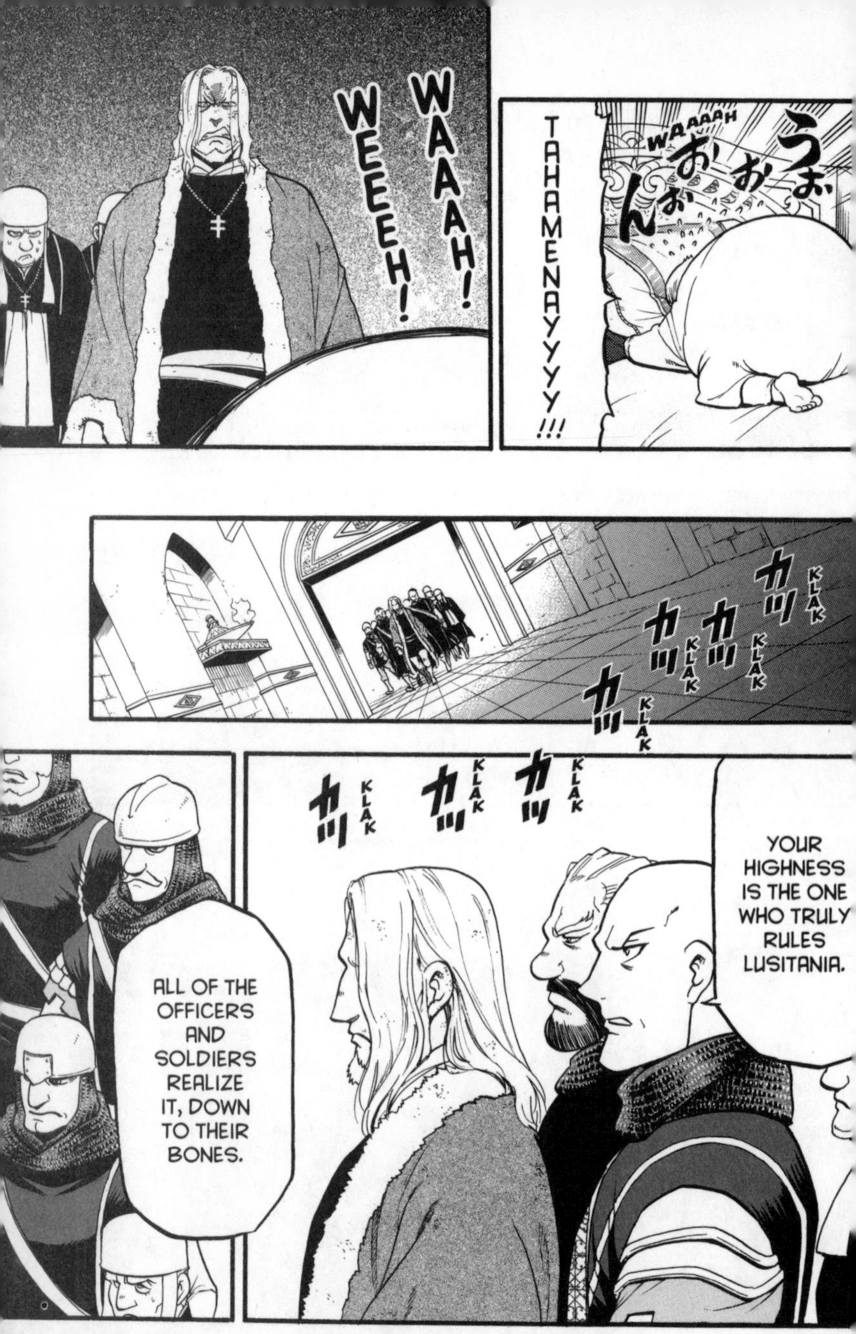
WAAAAH
TAHAMENAYYYYY!!!
WAAAAH!
WEEEEH!
KLAK
KLAK
KLAK
KLAK
KLAK
KLAK
KLAK
YOUR HIGHNESS IS THE ONE WHO TRULY RULES LUSITANIA.
ALL OF THE OFFICERS AND SOLDIERS REALIZE IT, DOWN TO THEIR BONES.

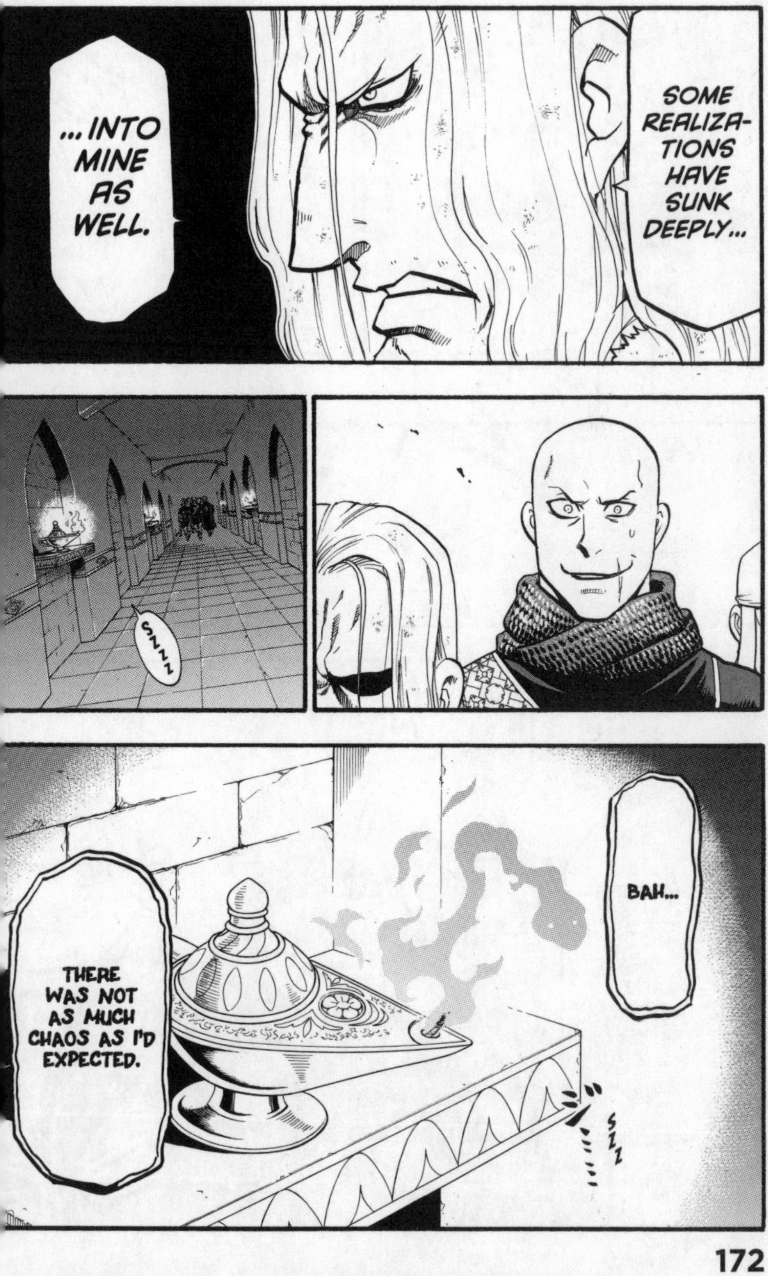
SOME REALIZATIONS HAVE SUNK DEEPLY...
...INTO MINE AS WELL.
SZZZ
BAH...
THERE WAS NOT AS MUCH CHAOS AS I'D EXPECTED.
SZZ

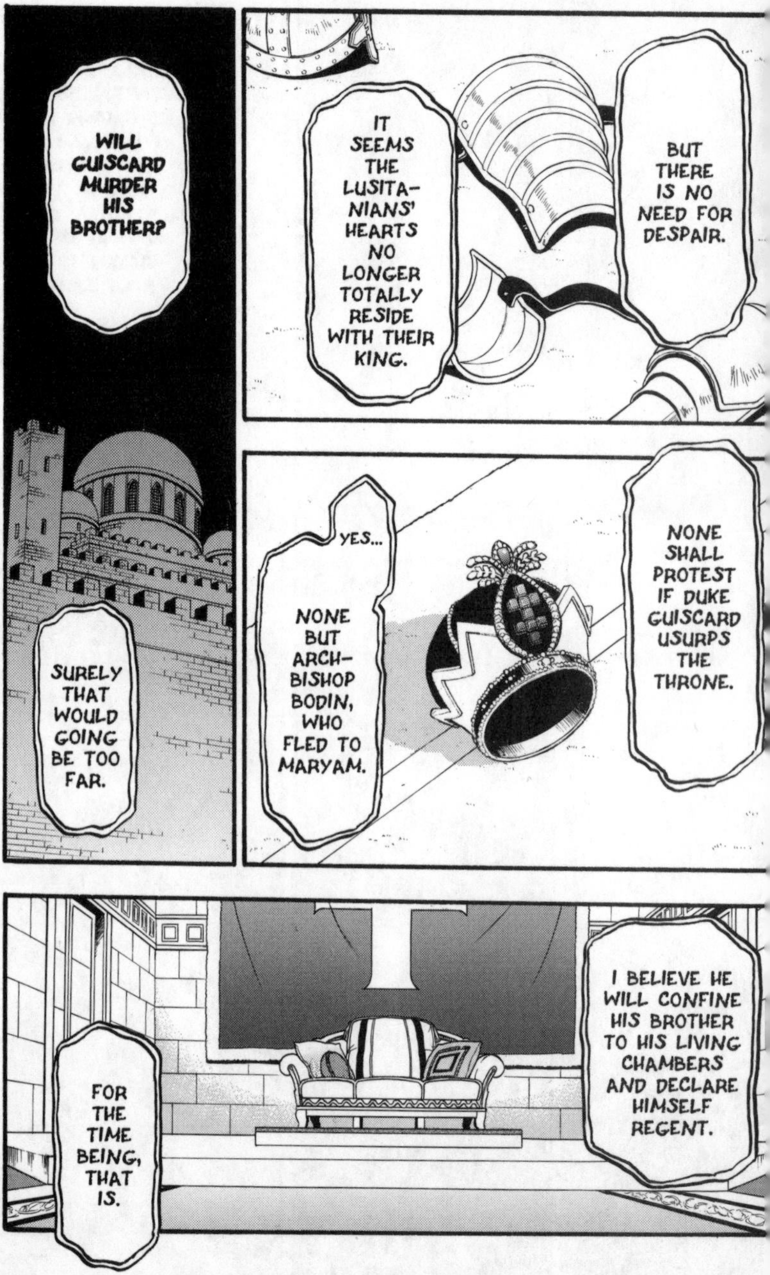
BUT THERE IS NO NEED FOR DESPAIR.
IT SEEMS THE LUSITA-NIANS' HEARTS NO LONGER TOTALLY RESIDE WITH THEIR KING.
NONE SHALL PROTEST IF DUKE GUISCARD USURPS THE THRONE.
YES...
NONE BUT ARCH-BISHOP BODIN, WHO FLED TO MARYAM.
WILL GUISCARD MURDER HIS BROTHER?
SURELY THAT WOULD GOING BE TOO FAR.
I BELIEVE HE WILL CONFINE HIS BROTHER TO HIS LIVING CHAMBERS AND DECLARE HIMSELF REGENT.
FOR THE TIME BEING, THAT IS.

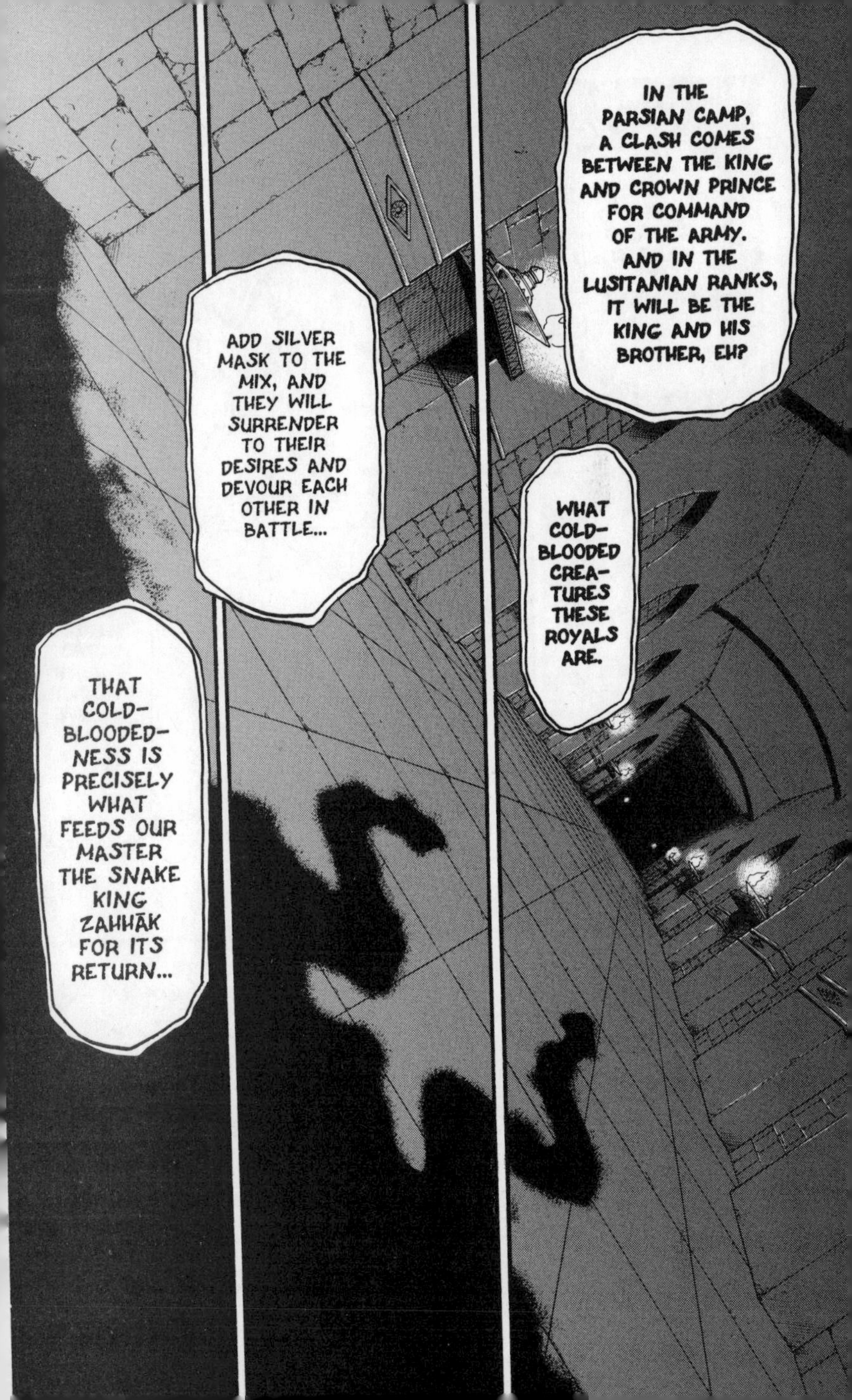
IN THE PARSIAN CAMP, A CLASH COMES BETWEEN THE KING AND CROWN PRINCE FOR COMMAND OF THE ARMY. AND IN THE LUSITANIAN RANKS, IT WILL BE THE KING AND HIS BROTHER, EH?
WHAT COLD-BLOODED CREATURES THESE ROYALS ARE.
ADD SILVER MASK TO THE MIX, AND THEY WILL SURRENDER TO THEIR DESIRES AND DEVOUR EACH OTHER IN BATTLE...
THAT COLD-BLOODEDNESS IS PRECISELY WHAT FEEDS OUR MASTER THE SNAKE KING ZAHHĀK FOR ITS RETURN...

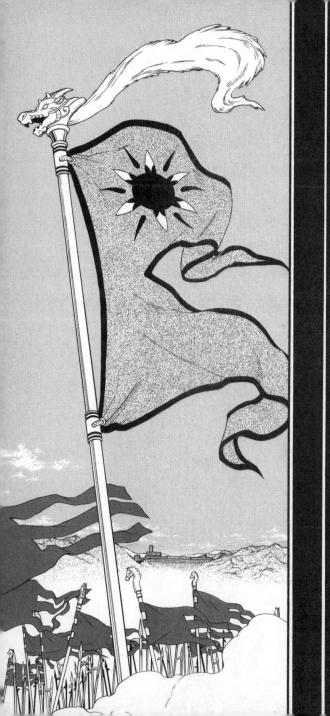

HE
HE
HE
HE
...

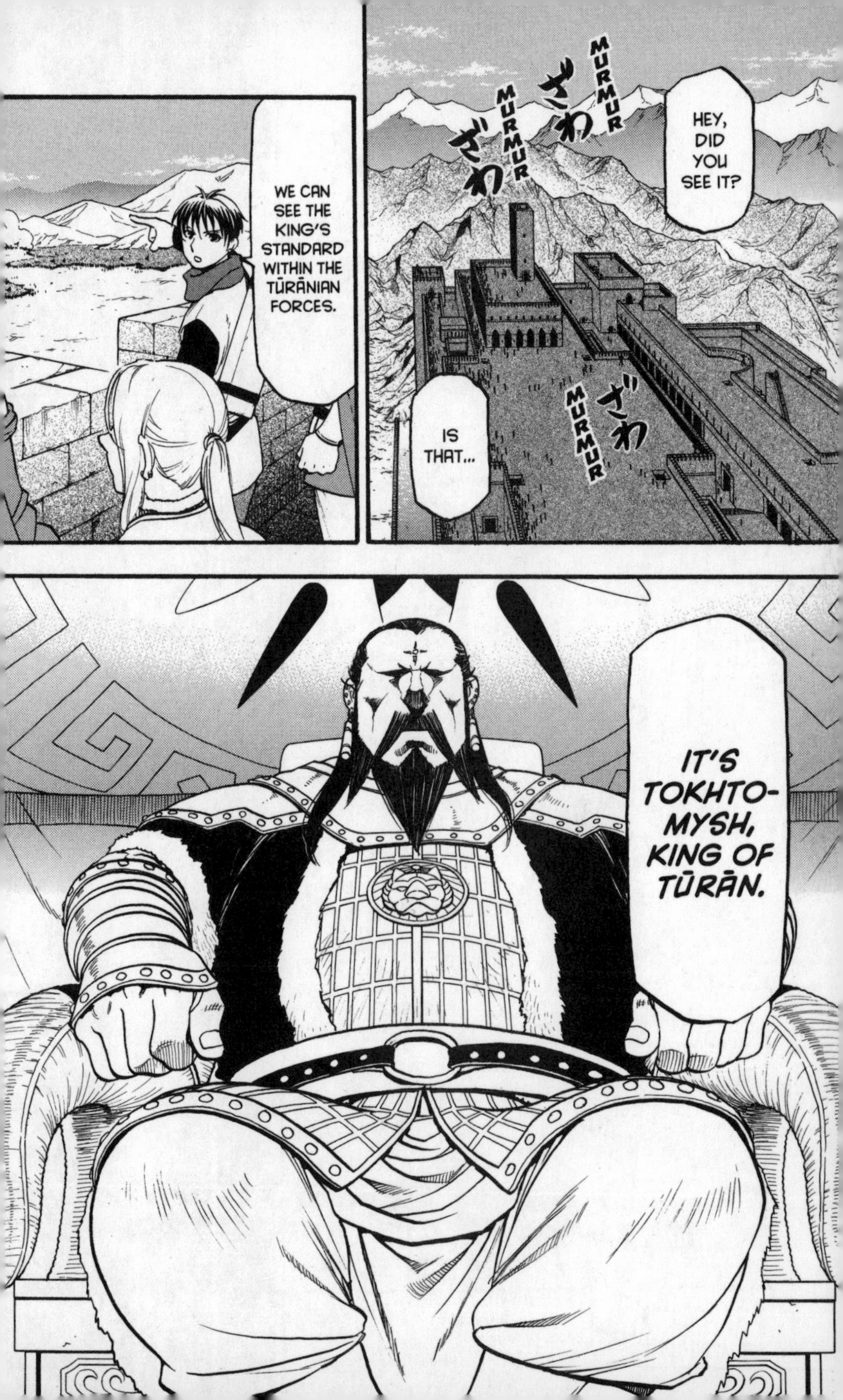

HEY, DID YOU SEE IT?
ざわ MURMUR
ざわ MURMUR
IS THAT...
ざわ MURMUR
WE CAN SEE THE KING'S STANDARD WITHIN THE TŪRĀNIAN FORCES.
IT'S TOKHTO-MYSH, KING OF TŪRĀN.

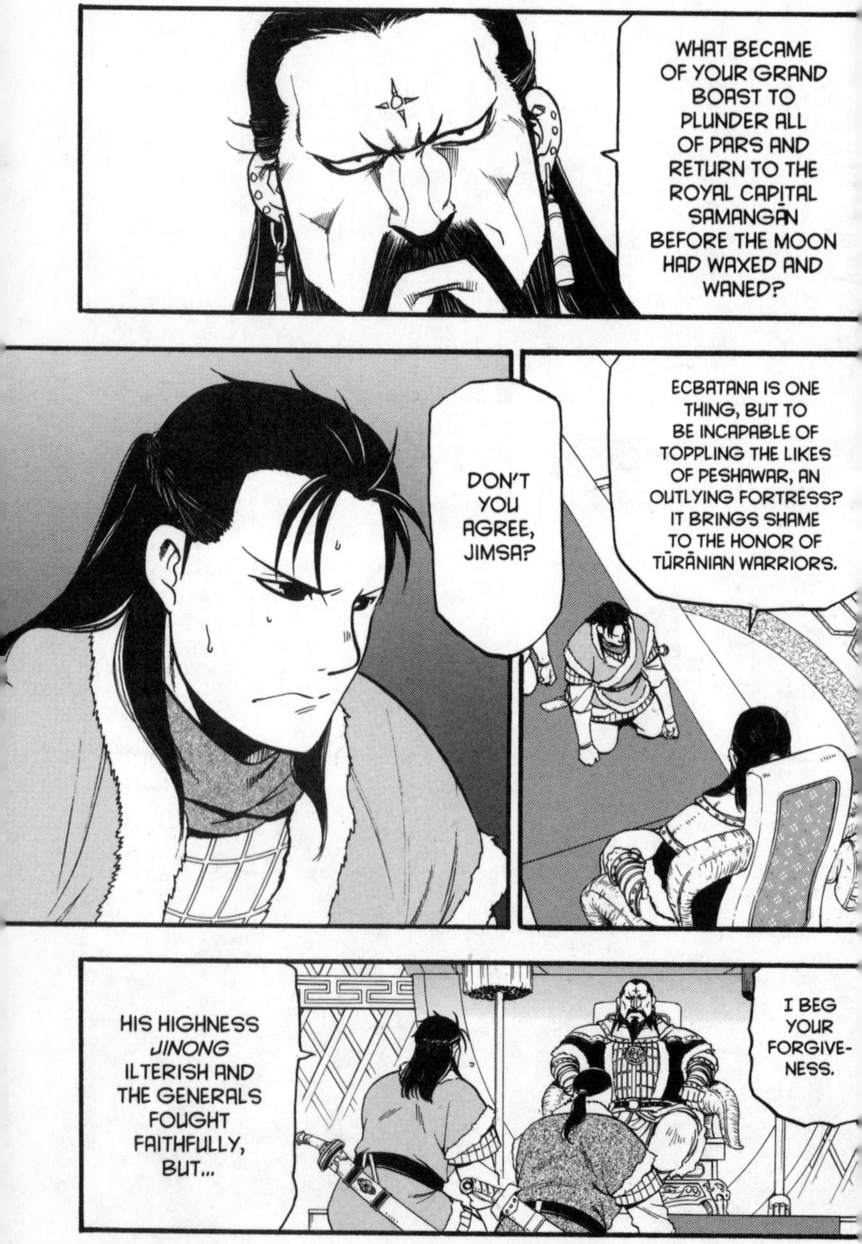
WHAT BECAME OF YOUR GRAND BOAST TO PLUNDER ALL OF PARS AND RETURN TO THE ROYAL CAPITAL SAMANGĀN BEFORE THE MOON HAD WAXED AND WANED?
ECBATANA IS ONE THING, BUT TO BE INCAPABLE OF TOPPLING THE LIKES OF PESHAWAR, AN OUTLYING FORTRESS? IT BRINGS SHAME TO THE HONOR OF TŪRĀNIAN WARRIORS.
DON'T YOU AGREE, JIMSA?
I BEG YOUR FORGIVE-NESS.
HIS HIGHNESS *JINONG* ILTERISH AND THE GENERALS FOUGHT FAITHFULLY, BUT...

JINONG: PRINCE OF THE BLOOD

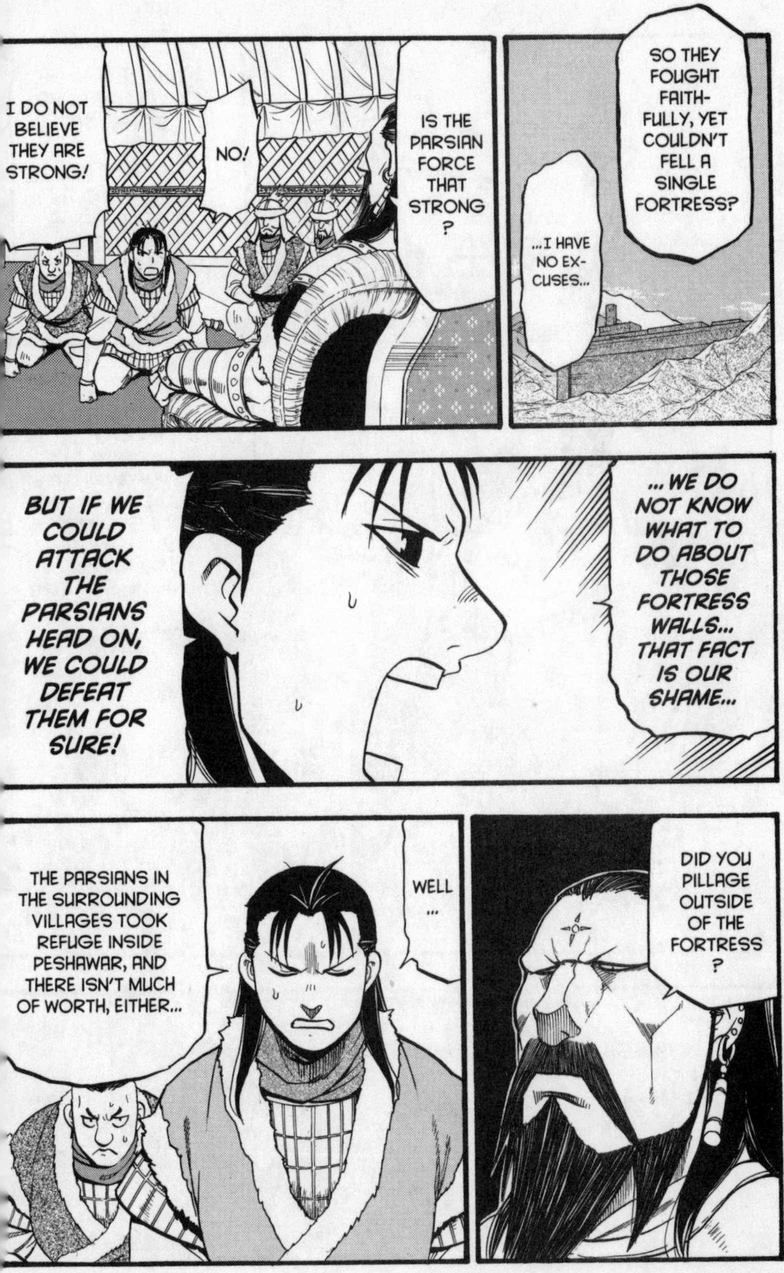
SO THEY FOUGHT FAITH-FULLY, YET COULDN'T FELL A SINGLE FORTRESS?
...I HAVE NO EX-CUSES...
IS THE PARSIAN FORCE THAT STRONG ?
NO!
I DO NOT BELIEVE THEY ARE STRONG!
...WE DO NOT KNOW WHAT TO DO ABOUT THOSE FORTRESS WALLS... THAT FACT IS OUR SHAME...
BUT IF WE COULD ATTACK THE PARSIANS HEAD ON, WE COULD DEFEAT THEM FOR SURE!
DID YOU PILLAGE OUTSIDE OF THE FORTRESS ?
WELL ...
THE PARSIANS IN THE SURROUNDING VILLAGES TOOK REFUGE INSIDE PESHAWAR, AND THERE ISN'T MUCH OF WORTH, EITHER...

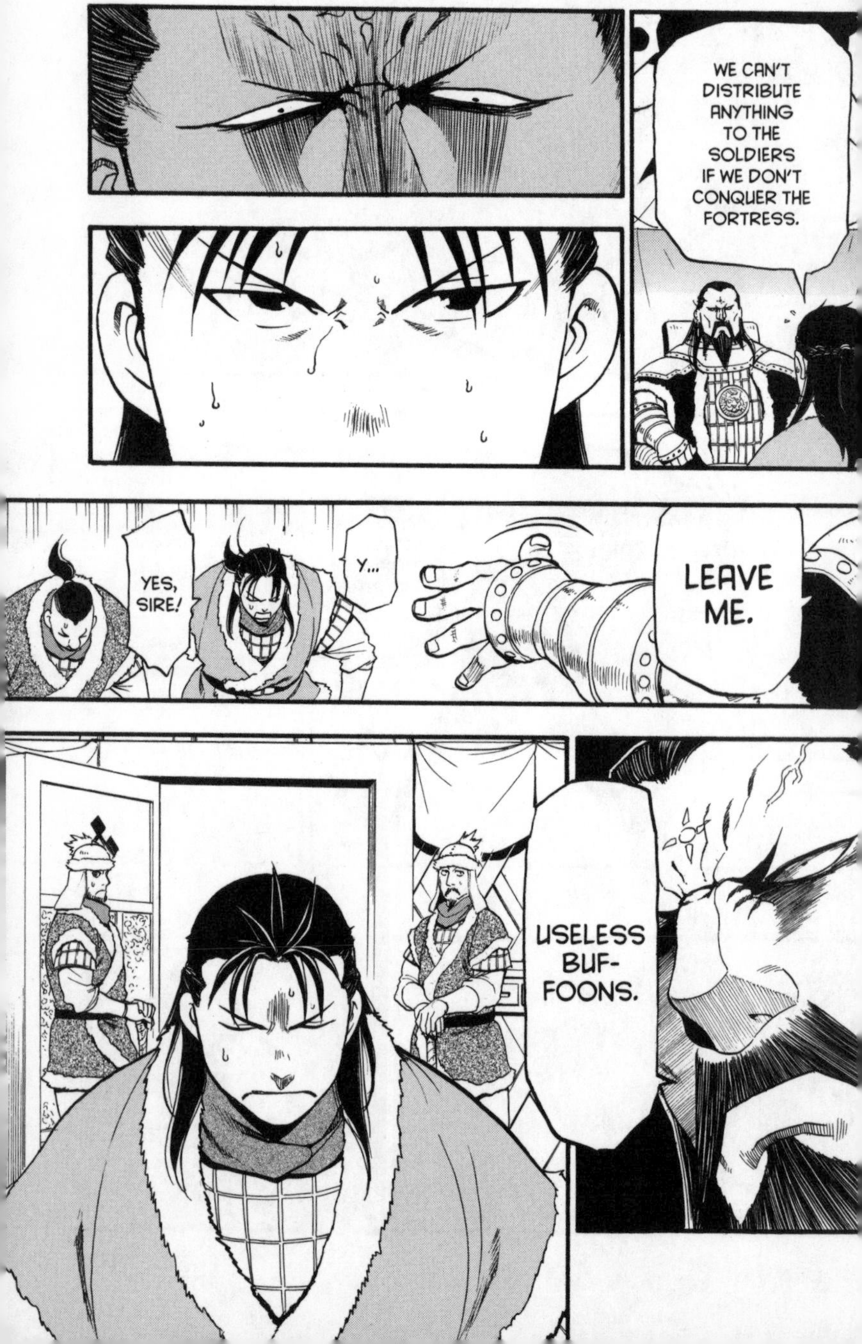

WE CAN'T DISTRIBUTE ANYTHING TO THE SOLDIERS IF WE DON'T CONQUER THE FORTRESS.
LEAVE ME.
Y...
YES, SIRE!
USELESS BUF-FOONS.

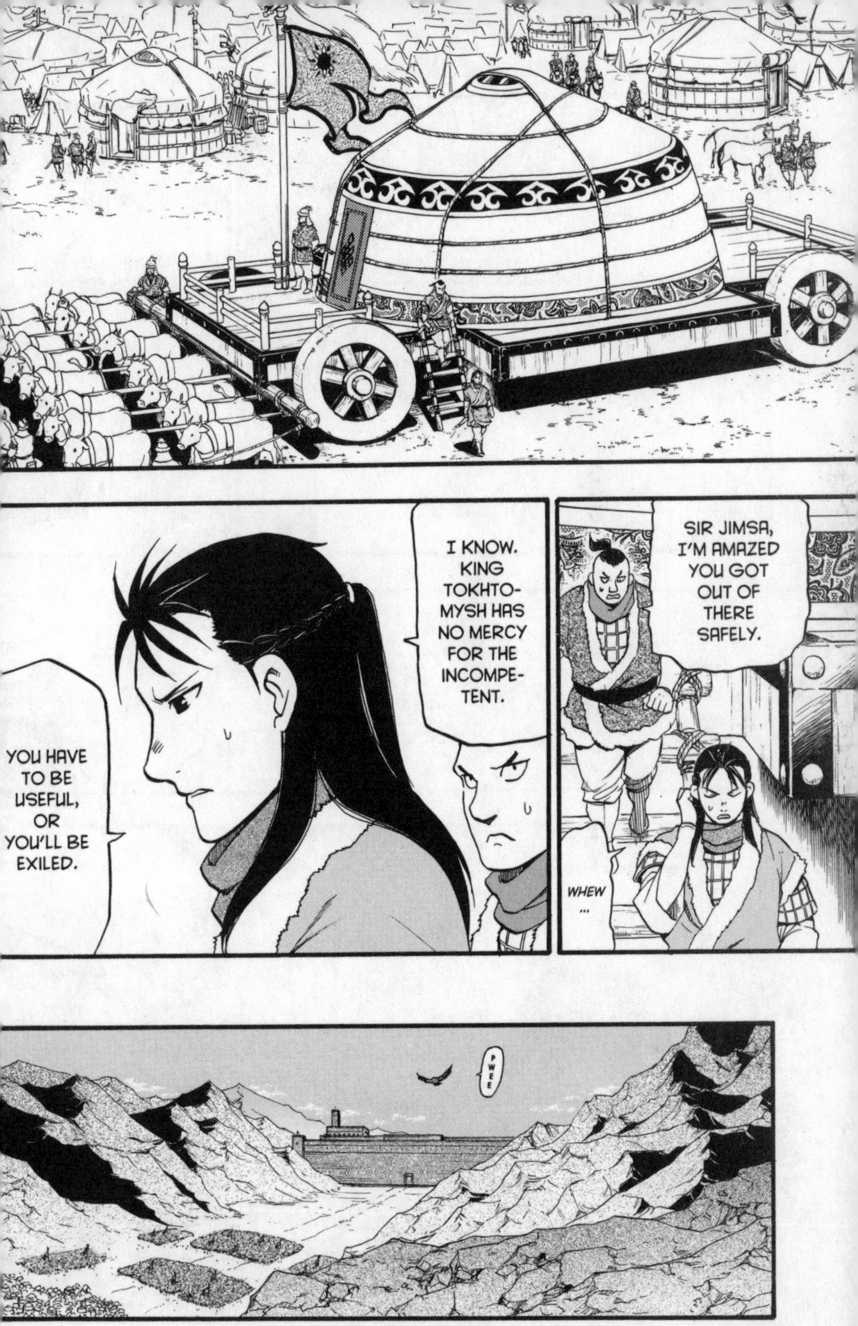
SIR JIMSA, I'M AMAZED YOU GOT OUT OF THERE SAFELY.
WHEW ...
I KNOW. KING TOKHTOMYSH HAS NO MERCY FOR THE INCOMPETENT.
YOU HAVE TO BE USEFUL, OR YOU'LL BE EXILED.
PWEE

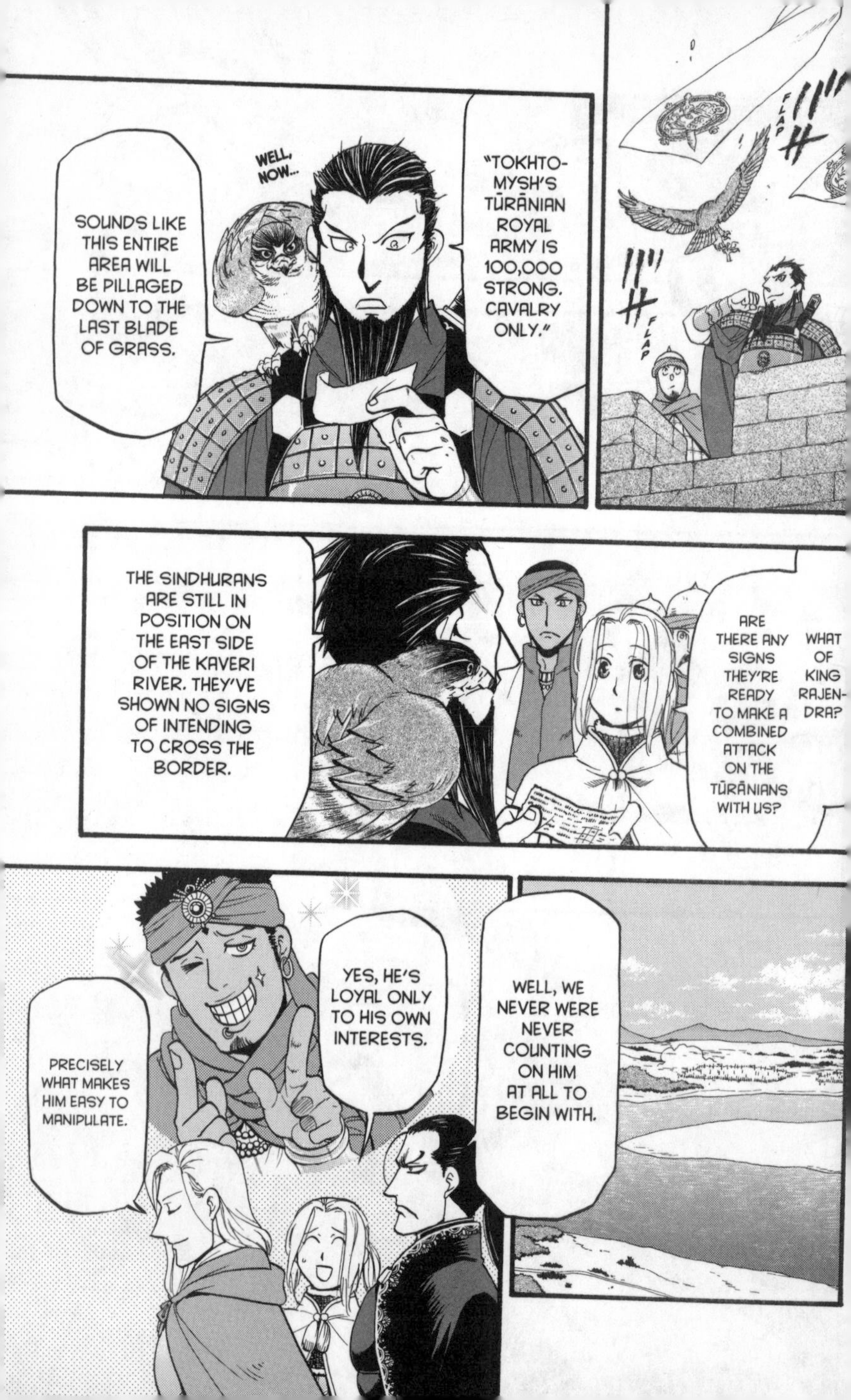
!
FLAP
FLAP
"TOKHTOMYSH'S TŪRĀNIAN ROYAL ARMY IS 100,000 STRONG. CAVALRY ONLY."
WELL, NOW...
SOUNDS LIKE THIS ENTIRE AREA WILL BE PILLAGED DOWN TO THE LAST BLADE OF GRASS.
WHAT OF KING RAJENDRA?
ARE THERE ANY SIGNS THEY'RE READY TO MAKE A COMBINED ATTACK ON THE TŪRĀNIANS WITH US?
THE SINDHURANS ARE STILL IN POSITION ON THE EAST SIDE OF THE KAVERI RIVER. THEY'VE SHOWN NO SIGNS OF INTENDING TO CROSS THE BORDER.
WELL, WE NEVER WERE NEVER COUNTING ON HIM AT ALL TO BEGIN WITH.
YES, HE'S LOYAL ONLY TO HIS OWN INTERESTS.
PRECISELY WHAT MAKES HIM EASY TO MANIPULATE.

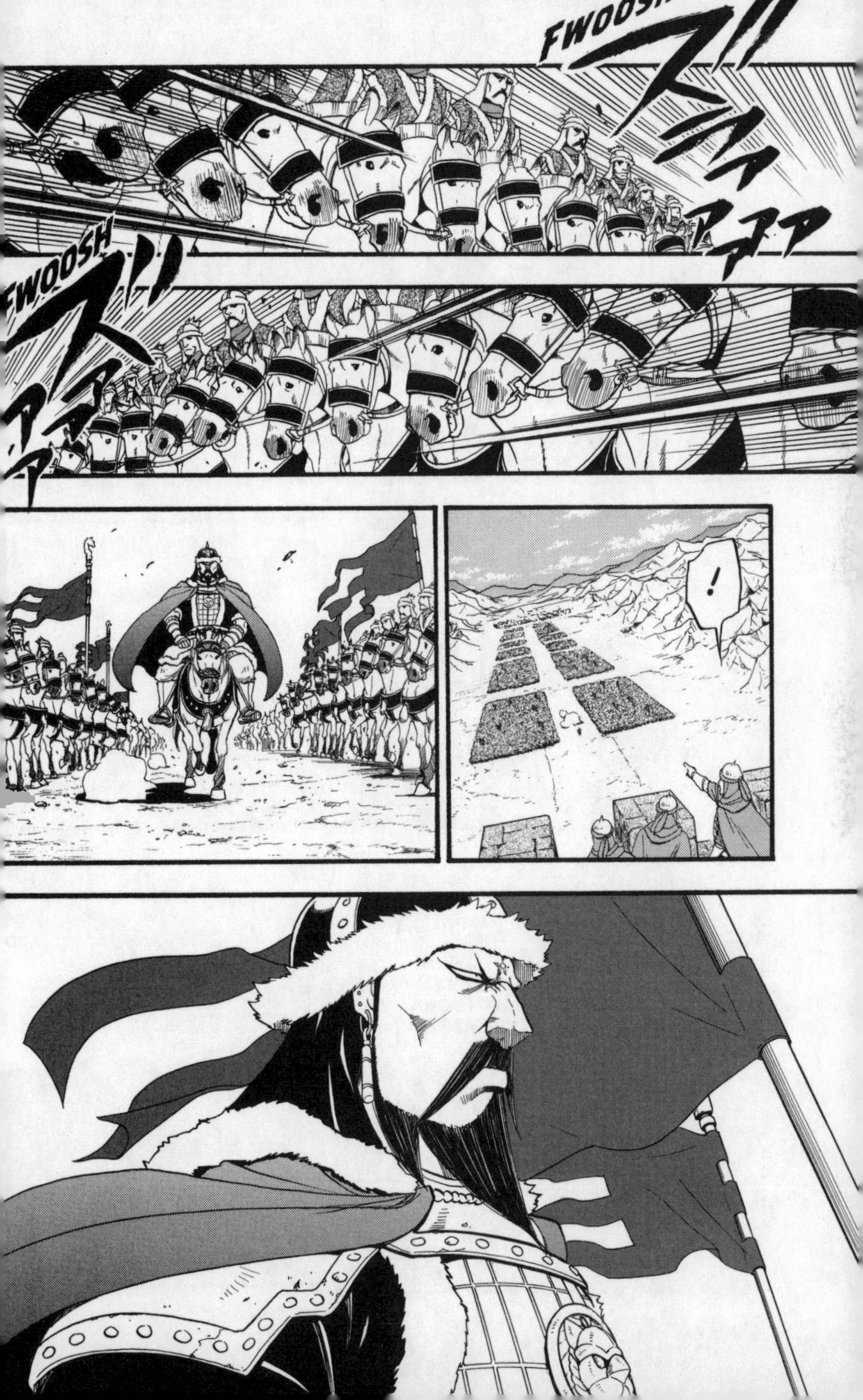
FWOOSH
FWOOSH
!

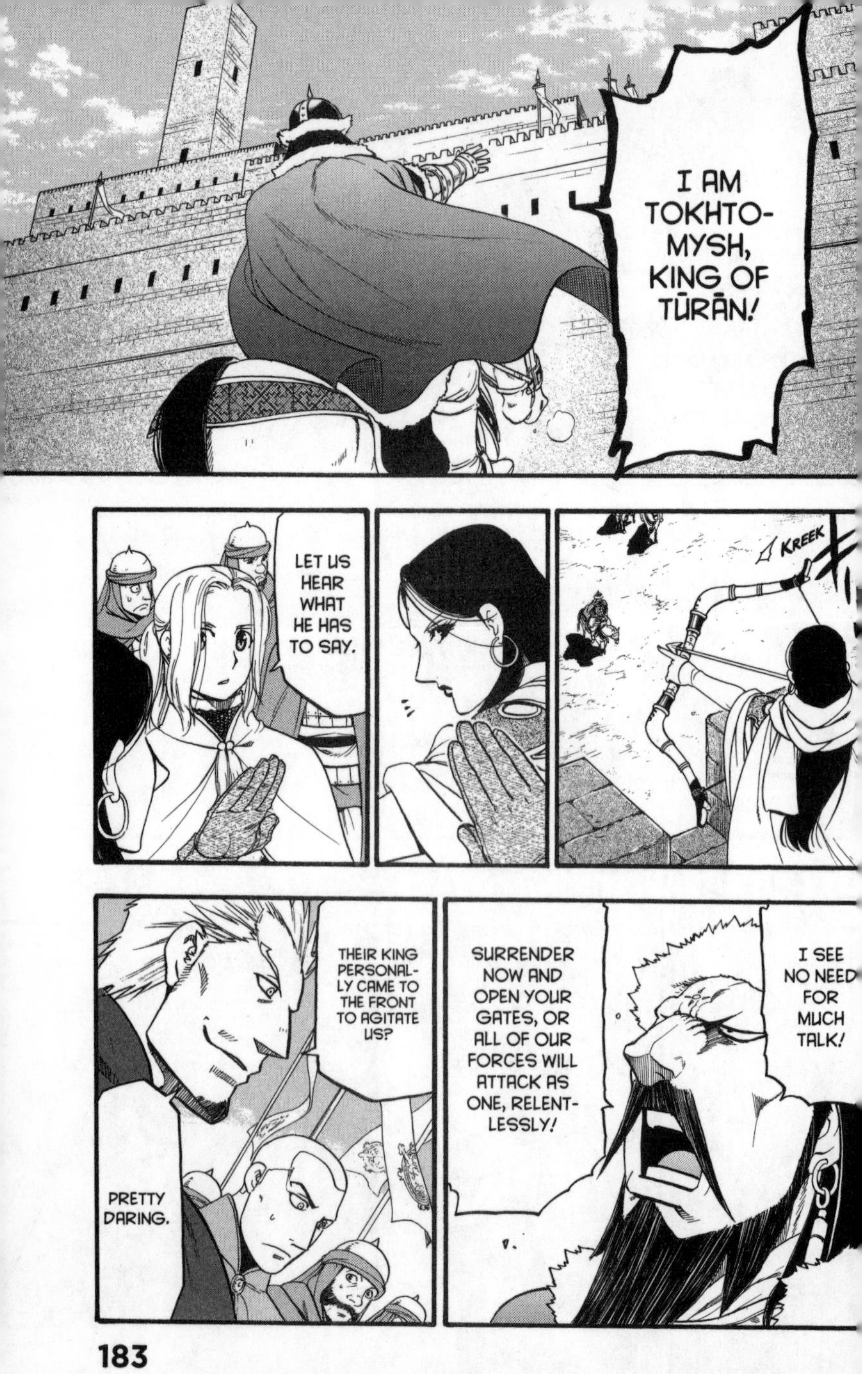
I AM TOKHTO-MYSH, KING OF TŪRĀN!
KREEK
LET US HEAR WHAT HE HAS TO SAY.
I SEE NO NEED FOR MUCH TALK!
SURRENDER NOW AND OPEN YOUR GATES, OR ALL OF OUR FORCES WILL ATTACK AS ONE, RELENTLESSLY!
THEIR KING PERSONALLY CAME TO THE FRONT TO AGITATE US?
PRETTY DARING.

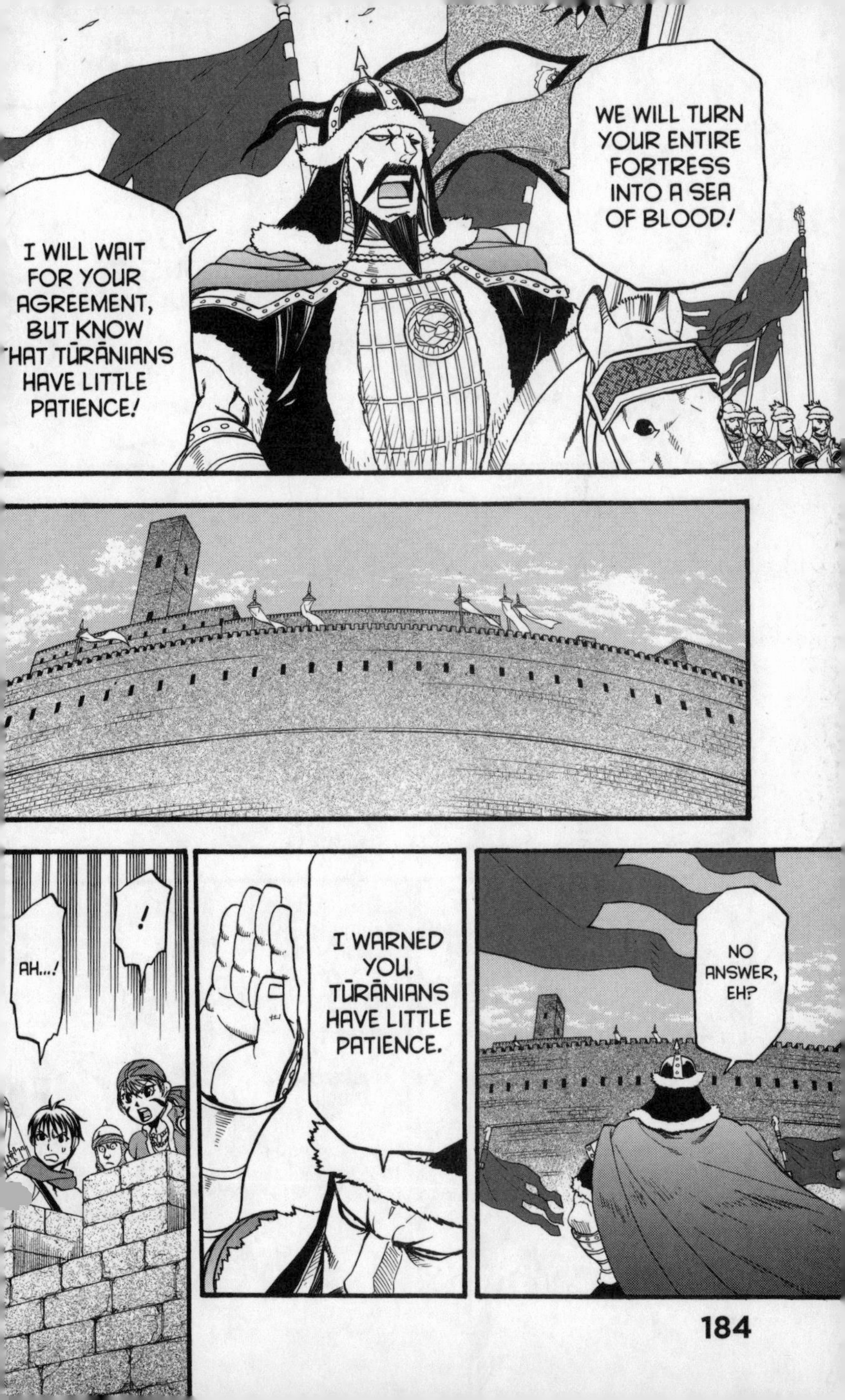
WE WILL TURN YOUR ENTIRE FORTRESS INTO A SEA OF BLOOD!
I WILL WAIT FOR YOUR AGREEMENT, BUT KNOW THAT TŪRĀNIANS HAVE LITTLE PATIENCE!
NO ANSWER, EH?
I WARNED YOU. TŪRĀNIANS HAVE LITTLE PATIENCE.
!
AH...!

END-OF-BOOK BONUS

THE HEROIC LEGEND OF ARSLAN

SINDHURA

KING: Rajendra III **CAPITAL:** Uraiyur

Located southeast of Pars. The might of its unique elephantry is known across the land. A battle for succession between two crown princes recently ended with the coronation of Rajendra, the younger of the two. On friendly terms with Arslan's forces, notwithstanding a degree of mutual suspicion.

KEY FIGURES

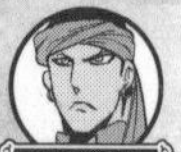
JASWANT

Originally a soldier on Gadhevi's side in the battle with Rajendra for the throne. Now one of Arslan's bodyguards.

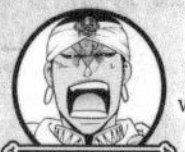
GADHEVI

Rajendra's older half-brother. Royal blood ran thick in his veins, but he was killed after his champion was defeated in the "duel before the gods."

RAJENDRA

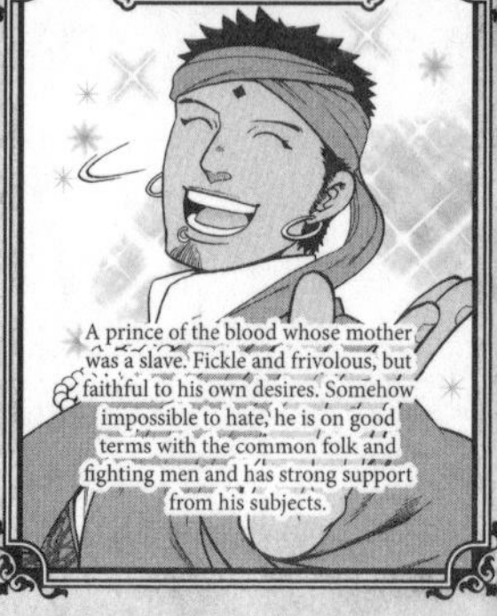
A prince of the blood whose mother was a slave. Fickle and frivolous, but faithful to his own desires. Somehow impossible to hate, he is on good terms with the common folk and fighting men and has strong support from his subjects.

MARYAM

PRINCESS OF THE BLOOD: Irina **CAPITAL:** Iraklion

Kingdom that lay northwest of Pars. Practiced the Faith of Yaldabaoth, but with teachings that differed slightly from Lusitania's. Destroyed in a Lusitanian invasion that wiped out the entire royal family except for Princess Ilana.

KEY FIGURES

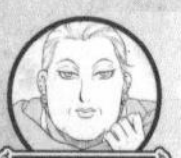
JOVANNA

Ilana's head lady-in-waiting. A spirited woman unfazed by even the fiercest enemy warriors.

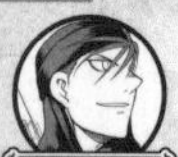
MERLAIN

A boy of the Zot Clan. Alfarīd's older brother. Offers Irina his assistance—or, rather, falls in love with her.

IRINA

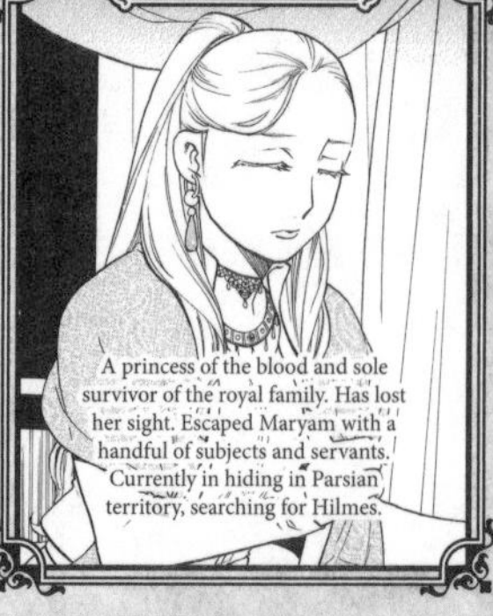
A princess of the blood and sole survivor of the royal family. Has lost her sight. Escaped Maryam with a handful of subjects and servants. Currently in hiding in Parsian territory, searching for Hilmes.

TŪRĀN

KING: Tokhtomysh **CAPITAL:** Samangān

A nation of horse-riding warriors known as the Rulers of the Grasslands northeast of Pars. At their strongest in mounted combat. Nomadic by nature, they are currently raiding in Parsian territory, and have engaged Arslan's forces at Peshawar Citadel.

KEY FIGURES

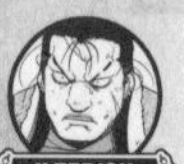
ILTERISH

Son of the king's brother and a prince in his own right. Led the first assault on Peshawar Citadel. A rather short-tempered warrior.

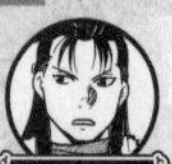
JIMSA

A young commander also participating in the attack on Peshawar alongside Ilterish and the other generals.

TOKHTOMYSH

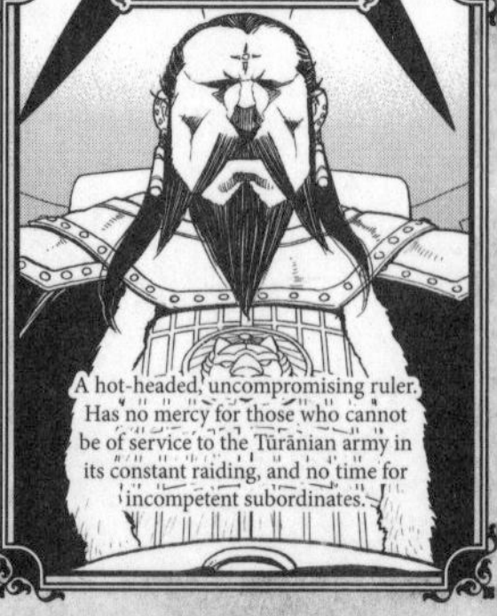
A hot-headed, uncompromising ruler. Has no mercy for those who cannot be of service to the Tūrānian army in its constant raiding, and no time for incompetent subordinates.

A Kodansha Comics Trade Paperback Original
The Heroic Legend of Arslan 13 copyright © 2020 Hiromu Arakawa & Yoshiki Tanaka
English translation copyright © 2020 Hiromu Arakawa & Yoshiki Tanaka

Published in the United States by Kodansha Comics, an imprint of Kodansha USA Publishing, LLC, New York.

Publication rights for this English edition arranged through Kodansha Ltd., Tokyo.

First published in Japan in 2020 by Kodansha Ltd., Tokyo as *Arslan Senki*, volume 13.

ISBN 978-1-64651-030-6

Printed in the United States of America.

www.kodanshacomics.com

9 8 7 6 5 4 3 2 1
Translation: Matt Treyvaud
Lettering: James Dashiell
Editing: Nathaniel Gallant
Kodansha Comics edition cover design by Phil Balsman

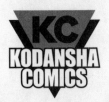

Publisher: Kiichiro Sugawara

Director of publishing services: Ben Applegate
Associate director of operations: Stephen Pakula
Publishing services managing editor: Noelle Webster
Assistant production manager: Emi Lotto, Angela Zurlo

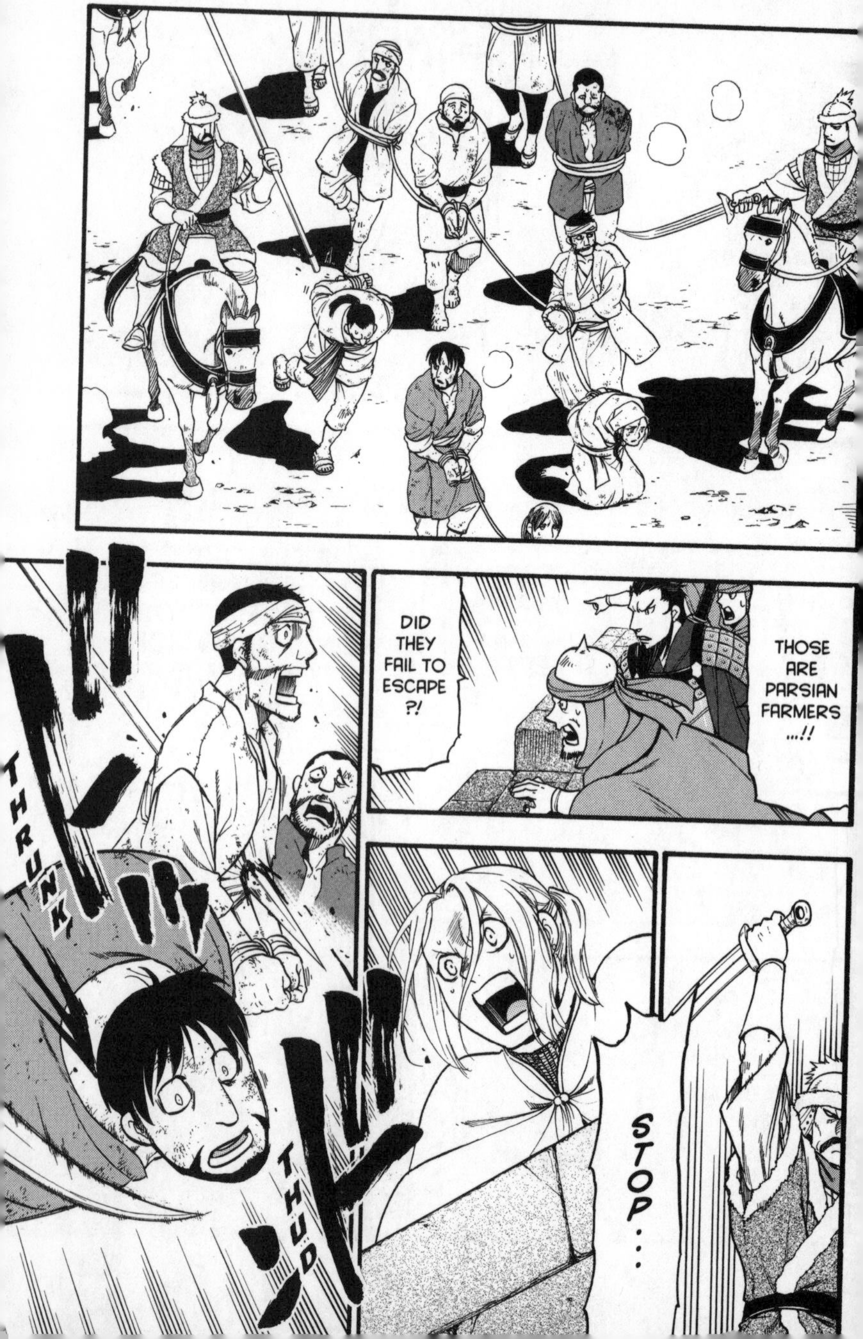
THOSE ARE PARSIAN FARMERS ...!!
DID THEY FAIL TO ESCAPE ?!
STOP...
THRUNK
THUD

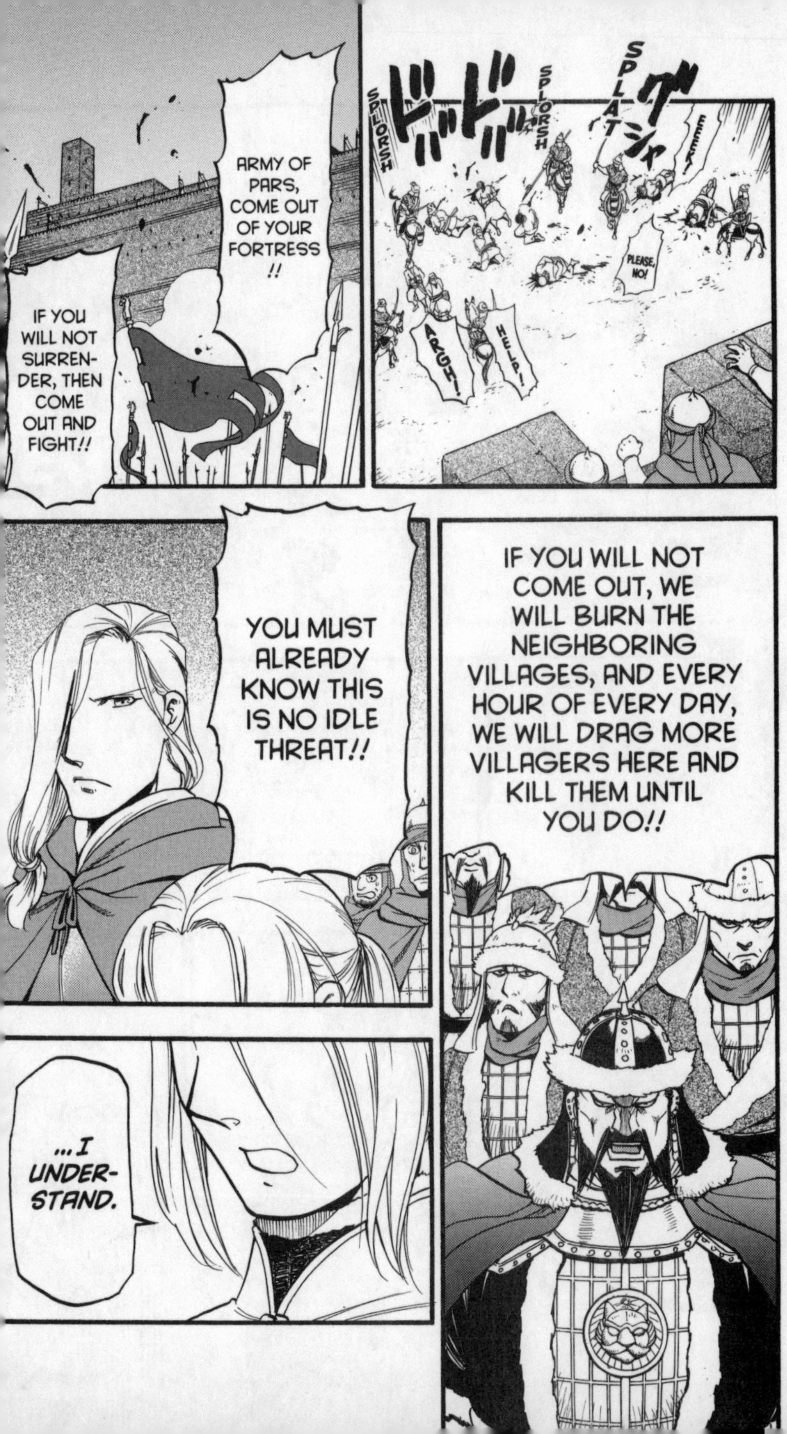
SPLAT
EEEEK!
SPLORSH
SPLORSH
PLEASE, NO!
HELP!
ARGH!
ARMY OF PARS, COME OUT OF YOUR FORTRESS!!
IF YOU WILL NOT SURRENDER, THEN COME OUT AND FIGHT!!
IF YOU WILL NOT COME OUT, WE WILL BURN THE NEIGHBORING VILLAGES, AND EVERY HOUR OF EVERY DAY, WE WILL DRAG MORE VILLAGERS HERE AND KILL THEM UNTIL YOU DO!!
YOU MUST ALREADY KNOW THIS IS NO IDLE THREAT!!
...I UNDERSTAND.

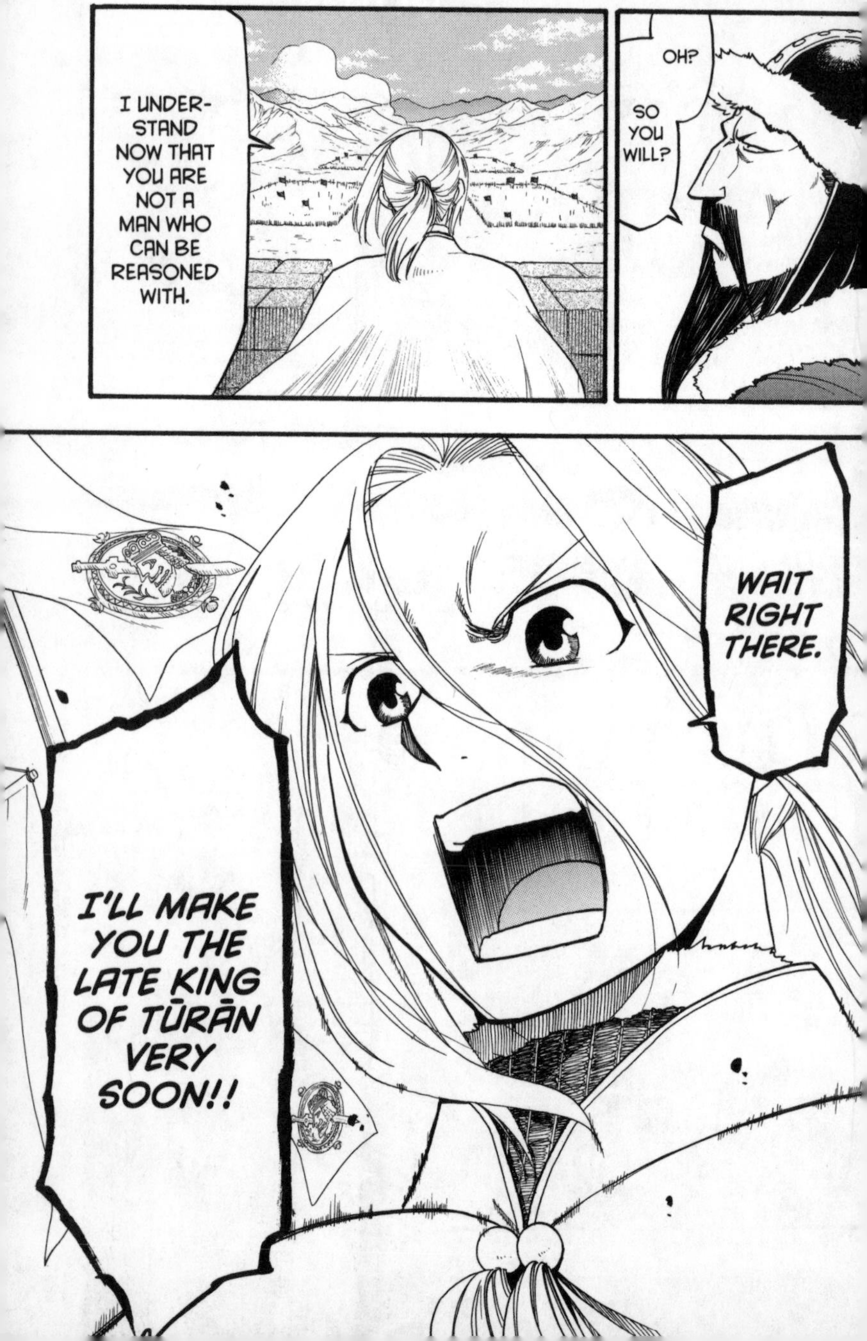
OH?
SO YOU WILL?
I UNDER-STAND NOW THAT YOU ARE NOT A MAN WHO CAN BE REASONED WITH.
WAIT RIGHT THERE.
I'LL MAKE YOU THE LATE KING OF TŪRĀN VERY SOON!!

ALL-NATION BREAK

Refresh your knowledge of the ... n the ... as of ... ors ... the course of battle!

PARS

KING: Andragoras III

CAPITAL: Ecbatana

A kingdom made rich and powerful by trade along the Continental Highway. Under the reign of Andragoras III, its undefeated army led by one *ēran* and twelve *marzbāns* struck fear in the hearts of the enemy. Suffered a shocking defeat at the hands of Lusitania during Crown Prince Arslan's first battle at the age of 14. Ecbatana, the capital, remains under Lusitanian military occupation.

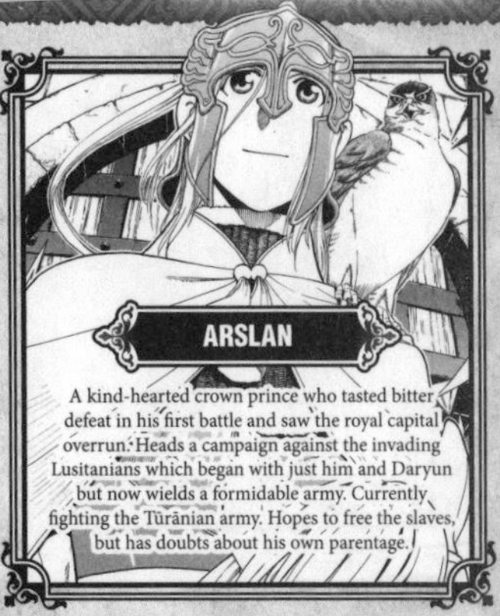

ARSLAN

A kind-hearted crown prince who tasted bitter defeat in his first battle and saw the royal capital overrun. Heads a campaign against the invading Lusitanians which began with just him and Daryun but now wields a formidable army. Currently fighting the Tūrānian army. Hopes to free the slaves, but has doubts about his own parentage.

KEY FIGURES

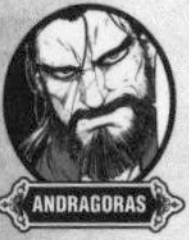

ANDRAGORAS

A king famed for being undefeated in battle. Solicitous of his queen, but cold to Arslan. Escaped from Lusitanian captivity to return to the fight.

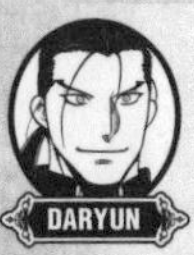

DARYUN

A *marzbān* who serves Arslan due to his uncle's dying wish and his own loyalty. Young and fierce, he is known as the "black-clad knight" and "warrior among warriors."

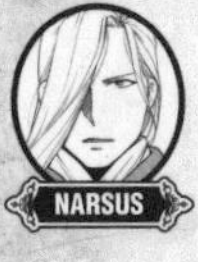

NARSUS

Finest strategist in Pars and future court painter. Had retired from public service, but now part of Arslan's forces. As a painter he is, in a way, without equal.

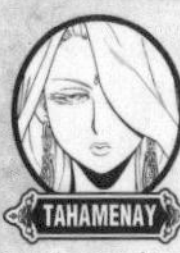

TAHAMENAY

Bewitching queen of Pars. So many powerful suitors vied for her affections that that she became known as a beauty for whom kingdoms might be forsaken. Treats Arslan coldly.

LUSITANIA

KING: Innocentis VII

*Currently occupying royal capital of Pars

A kingdom northwest of Pars devoted to the monotheistic Faith of Yaldabaoth. After invading and destroying the neighboring kingdom of Maryam, turned its attentions to Pars. Soundly defeating the Parsian army at the Battle of Atropatene and conquered the supposedly impregnable Ecbatana, which it currently occupies.

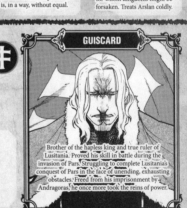

GUISCARD

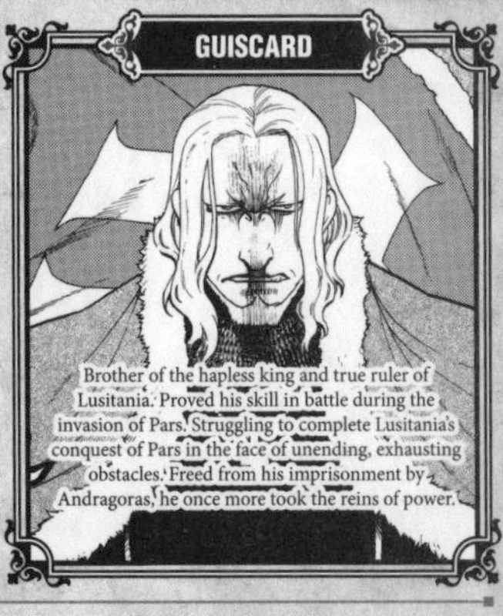

Brother of the hapless king and true ruler of Lusitania. Proved his skill in battle during the invasion of Pars. Struggling to complete Lusitania's conquest of Pars in the face of unending, exhausting obstacles. Freed from his imprisonment by Andragoras, he once more took the reins of power.

KEY FIGURES

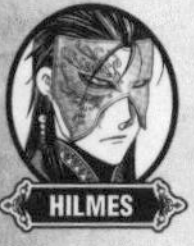

HILMES

As Parsian royalty by blood, believes he is the nation's rightful king. Joined Lusitania in a conspiracy to destroy the ruling royal family of Pars, whom he despises.

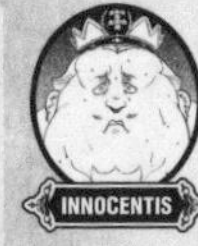

INNOCENTIS

Leaves ruling to his capable younger brother while he indulges his laziness and gluttony as king. Foolish by nature, with an insatiable appetite for sugar water. Utterly smitten with Tahamenay.

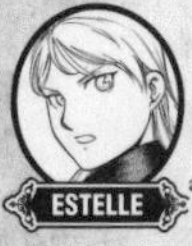

ESTELLE

A girl who once encountered Arslan posing as a boy soldier. Can be intolerant due to her faith, but not without kindness or a sense of justice.

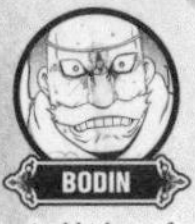

BODIN

Archbishop of Yaldabaoth. Fled to Maryam.

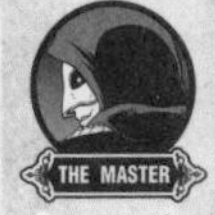

THE MASTER

A sorcerer who seeks to resurrect the Snake King, Zahhāk.